Crime and Justice

Crime and Justice
A Review of Research
Edited by Michael Tonry

VOLUME 29

The University of Chicago Press, Chicago and London

This volume was prepared under Grant Number 92-IJ-CX-K044 awarded to the Castine Research Corporation by the National Institute of Justice, U.S. Department of Justice, under the Omnibus Crime Control and Safe Streets Act of 1968 as amended. Points of view or opinions expressed in this volume are those of the editors or authors and do not necessarily represent the official position or policies of the U.S. Department of Justice.

Contents

Preface

Crime and Justice's mandate was to commission and publish state-of-the-art reviews of knowledge on topics relating to crime and the criminal justice system, and we have stuck to it. Subject to the implicit condition that essays be in English, there were and have been no constraints of time, geography, or discipline. A majority of writers have been based in the United States, but nearly a third have been from Australia, Canada, England and Wales, France, Germany, Holland, Hong Kong, New Zealand, Northern Ireland, Scotland, Sweden, and Switzerland. Disciplines have included anthropology, biology, criminology, developmental psychology, economics, history, law, neuropsychology, operations research, philosophy, political science, social psychology, sociology, and statistics. And periods covered have ranged from the thirteenth century to yesterday.

This volume reflects a not atypical diversity of topic and discipline. Philip J. Cook and John Laub extend through the late 1990s their analysis of trends in youth violence and victimization, and they document steep drops in youth violence since peaks in the early 1990s provoked claims that American society was beset by a new kind of youthful superpredator. Ronald Wright provides a policy history of twenty-five years of sentencing innovation in North Carolina. Nadine Lanctôt and Marc Le Blanc provide a rich and comprehensive look at what is known about the criminality and criminal trajectories of adolescent females. George Thomas and Richard Leo chart the controversial course and multiple meanings of America's quarter-century experience of the Miranda Rule. Paul Mullen and Michele Pathé examine policy and knowledge on stalking—a problem that, while no doubt long part of human experience, became a focus of policy making only in the 1990s. And Anthony Braga and colleagues use recently available data on gun traces to provide a closer examination than anyone has before of the sources and courses of guns used in crime.

With the 2002 publication of this volume, twenty-five years will have passed since the first *Crime and Justice* editorial board meeting in Reston, Virginia, in 1977. Neither we nor anyone else would have predicted or imagined the series would continue to exist and to thrive for so long. The participating National Institute of Justice (NIJ) officials (acting director Blair Ewing, Paul Cascarano, Bob Burkhart, Mort Goren, and John Gardner) all have retired, as have most members of that first editorial board. Only the two of us and Alfred Blumstein remain active, and only Franklin Zimring was among those who were board members before 1990. In previous prefaces we have listed and thanked the by-now long lists of NIJ directors and acting directors we have had the good fortune to work for, and to identify the many other NIJ staff—including, notably, Mary Graham, Virginia Baldau, Paul Estaver, Cheri Crawford, Ed Zedlewski, and Judy Reardon—we have had the good fortune to work with.

We have never before in one place listed all those who have over the years served on the editorial board: Alfred Blumstein, Ulla Bondeson, Anthony Bottoms, Jacqueline Cohen, Philip J. Cook, Robert Crutchfield, Shari Diamond, Anthony N. Doob, Felton Earls, Albin Eser, Jeffrey Fagan, Daniel Glaser, Ted Robert Gurr, Darnell F. Hawkins, Roger G. Hood, James B. Jacobs, Wade McCree, Sheldon Messinger, Terrie E. Moffitt, John Monahan, Mark H. Moore, Patrick V. Murphy, Charles J. Ogletree, Jr., Lloyd Ohlin, Joan Petersilia, Albert J. Reiss, Jr., Chase Riveland, Stuart O. Simms, Michael E. Smith, Patricia Wald, Nigel Walker, James Q. Wilson, and Franklin E. Zimring.

It is an impressive list, and *Crime and Justice* would have been something very different without them. Volume 20 contained an index of the 169 writers of essays to that point, and volume 30 will contain another. The names are many too many to list here without risking undue blearying of readers' eyes.

We have had the great good fortune to work with and learn from all of these many collaborators, advisors, and writers, cannot think of words that adequately express our gratitude to them, and hope they will accept these words of thanks as genuine and heartfelt.

Michael Tonry
Norval Morris
Cambridge, April 2002

Philip J. Cook and John H. Laub

After the Epidemic: Rece
Trends in Youth Violence
in the United States

ABSTRACT

The epidemic of youth violence in the United States peaked in 1993 and
has been followed by a rapid, sustained drop. We assess two types of
explanation for this drop—those that focus on "cohort" effects (including
the effects of abortion legalization) and those that focus on "period"
effects (including the effects of the changing crack-cocaine trade). We are
able to reject the cohort-type explanations yet also find contradictions
with an account based on the dynamics of crack markets. The "way out"
of this epidemic has not been the same as the "way in." The relative
importance in homicide of youths, racial minorities, and guns, all of which
increased greatly during the epidemic, has remained high during the
drop. Arrest patterns tell a somewhat different story, in part because of
changing police practice with respect to aggravated assault. Finally, we
demonstrate that the rise and fall of youth violence has been narrowly
confined with respect to race, sex, and age, but not geography. Given the
volatility in the rates of juvenile violence, forecasting rates is a risky
business indeed. Effectively narrowing the range of plausible explanations
for the recent ups and downs may require a long time horizon,
consideration of a broader array of problem behaviors, and comparisons
with trends in other countries.

Philip J. Cook is ITT/Terry Sanford Professor of Public Policy at Duke University,
Durham, N.C. John H. Laub is professor of criminology and criminal justice at the University of Maryland, College Park, and Affiliated Scholar, Henry A. Murray Center, the
Radcliffe Institute for Advanced Study, Harvard University. We gratefully acknowledge
the assistance of Michael Rand in providing unpublished NCVS statistics and James Alan
Fox for his help with SHR data. Bob Malme, Cumbuka Ortez, and Elaine Eggleston
provided excellent research assistance. Many thanks to all those who offered comments
on an earlier draft, including Frank Cullen, John Donohue, Ted Joyce, Gary LaFree,
Janet Lauritsen, Steve Levitt, Jens Ludwig, Roger Parks, Michael Tonry, and an anonymous referee—the final version is much improved for their efforts. The opinions and
any remaining errors are ours alone.

1

Philip J. Cook and John H. Laub

The epidemic of violence that began in the mid-1980s was of unprecedented intensity, but narrowly channeled, like a flood in a canyon; most of those caught up in this epidemic, either as victims or perpetrators, were young black or Hispanic males. That flood peaked in 1993–94 and has receded since. The huge swing in rates—a tripling of the homicide-commission rate by adolescents over just eight years—is a challenge to existing theories of the determinants of violence. The challenge for policy makers may be still more urgent: Has enough been learned from this epidemic to predict the next one, or to know what is needed to prevent it? To date both the upside and downside of the epidemic have received some systematic attention (see, e.g., Tonry and Moore 1998; and Blumstein and Wallman 2000), but there remains considerable uncertainty, not to mention disagreement, about what happened and why.

In our earlier analysis (Cook and Laub 1998), we characterized the major explanations as either "cohort" or "period." Cohort explanations interpreted the increase in violence as the direct result of an increase in the prevalence of exceptionally violent individuals, who in one prominent account were labeled "super-predators" (Bennett, DiIulio, and Walters 1996). Although influential politically, that type of explanation did not fit the facts of the epidemic. The super-predator theory suggested a secular increase in violence-involvement rates from one birth cohort to the next, but in fact there was an upsurge for a number of birth cohorts simultaneously. Further, the birth cohorts that were on the front lines as the epidemic peaked during the early 1990s were not at all exceptional with respect to their involvement in violence during their younger years. These facts strongly favor explanations that focus on environmental factors during the epidemic period rather than on trends in the violent propensities of youth cohorts.

The most widely accepted "period" explanation focused on the drug trade, especially crack cocaine, and the related increase in gun carrying and use by youths (Blumstein 1995). The importance of guns is evident from the homicide data: all of the increase in youth homicide was a result of guns, while the non-gun homicide rate remained essentially constant. Every category of homicide, including those associated with felonies, arguments, and gang conflict, experienced a relative increase in gun use (Cook and Laub 1998). Other studies have provided evidence that the timing of youth-homicide increases was closely linked to the introduction of crack (Cork 1999; Grogger and Willis 2000).

In this sequel, we extend our analysis to include an additional three or four years of data (through 1998 or 1999) in an effort to document the remarkable drop in youth violence that began around 1994. We are interested in assessing the two types of explanation for this drop, those that focus on "cohort" effects (the composition of the relevant cohorts with respect to violence proneness) and those that focus on "period" effects (contemporaneous environmental determinants of violence). The most prominent "cohort" explanation attributes falling crime rates to the legalization of abortion during the early 1970s (Donohue and Levitt 2001). But the facts of the epidemic increase and decline in youth violence do not fit this or any other cohort explanation. There are a variety of period explanations, but the most prominent is that the decline in violence followed the decline in conflict associated with the crack-cocaine trade and a concomitant decline in gun carrying and use by young minority males (Blumstein 2000, 2001). That explanation is plausible, but does not account for the fact that non-gun homicide rates declined almost as rapidly as gun homicide rates following the epidemic peak. Thus, the drop in youth violence has been something of a mystery, just as was the prior increase. Our purpose here is not to solve the mystery, but rather to bracket the domain of acceptable explanation.

A related issue is whether the "way out" of this epidemic has been the same as the "way in"; specifically, are the postepidemic patterns of youth violence with respect to age, race, weapon use, and geography similar to those that prevailed in the pre-epidemic period of the mid-1980s? Or is there a hangover from this binge of violence? The most complete data are for homicide, where a hangover is indeed evident. First, the relative importance of youths in the national violence picture, which increased greatly during the epidemic, has remained relatively high by historical standards; killers under age twenty-five accounted for 60 percent of homicides in 1998, compared to 43 percent in 1982 (before the epidemic began). Second, the relative involvement of blacks in homicide, which increased during the epidemic, has remained high during the downturn. Third, while gun homicides accounted for all of the youth homicide increase, they have shared the decline with non-gun homicides; the result is that the gun percentage in youth killings was almost as high in 1998 as in 1993, and much higher than in 1985.

For the broader array of violent crimes, including aggravated assault and robbery, the primary indicators are based on arrest data, which reflect police practice as well as the underlying crime patterns. The arrest trends help document the rise and fall of youth crime over the course of the epidemic and reveal some intriguing trends. In particular, for juveniles younger than eighteen, the long-term trend toward parity (documented in Cook and Laub [1998]) in both the male-female violence-arrest-rate ratio and the black-white violence-arrest-rate ratio has accelerated during the downturn.[1] In part this trend is due to a change in composition of juvenile arrests for serious violence: robbery has been declining relative to assault. (The predominance of males and blacks in assault is much less than in robbery.) And in part it is due to the intriguing fact that the composition of assault arrests has been approaching parity; the recent reduction in aggravated assault arrests for juveniles has been greater for males than females, and for blacks than whites. But it is important to note that the trend toward greater parity in assault is not present in the homicide data, and most likely is a consequence of changing police procedures rather than a reflection of underlying crime patterns (see Zimring 1998, pp. 38–47).

The epidemic of youth violence is treated in all these analyses as national in scope, but that is not self-evidently the case. It is certainly possible that the large movements in national aggregates conceal important regional differences. As one check on this possibility, we tabulate homicide rates for youthful black males for the fifteen jurisdictions that have the highest counts of such homicides. (These cities and counties collectively accounted for over half of all homicides involving young black male victims in the mid-1980s.) Every one of them experienced a substantial increase in homicide victimization for this group by the early 1990s; in all but two, that rate had fallen by 1997–98. This high degree of synchrony suggests that the epidemic was indeed nationwide.

The organization of this sequel follows the original article but with some omissions and additions. In particular, the discussion of data sources is not repeated here, and we relegate to an appendix some of the updated documentation of the "burden" of youthful violence on the criminal justice system (see app. table A1 and figs. A1 and A2). However, new material has been added to the analysis of homicide, including an analysis of birth cohorts and of synchrony among urban areas. The principal sections concern juvenile arrest and offending rates (I), homicide victim and offending patterns (II), and a review of the evidence concerning whether the epidemic was due primarily to

---

[1] Of course, a number of criminologists have analyzed trends in relative offending rates by gender and race. For a recent example on gender, see O'Brien (1999), and on race, see LaFree (1998a).

cohort or period effects (III). A final section (IV) recaps the evidence that period effects are paramount and discusses the implications for projecting future rates of youth violence.

Before setting out on this path, a note on the timing and age-group involvement of the epidemic is in order. With respect to age, the epidemic increase in violence was most concentrated on juveniles younger than eighteen, but also involved young adults age eighteen to twenty-four. (In discussing juveniles, we usually focus on ages thirteen to seventeen or twelve to seventeen, and refer to that group as "adolescents.") The relevant indicators all show that the epidemic of youth violence peaked in the early 1990s. The violent-crime arrest rate for adolescents peaked in 1994. For homicide, both the commission rate and the victimization rates peaked in 1993 for both adolescents and young adults ages eighteen to twenty-four. In what follows we use either 1993 or 1994 as the peak year.

I. Juvenile Arrest and Offending Rates

Based on national statistics, the upswing in violence during the late 1980s appears quite mild. In particular, the homicide rate increased from 8.2 (in 1985) to 10.4 (in 1991) per 100,000, a high but not unprecedented level.[2] But this overall pattern conceals a remarkable disparity among age groups. In fact, the increase was concentrated among youths under age twenty-five,[3] and was particularly intense for juveniles under age eighteen (Blumstein 1995, 2000). This was an epidemic of youth violence of unprecedented intensity, largely isolated from broader trends.

We begin our account with a focus on serious violence committed by juveniles. Here we have two indicators of the underlying phenomenon: arrest data from the FBI's Uniform Crime Reports (UCR) and victim reports in the National Crime Victimization Survey (NCVS). Both of these indicators confirm the epidemic increase and subsequent reduction in violence rates. The next section then provides a more extensive account focused on homicide, for which more detailed and accurate data are available.

For over two decades beginning in 1974, adolescent arrest rates for

---

[2] See webapp.cdc.gov/sasweb/ncipc/mortrate.html, accessed on June 5, 2001.
[3] Between 1985 and 1993, the homicide-victimization rate increased 74 percent for ages twenty to twenty-four, 25 percent for ages twenty-five to twenty-nine, and just 11 percent for ages thirty to thirty-four. For victims age thirty-five and over, the rate declined slightly.

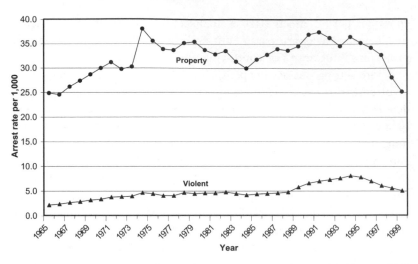

Fig. 1.—Arrest rates for youths ages thirteen to seventeen. Sources: FBI (1966–2000); U.S. Department of Commerce (1966–2000). Arrest rates have been adjusted to account for incomplete coverage by the Uniform Crime Reports.

the property crimes included in the FBI index (burglary, larceny, and auto theft) fluctuated in a relatively narrow band around thirty-five per 1,000 (fig. 1).[4] Arrest rates for the violent index crimes (rape, robbery, aggravated assault, and criminal homicide) were also quite static during the first half of this period, but then doubled between 1984 and 1994. The decline in both the property and violence arrest rates since 1994 has been rapid, with the result that by 1999 the violence arrest rates had returned to near the pre-epidemic level, and the property arrest rates declined to a level not seen since 1966.

While trends in arrest rates are mediated by police practice and do not necessarily track the underlying changes in criminal activity, evidence from the NCVS tells a similar story. In most cases respondents who report that they were victims of serious violent crime are able to estimate the age of the assailant. From these reports it is possible to estimate the rate of commission for broad age groups, including for adolescents ages twelve to seventeen. Commission rates for this group are reported in table 1 for five five-year periods through 1999. These commission rates are several times higher than the arrest rates but exhibit roughly the same pattern, albeit in more muted form. As with the

---

[4] See Cook and Laub (1986) for a commentary on the surprising stability of arrest rates in the face of criminogenic trends in the socioeconomic and family status of children.

TABLE 1

Juvenile Perpetrators in Serious Violent Crime, Rate per 1,000, NCVS Data, 1975–99

| Period | Commission Rate by Perpetrators Ages 12–17, No. of Crimes (Thousands)/No. of Youths (Millions), Rate per 1,000 | |
	Excluding Unknowns	Apportioning Unknowns
1975–79	505/25.0 = 20.2	599/25.0 = 24.0
1980–84	449/22.3 = 20.1	540/22.3 = 24.2
1985–89	376/21.0 = 17.9	464/21.0 = 22.1
1990–94	573/20.9 = 27.4	721/20.9 = 34.5
1995–99	471/22.8 = 20.6	524/22.8 = 23.0

SOURCE.—Unpublished data from National Crime Victimization Survey (1975–99), provided by Michael Rand.

NOTE.—NCVS = National Crime Victimization Survey. All statistics are for the crimes of rape, robbery, and aggravated assault. The NCVS statistics are based on respondents' reports of the age of the perpetrators. Crimes in which there are multiple perpetrators are counted as one.

arrest rates, the commission rates are highest during the early 1990s, dropping back to the previous level (of about twenty-three per 1,000) after 1994.

Figure 2 provides a broader context for the trends in adolescent-violence arrests by depicting the age profiles of violence arrest rates for males at three points in time. As expected, the youthful end of the profile shifts up sharply between 1985 and 1994, and then drops back most of the way by 1999. But this dynamic is not limited to youths. By 1994 arrest rates had increased by 40 percent for men in their twenties and 63 percent for men in their thirties, and while the rates for these groups have declined since 1994, they have remained substantially higher than in 1985.

Again, it is important to ascertain whether these patterns are tracking an underlying reality in terms of violent crime, or rather reflect changes in police practice in making and recording arrests. In this case, police practice is most likely the answer. The elevated rates of arrest for violence in recent years are mostly due to higher rates for aggravated assault, a crime that is closely linked both logically and etiologically to homicide. Yet the trend in homicide arrests tells quite a different story than the trend for aggravated assault arrests. Homicide arrest rates for those ages twenty-five and over were actually declining

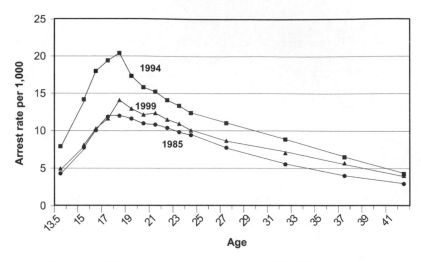

Fɪɢ. 2.—Age profiles of male violence arrest rates, 1985, 1994, and 1999. Sources: U.S. Department of Commerce (1966–2000); FBI (1986, 1995, 2000). Arrest rates have been adjusted to account for incomplete coverage by the Uniform Crime Reports.

during the surge of youth violence, and have continued to decline since 1994 (Blumstein 2000; Fox 2000; Rosenfeld 2000). It appears that the increases in adult arrests for aggravated assault are not the result of changes in offending but rather in police practice in domestic-violence cases (Cook and Laub 1998, p. 42; Blumstein 2000, pp. 17–19). The trend has been for police to treat such cases with greater formality and seriousness in processing and reporting. Zimring (1998, p. 46) provides compelling evidence that increases in aggravated assault arrests were due to a downward shift in the line that separated aggravated from simple assaults rather than a change in violent behavior among youth and adult offenders.

A. Sex and Race

Arrests for violent crime are highly concentrated with respect to sex and race. In 1999, males constituted 83 percent of juvenile violence arrestees (defined as under eighteen); thus, almost five times as many boys as girls were arrested. With respect to race, 41 percent of all juvenile violence arrestees were black, while 57 percent of the juvenile violent arrestees were white. Per capita violence arrest rates for blacks were almost four times as high as for whites.

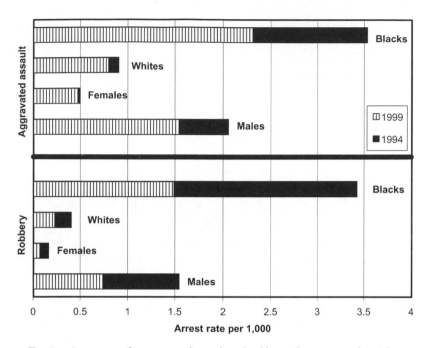

Fig. 3.—Arrest rates for aggravated assault and robbery of arrestees under eighteen, 1994 and 1999, by sex and race. Sources: U.S. Department of Commerce (1966–2000); FBI (1995, 2000). Arrest rates have been adjusted to account for incomplete coverage by the Uniform Crime Reports.

Figure 3 depicts arrest rates by race and sex for the two most common of the violent crimes, robbery and aggravated assault. Each bar in this chart represents both the 1994 and 1999 rates. Robbery has the greatest disparities by race and sex, and those disparities were largely preserved during the sharp drop in arrests during that five-year period. (The "white" rate, which incidentally includes most Hispanics, did not drop quite as much proportionately as the black rate.) Arrest rates for aggravated assault did not drop nearly as much as robbery overall, and dropped hardly at all for whites and females.

Both the relative decline in robbery arrests and the changing demographic composition of assault arrests have had the effect of reducing the race and sex disparities in arrests for violent crime during the late 1990s. (Over 90 percent of juvenile violent-crime arrests are for aggravated assault or robbery. Also included are rape and homicide.) Figure 4 reveals that this trend has actually been evident for at least three decades. In 1970 both the male-female and the black-white arrest ratios for juveniles

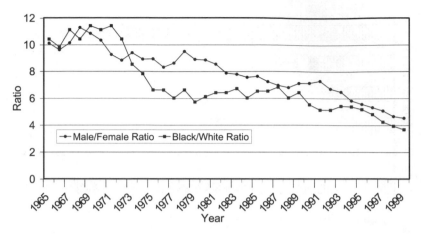

Fig. 4.—Juvenile arrest rate ratios for violence, 1965–99, males and females, blacks and whites. Sources: FBI (1966–2000); U.S. Department of Commerce (1966–2000).

exceeded ten. By 1999 they had declined to approximately four. The male-female ratio has declined steadily, while most of the decline in the black-white ratio occurred in the early 1970s and again in the 1990s.

B. Conclusion

From both UCR and NCVS data, it appears that adolescents committed violent crimes at a substantially higher rate during the early 1990s than either before or since. Based on the UCR arrest data, the national epidemic of juvenile violence began in 1984 and peaked in 1994. It is important to note that this epidemic did not reflect a general outbreak of lawlessness; while arrest rates for violence doubled, arrest rates for property crimes increased relatively little during this period.

Forty-one percent of juvenile violence arrests are for blacks, despite the fact that they constitute only about 14 percent of the relevant population. White or black, most of the violence arrestees are males. But these race and sex differences are less than half as large as they were during the 1960s. Thus arrests for violent offending are less concentrated demographically now than in previous decades. The epidemic did not interrupt that trend. But the trend in arrests for aggravated assaults probably has more to do with police practice than the underlying reality.

In any event, the story is quite different for homicide, as we shall see in the next section. For that important crime, the epidemic was to a remarkable degree limited to black males, and their role has remained elevated throughout the 1990s.

II. Homicide Victims and Offenders

An adequate description of the epidemic of youth violence requires a detailed look at homicide. While relatively rare, it is both the most serious and the best documented of the violent crimes. The homicide statistics suggest a somewhat different story about the epidemic than the arrest statistics for violence. The homicide epidemic appears more intense and more narrowly concentrated with respect to age and race than the epidemic of nonlethal youth violence.

There are two sources of detailed data on homicide (Wiersema, Loftin, and McDowall 2000). The Supplementary Homicide Reports (SHR) data compiled by the FBI from law enforcement agencies provide information on individual homicides, including what is known about the victim, the killer or killers, and the circumstances. Because some agencies fail to send in these reports, the SHR captures only 80–90 percent of all homicides. The other source, the mortality data from the National Center for Health Statistics Vital Statistics Program, includes individual records on all of the known homicides each year compiled from medical examiners' or coroners' reports. These data are useful as a check on the SHR but lack information on circumstances of the homicides and characteristics of the killers.

Figure 5 depicts the trend in homicide-commission rates and victimization rates in two age groups: adolescents (ages thirteen to seventeen) and young adults (ages eighteen to twenty-four).[5] The commission rates are not based on arrest data but rather are based on the SHR data concerning demographic characteristics of suspects. We have adjusted these statistics for both the underreporting in the SHR, and the fact that there are no suspects in some homicides.[6] If the SHR lists more

[5] The choice of 1976 as the first year in these charts is a reflection of SHR data availability.

[6] Data are missing for two reasons. Some law-enforcement agencies did not submit their SHR data to the FBI, and some of the homicide reports that were submitted included no information on the killer—presumably because the investigation had failed to yield an arrest or even a description. We correct for the failure to report by use of the Vital Statistics Program data, as explained in Cook and Laub (1998). For SHR homicides in which no suspect is listed, we impute demographic characteristics based on the characteristics of the victim. Victims were placed in sixteen categories based on sex, race (black or not), and age (0–12, 13–17, 18–24, 25 and over). The percentage distribution of suspect characteristics over these same sixteen categories was calculated for each of the sixteen victim groups, for each year. Those distributions were then treated as probability distributions in imputing suspect characteristics for cases in which no suspect was listed. It should be noted that this imputation procedure is more elaborate than used in Cook and Laub (1998); for that reason, and because we used somewhat different population estimates, the estimates presented here are slightly different from those presented in our earlier work. This imputation strategy is slightly different from that employed by Fox (2001). He infers the demographic characteristics of unidentified offenders from the

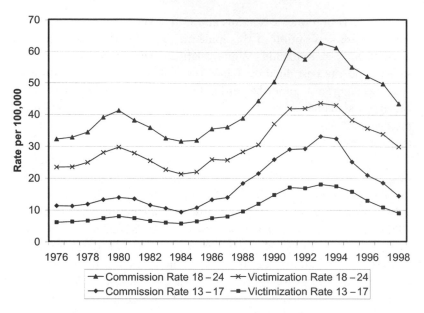

F<small>IG</small>. 5.—Homicide commission and victimization rates, males only, ages thirteen to seventeen and eighteen to twenty-four, 1976–98. Sources: ICPSR (2001a–f); CED (2001a). See appendix for details. Adjusted for unknowns and underreporting by police to match homicide counts in the Vital Statistics.

than one suspect, we include only one of them.[7] Thus our approach assigns one and only one suspect to each homicide. We prefer this approach to the use of arrest data, which include multiple suspects for some homicides and none for others. One attractive consequence of our approach is that the commission rates that we estimate for different demographic groups are directly comparable to the victimization rates.

Figure 5 and those that follow are limited to males since they account for most killings. In particular, in 1998 81.5 percent of victims

known offender profiles based on age, race, and sex of the victim, the state in which the homicide occurred, and the year of the offense. Of course, as Maltz points out, "unknown offenders are not necessarily representative of the knowns" (1999, p. 39). For a general overview of the quality of police data and efforts to impute missing data, see Maltz (1999).

[7] The Inter-University Consortium for Political and Social Research SHR data set used in the analysis (Study no. 3000vi) is a consolidated victim data set. Where there is more than one offender listed in the complementary offender data set (Study no. 3000of), only the characteristics of the first offender are listed in the victim data set. The concern is that the first offender listed is often chosen arbitrarily. Nevertheless, Maltz concludes that this is not a serious problem "since the great majority of homicides consist of one victim and one offender" (1999, p. 34).

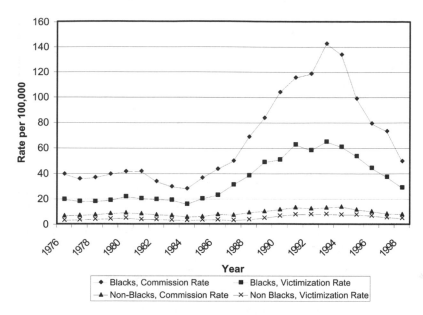

Fɪɢ. 6.—Homicide commission and victimization rates for black and nonblack males ages thirteen to seventeen, 1976–98. Sources: ICPSR (2001 a–f); CDC (2001a). See appendix for details. Adjusted for unknowns and underreporting by police to match homicide counts in the Vital Statistics.

ages thirteen to seventeen were male, while 92.5 percent of suspects in this age range were male. (The male percentages of victims and suspects for the eighteen to twenty-four age group are 86 and 93 percent, respectively.) Further, females were somewhat immune from the epidemic, exhibiting a more muted increase through 1993, and subsequent fall, in comparison with males.[8]

As seen in figure 5, male homicide rates were highly volatile during the epidemic period. For adolescents, homicide commission rates more than tripled between 1984 and 1993, while they doubled for young adults ages eighteen to twenty-four. Victimization rates followed the same intertemporal pattern, although at a lower level: youths are much more likely to kill than be killed. All rates fell sharply after 1994.

Figure 6 depicts the victimization and commission rates for the younger age group, males only, for blacks and nonblacks. Figure 7 provides the same information for ages eighteen to twenty-four. Both age

[8] The homicide-victimization rate for males ages ten to twenty-four doubled between 1985 and 1993, while the rate only increased by one-third for females. Following the peak in 1993, male and female rates declined by the same proportion through 1998.

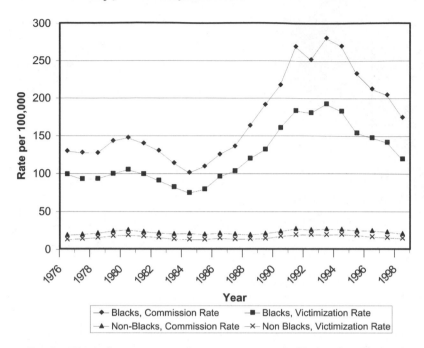

Fig. 7.—Homicide commission and victimization rates for black and nonblack males ages eighteen to twenty-four, 1976–98. Sources: ICPSR (2001 a–f); CDC (2001a). See appendix for details. Adjusted for unknowns and underreporting by police to match homicide counts in the Vital Statistics.

groups exhibit the same patterns as in figure 5. In addition, the figures make evident the vast racial disparities in the average rates and the volatility of those rates over the course of the epidemic. For blacks ages thirteen to seventeen, the homicide commission rate increased by a factor of five, and victimization rates increased by a factor of four. The rates for nonblacks (predominantly whites) also increased during this period, but proportionately much less; for adolescents, the increase in the rate of killing was by a factor of two, and in victimization by two and one-half.

The remarkable run-up in homicide rates shown in these figures was largely confined to youths. As a logical result, the relative importance of youths in the homicide picture increased. Figure 8 shows that as a percentage of all male killers, youths under age twenty-five accounted for about 43 percent in the early 1980s; that figure climbed over 20 percentage points by 1993, and has receded only marginally since then. Thus three out of every five homicides were committed by youths in 1998.

Given similar trends in commission and victimization rates, and the

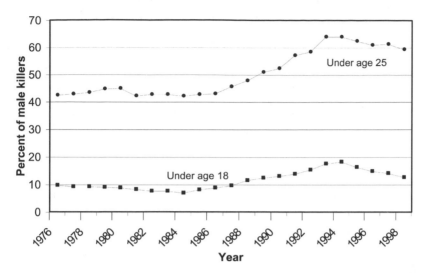

Fɪɢ. 8.—Age distribution of suspected male killers, 1976–98. Sources: ICPSR (2001a). See appendix for details.

all-too-vivid images of the recent school rampage shootings, it seems natural to conclude that youths are killing each other.[9] But the data suggest substantial age disparities. In 1998, for example, only 33 percent of adolescent victims (ages thirteen to seventeen) were killed by someone under age eighteen. In the other direction, only 28 percent of victims of adolescent killers were under age eighteen (table 2). While adolescents tend to fraternize and fight with schoolmates and others in their age group, homicide is a different story.

Tables 3 and 4 provide details regarding the age relationships between victims and killers. Starting with homicide victims ages thirteen to seventeen (table 3), we see that the majority of the suspected killers were at least three years older than the victim. This pattern is evident before the epidemic, during its peak, and during the decline. While the age gap seems to have narrowed during the epidemic, suggesting that conflicts among age peers became relatively more deadly, there has been some rebound since 1993. Nevertheless, 38 percent of the adolescent victims in 1998 were killed by someone five or more years older.

When we consider the ages of victims of adolescent killers, a different

---

[9] The conventional wisdom conveyed in criminology and victimology textbooks is that there is substantial age homogeneity among offenders and victims (see, e.g., Fattah 1991 and Siegel 1995). For a recent study emphasizing age homogeneity in homicide, see Maltz (1998).

TABLE 2

Age Patterns of Homicide Victimization and Commission:
SHR Data, 1994 and 1998

Age of Killer (Years)	Percent Distribution with Victims Ages 13–17*		Age of Victim (Years)	Percent Distribution with Killers Ages 13–17	
	1994	1998		1994	1998
<13	.5	.7	<13	5.8	6.0
13–17	37.2	32.1	13–17	25.9	22.1
18–24	47.2	46.1	18–24	30.0	31.1
>24	15.2	21.1	>24	39.4	40.8
N	1,036	549	N	1,489	795

SOURCE.—FBI, Supplementary Homicide Reports for 1994 and 1998.
NOTE.—SHR = Supplementary Homicide Reports. Excludes homicides not reported by local police agencies to the FBI as part of the SHR. Excludes negligent manslaughter and justifiable homicide. The total percent distribution for victims is 100.0 and for killers is 100.0.
* There were an additional 535 victims ages thirteen to seventeen in 1994 and 304 victims in 1998, for whom no suspects were listed. The SHR's victim data set lists no more than one suspect.
For eight of the cases in 1994 and fourteen in 1998 in which the suspect was thirteen to seventeen years old, the age of the victim was unknown. These cases were excluded.

portrait emerges. Table 4 indicates that most adolescent killers select older victims, and half select victims who are at least five years older. These patterns are suggestive of routine activities by violent adolescents that involve a good deal of conflict with people who are substantially older. But there has been little change over the course of the epidemic in

TABLE 3

Age Relationships between Victim and Killer, Victims Ages 13–17
(1985, 1993, and 1998)

	Percent of Homicide Victims		
	1985	1993	1998
Killer older than victim	79	74	77
Killer three or more years older than victim	61	50	56
Killer five or more years older than victim	47	32	38

SOURCE.—FBI, Supplementary Homicide Reports (1985, 1993, 1998).
NOTE.—Excludes homicides not reported by local police agencies to the FBI as part of the SHR. Excludes negligent manslaughter and justifiable homicide. Excludes cases in which no suspect was listed.

TABLE 4

Age Relationship between Victim and Killer, Killers Ages 13–17
(1985, 1993, 1998)

| | Percent of Homicide Victims | | |
	1985	1993	1998
Killer younger than victim	77	78	77
Killer three or more years younger than victim	65	64	62
Killer five or more years younger than victim	55	52	51

Source.—FBI, Supplementary Homicide Reports for 1985, 1993, and 1998.
Note.—Excludes homicides not reported by local police agencies to the FBI as part
of the SHR. Excludes negligent manslaughter and justifiable homicide. Excludes cases
in which no suspect was listed.

the age distribution of those who are killed by adolescents, despite enormous changes in the underlying homicide rates over this time period.

Figure 9 provides a look at the racial and ethnic composition of
youth homicide, this time focusing on victims. Unfortunately, the vital
statistics data do not include information on ethnicity before 1990, so
it is not possible before then to separate Hispanics from other whites.
As shown, black representation among male victims increased by about

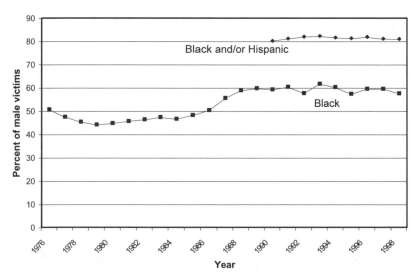

Fig. 9.—Race and ethnicity of male victims, ages thirteen to twenty-four, black and/
or Hispanic, 1976–98. Source: ICPSR (2001 a–f). See appendix for details.

13 percentage points in the early years of the epidemic and remained near 60 percent thereafter. Of the remaining 40 percent, over half were white Hispanics during the 1990s. Thus in recent years, while the epidemic peaked and then receded, over 80 percent of youth homicide victims have been blacks or Hispanics.

It is an open question whether non-Hispanic whites were affected by the epidemic. Youthful victimization rates of whites did increase during the late 1980s, but there is no precise way to apportion that increase between Hispanic and non-Hispanic whites. One approach is to compare white homicide trends in states that had relatively large Hispanic populations (the Southwest and Florida) with those that did not. The number of youthful white homicide victims nationwide increased by 37 percent between 1985 and 1993, but that increase was far from uniform; states with a high concentration of Hispanics experienced a 51 percent increase, while other states experienced only a 22 percent increase.[10]

To summarize, the homicide data confirm the existence of a great epidemic of youth violence, demonstrating that it was even more intense than indicated by trends in assault and robbery. As noted in the introduction, this epidemic was dominated by a particular demographic group—black males under age twenty-five. The image that comes to mind is of a flood in a canyon (Cook 1998). That flood receded after 1993–94, but the rates remained substantially higher by 1998 than prior to the epidemic's onset. Further, the shift in the racial and age profile of homicide during the run-up in homicide rates has not reverted during the decline.

While the epidemic was narrowly confined with respect to demographic characteristics, it affected all regions of the nation. Table 5 lists the fifteen jurisdictions with the highest homicide counts for black males ages ten to twenty-four in the mid-1980s. Every one of these jurisdictions experienced a sharp increase in homicide rates for this group by the early 1990s; in ten of these jurisdictions, the victimization rate more than doubled. In all but two of these jurisdictions (Cook County and Baltimore) the homicide rate declined again by 1997–98. The pervasiveness of this epidemic dictates that any satisfactory explanation be national in scope.[11]

[10] States included in the former group are California, Arizona, New Mexico, Texas, Florida, Nevada, Oklahoma, Utah, and Colorado. In 1993, 74 percent of the 1,489 white male homicide victimizations in these states were Hispanic, compared with 37 percent of the 1,130 such victimizations in the remaining states. The age group for these computations is ten to twenty-four.

[11] This observation raises the question of what can be learned from international comparisons, an issue we revisit in the last section of our essay.

TABLE 5

Homicide Victimization Rates for Black Males Ages 10–24: Fifteen Large Counties, Three Periods

Top 15 Jurisdictions by Total Homicide Count, 1984–86	1984–86		1991–94		1997–98	
	Average Annual Homicides	Annual Homicide Rate (per 100,000)	Average Annual Homicides	Annual Homicide Rate (per 100,000)	Average Annual Homicides	Annual Homicide Rate (per 100,000)
New York City	213	79.4	334	124.9	133	50.8
Los Angeles County, CA	168	127.5	221	183.4	121	100.5
Wayne County, MI	161	146.7	199	191.3	122	117.0
Cook County, IL	144	78.6	238	142.8	279	170.8
Baltimore (city), MD	62	109.3	109	229.2	111	245.7
Philadelphia County, PA	41	49.8	121	168.6	106	155.3
Orleans Parish, LA	40	90.8	139	346.6	82	207.7
Harris County, TX	38	50.9	91	125.4	38	49.0
St. Louis (city), MO	36	133.8	101	455.1	35	160.0
Dallas County, TX	36	75.1	82	166.8	48	88.8
District of Columbia	34	65.3	182	512.0	93	389.2
Dade County, FL	34	73.2	56	107.3	47	82.3
Fulton County, GA	28	66.7	93	149.6	32	67.8
Shelby County, TN	28	56.8	61	125.3	37	73.1
Cuyahoga County, OH	27	54.9	50	123.8	20	46.8
Total for period	1,086		2,047		1,303	
% of U.S. total	56.1		47.0		43.5	

Sources.—National Center for Health Statistics (1984–86, 1991–94, 1997–98); U.S. Department of Commerce, 1984–86. County populations for 1991–94 and 1997–98 are from CDC Wonder database.

It is also of interest that the decline in overall homicide rates in the 1990s has not been uniform but rather has been concentrated in the largest cities. The remarkable result has been a violation of one of the empirical verities of criminology, namely, that homicide rates tend to increase with the population size of the city (Blumstein 2000; Fox and Zawitz 2000). By 1999 the average homicide rate for cities with populations of 250,000 to 500,000 was as high as for the largest cities.

III. Cohort versus Period Explanations

When an adolescent commits criminal homicide, it is a natural presumption that the killer is a vicious, depraved, or psychologically disturbed individual. When an entire cohort of adolescents commits homicide at an unusually high rate, then it seems reasonable to conclude that such individuals are unusually prevalent in that cohort.

Explanations of this sort, that attribute trends in youth violence to underlying trends in the character of the youths, have been popular going back to the 1960s and probably long before (Cook 1985). The epidemic in youth violence that began in the mid-1980s was no exception. John DiIulio and his coauthors attributed that epidemic to the fact that "America is now home to thickening ranks of juvenile 'superpredators'—radically impulsive, brutally remorseless youngsters" (Bennett, DiIulio, and Walters 1996, p. 27), a trend caused by " 'moral poverty'—children growing up without love, care, and guidance from responsible adults" (p. 59). In our earlier article (Cook and Laub 1998), we pointed out a variety of ways in which this sort of explanation was contradicted by the facts.[12] Explanations that attributed rising violence rates to the character of the youths nonetheless proved influential with legislators, who in most states responded to the epidemic with more punitive policies for juvenile crime (Feld 1998).

The latest claim for the "cohort" explanation of the epidemic is from O'Brien, Stockard, and Isaacson (1999). This article attempts to distinguish between cohort and period effects in explaining age-specific homicide-arrest rates over the years 1960–95; one remarkable conclusion is that the "period" effect was actually smaller in the 1990s than in previous years, and the increase in the youth homicide-arrest rate was largely the result of characteristics of the relevant cohorts. They arrive at this conclusion by use of a regression analysis. The dependent variable is the homicide arrest rate, with data for each five-

---

[12] John DiIulio has recanted his earlier views on this subject (Becker 2001).

year interval in the 1960–95 period, and for each five-year cluster of birth cohorts. The independent variables include period and age indicators, and a two-variable characterization of each birth-cohort cluster. The two variables are the relative size of the cohort and the percent of the cohort born out of wedlock. The latter increases sharply for the birth cohorts that were on the front lines of the epidemic. O'Brien and his colleagues find that controlling for age and period, both cohort size and especially born-out-of-wedlock percentage are positively and significantly related to age-period-specific homicide rates. Moreover, the effect of nonmarital births on homicide is considerably stronger compared with the effect of relative cohort size.

The claim that the period effect was relatively small during the early 1990s is counterintuitive to say the least, given that youth homicide rates were at an all-time peak. The problem with their regression specification is that it forces the period effects to have the same proportional effect across all age groups. That assumption is not defensible in the recent epidemic, which, as we have seen, was concentrated among the youngest cohorts.[13] These same cohorts have had much more typical rates of homicide involvement before and after the epidemic, despite their high prevalence of out-of-wedlock births. A more flexible regression specification would be required to provide a valid characterization of the recent history of youth violence.

Rather than a change in the intrinsic violence-proneness of youth cohorts, it is more plausible that the upsurge in youth violence was the result of a youth-specific period effect, which is to say that something about the social, economic, or policy environment was more conducive to lethal violence by youths in the early 1990s than in previous or subsequent years.[14] In particular, there is a strong case that the introduction of crack cocaine in the mid-1980s in one city after another provided a new source of deadly conflict, and the resources and motivation

[13] One implication of the analysis in O'Brien, Stockard, and Isaacson (1999) is that adolescent homicide rates should have continued to increase strongly during the late 1990s, since the nonmarital birth rate continued to increase sharply during the relevant years (i.e., fifteen years earlier). In fact, the adolescent homicide rates have declined both absolutely and relative to that of older cohorts.

[14] Yet another possibility is that the epidemic increase and decline are the result of an endogenous, self-generating process, rather than exogenous environmental effects. For example, if youth violence is in some sense contagious, then the volatility of rates could be explained by the same internal dynamic as, say, a measles epidemic. While the possibility of contagion or other self-generating processes is entirely plausible in human behavior (Gladwell 2000) and has been discussed in the context of gun carrying and other aspects of youth violence (Hemenway et al. 1996; Fagan, Wilkinson, and Davies 2000), we limit our discussion to the more traditional cohort-period dichotomy.

for many young men to obtain guns (Blumstein 1995, 2000; Cork 1999; Grogger and Willis 2000). The subsequent drop in violence was in this account the result of reduced conflict over crack distribution as markets stabilized and became less lucrative. But that explanation is hypothetical and has not settled the matter.

A. Cohort Explanations for the Crime Drop

With the sustained drop in youth crime rates since 1993, there is renewed interest in cohort-type explanations. What might have happened to reduce the crime-proneness of recent cohorts? The most prominent hypothesis attributes a substantial portion of the crime drop to abortion legalization. Several states liberalized abortion restrictions in the late 1960s, and five legalized abortion by 1970. In 1973 the Supreme Court's ruling in *Roe v. Wade* (410 U.S. 113 [1973]) declared state laws prohibiting abortion to be unconstitutional. The upsurge in legal abortions could plausibly have reduced the criminal involvement of the birth cohorts that were affected by these changes by reducing the size of these cohorts, or, more interestingly, by reducing the prevalence of children born into circumstances that placed them at risk for becoming violent offenders.

There is strong evidence that abortion when legal is used selectively, in the sense that women are more likely to abort pregnancies that would otherwise result in the birth of children who would be unwanted or for whom there would be few child-rearing resources available. It is entirely plausible, then, that unwanted children "at the margin of abortion" would be more likely to be at risk for a variety of problems (Brown and Eisenberg 1995; Gruber, Levine, and Staiger 1999), including violence and crime. Hence abortion legalization could have reduced the per capita crime involvement for the cohorts that were affected.

Donohue and Levitt (2001) conclude from their analysis that abortion legalization accounts for as much as half of the crime drop during the 1990s—a finding that has received considerable attention in the popular press (Holloway 1999). Their analysis exploits the large differences among states in postlegalization abortion rates. They find that states with high abortion rates have enjoyed greater reductions in crime beginning in the late 1980s (when the relevant cohorts are entering their adolescent years) than states with lower abortion rates. This is a robust finding. The conclusion has not gone unchallenged, however. Joyce (2001), using a somewhat different empirical strategy that focuses on the contrast between states that legalized early with states that only legalized after the Court's decision, concludes that there is no evidence that abortion affected crime.

Note that there are two questions here. The first question is whether abortion legalization reduced crime rates relative to what they would have been otherwise. The second is whether abortion legalization is a good candidate for explaining the observed drop in violent crime among adolescents. To answer yes to the second question, the answer to the first question must be affirmative, and the crime-reducing effect of legalization must not have been concealed by other historical (period) effects. Without drawing a firm conclusion on that first and more fundamental issue, we can nonetheless offer an opinion on the second question. The timing of the downturn is simply wrong for legalized abortion to be the driving force.[15] As shown in previous sections, the adolescent arrest rate for property crime did not turn down until 1994, about eight to eleven years after what we would expect if abortion legalization were responsible.[16] The violent-crime trends are still more out of synch with the abortion explanation, since adolescent arrest rates and other measures of violence involvement were actually increasing through 1993. Further, the increases were greatest for black youths, even though a larger percentage of pregnancies by black women were aborted following legalization than for women of other races (Levine et al. 1996).[17]

The abortion-legalization hypothesis is not the only "cohort" explanation for the crime drop. Another focuses on the reduction in serum lead levels in young children, resulting in part from the ban on the use of lead paint in 1978, the ban of lead in gasoline in 1982, and regu-

[15] Donohue and Levitt (2001) use 1991 as the start of the crime drop. They write, "The year 1991 represents a local maximum for all three of the crime measures. Murder has fallen by 40 percent and the other two categories are down by more than 30 percent" (2001, p. 392). They also argue that ages eighteen to twenty-four are crime-prone years with age twenty being the peak of the age-crime profile. Thus, in 1991, the first cohort affected by *Roe v. Wade* would be seventeen to eighteen years old. In the early-legalizing states, the first cohort affected by legalized abortion would be twenty to twenty-one years old (2001, pp. 393–94). But for these age groups, we have seen that the homicide rate did not turn down until after 1993, so these cohorts were in fact two years older than that.

[16] The "seven to ten year" range is based on two dates for the liberalization of abortion: 1970, when California, New York, and several other states legalized abortion, and 1973, when the rest of the country legalized abortion. Then thirteen-year-olds in 1983 (given the early legalizers) or 1986 (given the later ones) should have had reduced crime involvement.

[17] It should be noted that Donohue and Levitt recognize that the "dampening effect" of abortion on crime "can be outweighed in the short term by factors that stimulate crime. Elevated youth homicide rates in this period [late 1980s and early 1990s] appear to be clearly linked to the rise of crack and the easy availability of guns" (2001, p. 395).

lations on lead in drinking water and consumer products. Epidemiological evidence suggests that ingesting even small quantities of lead may damage children in a variety of ways, including causing a reduction in IQ and emotional development (Nevin 2000). A recent study found a correlation across counties between lead in the air and homicide rates (Stretesky and Lynch 2001). Nationwide, serum lead levels in young children have declined at least since 1980 (Lutter and Mader 2001), suggesting the possibility that violence rates will decline as cohorts that have been less exposed reach adolescence and beyond. To illustrate this point, Nevin argues that "if the association between gasoline lead and social behavior continues into the future, then violent crime and unwed teen pregnancy could show dramatic declines over the next five to ten years" (2000, p. 19). Yet while the "lead" hypothesis is certainly intriguing and may, like liberalized abortion, have an effect on violence and other behavior, it does not account for the movements in cohort-specific homicide rates that have been observed since 1985.

Any "cohort" account of why violence rates have been dropping requires demonstration of a downward trend in violence involvement from one birth cohort to the next. To explore this possibility, we analyze homicide victimization rates for black males born in 1969, 1974, 1977, and 1981. (As we have seen, victimization rates have been highly correlated over time with rates of commission, and can be measured more accurately.) Figure 10 depicts annual victimization rates for each of these cohorts relative to average same-age victimization rates for a baseline period, 1976–84. (This baseline period was chosen because it preceded the epidemic.) For example, the 1990 point on the graph for the 1969 birth cohort is the ratio of the homicide-victimization rate for twenty-one-year-olds in 1990 to the average victimization rate for twenty-one-year-olds during the baseline period. In that sense we have controlled for the effect of age, revealing the period effects and differences among the cohorts. If the age profiles for these four cohorts had been similar to the age profile during the baseline period, then all four lines would be flat and equal to 1.0 throughout.

What the data in figure 10 reveal, however, is that all four cohorts have elevated rates during the epidemic period, with peaks in the early 1990s. Note that the three younger cohorts were born after abortion was legalized, but there is no indication that they have been less likely to experience violence than the oldest cohort (born in 1969, before legalization); indeed, all three of these later cohorts have higher ratios

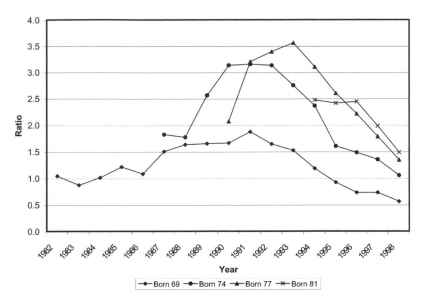

Fɪɢ. 10.—Ratio of homicide victimization rates to pre-epidemic base rate (1976–84), four birth cohorts of black males. Sources: ICPSR (2001a–f); CDC (2001a, c). See appendix for details.

than the 1969 birth cohort throughout the period depicted here. If there is a trend from one cohort to the next, it appears to be in the direction of greater violence rather than less.[18] In any case, the period effects dominate this picture.[19]

These results do not rule out the possibility that abortion legalization or other influences on the violence-proneness of youth cohorts have had an ameliorative effect on youth violence rates but do indicate that that effect, if it exists, has been well concealed by historical events. The evidence against the "super-predator" explanation for the upside of the epidemic is compelling (Cook and Laub 1998), and we find the evidence against a cohort explanation for any substantial portion of the downside just as compelling.

[18] Another possibility is that the "period" effects were strongest for adolescents and declined across the age spectrum. That possibility accords with the economics of the crack trade, which recruited adolescents to sell crack in public places, thus putting them in harm's way. An "age-differential period effect" cannot be logically distinguished from a trend in cohort effects.

[19] Again, it is very difficult to see how the period effect for homicide could be declining from 1970 to 1995, as the regression results in O'Brien, Stockard, and Isaacson (1999, p. 1078) suggest.

B. Gun Use during the Crime Drop

On the upside, the epidemic of youth homicide was entirely a gun-homicide epidemic: non-gun rates remained essentially unchanged. The conventional explanation attributes the increase in gun use to the introduction of crack cocaine, which recruited youths into the business and provided them with the means and motivation to acquire guns. That by itself would not explain why gun killings increased in domestic arguments and routine altercations, unless the habit of gun carrying spread beyond the drug trade as a matter of fashion or self-defense (Fagan and Wilkinson 1998).

Several commentators have suggested that the way out of the epidemic has been the same as the way in, with declining gun use leading the way (Blumstein 2001). But the data indicate that non-gun homicide rates have declined along with gun rates, an important difference with the upside of the epidemic. At the peak of the epidemic in 1993, the gun percentage in homicide victimization had reached 90 percent for males ages thirteen to seventeen, and 88 percent for those ages eighteen to twenty-four. By 1997 each of those percentages had dropped by just one point.

Figure 11 places recent trends in historical context, showing that the gun percentage in male-youth-homicide victimization increased about 17 percentage points during the period 1985 to 1993, and has re-

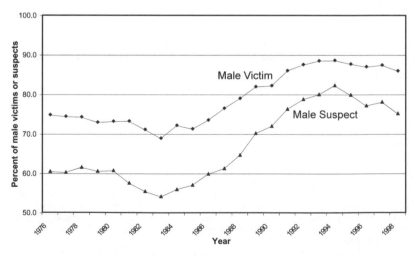

Fig. 11.—Percent gun use in homicides involving males ages thirteen to twenty-four, 1976–98. Sources: ICPSR (2001a–f); CDC (2001a). See appendix for details.

TABLE 6

Homicide Gun Percentage by Circumstance, Male Killers
Ages 13–24 (1982–85, 1990–92, 1997–98)

Circumstances	Percent with Guns		
	1982–85	1990–92	1997–98
Family and intimates	52.0	55.3	37.0
Felony type	53.5	73.1	79.4
Brawls and arguments	56.6	73.6	71.2
Gang related	78.9	90.5	93.4
Other known circumstances	50.3	69.8	62.7
Unknown circumstances	56.8	77.6	70.2
All circumstances	54.7	72.3	70.7

SOURCE.—FBI, Supplementary Homicide Reports (1982–85, 1990–92, 1997–98).
NOTE.—Excludes homicides not reported by local police agencies to the FBI as part of the SHR. Excludes negligent manslaughter and justifiable homicide. "Family and intimates" is not a circumstance but was defined to supercede other categories in this list.

mained near that very high level for the first few years of the drop. This figure also includes the trend line for the gun percentage in homicide commission by youths, which follows the same pattern but at a lower level.[20] Thus it appears that guns remained prevalent in deadly conflicts involving at-risk youths even while such conflicts were becoming less common.

Some detail is provided in table 6, which gives the percentage of gun use in homicide by circumstance for three periods. On the upside of the epidemic, the prevalence of guns increased sharply in all types of homicide, including domestic, gang-related, felony-related, and so forth. (Technically the "domestic" category is not a circumstance as designated by the SHR. That line in table 6 includes all cases of killings within the family, regardless of SHR-designated circumstance.) After the peak, the gun percentage dropped very little except in domestic cases, and for two categories—felony-type and gang-related—it actually increased. Thus the "hangover" from the epidemic appears to include a broader access to guns by violent youths.

[20] Cook (1991) found that the gun percentage in homicide was closely related to the physical strength and robustness of the victims. Thus the gun percentage is higher for males than females, and higher for young adults than for children or older people. Confirming the importance of the victim characteristics in influencing weapon type, we find that when young men kill each other, they are as likely to use a gun as are women or older men who kill young men. But when young men kill less robust victims, they (like other killers) are less likely to use a gun.

IV. Concluding Thoughts

The epidemic of youth violence began in the mid 1980s, peaked in 1993–94, and had subsided to near the original levels by 1999. This volatility has provided a profound challenge to criminologists. The scientific effort to explain why some individuals or groups or communities or nations have higher violence rates than others is well advanced but provides little guidance to understanding how, for example, the homicide rate for black adolescents nationwide could triple in just a few years.

James Q. Wilson recently observed that "social scientists have made great gains in explaining why some people are more likely than others to commit crimes but far smaller gains in understanding a nation's crime rate" (2002, p. 537). As Wilson points out, the two tasks are not the same thing at all.[21] Yet there is a natural presumption among many criminologists that the first place to seek an explanation for a change in the nation's crime rate is in changes in the composition of the population. More crime suggests more crime-prone people; a vast increase in youth violence of the sort experienced in the late 1980s suggests a correspondingly vast increase in the number of violence-prone youth. And similarly for the downside.

As we have seen, this sort of "cohort" explanation for the epidemic increase or the subsequent decline has not squared with the facts. The same birth cohorts that appeared quite typical in their violence involvement before and after the epidemic were not at all typical during the peak years of the epidemic. The evidence seems to rule out cohort-type explanations as the primary source of the observed volatility. That does not mean that cohort size, being born out of wedlock, abortion availability, serum blood levels, and so forth are irrelevant to crime and violence rates. It does mean that such explanations cannot account for this epidemic.

That narrows the search to "period" or environmental effects as the primary driving force. We have attempted to narrow the search still further by documenting the structure of violence rates over time. The second most remarkable feature of the epidemic (after the sheer amplitude of the rate swings) has been the extent to which it was narrowly channeled demographically. Hispanic and most especially black males

---

[21] Levitt and Lochner document a variety of determinants of juvenile crime from their multifaceted study but conclude that "none of these determinants of crime . . . do a particularly good job of explaining the time-series pattern of juvenile crime over the last two decades" (2001, p. 371).

under age twenty-five did most of the additional killing and provided most of the additional victims. Young females and non-Hispanic whites, and adults in their thirties or older, were left on the sidelines for the most part. Yet within its demographic confines, the epidemic was national in scope. The appeal of what has become the conventional explanation, the introduction of crack cocaine in one city after another across the nation, is that it has the right timing and can accommodate all these facts.

To further limit the domain of acceptable explanations, it may be of value to compare trends in the United States with those in other countries, especially Canada and Europe. For example, Pfeiffer (1998), in a review of youth-violence trends in Europe, concludes that ten European countries experienced increases in youth violence beginning in the early to mid-1980s, suggesting that the U.S. experience is not unique in that respect (see also Killias and Aebi 2000). The shared trend may call into question the crack-market explanation for the U.S. epidemic, and in any event encourages a search for other underlying causal factors that are operating in parallel.

A consensus explanation for the downside of the epidemic has not yet emerged. We do know that the downside has not been a mirror image of the upside. The "way out" has not been the same as the "way in" with respect to sex, race and ethnicity, and perhaps most important, weapons. In each of those dimensions, the postpeak period has seen more balanced declines in the homicide rates. As a result, the youth homicide rate in 1998 was substantially lower than 1993 but was similar in composition with respect to sex, race and ethnicity, and weapon type. Thus the high concentration among minorities and males, and the prevalence of guns, may be long-lasting hangovers from the epidemic.

Also relevant in seeking a satisfactory explanation for the downside is that the declining rate for youths occurs in a context of overall declines in homicide. While the youth-violence epidemic was bucking the prevailing trend and hence requires a "youth only" explanation, that is not the case for the downside, where it may reasonably be supposed that the youths are responding to the same environmental factors associated with law enforcement, the economy, cultural change, routine activities, drug and gun markets, and so forth as are older adults. But that observation does not provide much leverage, since the relative contribution of these factors to adult crime has not been well established (Blumstein and Wallman 2000), and it is in any event likely to be differ-

ent for youths than adults. For example, while Spelman (2001) estimates that the incapacitation effect of increased imprisonment could account for 25 percent of the overall crime drop, it is unlikely that
incarceration of juvenile offenders played such an important role.

For policy makers, the lesson here is not very reassuring. If cohort
characteristics reliably predicted violence involvement, then future
trends in violence rates might at least be foreseeable.[22] At the most basic
level, the size of cohorts has long been used to predict rates of crime
and violence, on the reasonable assumption that relatively large cohorts
passing through the crime-prone years of adolescence and young adulthood will be associated with relatively high crime rates for the nation as
a whole (Fox 2000). But even this commonsense observation has proven
of little use in projecting violence rates, simply because the volatility in
per capita commission rates has dominated the picture for youths. In
our earlier article, we reported a negative correlation for the period
1965–95 between the number of people ages thirteen to seventeen and
the number of homicides in this age group (Cook and Laub 1998, p. 59).
Unfortunately for forecasting purposes, demography is not destiny, and
forecasts based on demographics and an assumption of constant age-
specific offending rates have been notable for their large errors.[23] We
agree with Land and McCall (2001), who suggest that analysts have
tended to place too much faith in demographic-based forecasts and
should acknowledge the great uncertainty inherent in such efforts.

Forecast uncertainty of course increases as we attempt to look farther into the future. But our understanding of crime trends may improve if we look farther into the past. If we define the problem as understanding the crime drop during the 1990s, then that encourages a
focus on policy innovations and other changes during that period. A
longer historical perspective on crime "booms" and "busts" may encourage a deeper analysis (LaFree 1998a, 1998b, 1999, 2000). For example, the most recent epidemic of youth violence was closely tied to
a parallel epidemic of crack cocaine. If we look back to the 1960s, or
all the way back to Prohibition, then the question arises of how other
epidemics of illicit drug use have influenced violence rates and why the

---

[22] For example, Donohue and Levitt conclude that, "all else equal, legalized abortion
will account for persistent declines of 1 percent a year in crime over the next two decades" (2001, p. 415).
[23] For documentation and discussion, see Cohen and Land (1987), Zimring (1998),
Levitt (1999), and Steffensmeier and Harer (1999).

market for some drugs, particularly marijuana, appears to be more benign than for others, including heroin, powder cocaine, and crack.[24]

We may also gain additional insight by casting a broader net, considering other forms of problematic behavior besides crime and violence. The fact that teen childbearing began a sustained decline after a peak in 1991, and that teen suicide rates declined substantially after 1994, invites speculation that there is more than mere coincidence with the downward trend in violence. If teenagers as a group became more hopeful and future-oriented over the course of this decade, that would account for a variety of healthy trends—but leave us with a new question.

APPENDIX

Source Information for Data Used to Generate Figures

Homicide
ICPSR 2001a: FBI, Supplementary Homicide Reports, 1976–98. Obtained from the Inter-University Consortium for Political and Social Research Web site, www.icpsr.umich.edu. Study no. 3000, dataset da3000vi.

Vital Statistics—Mortality
ICPSR 2001b: National Center for Health Statistics, Vital Statistics Mortality, 1976–91. Obtained from the Inter-University Consortium for Political and Social Research Web site, www.icpsr.umich.edu. Study no. 7632, Mortality Detail Files 1968–91, datasets da7632.y76 to da7632.y91.

ICPSR 2001c: National Center for Health Statistics, Vital Statistics Mortality, 1992. Obtained from the Inter-University Consortium for Political and Social Research Web site, www.icpsr.umich.edu. Study no. 6546, Multiple Causes of Death 1992, dataset da6546.

ICPSR 2001d: National Center for Health Statistics, Vital Statistics Mortality, 1993. Obtained from the Inter-University Consortium for Political and Social Research Web site, www.icpsr.umich.edu. Study no. 6320, Multiple Causes of Death 1993, dataset da6320.

ICPSR 2001e: National Center for Health Statistics, Vital Statistics Mortality, 1994. Obtained from the Inter-University Consortium for Political and Social Research Web site, www.icpsr.umich.edu. Study no. 2201, Multiple Causes of Death 1994, dataset da2201.

ICPSR 2001f: National Center for Health Statistics, Vital Statistics Mortality, 1995. Obtained from the Inter-University Consortium for Political and Social

---

[24] Fagan, Zimring, and Kim point out that "homicide and drug epidemics have been closely phased, both temporally and spatially, in New York and nationwide, for nearly thirty years. Homicide peaks in 1972, 1979, and 1991 mirror three drug epidemics: heroin; cocaine hydrochloride (powder); and crack cocaine" (1998, p. 1306).

Research Web site, www.icpsr.umich.edu. Study no. 2392, Multiple Causes of Death 1995, dataset da2392.

ICPSR 2001g: National Center for Health Statistics, Vital Statistics Mortality, 1996. Obtained from the Inter-University Consortium for Political and Social Research Web site, www.icpsr.umich.edu. Study no. 2702, Multiple Causes of Death 1996, dataset da2702.

CDC 2001a: Centers for Disease Control, National Center for Injury Prevention and Control, WISQARS database, www.cdc.gov/ncipc/wisqars/; U.S. gun and total homicide statistics, 1997–98.

CDC 2001b: Centers for Disease Control, National Center for Injury Prevention and Control, WISQARS database www.cdc.gov/ncipc/wisqars/; U.S. gun and total homicide statistics, Hispanic males thirteen to twenty-four, 1990–98.

Population Estimates
USDC 2001: U.S. Department of Commerce, U.S. Census Bureau, Quarterly Population estimates, by single year of age, race, and sex, 1980–89. Data obtained from www.census.gov/population/www/estimates/nat_80s_detail html, files e8081rqi.zip through e8990rqi.zip.

CDC 2001c: Centers for Disease Control, National Center for Injury Prevention and Control, WISQARS database www.cdc.gov/ncipc/wisqars/; Population totals, black, Hispanic, and total U.S. males thirteen to twenty-four, 1990–98.

TABLE A1

Juvenile Perpetrators in Serious Violent Crime: Percentage of Victimizations, 1975–99

Period	FBI Data, Crimes Cleared by Juvenile Arrests as a Percentage of All Crimes Cleared	NCVS Data, Victimization in Which Perpetrators Are Less than Age 18	
		Excluding Unknowns	Percentage of All Victimizations
1975–79	12	25	23
1980–84	10	23	21
1985–89	9	22	20
1990–94	13	27	25
1995–99	13	27	25

Sources.—FBI data are from *Crime in the United States* (1976–2000). Unpublished NCVS data were provided by Michael Rand, Bureau of Justice Statistics.
Note.—NCVS = National Crime Victimization Survey. Percentages are for the crimes of rape, robbery, aggravated assault, and (for the FBI statistics only) criminal homicide. The NCVS statistics are based on respondents' reports of the age of the perpetrators. In the case when there was more than one perpetrator in the incident, the incident was included in the "juvenile" category if there was at least one perpetrator under eighteen.

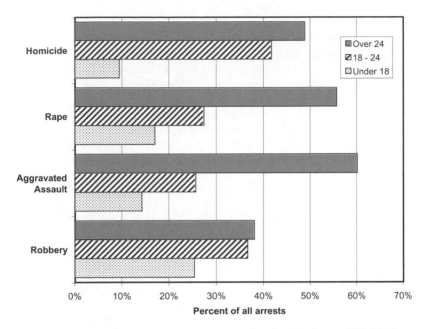

Fig. A1.—Arrests by age group as percentage of total, 1999. Source: FBI (2000).

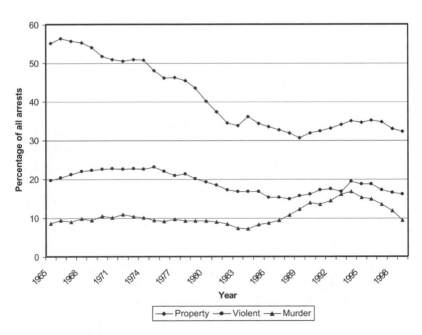

Fig. A2.—Arrests for juveniles under eighteen as percentage of total, 1965–99. Source: FBI (1966–2000).

REFERENCES

Becker, Elizabeth. 2001. "As Ex-Theorist on Young 'Superpredators,' Bush Aide Has Regrets." *New York Times* (February 9), p. A19.

Bennett, William J., John J. DiIulio, and John P. Walters. 1996. *Body Count: Moral Poverty and How to Win America's War against Crime and Drugs.* New York: Simon & Schuster.

Blumstein, Alfred. 1995. "Youth Violence, Guns, and the Illicit-Drug Industry." *Journal of Criminal Law and Criminology* 86:10–36.

———. 2000. "Disaggregating the Violence Trends." In *The Crime Drop in America*, edited by Alfred Blumstein and Joel Wallman. New York: Cambridge University Press.

———. 2001. "Why Is Crime Falling?—or Is It?" Paper presented in Washington, D.C., February 14.

Blumstein, Alfred, and Joel Wallman, eds. 2000. *The Crime Drop in America.* New York: Cambridge University Press.

Brown, Sarah S., and Leon Eisenberg. 1995. *Unintended Pregnancy and the Well-Being of Children and Families.* Washington, D.C.: National Academy Press.

Cohen, Lawrence E., and Kenneth C. Land. 1987. "Age Structure and Crime." *American Sociological Review* 52:170–83.

Cook, Philip J. 1985. "Is Robbery Becoming More Violent? An Analysis of Robbery Murder Trends since 1968." *Journal of Criminal Law and Criminology* 76:480–89.

———. 1991. "The Technology of Personal Violence." In *Crime and Justice: An Annual Review of Research*, vol. 14, edited by Michael Tonry. Chicago: University of Chicago Press.

———. 1998. "The Epidemic of Youth Gun Violence." In *Perspectives on Crime and Justice: 1997–1998 Lecture Series.* NCJ172851:107–16. Washington, D.C.: National Institute of Justice.

Cook, Philip J., and John H. Laub. 1986. "The (Surprising) Stability of Youth Crime Rates." *Journal of Quantitative Criminology* 2:265–77.

———. 1998. "The Unprecedented Epidemic in Youth Violence." In *Youth Violence*, edited by Michael Tonry and Mark H. Moore. Vol. 24 of *Crime and Justice: A Review of Research*, edited by Michael Tonry. Chicago: University of Chicago Press.

Cork, Daniel. 1999. "Examining Space-Time Interaction in City-Level Homicide Data: Crack Markets and the Diffusion of Guns Among Youth." *Journal of Quantitative Criminology* 15:379–406.

Donohue, John J., III, and Steven D. Levitt. 2001. "The Impact of Legalized Abortion on Crime." *Quarterly Journal of Economics* 116:379–420.

Fagan, Jeffrey, and Deanna L. Wilkinson. 1998. "Guns, Youth Violence, and Social Identity in Inner Cities." In *Youth Violence*, edited by Michael Tonry and Mark H. Moore. Vol. 24 of *Crime and Justice: A Review of Research*, edited by Michael Tonry. Chicago: University of Chicago Press.

Fagan, Jeffrey, Deanna Wilkinson, and Garth Davies. 2000. "Social Contagion of Youth Violence." Paper presented at the Urban Seminar Series on Children's Health and Safety, Urban Poverty Research Program, John F. Kennedy School of Government, Harvard University.

Fagan, Jeffrey, Franklin E. Zimring, and June Kim. 1998. "Declining Homicide in New York City: A Tale of Two Trends." *Journal of Criminal Law and Criminology* 88:1277–1323.

Fattah, Ezzat A. 1991. *Understanding Criminal Victimization: An Introduction to Theoretical Victimology.* Scarborough: Prentice-Hall Canada.

Federal Bureau of Investigation. 1966–2000. *Crime in the United States.* Washington, D.C.: U.S. Government Printing Office.

Feld, Barry C. 1998. "Juvenile and Criminal Justice Systems' Response to Youth Violence." In *Youth Violence*, edited by Michael Tonry and Mark H. Moore. Vol. 24 of *Crime and Justice: A Review of Research*, edited by Michael Tonry. Chicago: University of Chicago Press.

Fox, James Alan. 2000. "Demographics and U.S. Homicide." In *The Crime Drop in America*, edited by Alfred Blumstein and Joel Wallman. New York: Cambridge University Press.

———. 2001. "National and State Level Gun and Total Homicide Victimization and Offending Rates by Age, Sex, and Race, 1976–99." Unpublished report. Boston: Northeastern University.

Fox, James Alan, and Marianne W. Zawitz. 2000. *Homicide Trends in the United States: 1998 Update.* NCJ 179767. Washington, D.C.: Bureau of Justice Statistics.

Gladwell, Malcolm. 2000. *The Tipping Point: How Little Things Can Make a Big Difference.* Boston: Little, Brown.

Grogger, Jeffrey, and Michael Willis. 2000. "The Emergence of Crack Cocaine and the Rise of Urban Crime Rates." *Review of Economics and Statistics* 82:519–29.

Gruber, Jonathan, Phillip B. Levine, and Donald Staiger. 1999. "Abortion Legalization and Child Living Circumstances: Who Is the 'Marginal Child?'" *Quarterly Journal of Economics* 114:263–91.

Hemenway, David, Deborah Prothrow-Stith, Jack M. Bergstein, Roseanna Ander, and Bruce P. Kennedy. 1996. "Gun Carrying among Adolescents." *Law & Contemporary Problems* 59:39–54.

Holloway, Marguerite. 1999. "The Aborted Crime Wave?" *Scientific American* 281:23–24.

Joyce, Ted. 2001. "Did Legalized Abortion Lower Crime?" Working Paper Series no. 8319. New York: National Bureau of Economic Research.

Killias, Martin, and Marcelo F. Aebi. 2000. "Crime Trends in Europe from 1990 to 1996: How Europe Illustrates the Limits of the American Experience." *European Journal on Criminal Policy and Research* 8:43–63.

LaFree, Gary. 1998a. *Losing Legitimacy: Street Crime and the Decline of Social Institutions in America.* Boulder, Colo.: Westview.

———. 1998b. "Social Institutions and the Crime 'Bust' of the 1990s." *Journal of Criminal Law and Criminology* 88:1325–68.

———. 1999. "Declining Violent Crime Rates in the 1990s: Predicting Crime Booms and Busts." *Annual Review of Sociology* 25:145–68.

36   Philip J. Cook and John H. Laub

———. 2000. "Explaining the Crime Bust of the 1990s: A Review Essay of 'The Crime Drop in America.'" *Journal of Criminal Law and Criminology* 91: 269–306.

Land, Kenneth C., and Patricia L. McCall. 2001. "The Indeterminacy of Forecasts of Crime Rates and Juvenile Offenses." In *Juvenile Crime, Juvenile Justice*, edited by Joan McCord, Cathy Spatz Widom, and Nancy A. Crowell. Washington, D.C.: National Academy Press.

Levine, Phillip B., D. Staiger, Thomas J. Kane, and D. J. Zimmerman. 1996. "*Roe v. Wade* and American Fertility." National Bureau of Economic Research Working Paper no. 5615, June.

Levitt, Steven D. 1999. "The Limited Role of Changing Age Structure in Explaining Aggregate Crime Rates." *Criminology* 37:581–98.

Levitt, Steven D., and Lance Lochner. 2001. "The Determinants of Juvenile Crime." In *Risky Behavior among Youths: An Economic Analysis*, edited by Jonathan Gruber. Chicago: University of Chicago Press.

Lutter, Randall, and Elizabeth Mader. 2001. "Litigating Lead-Based Paint Hazards: Is It a Solution?" Paper prepared for the American Enterprise Institute–Brookings Institution Joint Center Conference on Regulation through Litigation, April 26.

Maltz, Michael D. 1998. "Visualizing Homicide: A Research Note." *Journal of Quantitative Criminology* 14:397–410.

———. 1999. *Bridging Gaps in Police Crime Data*. Washington, D.C.: Bureau of Justice Statistics.

Nevin, Rick. 2000. "How Lead Exposure Relates to Temporal Changes in IQ, Violent Crime, and Unwed Pregnancy." *Environmental Research Section A* 83:1–22.

O'Brien, Robert M. 1999. "Measuring the Convergence/Divergence of 'Serious Crime' Arrest Rates for Males and Females: 1960–1995." *Journal of Quantitative Criminology* 15:97–114.

O'Brien, Robert M., Jean Stockard, and Lynne Isaacson. 1999. "The Enduring Effects of Cohort Characteristics on Age-Specific Homicide Rates, 1960–1995." *American Journal of Sociology* 104:1061–95.

Pfeiffer, Christian. 1998. "Juvenile Crime and Violence in Europe." In *Crime and Justice: An Annual Review of Research*, vol. 23, edited by Michael Tonry. Chicago: University of Chicago Press.

Rosenfeld, Richard. 2000. "Patterns in Adult Homicide: 1980–1995." In *The Crime Drop in America*, edited by Alfred Blumstein and Joel Wallman. New York: Cambridge University Press.

Siegel, Larry J. 1995. *Criminology*. Minneapolis: West.

Spelman, William. 2001. "The Limited Importance of Prison Expansion." In *The Crime Drop in America*, edited by Alfred Blumstein and Joel Wallman. New York: Cambridge University Press.

Steffensmeier, Darrell, and Miles D. Harer. 1999. "Making Sense of Recent U.S. Crime Trends, 1980 to 1996/1998: Age Composition Effects and Other Explanations." *Journal of Research in Crime and Delinquency* 36:235–74.

Stretesky, Paul B., and Michael J. Lynch. 2001. "The Relationship between

Lead Exposure and Homicide." *Archives of Pediatric and Adolescent Medicine* 155:579–82.

Tonry, Michael, and Mark H. Moore, eds. 1998. *Youth Violence.* Vol. 24 of *Crime and Justice: A Review of Research,* edited by Michael Tonry. Chicago: University of Chicago Press.

U.S. Department of Commerce, Economics and Statistics Administration, Bureau of the Census. 1966–2000. *Statistical Abstract of the United States.* Washington, D.C.: U.S. Government Publishing Office.

Wiersema, Brian, Colin Loftin, and David McDowall. 2000. "A Comparison of Supplementary Homicide Reports and National Vital Statistics System Homicide Estimates for U.S. Counties." *Homicide Studies* 4:317–40.

Wilson, James Q. 2002. "Crime: Public Policies for Crime Control." In *Crime,* 2d ed., edited by James Q. Wilson and Joan Petersilia. Oakland, Calif.: ICS Press.

Zimring, Franklin E. 1998. *American Youth Violence.* New York: Oxford University Press.

Ronald F. Wright

Counting the Cost of Sentencing in North Carolina, 1980–2000

ABSTRACT

North Carolina's Fair Sentencing Act of 1979 emphasized the need to reduce sentence disparities. Because the statute lacked any enforcement mechanism, judges reverted to earlier practices within five years. In the Structured Sentencing Act of 1993, legislators put concerns about disparity to the side and concentrated on changing the state's prison use priorities. The new law lengthened prison terms for violent crimes and assigned more property offenders to nonprison sanctions. It also guided judicial choices among "intermediate" and "community" punishments for lesser crimes. Tight controls on judges made it possible to match corrections resources to sentencing practices. The intended effects took hold during the first five years. Judges imposed longer prison terms for violent crimes and sentenced a larger proportion of property felons to intermediate and community sanctions. The longer-term effects may prove more difficult to manage. Appellate judges have remained uninvolved in sentencing policy; no "common law" of sentencing is developing. Prosecutors are dismissing and discounting more charges while at the same time obtaining more serious felony convictions overall.

The sentencing system in North Carolina has changed even faster over the last two decades than the state's demographics, and that is saying a lot. A state that once had the highest rate of imprisonment in the nation now has a rate just under the national average. A state that once devoted almost no money to community corrections now publishes an

Ronald F. Wright is professor of law at Wake Forest University.

annual compendium of programs to keep judges updated on the options available. Where the state once assumed that prison space would be available for whatever punishments the legislatures and judges together might impose, today it forecasts prison populations twenty years into the future. The route from the old system to the new has been erratic and eventful.

This essay records the key events in the development of sentencing policy in North Carolina since 1980. The plans and motives of the people involved are difficult to reconstruct and in some cases remain unrecorded today. The essay also explores the free movement of ideas in sentencing policy. Some features of the North Carolina experience may be transferable elsewhere; others might not. But North Carolina's efforts do confirm that sentencing ideas can move from state to state, because events in other states shaped North Carolina's choices.

This case history covers a full twenty years because in North Carolina there were two distinct phases to the redesign effort, and the second played out differently than the first. The first phase began as a reaction to the uncontrolled growth of expensive prisons and to concern about the unequal distribution of sentences. The remedy at the time was to send stronger signals to judges about the proper sentences in normal cases. The legislature chose "presumptive" sentences for judges to impose for each class of crime. But the new system's lack of an enforcement mechanism, together with its failure to link corrections resources with the sentences that judges were handing down, proved fatal. Within five years, the system was in trouble.

The second phase focused more emphatically on prison costs as the problem, and it relied on centralized control over judges as the solution. A commission created a set of sentencing guidelines that gave judges less power to sentence outside the preferred range for each class of crime. Overall size was the key to this new system; equality of sentences among individual offenders (or among racial groups) was not a concern this time around. The new sentencing rules lengthened prison terms for violent offenders and diverted many less serious offenders into nonprison punishments.

The second revamped system—the one operating today—is a fiscal planner's approach to sentencing. The key question is not the effect of the sentence on the criminal or on crime rates; instead, the key questions are how sentences affect the ability of the state to plan what it needs, and how sentences affect the overall credibility of the system with the public. This approach bypasses many of the impenetrable questions of sentencing philosophy. Throughout the second redesign of sentencing policy in North Carolina, the participants debated in terms of cost. Most debaters presumed that longer prison terms would be the ideal for the great majority of offenders, but an equally important starting assumption was the public's limited willingness to pay for this public good. So the debate returned time and again to ways of getting the most out of a regrettably limited resource. Over the last twenty years, money became the universal solvent of sentencing disputes in North Carolina.

The system that emerged from these two phases of reform is distinctive in several ways. First, the new laws place unusually tight controls on sentencing judges: the laws provide for three fairly generous ranges of sentences (mitigated, presumptive, and aggravated ranges) but do not allow the judge to "depart" from the guidelines to impose some different sentence in an unusual case. Second, the structured sentencing laws place an unusual emphasis on integrating prison and non-prison sanctions. The felony and misdemeanor rules include detailed guidance for the selection of nonprison sanctions, while systems in other states offer more open-ended instructions for nonprison sentences. The funding for prison and nonprison sanctions is also tightly connected. Finally, the North Carolina system is distinctive in its routine use of prison population projections. While most states project prison populations on a regular basis, the projections in North Carolina became part of an iterative process during the drafting of guidelines. The projections also became a routine feature in all legislative debate on crime measures.

An observer, with the benefit of twenty years of perspective, might draw a few lessons from North Carolina. The state illustrates both the limits and virtues of a managerial approach to sentencing. Rather than reacting to periodic problems in the prisons and courts, legislators and other officials in North Carolina have paid steady attention to the link between sentencing policy and corrections resources. The sentencing laws no longer benefit from periods of benign neglect. The emphasis on prison costs has squelched debate on some fundamental ethical questions, such as the proper reach of the criminal law and the equality of sentences among similar offenders. But on the positive side, legislators now expect systematic rather than anecdotal information during debates on crime and normally consider the long-term fiscal consequences of their actions.

North Carolina also shows that relatively subtle arguments can sometimes succeed in the politics of crime. Political leaders can sell new sentencing laws as a package making the best use of scarce prison resources, by trading less prison time for some low-priority crimes and thereby freeing up more prison beds for high-priority crimes. Although these ideas are relatively complex because they involve the interaction among sentences for many different people and many different crimes, they translate well into everyday public debate. This political outcome is easiest to achieve in a setting where the corrections system is still growing, as it was in North Carolina during the 1990s.

The state also offers some interesting lessons about the role of judges in sentencing reforms. Appellate judges played virtually no part in shaping structured sentencing in North Carolina. All the judicial input came from individual judges who worked with the commission and from the shifting patterns of sentences that trial judges imposed. Appellate courts can surely develop useful sentencing doctrine to redirect or reinforce new statutes, but a "common law" of sentencing is not necessary for a system to succeed.

This essay takes the following route through the North Carolina experience. Section I summarizes the first phase of sentencing reform under the Fair Sentencing Act (FSA), from 1981 to 1988. Section II revisits the period from 1988 to 1991, when Democratic leaders in the legislature reevaluated the Fair Sentencing Act and diagnosed the reasons for its failure. Section III then describes the efforts of the legislature and the sentencing commission to create a new structured sentencing system. The section ends with some observations about the features that make North Carolina's system distinctive when compared to the sentencing laws in other states.

Section IV recounts events in the legislature just after the passage of the Structured Sentencing Act, when the legislators very nearly undermined their earlier work by returning to uncoordinated crime legislation. Section V reviews the major effects of the new sentencing laws on prison sentences and community corrections, along with the shifts in charging and sentencing practices that have occurred as prosecutors, judges, and others have adjusted to the system. Section VI, the conclusion, surveys some of the challenges now facing North Carolina and some of the implications of two decades of sentencing upheaval in the state.

I. Fair Sentencing Act Era, 1981–88

The first phase of the transformation of North Carolina sentencing was embodied in the Fair Sentencing Act of 1979. The FSA placed tighter statutory controls on the sentences that judges imposed, while eliminating parole. The creators of the new law hoped that it would produce less disparity among similar defendants and eliminate over-crowding in the state prison system. After some initial success, how-ever, the FSA failed on both counts. Because judges routinely avoided the presumptive sentences set out in the statute, the system drifted for a decade without any centralized coordinating force. A second phase in the transformation of North Carolina sentencing became necessary, and the failures of the FSA shaped the priorities of reformers in the second phase.

A. The Brief Promise of the Fair Sentencing Act

Before 1981, North Carolina's sentencing system used a division of labor that was typical for the times. The criminal code, created and amended in a haphazard way over the years, authorized a broad range of sentences for each crime. The sentencing judge in a particular case chose both the disposition (prison or some other sanction such as sim-ple probation) and the duration of the sentence from within the statu-tory range. The parole commission released some offenders serving prison terms before the announced sentence was complete. For most crimes, the offender had to serve at least one quarter of the minimum sentence imposed before becoming eligible for parole (N.C. Gen. Stat. sec. 15A-1371).

By the 1970s, this uncoordinated and discretionary system was draw-ing criticism from several different quarters. Increasing prison costs prompted Governor Bob Scott to ask the North Carolina Bar Associa-tion to study the state's corrections and sentencing. The Bar Associa-tion's Penal System Study Committee published two reports that rec-ommended ways to move some offenders—such as public drunkenness and nonsupport cases—out of the prison system (North Carolina Bar Association 1971, 1972). Many of the recommendations in these re-ports dealt with ways to reduce the caseload for probation officers and to improve the rehabilitative effects of prison programs. The commit-tee also emphasized the need for further study of the "great disparity between lengths of sentences imposed upon individuals with like back-grounds for like offenses" (North Carolina Bar Association 1972, p. 14).

Meanwhile, the prison system continued to grow rapidly (Clarke and Pope 1982). The per capita rate of imprisonment in North Carolina was the highest in the nation in 1973—the state's prisons and jails held 184 out of every 100,000 residents, compared with the national average of eighty-seven for state systems. North Carolina's rates were higher than any other state's for much of the decade, occasionally finishing a close second to Georgia (Bureau of Justice Statistics 1992, table 6.72). The Department of Correction was submitting ever-larger requests for construction funds (Legislative Commission on Correctional Programs 1977, p. 3).

In response to the two concerns of prison overcrowding and disparate sentences, the legislature in 1974 appointed the Legislative Commission on Correctional Programs, dubbed the "Knox commission" for its chair, state senator Eddie Knox (1973 N.C. Session Laws, 2d Sess. 1974, Res. 184). Knox was an attorney and a friend and former university classmate of Democratic lieutenant governor (and senate president) Jim Hunt. Changes in the sentencing laws were a priority for Hunt.

The commission set out to develop a coordinated state corrections policy that would depend less heavily on prison and produce more consistent sentences for felons. The Knox commission issued its major recommendations in its 1977 final report. The report began with a discussion of increasing crime rates during the 1970s and pointed to disparity in sentences as the key shortcoming of the system that undermined public confidence and the deterrent value of the criminal law. It recommended sentences that were "shorter," more "certain," and more "uniform" (Legislative Commission on Correctional Programs 1977, pp. 6–8, 34–35). To that end, the commission called for revised sentencing statutes that would assign all felonies to a small number of classes and set a "presumptive penalty" for each class of felonies. Although the proposal permitted judges to decide on the disposition (prison or some other sanction), it controlled durations more closely. Judges would be required to impose the presumptive prison term unless some statutorily defined aggravating or mitigating factor was present in the case. Appellate review would ensure that trial judges complied with the presumptive sentences.[1]

[1] The Knox commission based its presumptive sentence concept on the work of Alan Dershowitz and the Twentieth Century Fund Task Force on Criminal Sentencing (1976). The final report also discussed the work of Marvin Frankel, dealing with the need to constrain the discretion of sentencing judges through legal rules (Frankel 1973).

The general assembly voted down the earliest version of the bill, based mostly on the objections of judges and lawyers. Both groups hoped to retain the judge's power to individualize sentences. Attorneys were concerned that the presumptive terms would limit their ability to influence sentence outcomes during plea bargaining. But the legislation still got vocal support from Jim Hunt (by now the governor), who believed that more "certain" sentences were consistent with the anticrime agenda of his 1976 campaign (Clarke 1984). After the Bar Association failed to produce a serious alternative to the Knox commission package, the legislation finally passed in 1979. The Fair Sentencing Act took effect in 1981.

The strategy of the FSA (like the Knox commission proposal) was to eliminate parole and to control sentences more closely on the front end. The statute retained the old maximum and minimum boundaries for authorized sentences but also designated for each crime a new "presumptive" sentence within those ranges for judges to impose. The presumptive sentences would, on average, provide shorter but more certain prison terms for felons. For instance, the FSA assigned a presumptive sentence of three years for crimes such as involuntary manslaughter, assault with a deadly weapon inflicting serious injury, and felonious larceny. A presumptive term of twelve years applied to second degree murder, rape, armed robbery, and burglary.

In place of parole, the FSA created appellate review of sentences above the presumptive level. Trial judges had to provide written reasons for prison terms lasting a longer or shorter time than the presumptive term. The FSA also established automatic reductions in sentences for "good time" (one day reduction for each day without major misconduct in prison) and "gain time" (the amount varied, based on participation in prison work or education programs).

But the presumptive sentences of the FSA had no real power to control the sentences that judges selected, so long as they remained within the existing statutory maximum and minimum. For instance, there was usually no presumptive outcome for the judge's disposition decision, leaving the judge free to select prison, probation, or some other sanction. Furthermore, the judge could depart from the presumptive duration for any legally adequate "aggravating" or "mitigating" factor, so long as written reasons for the departure were given (N.C. Gen. Stat. sec. 15A-1340.4; Clarke 1991; Meyer 1993). Even a perfunctory mention of one mitigating or aggravating factor was an acceptable statement of reasons.

TABLE 1

Fair Sentencing Act Effects on Prison Sentences for Felonies,
1981–86

	Median Length Imposed (Months)	Mean Length Imposed (Months)	Standard Deviation (Months)	Percent of Active Sentences above Presumptive
1976–81	60	108	143–67	...
1981–82	36	78	112	35
1982–83	36	87	...	41
1983–84	48	91	...	46
1984–85	54	96	...	51
1985–86	60	98	156	53

SOURCE.—Clarke 1987, pp. 11–12.

Although the Knox commission report never specified the aggravating and mitigating factors that would authorize a sentence above or below the presumptive level, the legislation created long lists of such factors—sixteen aggravators and fifteen mitigators. The FSA (unlike the Knox commission package) also empowered trial and appellate courts to add to these lists over time (N.C. Gen. Stat., sec. 15A-1340.4). Trial judges and prosecutors in particular were concerned about possible increases in trial rates, so they convinced the legislature to amend the FSA in 1980 (a year before the bill took effect) to treat a plea of guilty as a mitigating factor that would authorize a sentence below the presumptive level (Clarke 1987, p. 3). This became the largest exemption from the FSA, taking most felony cases outside the reach of the presumptive sentences.

Despite these limits, the FSA had the desired effects for the first few years after passage. Sentences did cluster close to the presumptive level, the length of active terms imposed moved down, and growth in the prison population slowed. Although the judges usually could find a way to avoid a presumptive sentence, that presumptive sentence gave a more precise benchmark than before, and many judges chose a sentence at or near the benchmark (Clarke et al. 1983, pp. 6–11). Racial differences in sentencing outcomes also became smaller under the FSA (Clarke 1987, pp. 19–20).

But the unifying and moderating effects did not last long. By the mid-1980s, judges treated most cases as aggravated cases, and their sentences started drifting away from the presumptive level. Table 1 summarizes evidence that Clarke (1987, pp. 11–12) assembled in his study of the effects of the FSA. The mean and median length for felony prison sentences imposed, the standard deviation among felony prison sentences, and the percentage of active sentences above the presumptive level all crept up after 1982. The gap in imprisonment rates among blacks and whites began to grow again (Clarke 1997, p. 72). By 1986, sentences looked much as they did before the FSA took effect.

Why did the effects of the FSA on judges last for such a short time? There are several possible reasons. First, the percentage of the active felony sentences that defendants actually served continued to go down after the FSA took effect (Clarke 1987, fig. 24). The average felony defendant sentenced in 1979–80 to a term under four years served just under 40 percent of the sentence imposed (down from about 50 percent in 1973–74). By 1981–82, the median dropped under 35 percent. Although the downward trend was already happening before the FSA era, judges were keenly aware of early releases allowed through automatic statutory grants of good time and gain time, as opposed to the less predictable releases through parole under the old system (Clarke 1991, pp. 44–48).

Second, the appellate courts made clear in their earliest rulings on the FSA that they would not actively monitor the sentences imposed above the presumptive levels. Because the statute did not specify how a court should weigh the aggravating and mitigating factors present in a case, the sentencing judge was safe from review if he or she found one very clear aggravating factor along with any mitigating factors arguably present and then imposed a sentence above or below the presumptive level (*State v. Baucom*, 66 N.C. App. 298 [1984]; *State v. Parker*, 315 N.C. 249 [1985]).

Thus, by the middle of the 1980s the FSA became almost irrelevant to the sentencing practices of judges. Without any meaningful control over sentences on the front end, and no parole authority to adjust sentences on the back end, there was no centralizing force in North Carolina sentencing. No institution had the power to draw case-level sentences into a statewide policy that would match the available corrections resources.

B. New Limits on Prison Space

Even before the FSA started operating, many observers in the state worried that the new statute would not change sentencing practices enough. Two influential in-state foundations funded a study commission whose name clearly indicated its purpose: the Citizens Commission on Alternatives to Incarceration. The commission, chaired by Judge Willis Whichard of the state's court of appeals, issued a report in 1982 that outlined "the case for community-based penalties rather than prison for appropriate offenders" (Citizens Commission on Alternatives to Incarceration 1982, p. 4).

The legislature responded to this report in 1983 with the passage of the Community Penalties Act (N.C. Gen. Stat., secs. 143B-500 to -507). The new Community Penalties Program authorized private nonprofit agencies to create (at state expense) "client-specific plans" for the sentencing judge, recommending community penalties for some defendants who might otherwise receive a prison term. These agencies, in turn, encouraged the development of new or expanded community penalty programs at the local level.

But at this point, such nonprofit agencies only appeared in a few of the more populous counties. For the time being, community corrections programs offered alternatives to prison in very few cases. Meanwhile, increases in the state's population, with correspondingly higher levels of crime in the state, pushed up the number of convictions and prison admissions. The prison population at the end of 1981 was 15,786; by 1988, the population was 17,292.

By some measures, this level of growth was modest. The prison population increased at the same pace as the state's overall population, and this happened during a period when the rate of incarceration in the United States as a whole was moving up steeply. As table 2 shows, North Carolina's rate of incarceration stayed flat between 1981 (when it was 248 per 100,000) and 1988 (when it was 249), while the national rate—that is, the average rate for state systems in the country—went from 144 to 227.

But hidden beneath this unchanged incarceration rate in the late 1980s was an ever greater demand for prison space. Because there was no major building program underway in the early or mid-1980s, the prison system was housing far more people than its rated capacity. Judges wanted to impose longer prison terms on more offenders, but there was no room for them. Thus, the number of prison admissions was moving up faster than the prison population, meaning that prisoners were staying in the system for shorter periods of time (Clarke 1997).

The federal courts entered the scene at this point and played a pivotal role. Attorneys for state prisoners, including attorneys at North

TABLE 2

Incarceration Rates (per 100,000) and Prison Populations, 1971–99

	Prison Population	North Carolina Rate of Incarceration	Southeast Region Rate	National Rate
1971	7,795	153	124	86
1972	8,263	160	125	84
1973	9,641	184	128	87
1974	11,006	207	135	93
1975	11,449	210	150	102
1976	13,257	214	161	111
1977	14,250	234	169	116
1978	13,252	223	181	123
1979	14,255	240	196	126
1980	15,382	244	188	130
1981	15,786	248	201	144
1982	16,660	255	224	160
1983	15,485	233	225	167
1984	16,469	246	231	176
1985	17,501	254	236	187
1986	17,912	257	248	201
1987	17,404	250	255	211
1988	17,292	249	266	227
1989	17,665	250	292	253
1990	18,619	265	316	272
1991	19,116	269	333	287
1992	20,454	290	355	305
1993	21,892	305	380	322
1994	23,648	323	454	356
1995	29,253	384	478	378
1996	30,647	376	490	394
1997	31,612	370	506	410
1998	31,961	358	520	423
1999	31,086	349	543	434

SOURCE.—Bureau of Justice Statistics 1992, 2000.

Carolina Prisoner Legal Services (an offshoot of North Carolina Legal Services), filed several class action lawsuits in federal district court in the early 1980s. In the most important of the cases, *Small v. Martin* (No. 85-987-CRT, E.D.N.C., April 3, 1989), the plaintiffs asked Judge Earl Britt to declare that overcrowded conditions in forty-nine of the state's ninety-seven prisons amounted to cruel and unusual punishment in violation of the Eighth Amendment.[2] The same argument had

[2] Prisons elsewhere in the state were covered in companion cases such as Thorne v. Martin, No. 87-446-CRT (E.D.N.C., April 3, 1989).

worked for prisoners in earlier litigation affecting a smaller group of prisons in the state; the odds of success for these prisoners looked very strong. The state resisted gamely at first. The plaintiffs filed suit early in 1985, and the court arranged for settlement negotiations (with a magistrate presiding) to begin by the end of the year. Those negotiations did not produce an agreement until December 1988.

Although the effect was not immediate, the federal litigation eventually spurred the state into action. Major expansion of the prison system would take time and would be very costly, so the first legislative responses limited the demand for prison space, without increasing supply. In 1985, the legislature passed the Emergency Powers Act, restoring to the parole commission a limited power to release felons 180 days before their release dates (N.C. Gen. Stat., sec. 15A-1380.2[h], 148-4.1). These powers were strengthened in 1986 and 1987. The pending federal litigation created an urgent need to control overall prison population and muted any opposition to the act.

The Democratic lieutenant governor (and senate leader) Bob Jordan, along with the longtime house speaker, Democrat Liston Ramsey, also appointed a special committee on prisons late in 1985, with eight members from the North Carolina House of Representatives and eight from the North Carolina Senate. Representative Ann Barnes and Senator David Parnell served as cochairs of the special committee, and from that position they became the most influential legislators on sentencing and corrections questions for several years to come. The legislative leaders chose Barnes and Parnell for these positions because they both already chaired the key committees dealing with appropriations for prisons.

The first order of business was to neutralize the threat from the federal litigation. Soon after the trial began in late 1985, the state entered settlement negotiations in *Small v. Martin.* Representative Barnes served with other legislators on the "Settlement Committee," along with designees of Republican governor Jim Martin, whose election in 1984 preceded the start of the lawsuit. Through these negotiations, it became plain to the state what prison changes would be necessary to satisfy the federal court. As in other prison litigation around the country, the judge seemed inclined to require the elimination of triple bunking and to impose some minimum square footage for each prisoner.

On the recommendation of the special committee, the general assembly in 1987 passed the Emergency Prison Population Stabilization

Act (North Carolina Special Committee on Prisons 1987). This legislation anticipated a way out of the federal litigation. It established a
formula for setting a "prison cap," originally limiting the population
to 17,640 inmates. As the state built more prison facilities, it was able
to increase the prison cap to 19,324 in November 1990 and again to
21,400 in March 1994. The act also gave the parole commission the
authority to release the number of offenders necessary to remain under
the cap, although they could not release those sentenced under certain
mandatory minimum statutes, including some narcotics crimes.

By March 1989, the settlement committee completed its work, and
the legislature ratified the agreement. As anticipated by the prison cap
legislation, the state agreed to eliminate triple bunking by July 1989
and to attain fifty square feet of living space per inmate by 1994. Given
the representation from both political parties on the settlement committee during its three years of work, there was not much opposition
to the final outcome. Judge Britt might have required even more from
the state if there had been no agreement.

To keep the system within the limits of the prison cap despite the
increased admissions and the longer durations that judges were an-
nouncing in their sentences, the parole commission had to release
more offenders before the end of their prison terms, sometimes several
hundred per week. The percentage of the announced sentence that an
average felon actually served dropped quickly; it eventually reached
less than 20 percent for some felony classes (North Carolina Sentencing and Policy Advisory Commission [NCSPAC] 1992a; Lubitz 2001).
By 1991, misdemeanants served 6 percent of their sentences. Felons
served as much as 35 percent of their sentences for the most serious
violent felonies, and as little as 19 percent for the least serious. Judges
responded by increasing the lengths of the prison terms they imposed,
in the (mostly futile) hope of influencing the parole commission in a
particular case.[3] Thus, the average sentence lengths announced by
judges were increasing at the same time that the average times served
were declining.

Offenders who committed misdemeanors or low-level felonies could

[3] Under earlier parole provisions, a felon was not eligible for parole until he or she
had served the minimum sentence announced by the judge, provided that the judge's
minimum was no more than one-fifth the length of the maximum term. However, legislation in 1987 allowed the parole authority to ignore these limits for most offenders—
sex offenses, murders, and drug trafficking convictions were excluded—when necessary
to stay under the prison cap (N.C. Gen. Stat., sec. 148-4.1).

count on being released immediately—or being held only as long as it took the Department of Correction to complete the paperwork and fax it to the prison (Governor's Advisory Board on Prisons and Punishment 1990, p. 11; Peek 1992). The state also released probation violators almost immediately, which meant that probationers no longer had much incentive to comply with conditions. Many offenders facing a choice of lengthy probation terms or shorter prison terms opted for prison, knowing that they would be released immediately and could avoid months of supervision by probation officers. (The state constitution gave this choice to convicted offenders, since it required consent from offenders before judges could impose conditions of probation.) Because neither prison nor alternative sanctions were credible, North Carolina had effectively decriminalized most misdemeanors and a few lower-level felonies.

II. Creating a Commission, 1988–90

When the immediate threat of federal court intervention in the state prisons dissipated in 1988, legislators stepped back to look for a longer-term solution. They drew some lessons from the FSA. The second phase of reform would require tighter centralized control over judicial sentencing, more effort to develop attractive nonprison options for the sentencing judge to choose, and greater ability to adjust quickly as practices changed over time.

A. Leadership from the Special Committee

Between 1988 and 1990, the special committee on prisons in the general assembly and the governor cast around for ideas that would succeed where the FSA had failed. This dialogue with the governor led the general assembly to characterize the state's problem in terms of cost: the prisons were overcrowded, and a major expansion would be expensive. As a secondary matter, the special committee came to believe that the gap between the sentence announced and the sentence served was a major blow to public credibility for the system. In contrast to the debate leading up to the FSA in 1979, the debate this time placed only minor emphasis on the distribution of sentences within the state. Sentence disparity generally, and racial disparity in particular, played only a peripheral part in the debate.

Republican governor Jim Martin played an active role in the protracted negotiations over the federal prison litigation. The litigation convinced him that some major changes were necessary in the sentencing system. He believed that "alternative" sanctions were ineffective and made frequent public statements about the need to add enough prison capacity in North Carolina to give judges "alternatives to the alternatives" (North Carolina Public Television 1991; Drennan 2001). In February 1989, he appointed an advisory panel chaired by supreme court justice Burley Mitchell that recommended in 1990 a major increase in prison construction. The panel's final report reviewed the downward trend in North Carolina's rate of imprisonment (see table 2) and noted an increase in the amount of reported crime in the state. The report also pointed—selectively—to states that had increased imprisonment rates and decreased reported crimes in recent years. The conclusion for the panel was clear: it endorsed Martin's proposal to seek $400 million in bond funds for prison expansion and proposed using that money to increase system capacity to 29,000 within five years. Prison capacity at the time was 18,000 (Governor's Advisory Board on Prisons and Punishment 1990).

Meanwhile, the general assembly's special committee on prisons showed little interest in such a large-scale expansion. Despite forceful requests by the Department of Correction for new construction funds every year from 1986 through 1990, the legislature paid for new facilities only grudgingly. It authorized $154 million for prison construction between 1985 and 1990, after authorizing $100 million the previous decade (North Carolina Special Committee on Prisons 1990, p. 3).

Representative Barnes and Senator Parnell came to view these appropriations as piecemeal responses to an unchanging problem. So in February 1988, they wrote a "Proposal" to the special committee, designed to break out of this cycle (North Carolina Special Committee on Prisons 1990, p. 71). While acknowledging that the committee's early willingness to fund new prisons had strengthened the state's negotiating position in prison litigation, the "emergency" had now passed. The time had arrived, said Barnes and Parnell, to develop a "balanced system of justice." The state needed to create a fuller "continuum" of sanctions and rehabilitation services. To achieve this balance, it was necessary to use nonprison sanctions and to control more closely the power of sentencing judges who were "allocating the State's penal resources." A sentencing guidelines commission could make this possible by developing more specific crime categories and punishment ranges (North Carolina Special Committee on Prisons 1990, p. 71).

The special committee endorsed the Barnes-Parnell Proposal, and House Speaker Liston Ramsey and Lieutenant Governor Bob Jordan used it as the basis for a "clarification" of their charge to the special committee in March 1988 (North Carolina Special Committee on Prisons 1990, p. 74). This was a critical moment in the transition to a new sentencing structure. Even though the threat of federal litigation was now defused, and even though the governor was speaking often in public about the need to emphasize major growth in the prison system, the Democratic leadership in the legislature wanted to shift more money and attention to alternative sanctions.

Why were the legislative leaders so reluctant to endorse prison expansion? The full answer is unknowable. But their attitude toward prison expansion was driven more by money than by prison's effects on crime rates. In a weakened economy, the state at that point (unlike the more prosperous mid-1990s) struggled to balance its budget as required by the state constitution. In 1990, Standard & Poor's credit rating service placed some of North Carolina's AAA-rated debt on "CreditWatch" because of the state's growing estimated deficit (Yacoe 1990). In a state that treasured its traditionally sound credit rating, this was serious business.

Moreover, this tight budget was threatening another major priority. State leaders were especially concerned about the weak system of primary and secondary schools in the state. They were tired of the annual low ratings of North Carolina students on standardized tests and were determined to spend more on education. The legislative leaders saw that a major shift of resources into prisons would wreck their plans to transform education. Key leaders, such as Ann Barnes and David Parnell, were elected from safely Democratic districts where the constituents shared their concern for public education.

After receiving its "clarified" charge, the special committee set to work, hiring consultants from the National Institute of Sentencing Alternatives (NISA) at Brandeis University and the Community Justice Resource Center in Greensboro, North Carolina. The members heard testimony from state corrections officials, county commissioners, and many others. These witnesses highlighted the popularity of the "truth in sentencing" concept, and the special committee started describing its legislative package in these terms, rather than in terms of "sentencing disparity."

The special committee's choice of NISA to serve as a consultant showed the high priority that Barnes and Parnell placed on nonprison sanctions as part of a "balanced" sentencing policy. Although the legislature had passed the Community Penalties Act in 1983, the special committee found that community penalties had not progressed nearly far enough. The first phase of a report from the consultants at NISA in 1988 analyzed profiles of the prison and probation populations and pointed to a pool of 4,000–5,000 low-risk offenders (25–30 percent of the prison population at the time) who could be moved from prison into other corrections programs (Corrigan 1989*a*). To make this growth possible, the state needed to develop for itself—or convince local governments to develop—more openings in a greater variety of community sanctions.

Even if the additional program slots became available, experience under the FSA showed that judges might not use the slots. To make this growth in nonprison sanctions possible, the special committee looked for ways to increase centralized control over sentencing judges.

The NISA report pointed to states with sentencing commissions— such as Minnesota, Washington, and Delaware—as the answer to the question of centralized control (Corrigan 1989*b*).[4] The special committee became convinced that a sentencing commission combined several attractions. A commission could create sentencing standards that combined clear rules for ordinary cases with more judicial flexibility for unusual cases. Further, a commission could respond quickly to changes in practice by amending the existing rules (Corrigan 1990). Legislators who had seen their good intentions in the FSA turn to ashes in less than a decade knew how important it was to have responsive sentencing rules. But the central attraction of a sentencing commission was its ability to serve as a "vital link" between sentencing policy and the available corrections resources (North Carolina Special Committee on Prisons 1990, p. 22). Unlike under the FSA, sentencing judges using guidelines would not promise more than the state was willing to deliver.

B. Directives to the Commission

The legislature met in "short session" in 1990, a session meant to address only budgetary matters and noncontroversial issues. The special committee's recommended bill had the support of the Democratic leadership in the house and senate; most prominently, Barnes and Parnell obtained the backing of House Speaker Dan Blue. Blue, who was newly elected to the post of house speaker, was the first African-

---

[4] The academic consensus was also shifting strongly in this direction (Tonry 1979; Frankel and Orland 1984; Clarke 1987).

American to hold that office. He had served on the settlement committee in the federal litigation and was acutely interested in ways to control prison costs.

The committee's bill passed through the legislative process without attracting much attention. With both chambers firmly in Democratic hands (Republicans had not controlled either the house or the senate since Reconstruction), the party leadership called the shots in the streamlined proceedings of the short session. The house and the senate both adopted the final conference committee version by unanimous votes.

The Sentencing and Policy Advisory Commission Act of 1990 devoted careful attention to the membership and powers of the commission. The twenty-three members of the commission obtained their seats through a balkanized appointment process. Some appointments came from the Republican governor and lieutenant governor; others came from the Democratic chief justice of the supreme court and the Democratic leadership of the house and senate. Various units of state government with criminal justice responsibilities named other appointees, including the Department of Correction, the Department of Crime Control and Public Safety, and the Parole Commission. Some commissioners came from the professional associations for sheriffs, county commissioners, chiefs of police, district attorneys, district court judges, superior court judges, and criminal defense lawyers. Still other members came from advocacy organizations, such as the Victim Assistance Network and the North Carolina Sentencing Alternatives Association (N.C. Gen. Stat., sec. 164-37). Although the twenty-three-member commission was larger than usual for a sentencing commission (Austin et al. 1996, p. 36), the wide representation on the commission would ultimately become one of its strengths.

But the 1990 law was short on specifics to guide the commission once the appointments were in place. The act instructed the commission to create a few analytical tools but left the uses of those tools wide open. The legislature told the commission to "develop a correctional population simulation model" to estimate the impact of any proposed sentencing rules (N.C. Gen. Stat., sec. 164-40), and it directed the commission to "classify" criminal offenses into categories of felonies and misdemeanors "on the basis of their severity" (N.C. Gen. Stat., sec. 164-41). The commission's most important tasks were to recommend a "comprehensive community corrections plan" and "structures for use by a sentencing court in determining the most appropriate sentence to be imposed in a criminal case." But the statute was opaque about the content of these "sentencing structures" (N.C. Gen. Stat., secs. 164-42, 42.2).[5]

The 1990 act merely listed factors for the commission to "consider" as it created the sentencing structures. The factors included the nature of the offense, the characteristics of the defendant (including prior convictions), the available corrections resources, and the rights of victims. The one clear legislative instruction about the sentencing structures embodied the truth-in-sentencing concept: felons and misdemeanants were to serve "a designated percentage of their sentences" before becoming eligible for parole, although the statute did not designate what that percentage should be (N.C. Gen. Stat., sec. 164-42[b]).

The act declared that the sentencing structures should be consistent with the "policies" and "purposes" of sentencing. It then listed, in no particular order, some traditional purposes of sentencing, including protection of the public, punishment of offenders, and rehabilitation of offenders. The same section listed several "policies" for sentencing, including a policy favoring restitution for crime victims and a declaration that convicted offenders "should work when reasonably possible," either in the private sector or in community service (N.C. Gen. Stat., sec. 164-35).

The vagueness of these statutory terms contradicted the advice that the special committee received from its consultants. Consultants had advised the legislature to select the sentencing purposes that deserved the most weight and to treat the capacity of the correctional system as a hard constraint on the sentencing rules (Corrigan 1989*b*; North Carolina Special Committee on Prisons 1990; Tonry 1991; cf. von Hirsch 1987, pp. 65–70). The legislature, it was suggested, should make the important value choices, and the commission should implement them. But the 1990 act merely collected relevant—and contradictory—values and left the commission to choose among them. In this respect, the North Carolina legislation was typical of statutes creating sentencing commissions in other states (Austin et al. 1996).

Although the legislature did not explicitly tell the commission in the 1990 act what amount of growth in the prison system it would accept, other events left a powerful clue regarding this question. Throughout the drafting of the statute creating the sentencing commission, mem-

---

[5] The legislature deliberately avoided use of the term "guidelines" to describe the work of the commission because the newly created federal sentencing guidelines were uniformly unpopular among judges and lawyers in the state (Orland and Reitz 1993).

bers of the special committee on prisons negotiated with representatives of the governor on the question of building new prisons. Governor Martin made public appeals for $490 million in construction funds, with $400 million financed by a new bond issue. This money, he believed, would add 9,500 beds to the prison system (Governor's Advisory Board on Prisons and Punishment 1990). The legislators, on the other hand, held out for a smaller construction package and a smaller bond package.

In the end, they adopted a compromise bond package. In July 1990, the general assembly authorized the sale of $75 million in bonds for prison expansion—the maximum allowed under state law without presenting the bond issue to the voters.[6] The legislature also placed on the November ballot a request to issue an additional $200 million in bonds—at that point, the largest single appropriation for prison construction in the state's history. Together, the funds would add almost 7,000 new beds. Although the package was smaller than Martin had requested, he publicly supported the bond referendum.

Much to the surprise of everyone involved, the vote was extremely close despite the lack of any organized campaign against the bonds. The referendum passed by less than 0.5 percent of the vote (Case 1990). Indeed, the vote would have been negative without strong support from the Charlotte area, where news stories and public debate spotlighted the unsafe and overcrowded local jail (Stahl 2001). This close outcome had a lingering effect. For some years to come, the state's leaders took it as a sign that North Carolina citizens had reached the outer limits of their willingness to spend on prison expansion (North Carolina Public Television 1991).

III. Creating Guidelines, 1991–93

The commission was large—twenty-three members—and many of the individual commissioners were sharply ideological figures. Nobody expected easy compromise from William Webb (the governor's appointee from the Department of Crime Control and Public Safety) or from Lao Rupert (from the North Carolina Community Sentencing Association). Other commissioners, while personally more open to debate and compromise, carried institutional ties that gave them strong views on sentencing matters. These included Jim Coman, the senior deputy

---

[6] The state constitution allows the general assembly to approve the sale of bonds without obtaining voter approval, but only up to two-thirds of the amount of debt retired the previous year.

attorney general; Roger Smith, from the Academy of Trial Lawyers; and Gregg Stahl, from the Department of Correction.

The commissioners had every inclination to disagree and to deadlock on questions of criminal justice when framed in global terms. But the commission leadership and staff created a sequence of decisions that avoided deadlock and allowed the commissioners to reach agreement on preliminary questions. The sequence of decisions postponed the most difficult choices until later in the process, when cost estimates and some timely signaling from the legislature made all the difference. They pushed the commission in the direction of modest prison growth and heavier reliance on community and intermediate sanctions.

A. Sequence of Decisions at the Commission

The 1990 act called for the chief justice of the supreme court to appoint a judge to chair the commission. Chief Justice James Exum was exceptionally knowledgeable about sentencing policy. He served as chair of the American Bar Association's Criminal Justice Standards Committee, which was redrafting its sentencing standards during this period (American Bar Association 1994). Exum appointed superior court judge Thomas Ross to the post. Before his appointment to the superior court bench in 1984, Ross had practiced law and had worked as a professor at the Institute of Government, a university-based center for training and research related to state government operations.

During its initial organizational meetings, the commission hired Robin Lubitz as executive director. Lubitz came to North Carolina from Pennsylvania and had no familiarity with North Carolina politics. But his experience as the associate director of the Pennsylvania Sentencing Commission appealed to the North Carolina commissioners, and their decision to hire Lubitz demonstrated their interest in looking to developments outside the state (NCSPAC 1990).

The commission's first substantive meetings took place at a multiday retreat in January 1991. The proceedings took place under the glare of camera lights; a film crew for a public broadcasting system documentary was on hand to record the meeting. The discussions began with general comments from commissioners about the nature of the sentencing and corrections problems in North Carolina. The list was long: lack of meaningful alternatives to prison, lack of prison capacity, de facto legalization of misdemeanors, disparity in sentencing, no truth in sentencing, and so forth. The group did not prioritize or explain the sources of these problems. The conversation then turned to a question that revealed the depth of disagreement among the commissioners: the overall purposes of criminal sentences. Some emphasized deterrence and protection of the public and argued for major additions to the prison system. Others spoke passionately about the need for community sanctions and restitution as part of a rehabilitative program that would cost less to operate (NCSPAC 1991a, January 22).[7] The prospects were dim for translating these disparate ideas into a coherent sentencing system.

However, the next phase of the January 1991 meeting offered a way out of the thicket. Lubitz and the staff proposed a detailed work plan that would ultimately allow the commissioners to reach agreement. The staff surveyed the structured sentencing systems from a long list of other states—Delaware, Florida, Massachusetts, Maryland, Michigan, Minnesota, Oregon, Pennsylvania, Tennessee, Utah, Virginia, and Washington—and found some common elements in those systems. On the basis of these common elements from other states, the staff's plan then divided the work into four stages and created subcommittees of commissioners to carry the load for each of the stages.

The first stage involved a major input into the sentencing decision: how to account for various aspects of the offense conduct (the "offense structure"). The second stage asked about a second major input: what aspects of an offender's background to consider (the "defendant structure"). The third stage involved a major choice among sentencing outcomes, the decision of whether to use prison or some other form of punishment (the "dispositional structure"). The fourth involved another choice among sentencing outcomes, the length of the sentence imposed (the "durational structure"). This work plan largely tracked the work of the Minnesota Sentencing Commission (Parent 1988, pp. 51–114).

Some commissioners at first mistrusted the work plan. In particular, commissioners such as David McFadyen (representing the district attorneys), Jim Coman (from the attorney general's office), and William Webb (from the state Department of Crime Control and Public Safety) were concerned that the agenda might prevent the commission from considering major increases in the scale of the prison system. The key to obtaining approval for the work plan was a promise from Ross

---

[7] The commission kept minutes of all its plenary meetings and of each subcommittee meeting. Staff members were present at each meeting and wrote the minutes within a few days. The minutes are unpublished but are open to public inspection.

that the commission could revisit any particular component of the plan later (NCSPAC 1991*a*, January 23; Ross 1992; McFadyen 1993).

The staff, with guidance from Lubitz and Ross, set the subcommittee membership to reflect the ideological balance of the commission as a whole (Ross 1992). Each subcommittee included practicing attorneys, judges, and law enforcement officials. Each included members who could later vouch for the subcommittee's work to other like-minded commissioners. The chair or vice chair of each subcommittee had criminal justice experience or strong influence with constituency groups. For instance, Senator Parnell chaired both the durational subcommittee and the dispositional subcommittee. Gregg Stahl from the Department of Correction was vice chair for the defendant structures subcommittee. Jim Coman from the Department of Justice chaired the offense structure subcommittee.

For the first few months, the commissioners treated recommendations from the subcommittees as reasonable compromises and accepted explanations from sympathetic members on the subcommittee. Only later did the divisions on the commission make the subcommittees less important.

1. *Offense and Defendant Structures.* The offense structures subcommittee began with the question of whether to use the Fair Sentencing Act, which already divided felonies into categories, as a starting point. There was some sentiment that the new legislation required only a modest reworking of the FSA, but most subcommittee members agreed that the legislature was expecting more comprehensive changes (NCSPAC 1991*b*). The subcommittee did, however, retain one key feature of the FSA: the sentencing structure would be based on the offense as charged, rather than the "real" conduct of the offender. The members were aware of serious problems with the new federal sentencing guidelines, based partly on "real" offense conduct, and decided to avoid the proof problems and controversy involved in that strategy (NCSPAC 1991*a*, 1991*b*; Stith and Cabranes 1998).

The offense structure subcommittee began its grouping task by drafting a set of general criteria for classifying crimes. The criteria were based on types of harm that various crimes cause. Serious, permanent personal injury was at the top of the scale, less serious and more temporary personal injury came next, while injuries to the social order and to property appeared at the lowest levels. The subcommittee settled on nine categories of felonies, with a tenth category for misdemeanors (NCSPAC 1991*b*).

The subcommittee was on unfamiliar ground here. Commissions in other states, such as Minnesota, relied on the intuitive judgments of commissioners about the seriousness of offenses (Parent 1988, pp. 55–60). The commissions in Louisiana and Oregon created general ranking criteria along the lines of those used in North Carolina (Bogan 1990; Austin et al. 1996). Outside of that, however, there was little precedent for sentencing commissions describing groups of crimes in general terms. Indeed, such a task resembled the work of commissions trying to rewrite substantive criminal codes, an unpromising point of comparison (Joost 1994).

The North Carolina commissioners hoped that their ranking criteria would allow them to make more consistent classifications. They also anticipated that general criteria would make it easier to explain their ranking choices to legislators and the public (North Carolina Public Television 1991). But the most important effect of the criteria was to establish that property crimes should be sentenced less severely than crimes against the person. North Carolina practice, as in other states in the region, was to treat property crimes as seriously or more seriously than some crimes of personal violence (NCSPAC 1991b; Spelman 2000, fig. 6). While the committee members disagreed about how severely to punish particular property crimes, they did all agree in the abstract that personal injury crimes were more important.

With the criteria in place for the nine felony categories, the subcommittee assigned specific crimes to each category. The members began with the most frequently charged felonies and concentrated on typical offense conduct rather than the extremes of conduct that a given charge might reach (NCSPAC 1991b, February 25; Knapp 1993). The views of practicing attorneys and judges on the subcommittee were especially important in deciding what offense conduct was typical. The chair of the subcommittee was James Coman, the senior deputy attorney general, who became an exceptionally important figure on the commission. Other members of the subcommittee with extensive practice experience included Judge Ross, Judge Jack Lewis, District Attorney David McFadyen, and defense attorney Roger Smith.

After the frequently charged felonies were in place, the subcommittee added the more unusual felonies. Table 3 sets out a few representative felonies for each class. They also selected a few misdemeanors whose statutory elements were similar to felonies and recommended that they be raised to felony status.

One key decision was to exclude driving while intoxicated (DWI)

TABLE 3

Representative Felony Classifications as Proposed in 1993

	Class Criteria: Crime Reasonably Tends to Result in . . .	Representative Crimes
Class A		Murder in the first degree
Class B	Serious debilitating long-term personal injury	Rape in the first degree Murder in the second degree
Class C	Serious long-term personal injury Serious long-term or widespread societal injury	Kidnapping in the first degree Assault with deadly weapon with intent to kill inflicting serious injury
Class D	Serious infringements on property interests that also implicate physical safety concerns by use of a deadly weapon or an offense involving an occupied dwelling	Burglary in the first degree Robbery with firearms Arson in the first degree
Class E	Serious personal injury	Assault with deadly weapon with intent to kill Child abuse, sexual act
Class F	Significant personal injury Serious societal injury	Extortion Dumping of toxic substances
Class G	Serious property loss: loss from the person or from the person's dwelling	Burglary in the second degree Arson in the second degree Sale of Schedule I or II controlled substance

Class H	Serious property loss:
	  Loss from any structure designed to house or secure any activity or property
	  Loss occasioned by the taking or removing of property
	  Loss occasioned by breach of trust, formal or informal
	  Personal injury
	  Significant societal injury
		Breaking or entering buildings
		Larceny of property worth more than $1,000
		Sale of Schedule III–VI controlled substance

Class I	Serious property loss: all other felonious property loss Societal injury	Forgery False statements in affadavit Assault with deadly weapon Possession of Schedule I controlled substance

SOURCE.—North Carolina Sentencing and Policy Advisory Commission 1993a.

crimes entirely from the classification scheme (NCSPAC 1991*b*, April 26). The existing sentencing statutes treated DWI crimes separately from the FSA, and the commissioners were concerned that the legislature would reject or amend any package that lumped the DWI crimes together with others. The same was true for the most serious drug crimes (Coman 1992). In the end, the commission included lower-level drug crimes in the structure without reference to the general criteria, and without changing the average time served for those crimes under the FSA. The commissioners left DWI crimes and the larger drug-trafficking crimes untouched.

The defendant structures subcommittee also met regularly during the first half of 1991. Their assignment was to decide which characteristics of a defendant should become a regular part of the sentencing decision. Attention moved quickly to the prior criminal record of the offender, by default. Other individual characteristics—such as substance abuse or juvenile delinquency—seemed important in assessing the defendant's chances of committing future crimes. But the subcommittee was convinced that reliable information was not routinely available for these characteristics. Such factors, they decided, should be left as grounds to aggravate or mitigate the ordinary sentence in a particular case (NCSPAC 1991*b*, Feb. 22, April 19).

Prior criminal record, on the other hand, would become part of the sentence in every case. After a review of the treatment of prior criminal records in other states, the subcommittee opted for a point system that would assign different amounts to defendants for various types of convictions. More serious offenses would receive more points, and offenses similar to the current crime would also receive more points. Defendants who committed new crimes while still on parole or probation for some previous offense would also receive extra points.

Two considerations loomed large in each of these choices. First, the subcommittee was concerned about the reliability and ease of use for each type of record in question. Second, the staff surveyed for the subcommittee the practices among about twenty "structured sentencing" states, with special attention to Pennsylvania, Washington, Oregon, and Minnesota (NCSPAC 1991*b*, February 22, April 19). Most of the decisions, such as the use of a point system and the weighting of prior offenses based on their severity, tracked the majority approach in those states. However, the subcommittee declined to follow the lead of other states that provided for "decay" of an offender's criminal record points after a crime-free period; they wanted to avoid complex calculations and disputes over the age of prior convictions. The subcommittee also diverged from common practice in other states when it assigned an extra point for an offender whose current offense was "the same or similar to" a previous offense.

The subcommittee then estimated the number of offenders currently in the system who would receive various point totals and, on the basis of that estimate, decided how to group the defendants into six different prior record levels. The decision was ad hoc, rather than a deliberate choice about the relative importance of criminal history and the current crime of conviction. The dividing lines the subcommittee chose made it relatively easy to move to the highest levels of prior record (NCSPAC 1991*b*, February 22, May 10). It later became clear that this fast progression up the scale would contribute heavily to the expense and severity of the system, but that was not apparent at the start.

2. *Disposition and Duration Structures.* The work of the first two subcommittees combined to form a sentencing "grid," familiar in many states with sentencing commissions and guidelines (Frase 1993*b*). The offense structures subcommittee classifications became the vertical axis of the grid (with the most serious felonies occupying rows at the top of the grid), while the offense-level classifications of the defendant structures subcommittee became the horizontal axis (placing offenders with no prior record on the left side, and offenders with more serious criminal records in columns further to the right). But the boxes in the grid remained empty for now.

Two subcommittees filled in the dispositions available to the judge within each of the grid boxes: the dispositions structure subcommittee and the community corrections subcommittee. The first of these subcommittees designated either an active prison term or a nonprison sanction for each box of the grid. The community corrections subcommittee developed in more detail the nonprison punishments that would be available in the relevant boxes (see fig. 1).

The FSA allowed the judge complete discretion over the "in-out" decision. The commissioners believed that this needed to change; centralized control over the decision to use prison or some other sanction was crucial to the state's ability to plan its corrections resources. The disposition structure would need to bind sentencing judges.

In its earliest meetings, the dispositions structure subcommittee members discussed the purposes of sentencing more extensively than any other commissioners. They agreed right away that punishment and incapacitation of offenders were the leading purposes of active prison

Offense Class	I	II	III	IV	V	VI	Disposition
A	Mandatory life or death as established by statute						
	A *180–225*	A *216-270*	A *252-315*	A *288-360*	A *324-405*	A *360-450*	Disposition *Aggravated range*
B	**144-180**	**173-216**	**202-252**	**230-288**	**259-324**	**288-360**	PRESUMPTIVE RANGE
	108-144	*130-173*	*152-202*	*173-230*	*194-259*	*216-288*	*Mitigated range*
	A *84-105*	A *115-144*	A *134-168*	A *152-190*	A *172-215*	A *192-240*	
C	**67-84**	**92-115**	**107-134**	**122-152**	**138-172**	**154-192**	
	50-67	*69-92*	*80-107*	*92-122*	*104-138*	*116-154*	
	A *74-93*	A *89-111*	A *118-148*	A *135-169*	A *152-190*	A *168-210*	
D	**59-74**	**71-89**	**94-118**	**108-135**	**122-152**	**134-168**	
	44-59	*53-71*	*71-94*	*81-108*	*92-122*	*101-134*	
	A *31-39*	A *36-45*	A *42-53*	A *56-70*	A *64-80*	A *72-90*	
E	**25-31**	**29-36**	**34-42**	**45-56**	**51-64**	**58-72**	
	19-25	*22-29*	*26-34*	*34-45*	*38-51*	*44-58*	
	I/A *21-26*	I/A *24-30*	A *26-33*	A *31-39*	A *42-53*	A *48-60*	
F	**17-21**	**19-24**	**21-26**	**25-31**	**34-42**	**38-48**	
	13-17	*14-19*	*16-21*	*19-25*	*26-34*	*29-38*	
	I/A *16-20*	I/A *19-24*	A *21-26*	A *25-31*	A *28-35*	A *36-45*	
G	**13-16**	**15-19**	**17-21**	**20-25**	**22-28**	**29-36**	
	10-13	*11-15*	*13-17*	*15-20*	*17-22*	*22-29*	
	C/I *8-10*	I *9-11*	I/A *11-14*	I/A *14-18*	A *18-23*	A *24-30*	
H	**6-8**	**7-9**	**9-11**	**11-14**	**14-18**	**19-24**	
	5-6	*5-7*	*7-9*	*8-11*	*11-14*	*14-19*	
	C *6-8*	C/I *7-9*	I *8-10*	I/A *9-11*	I/A *10-13*	A *12-15*	
I	**4-6**	**5-7**	**6-8**	**7-9**	**8-10**	**10-12**	
	3-4	*4-5*	*5-6*	*5-7*	*6-8*	*8-10*	

FIG. 1.—Felony punishments as proposed by commission, 1993. A = Active punishment; I = intermediate punishment; C = community punishment. Cells with a slash allow either disposition at the discretion of the judge. Sentence ranges are in months. Source: North Carolina Sentencing and Policy Advisory Commission 1993*a*.

terms. Rehabilitation seemed more important to the commissioners for nonprison sanctions, though punishment remained a relevant purpose here, as well (NCSPAC 1991*b*, August 6; Lubitz and Ross 2001). But the discussion of sentencing purposes made no real difference in the subcommittee's central task: deciding which offenders were best suited to receive various types of sanctions (Stahl 1992). Sentencing purposes mattered less than past sentencing practices and future cost estimates.

The subcommittee began by estimating the proportion of offenders in each grid box who were receiving prison and nonprison sanctions under the FSA. They designated the grid boxes at the top of the scale (involving the most serious felonies) as "active" boxes. Only an active sentence was available to the judge for those cases, even though a few offenders in those boxes received nonprison punishments under the FSA.

Then the subcommittee made a remarkable choice. In an effort to conserve prison space for the most violent and serious felonies, the members decided that some grid boxes in the bottom left corner of the grid (those involving the least serious crimes and the least serious prior criminal records) would offer only nonprison sanctions. Even though the strong majority of the least serious felons were already receiving no active prison time under the FSA, it was provocative to declare openly that prison sentences should not be available at all for some felonies. At this point, the commission had not addressed the "departure" provisions. Perhaps commissioners supported this restriction on the use of prison based on the prospect that judges could "depart" in unusual cases and impose an active term.

A few of the boxes in the middle of the grid allowed sentencing judges the option of choosing either prison or nonprison sanctions. These areas became known as "border boxes."

The community corrections subcommittee developed in more detail the different types of nonprison sanctions that judges could use in the lower boxes. They reviewed existing community sanctions and placed them on a "continuum," depending on the amount of supervision the program offered. The nonprison sanctions fell into two groups: the least restrictive programs such as ordinary probation or community service were labeled "community" sanctions, while more intrusive sanctions such as residential drug treatment programs were called "intermediate" punishments. The dispositional structure subcommittee recommended the term "punishments" rather than "sanctions" to make them more acceptable to the public (NCSPAC 1991b, June 7). The community punishments became the dispositions at the lowest levels of the grid, while the intermediate punishments became available to judges at slightly higher levels, before the active prison terms came into play. Again, border boxes in between these areas on the grid gave judges a choice between community or intermediate punishments.

Perhaps the most significant work of the community corrections subcommittee involved misdemeanors. This subcommittee attracted large groups of visitors to its meetings, and many of the visitors (such

| | | Prior conviction level | |
Misdemeanor offense class	Level I No prior convictions	Level II One to four prior convictions	Level III Five or more prior convictions
1	1–60 days C	1–120 days C/I/A	1–180 days C/I/A
2	1–45 days C	1–60 days C/I	1–120 days C/I/A
3	1–30 days C	1–30 days C/I	1–60 days C/I/A

FIG. 2.—Misdemeanor grid as proposed in 1993. A = Active punishment; I = intermediate punishment; C = community punishment. Cells with a slash allow either disposition at the discretion of the judge. Source: North Carolina Sentencing and Policy Advisory Commission 1993*a*.

as Patrice Roesler from the County Commissioners' Association) were concerned about the costs of criminal punishments for local governments. The subcommittee members understood that limits on the use of state prisons could translate into major increases in the use of local jails for misdemeanors. In North Carolina, any misdemeanant sentenced to more than a six-month active term served the sentence in state prison. In the early 1990s, about 15,000 misdemeanants every year passed through the state prisons, occupying about 1,500 prison beds on an average day (NCSPAC 1991*b*, December 6). If the new law simply shifted those misdemeanants into local jails, the cost to local government would be enormous. Furthermore, limits on low-level felony sentences could have an impact on local jails. Prosecutors could start charging misdemeanors rather than low-level felonies if they wished to see an active prison term even when the felony grid blocked such a sentence. Once again, local jails would bear the weight of this change.

As a method of preserving local resources to develop community sanctions, the subcommittee created a simplified grid system for misdemeanors (see fig. 2; NCSPAC 1991*b*, September 13, November 26). Patterned roughly on the work already done for felonies, the misdemeanor grid contained fewer offense and prior record categories and simpler point systems, making it easier to use for busy district court judges (Coman 1992).

The durations structure subcommittee created the final missing piece. Its task was to designate a range of months that a judge should normally choose as the duration of an active prison term for offenders within each grid box. In its earliest meetings, the subcommittee emphasized "truth in sentencing" and decided that all offenders would serve 100 percent of the minimum announced sentence. Prisoners would serve the maximum, set 20 percent higher than the minimum, only when they failed to comply with institutional rules. Commissioner Gregg Stahl from the Department of Correction assured other subcommittee members that the 20 percent difference gave prison administrators enough leverage over inmate behavior (NCSPAC 1991*b*, December 6).

This subcommittee choice effectively abolished parole.[8] Although it was a major landmark in the design of the system, it happened with no fanfare. The enabling legislation left open the possibility of a parole system (N.C. Gen. Stat., sec. 164-37). Pennsylvania and other states with sentencing commissions and guidelines still retained parole within limits (42 Pa. Cons. Stat., secs. 2153[a][1], 2154[a]; 61 Pa. Cons. Stat., sec. 331.2). But the North Carolina commission never seriously discussed keeping parole alongside its sentencing structures. The association between parole and the emergency releases over the previous decade made parole unpopular. Senator David Parnell, as chair of the subcommittee, anticipated no difficulty in the legislature on this question (NCSPAC 1992*b*, January 3).

The durations structure subcommittee also left in the hands of the sentencing judge some real control over the duration. It created three ranges for each grid box: a "presumptive" range, an aggravated range that expanded 25 percent higher than the top of the presumptive range, and a mitigated range that dipped down 25 percent lower than the bottom of the presumptive range. (The only state with a similar structure with three sentencing ranges was Pennsylvania, where Lubitz had served on the commission staff.) The judge had to find an aggravating or mitigating factor present in the case before moving to the higher or lower ranges of months, but it would be quite easy to make such a finding. The subcommittee, for ease of administration, kept the existing aggravators and mitigators from the FSA, except for the removal of a prior record and a few other factors they had already built into the new structure (N.C. Gen. Stat., sec. 15A-1340[a],[b]). The subcommittee also left judges to decide whether to impose concurrent or consecutive sentences in cases with multiple counts. This choice was typical of sentencing guidelines in other states (Austin et al. 1996).

[8] Fourteen states have abolished parole release for all offenders (Bureau of Justice Statistics 1999, p. 3).

For intermediate and community punishments, the judge would select the length of a suspended prison term to impose, a term the offender would serve only after violating the terms of probation. The structure also limited the durations of the intermediate and community punishments. Normally, intermediate punishments lasted between eighteen and thirty-six months; the presumptive range for community punishments was twelve to thirty months. Even in exceptional cases, five years was the maximum probation term.

With these structural decisions in place, the subcommittee started to fill in the numbers. Senator Parnell called this the commission's most "interesting" and "difficult" work to date (NCSPAC 1991*b*, October 11). The staff presented a starting point for discussion by placing into each grid box a presumptive range reflecting the average time currently served by defendants sentenced under the FSA. Although the guidelines began as "descriptive" of current practice, the commissioners soon gave them a clear "prescriptive" cast. Over the course of several meetings, the subcommittee members identified crimes that ideally should be punished more severely. In some cases, commissioners argued against the largest proposed increases by showing that the proposal would double or triple the time served currently in North Carolina or in other states. But the general thrust of the committee's work called for major growth. When the bidding ended, the staff compiled cost estimates to present to the commission as a whole.

3. *Scaling Back, Round 1.*   The system based on the wish list of the durations subcommittee produced astonishing cost estimates. The plan required $1 billion in new construction and an annual operating budget of $1.5 billion dollars. It would nearly have doubled the size of the prison system, adding 20,000 new beds right away (NCSPAC 1992*a*). Even more beds would be needed over the next ten years to handle the predicted increases in conviction rates. At first, the commissioners hoped to find some solution other than scaling back their ideal proposal. Judge Herbert Small convinced the commission to adopt a resolution calling on the governor and legislature to "use every resource available . . . to increase the prison capacity of this State" (NCSPAC 1992*a*, January 16–17).

However, political reality soon took hold. At the pivotal February and March 1992 meetings, a majority of commissioners declared that they were willing to scale back their plans to require only "reasonable" growth. Most still said that the previous version was ideal, but it was not politically realistic. Senator Parnell warned that such an expensive plan would be "dead on arrival" in the legislature (NCSPAC 1992*a*, February 21). It was now clear, for the first time, that the current capacity of the prison system would place some constraint on the system the commission would recommend.[9]

The debate turned to the best method to make the cuts. Commissioner Lao Rupert (from the Alternative Sentencing Association) proposed the deepest cuts, designed to remain strictly within the existing prison capacity. Her proposal changed the dispositions in several grid blocks from "active" to "intermediate." It also scaled back the durations for all crimes, taking the largest amounts from the least serious crimes.

Commissioner Gregg Stahl from the Department of Correction produced a plan that revisited an earlier subcommittee decision: it cut overall sentence levels by reducing the importance of prior criminal record. The Stahl plan required a more extensive criminal record to move into the right side columns in the grid and made the crime of conviction more important than the prior record. Stahl argued that this philosophy was consistent with the basic premises of the criminal law, punishing a person for criminal acts rather than for criminal propensities (Stahl 1992).

Judge Small continued to insist that the commission should not worry about cost. He proposed increases in the lowest levels of the grid, to make six months the shortest duration for an active prison term for any class of felony.

But the decisive proposal came from the chair, Judge Ross. The Ross plan did not rework the basic choices of the subcommittees and changed none of the recommended dispositions in the grid blocks. Instead, it cut all durations—by 20 percent at the top and bottom of the grid, and by 30 percent in the middle levels—until the projected use of prison space for new felons reached the level already projected to be built by 1994, about 24,000 beds. But unlike the Rupert plan, the Ross plan did call for some serious growth in the prison system. Some immediate building (over 3,000 beds) would be necessary to handle the misdemeanants who remained in the state system, along with proba-

---

[9] North Carolina followed the same path as commissions in some other states on the best response to ambiguous statutory instructions on prison capacity. The commission in Minnesota read its statute to limit its recommendations within existing capacity (Martin 1984). The statute in Washington instructed the commission to make "frugal use" of corrections resources, and the commission interpreted this as a real constraint on system capacity (Austin et al. 1996, p. 43). However, the North Carolina commission made no conscious use of these other states as a model on this particular point.

tion violators. And some further building would need to happen to anticipate increased prison admissions after 1994. These additional needs would require new construction of over 15,000 new prison beds over the next ten years (NCSPAC 1992*a*). But the price tag for the Ross plan was within the realm of political reality: less than half the cost of the committee's first draft, and roughly on a scale with Governor Martin's proposal of 9,500 new beds discussed during the 1990 bond campaign.

With time running out, the weight of opinion on the commission gathered around the Ross plan. Jim Coman from the attorney general's office brought into the coalition some of the key conservatives who trusted his judgment. Roger Smith, the defense attorney, brought along enough liberals. The commission settled on this scaled-down package just in time to include it in an interim report to the legislature (NCSPAC 1992*c*).

A few commissioners, led by Art Zeidman (from the Department of Crime Control and Public Safety) and Judge Herbert Small, drafted a minority report for the legislature. The minority report insisted that the role of the commission was to give its expert opinion about what North Carolina needed, and to let the legislature worry about the political and fiscal costs. The report also suggested that the commission's deliberations were a sham; it was reaching a preordained outcome. The minority report complained that legislators were using the commission merely to avoid political responsibility for their unpopular and unwise decision not to invest in prison expansion. In the eyes of the minority, a few commissioners (presumably Senator Parnell and Judge Ross) prevented the commission from exploring any different options. But the legislature was about to show that the commission was not perfectly in tune with its wishes, after all.

B. *Legislative Signals and Approval*

According to the 1990 legislation, the commission was to present its final report by the summer of 1992. But this proved to be too short a time, so the commission instead delivered an interim report, along with a request for an extension of their deadline and a reauthorization of their operating budget. The legislature was meeting again in short session that year. The request for a delay came as no surprise, since Lubitz and Ross provided occasional updates to House Speaker Dan Blue, and Senator Parnell kept his senate colleagues updated.

But legislators reacted coolly to the Ross proposal because it still called for prison growth. The legislature spent much of the session deciding how to spend the final $87.5 million from the bond issue that the voters narrowly approved in 1990. Given the weak economy and the exceptionally tight state budget, the legislature was finding it difficult to pay for the full amount—they delayed issuing the last of the bonds for a year, from 1992 until 1993 (North Carolina Public Television 1992*b*). Furthermore, much of the agenda in the short session dealt with health care, one of the major competitors for state funding at the time (Denton 1992; Moore 1992). In this setting, legislators considered any extra prison spending above the amounts already in the pipeline to be financially unrealistic.

Hence, the legislation authorizing the commission to continue work added some pointed instructions. It required the commission to submit at least one proposal that required no growth above current prison resources. And to drive the point home, the legislation added four new commissioners, two senators and two representatives (N.C. Session Laws 1991, 2d Sess., chap. 816). The new members, it was thought, would enforce a sense of political reality as the commission completed its work (Coman 1992; Moore 1992; Stahl 1992). The strengthened ties to the legislature were especially important on the house side, where the original 1990 appointee took no active part in the process after deciding to run for lieutenant governor. Ann Barnes—a major force in the 1990 legislation—and David Redwine became the two new commissioners from the house.

In response to the new legislative instructions, the commission appointed a standard operating capacity (SOC) subcommittee to develop the "bed-neutral" plan required by law. The subcommittee members used a combination of techniques to achieve this second round of cuts. They added a few more "border boxes" to give judges more opportunities to choose nonprison punishments for some midlevel crimes. They reduced all sentences, and reduced some of the most serious felonies (Classes B–D) even more. They also adjusted the prior record point system to move offenders less quickly into the right-hand columns on the grid.

While the SOC subcommittee was at work, the rest of the commission reinforced controls on sentencing judges. The sentencing structures in most states allowed judges to depart from the presumptive sentence in unusual cases. Various formulations of the departure power in different states made it easier or harder for the sentencing judge to depart. Appellate courts were available to block possible abuses of the departure power (Austin et al. 1996; Reitz 1997). Departures were the leading source of flexibility in sentencing structures, the usual method for individualizing sentences when the circumstances of the case called for an unusual outcome.

Experience in other jurisdictions suggested that judges could use departures responsibly, without undermining the predictability of the sentencing guidelines (Ashford and Mosbaek 1991, pp. vii–ix; Frase 1993a; Tonry 1996, p. 38). Nevertheless, the commissioners in North Carolina decided not to allow departures. In light of the FSA experience, they believed that departures presented too great a temptation for judges. Predictability was too important to risk. Although judges would be able to choose dispositions in a few grid boxes (the "border" boxes), and could choose among three generous ranges for the duration of an active sentence, the commission voted not to allow departures. The sentencing structure would bind the judge in all cases, both for the disposition and for the duration of the sentence.

As the commissioners assembled their final report for the legislature, they expressed their disapproval of the SOC plan. A few considered the plan irresponsible and argued that the commission should ignore the legislature's instruction to create a bed-neutral plan. In the end, the commission submitted its recommended plan (tracking the outlines of the plan submitted in the interim report), followed by the SOC plan (with no recommendation), and a minority report calling for more extensive use of prison and continued judicial discretion in sentencing. The commission's recommendation called for $300 million in new construction over five years (NCSPAC 1993a).

Discontent with the commission's final package went beyond the four commissioners who signed the minority report. Shifting majorities of commissioners voted for each component of the structure. Several commissioners stated openly that they would lobby for some components and against others. There is some question whether the package would have survived a simple up-or-down vote at the end of the process, but Ross never forced the issue (NCSPAC 1992d, p. i; McFadyen 1993). After the commissioners voted the final pieces of the package into place, the staff drafted the legislation and report and sent them to the legislature.

Both the senate and the house assigned the bill to their judiciary committees. The package received more attention in the house than in the senate. For weeks, the relevant subcommittee in the house met every morning at 7:30 for substantive hearings. The members reviewed the package piece by piece and heard complaints from critics of the bill. Representative Robert Hensley, a Democrat from Raleigh who chaired the hearings, routinely allowed Lubitz to explain the commission's rationale for each piece of the package and to respond after testimony from critics.

Two leading opponents of the bill were criminal defense attorneys and the parole commission. The defense attorneys objected that the guidelines limited judicial discretion "in an attempt to solve problems that the judiciary did not create." Furthermore, they said, the sentencing structure ignored the "unique facts of each individual case" and would result in "staggering" costs for the state (North Carolina Bar Association, Criminal Justice Section 1993, pp. 1–2). They tried to persuade the North Carolina Bar Association to oppose the bill, but Judge Ross met with bar leaders during their annual summer meeting in 1993 and persuaded the board to support the bill.

The parole commission issued a report collecting evidence about the difficulties other states encountered when they abolished parole (Lewandowski 1992). These troubles included massive overcrowding of prisons and poorly planned releases of inmates. The parole commission favored, in the place of structured sentencing, the widespread use of mandatory minimum sentences, coupled with maximum sentences much higher than the minimum (Boyd 1992). This would allow greater latitude for the parole commission to identify the most dangerous felons and to incapacitate them for a longer time.

But the parole commission's document was not credible. Its examples of overcrowding in states abolishing parole came from California and a few other states that eliminated parole without creating sentencing guidelines and without using computer projections of prison growth. While there was a serious case to be made for a parole authority rather than judges as the coordinating force in sentencing law, the North Carolina parole commission never made the case. Their arguments never swayed many legislators.

By the time the bill emerged from the committee hearings in the house, it was clear that the SOC plan would attract enough votes, while there was little support for the commission's more expensive plan. The agenda for the 1993 session included some major spending proposals for education and health, two of the traditional budgetary competitors with criminal justice (Moore 1992; Miller 1997). The desire to save state money for these other priorities focused the legislature on the least expensive sentencing package. The sentencing reform package, based on the prison capacity already available to the state, passed the house 91 to 2 and the senate 38 to 0.

These were exceptionally wide margins of victory. Given the public concern about the large numbers of early parole releases, there was widespread agreement in the legislature that major changes to the sentencing laws were necessary, and right away (Drennan 1992). It was also easy to recognize that no single piece of the complicated system was to blame. A complete overhaul was necessary. The sentencing commission produced the only plausible plan for overhaul, and the commission staff emphasized the risks of changing isolated parts of the integrated whole. Representative Ann Barnes endorsed the SOC plan, and the key Democratic leaders in both houses (Dan Blue in the house and Marc Basnight in the senate) were supporters. Surely there were alternatives to a "yes" vote, but none were anywhere in sight.

Apart from the choice of the SOC plan over the durations that the commission recommended, the new law made only a handful of changes from the commission's proposal. For one thing, the legislature trimmed back the "habitual felon" provision. Under the FSA, a prosecutor could charge a defendant with a Class C felony if the defendant had been convicted of three previous felonies. Some members of the sentencing commission tried to abolish this crime, arguing that it double-counted the criminal record that was already factored into the grid. Nevertheless, David McFadyen from the Conference of District Attorneys made this provision his highest priority. Believing that support from prosecutors was crucial to the proposal's success in the legislature, the commission kept the habitual felon provision but demoted it from a Class C to a Class D felony. The legislature further weakened the provision by adding a new requirement: only one of the previous felonies could be from Class H or I (N.C. Session Laws, 1993, chap. 538, sec. 9).

In retrospect, the political timing of the legislative debate was fortunate. If the commission had met its original 1992 deadline, the general assembly would have debated the whole package during a session just months before an election. Legislators would have worried about voters' reactions to a bill that reduced maximum sentences, even though it meant an increase in actual time served for many crimes.

The outcome of the 1992 gubernatorial election was also important to the outcome of the sentencing debate. Democrat Jim Hunt defeated Republican Jim Gardner in the election. Gardner campaigned actively against the work of the sentencing commission and surely would have worked to block its passage in 1993 if he had won the race. Although the North Carolina governor has no veto power, vocal opposition from a governor still makes it difficult to pass a bill.

Governor Hunt, on the other hand, mentioned sentencing hardly at all during the campaign and remained noncommittal about the work of the sentencing commission. Hunt strongly supported the FSA during his first two terms (1977–85) and continued to view favorably the idea of "determinate" and uniform sentencing. In a campaign brochure, he kept his distance from the sentencing commission: "I hope the Commission's proposals will bring us closer to the original goals of the Fair Sentencing Act: more certainty and more deterrence. If they do, I will support the proposals" (Hunt 1992, p. 35). After he took office in 1993, he remained on the sidelines as the house and senate debated the new package. It was only a year later that Governor Hunt became an important player in sentencing.

C. Distinctive Features of the Final Product

The North Carolina commission drew explicitly on the work of other states, most frequently the sentencing guidelines in Pennsylvania (Robin Lubitz's previous employer), Oregon, Washington, and Minnesota. In the creation of the work plan, and in setting out the structural options available to the commissioners, staff members typically described practices in about twenty other states to illustrate a few leading options (Drennan 1992). These state surveys were especially influential in dealing with prior criminal record—the North Carolina commission deliberately followed the "majority" approach to most questions involved in calculating the seriousness of a prior criminal record. Comparisons to the average time served for crimes in other states also figured in the setting of durations for prison terms.

These other states were not simply a source of ideas; they were also a source of confidence. A state with experience using a feature gave the North Carolina commissioners some assurance that the approach was politically and administratively workable. The recent passage of a Community Corrections Act in Texas was encouraging to the North Carolina commission. The generous funding of such programs in Texas suggested that they were politically saleable (North Carolina Public Television 1992a). Some commissioners also drew on other states as negative examples: they referred to California and Florida from time to time as states that were failing in their efforts to "spend their way out" of prison crowding problems (Ross 1992).

Despite the importance of models from other states, the North Carolina version of structured sentencing did follow its own path at some points. North Carolina's commission created its own distinctive selling point for this system. Structured sentencing, they said, was the most reliable way to increase prison terms for serious and violent felonies. If prison is used indiscriminately, it requires enormous recurring costs—especially in a state with a growing population and a resulting growth in crimes and convictions. The competing fiscal demands on state government make it unlikely that the legislature will devote such resources to prison every year. Given the episodic political support for prison growth, it is important to conserve scarce space for the most important cases. Thus, the best way to increase prison terms for serious felonies is to decrease the use of prison for less serious crimes.

Limits on the use of prison for the least serious felonies were crucial if the system was to control prison costs while sending serious felons to longer prison terms. But the limit also proved unpopular with judges, prosecutors, and other important constituent groups. So the North Carolina sentencing commission turned to another innovation to make these alternatives less unpopular. The commission emphasized the range of nonprison punishments available by dividing them into "community" and "intermediate" punishments, highlighting the heavy supervisory component of intermediate punishments.

The range of available community corrections under the new sentencing structure made the trade-off more palatable for many groups. Too often, the choice between an active prison term and a sentence to probation is perceived as an all-or-nothing choice for the sentencer (Morris and Tonry 1990). In light of the large caseload of the ordinary probation officer, it was probably true that probation was not an onerous or effective punishment for many offenders. But the North Carolina guidelines did not present the sentencing judge with a stark choice. Under structured sentencing, there was no immediate drop-off from active prison terms to ordinary probation.

North Carolina's system was also distinctive in the amount of centralized control it offered. This emphasis was likely the product of the unhappy experience with nominally "determinate" sentences that were decentralized in fact under the FSA. Thus, the new system covered both misdemeanors and felonies. Frase (1995) surveyed seventeen guideline systems, including North Carolina, and found only four that covered misdemeanors.

The new North Carolina system also created no departure power for judges. Although the sentencing judge could choose from within an ample range of durations, the judge could not go above or below the specified range in special cases. The structure also controlled the type of nonprison punishments that the judge would choose. In some boxes, only community punishments were available. In others, only intermediate punishments were available. Once the judge decided (or was required) to impose an intermediate or community punishment, the structure limited the length of the available probation terms and required certain conditions of probation in all cases. This was one of the few features of the North Carolina system that varied from the loose guidance offered under the American Bar Association Criminal Justice Standards on Sentencing (American Bar Association 1994, standards 18-3.7 and 18-3.8).

Because the most important work of appellate judges flows from their review of departures, the North Carolina system left appeals courts with little meaningful role to play. One might view aggravated and mitigated sentences as the functional equivalent of durational departures. But North Carolina appellate judges also said very little about the use of these substitutes for departures. Frase (1999) surveyed state sentencing guideline systems and found that six of the seventeen states have "effective appellate review," while North Carolina and three other states have "some" appellate review. Appellate courts in states such as Washington and Kansas have placed important boundaries on the acceptable grounds for departures from the presumptive sentence. Those rulings reinforced the power of sentencing guidelines to produce more uniform outcomes in similar cases.

The final distinctive feature of the North Carolina system relates to the roles of different institutions. The legislature and the sentencing commission in North Carolina reversed the customary roles that such institutions played in sentencing reform elsewhere. In states that passed guidelines prior to 1993, sentencing commissions showed less enthusiasm than legislatures for a growing prison system. For instance, in Pennsylvania, the legislature rejected the original proposed guidelines from the commission because they were too lenient and too restrictive on judicial discretion (Kramer 1997). In North Carolina, however, the politically insulated sentencing commission called for faster growth in the prison system, while the general assembly held out for cheaper alternatives to prison, at least for some lower-level felons (Wright and Ellis 1993, pp. 457–58).

The slow economy and shaky state revenues in the early 1990s gave the general assembly strong reasons to play this limiting role. While the general assembly was a politically responsive body that understood the political popularity of crime-fighting measures, it also worked from a generalist rather than specialist point of view. The legislature's responsibility to balance criminal justice spending against spending on health care and other needs of the state gave it a different perspective from the sentencing commission, which devoted two years of attention to one set of problems. The balanced budget provision in the state constitution, combined with a rhetorical tradition of praising fiscal conservatism in North Carolina, reinforced the legislature's chosen role. Those same factors would also help the sentencing guidelines survive a threat in the legislature during its first two years.

IV. Developing Legislative Discipline, 1994–98

The first few years after the passage of the Structured Sentencing Act were marked by second thoughts in the legislature. During 1994 and 1995, as the new sentencing system was getting underway, the legislature debated a string of proposals that would have dramatically increased the use of prison and reversed the basic direction of structured sentencing. In each case, the key to the outcome was—once again— the money.

A. Impact Projections in the 1994 Session

Although Governor Hunt had no major effect on the 1993 debate over the passage of structured sentencing, he did create the first major test for the new system. In 1993, a man who was released from prison after serving two years of a six-to-ten year prison term murdered the father of basketball star Michael Jordan in eastern North Carolina. Men released early from prison also were involved in the killings of two Charlotte policemen. Newspapers reported on other parolees charged with murders. To top it off, a group of crime victims filed a class action suit to force the state to repeal the prison cap, which was being phased out slowly as structured sentencing took effect (Eubank 1993).

Governor Hunt, referring to these events, called a special session of the general assembly to deal with crime. For seven weeks in February and March 1994, legislators introduced over 400 new crime bills. Many dealt with punishments for sexual assault and the use of weapons. Others embodied some variety of "three strikes and you're out" punishments—sentencing repeat felons to life imprisonment without possibility of parole—which were gaining attention at the same time in about half the state legislatures (Wright 1998*b*).

At the time, the commission staff members were occupied with the huge job of educating judges, prosecutors, defense attorneys, probation officers, and clerks about the new system. They developed training materials and conducted seminars around the state. At the start of the special session, however, some staffers dropped their more routine work to respond to the new sentencing proposals popping up in the legislature.

Under the 1993 sentencing legislation, any new sentencing bill introduced in the general assembly required a "fiscal note" (N.C. Gen. Stat., sec. 164-43). The sentencing commission estimated the number of new convictions or lengthened prison terms a crime bill would add to the system, then used a computer simulation model to calculate the number of prison beds that would be necessary over different time intervals. The projections moved in one-year increments for the first ten years, and then in five-year increments. The research arm of the state legislature supplemented this information with its own estimate of construction costs for new prison facilities necessary to handle the increased prison population. The estimates were based on the assumption that all convicted defendants were sentenced to the midpoint of the punishments designated in the bill. One difficult component of the estimates involved a prediction about future increases in the number of convictions in the state. An advisory panel recommended to the sentencing commission periodic changes to the "multiplier" for changing conviction rates.

Robin Lubitz, sometimes working alone and sometimes with Judge Ross, delivered these impact statements to legislators personally, during private conversations in the lawmakers' offices. By delivering the impact statements early and in private, Lubitz hoped to make it more palatable for the sponsor to alter or withdraw the bill. While some legislators did not at first believe the impact statements, after a methodical explanation of how the commission created its estimates, most legislators considered the numbers trustworthy. Many then worked with the commission staff to amend their bills in ways that still accomplished many of their goals with a lower impact on prison populations (Lubitz 1994).

By the end of the special session on crime, the legislature passed a "three strikes" law, a gun-enhancement law, and new punishments for rape. In each case, the commission's analysis had a sobering effect on the legislators, who amended each of the bills to reduce their impact on prison population. The bills, as introduced, would have increased the population by well over 20,000 beds within ten years. The bills that actually passed during the 1994 special session required about 2,000 new beds within ten years (Bennett 1994; Wright 1998a).

One legislative change to structured sentencing in 1994—revisions to the habitual felon law—had a larger potential to expand the prisons. The 1993 version of the habitual felon law allowed a prosecutor to charge a separate Class D felony upon conviction of three prior felonies, but two of the three felonies had to be more serious than Class H. The 1994 amendment increased the habitual felony crime itself from Class D to Class C, and the new law applied after any three prior felonies (N.C. Gen. Stat., secs. 14-7.1 et seq.). The habitual felon law now enabled prosecutors to increase a presumptive sentence for almost all the offenders in about twenty of the fifty-four cells in the felony sentencing grid, the lower right-hand corner of the grid.

This was a legislative battle the Association of District Attorneys lost in 1993, and it was at the top of their priority list for the 1994 legislative session. This time around, the prosecutors won. They pointed out that very few offenders were actually convicted of the habitual felon crime and that its real value was to give them leverage during plea negotiations. The sentencing commission, relying on this pattern of charges in the past, predicted a small impact on prisons. For a few years after the passage of the new habitual felon law, prosecutors continued to use it sporadically. The commission did not count on prosecutors changing their patterns of charging, but that is what eventually happened.

B. Legislative Newcomers in the 1995 Session

The November 1994 elections created another early test for the viability of structured sentencing. While governors changed during the debates over structured sentencing (Democrat Jim Hunt from 1977 to 1985, Republican Jim Martin from 1985 to 1993, followed again by Jim Hunt in January 1993), the legislature remained stable. Democratic leaders in the general assembly dominated the special committee on prisons, formulated the instructions for the sentencing commission, appropriated the funds for new prison space and corrections programs, and adopted the Structured Sentencing Act.

But in 1994, for the first time since the Reconstruction Era, North Carolinians gave Republicans a majority in the house of representatives

(68 of 120 seats). The senate remained in Democratic hands, but barely; they held only 26 of 50 seats. The question was whether the sentencing commission could sustain support for structured sentencing across party lines.

Incumbent Republicans overwhelmingly supported the 1993 Structured Sentencing Act. When they moved into leadership roles, Republican legislators spoke in general terms about North Carolina lagging behind other states in the punishment of criminals, but they never attempted to rework the new sentencing structure (Wright 1998a, pp. 11–12). One of the most influential Republican leaders, Representative Leo Daughtry from Smithfield, worked actively to repeal the statute requiring a "fiscal note" for any sentencing bill introduced in the general assembly. Daughtry believed that the fiscal notes made legislators overly timid and caused them to ignore the long-term benefits of crime reduction. But other Republican lawmakers convinced Daughtry that the fiscal notes were a useful discipline containing accurate information. The alternative did not inspire confidence: as Representative Dan Blue put it, in about two-thirds of the debates on crime bills before 1993, "We just guessed" (Bennett 1994). The fiscal notes requirement stayed in place.

The 1995 general assembly passed sentencing laws that made only modest long-term changes in the system. The combined effect of the 1995 changes to structured sentencing was, to be sure, larger than the impact of the 1994 statutes. The 1994 statutes carried a predicted increase of about 2,000 new prison beds over ten years. The 1995 amendments to the structured sentencing statutes combined for an estimated increase of about 3,200 beds over ten years. Nonetheless, the statutes that finally passed the legislature were once again considerably less expensive than the bills initially proposed.

The largest prison increases flowing from the 1995 amendments came from changes in the handling of assault cases. The 1993 statutes contained a gap in the treatment of assaults: a few assaults (such as assault with a deadly weapon) could be treated as serious Class E felonies, while simple assaults on a citizen received misdemeanor status. This meant that some crimes of real concern to judges and victims— particularly some domestic assaults—could not receive any prison time. The commission heard repeated complaints from judges and prosecutors about this "gap" in the assault sentences and proposed a set of amendments for the legislature. The 1995 legislation mostly tracked the commission proposals. It created a new intermediate category for assaults and changed the felony sentencing chart to allow judges to choose an active prison term as the punishment for more assault defendants (Wright 2001).

In the long run, the changes to the assault laws gave prosecutors more latitude to select charges for a high-volume class of crimes. But in the short run, none of these 1995 amendments rejected the basic principles of structured sentencing. The essential compromises held together.

A consensus settled into place: the sentencing structure, like the sentencing commission itself, was perceived to be apolitical. It was a planning device that allowed the state to link its sentencing aspirations with the corrections resources at hand. This role as a credible and nonpartisan technical advisor allowed the sentencing commission and the sentencing structure to remain intact even after the legislators who created them were no longer in leadership roles (Lubitz and Ross 2001).

The commission's prison projections created much of this good will in the general assembly. Legislators who remembered the mass releases of felons on short notice under the FSA and the prison cap were impressed that the sentencing commission's projections of prison populations were reasonably accurate (Ross and Katzenelson 1999).

When the commission issued its "population projections" each fiscal year, it attached a nontechnical explanation of the assumptions involved. These included the commission's estimates of the rate of parole for the FSA offenders remaining in the "stock" population, the percentage of the maximum sentence that structured sentencing offenders would serve, the growth rate for felony convictions, the rate of active sentences imposed, and so forth. This document gave legislators just enough detail to appreciate the difficulty of making good projections ten years into the future. The commission also revised its projections each year. For instance, the commission in 1997 projected a prison population of 30,060 for fiscal year 2000; by January 2000, the projection for that year shifted to 32,113. The actual population at the end of the fiscal year was 31,899. The commission's ability to offer more accurate predictions as the relevant year approached was unsurprising. However, the ability to explain projections and to earn the trust of legislators was a real communications achievement.

C. Community Corrections Funding

In 1993, the general assembly fully funded the prison construction necessary to operate within the sentencing guidelines until 2001. During the first two years after passage of the new sentencing structure, the time arrived to make appropriations for the planned expansion in community corrections programs and budgets. Corrections officials were concerned that the legislature would fail to follow through on the funding necessary for these programs. But during its 1994 and 1995 sessions, the legislature funded the expansion in corrections programs without controversy. The link between prison and nonprison punishments remained intact.

The sentencing structure determined the total number of intermediate and community punishment slots needed. The 1993 legislation anticipated more use of probation officers. It established specific targets for an upper limit on the caseloads of probation officers—ninety regular cases or twenty-five intensive cases per officer—and included funds to hire over 500 new probation officers (Gen. Stat., sec. 15A-1343.2). But the structure did not decide which other existing or potential new programs would expand to fill the increased need. The 1993 legislation depended on several state agencies, along with local governments and local agencies, to develop the programs, using state funding and some general state standards of accountability (NCSPAC 1993*b*).

The sentencing commission contacted administrators of the existing community corrections programs and asked for a "five year plan" for expansion under the new sentencing structure (Lubitz 1996). Planners at various state agencies, including the Department of Correction and the Department of Health and Human Services, met regularly to coordinate their requests. In the past, each of the existing community corrections programs had submitted independent budget proposals. Under the auspices of the sentencing commission and the Department of Correction, these programs submitted a budget proposal to the legislature that unified what had once been diffuse political support for community corrections (Pearce 2001). This planning process made it possible to present a unified vision to the general assembly.

Under the new administrative structure, state and local government shared the responsibility. The state continued to fund and administer most of the largest programs, including those—such as intensive probation and electronic house arrest—that were expected to grow most quickly. Local governments continued to fund and administer the small number of programs already in place.

The centerpiece of the new partnership was an appropriation every year—$12 million each year for the first few years—available for grants to local governments. The state disbursed 80 percent of the money in "formula" grants, with each county eligible for a different amount depending on population. The state reserved the remaining 20 percent for "discretionary" grants. Each county could appoint a local advisory board and submit to the Department of Correction a plan to expand an existing program or to create a new one. The discretionary grants often funded one-time capital expenses, such as renovating a building to house a day reporting center. Counties obtained operating expenses through the discretionary grants only for the first few years of a new program; after that time, state officials hoped that the local government would see the value of the program and fund it for themselves.

In the first few years under the new law, eighty-two of the state's 100 counties applied for grants, and seventy were funded right away (Lubitz 2001). By 2000, ninety-three counties were receiving state grant funds to operate community corrections programs (Stahl 2001). The annual expense was relatively small: about $12 million, compared with a $200 million budget for the state's probation and parole division and a $660 million operating budget for prisons. But the extra program slots generated with this money were critical to the credibility of structured sentencing with judges.

V. Changing Sentence Patterns, 1995–2000

The central goal of structured sentencing was to direct prison resources more emphatically to violent felonies while controlling prison costs by expanding the use of nonprison sanctions for lesser felonies. A secondary goal was to promote more deliberation in the legislature about new sentencing laws and perhaps to restrain any new growth in the use of prison. Other goals were to remove the gap between the announced sentence and the time served and to monitor sentencing practices so the system could adjust over time. Have sentencing practices actually changed in the direction that the system's creators hoped they would? Although a complete review of the impact of structured sentencing goes beyond the scope of this historical overview, analysis of commission reports and the one independent evaluation completed thus far (Collins et al. 1999) offer partial answers.

A. Prison and Jail Terms

The basic objectives of structured sentencing were accomplished during its first few years of operation. The objective of "truth in sentencing" was the first and most straightforward achievement: all of-

TABLE 4

Percentage of Active Terms Imposed for Felony Convictions

	1993–94	1995–96	1996–97	1997–98	1998–99	1999–2000
All felonies	48	28.1	31.5	33.1	33.7	32.6
Violent crimes	66	64.0	63.2	64.1	64.8	60.4
Property crimes	45	24.7	26.9	28.5	28.4	27.8
Lesser drug crimes	36	12.0	17.1	16.9	18.1	19.0
Other felonies	65	49.2	55.5	55.5	52.8	52.9
Number of convictions	21,395	17,871	20,531	20,495	20,536	24,146

SOURCE.—North Carolina Sentencing and Policy Advisory Commission 1994, 1996, 1998, 1999, 2000, 2001*b*.

fenders sentenced under the new law serve 100 percent of the minimum term, unless the legislature later amends the sentencing laws to revive the dormant parole authority. Parole is a resilient practice, as the FSA experience in North Carolina—and similar episodes in states such as Florida—can attest (Handberg and Holten 1993). But at this point, its return in North Carolina does not seem likely.

The central priority of structured sentencing—sending fewer property crime offenders to prison, thereby allowing longer prison terms for violent offenders—also has taken hold as expected. As table 4 shows, fewer felons overall have gone to prison.

During fiscal year 1993–94,[10] just prior to the beginning of structured sentencing, 48 percent of the felony convictions resulted in an active prison sentence. Under structured sentencing, the percentage dropped and remained between 28 and 34.

Much of the decline came from property crimes, as intended. As table 4 indicates, the proportion of active prison sentences imposed in property crimes fell from 45 percent in 1993–94 to somewhere between 24 and 29 percent for each year after the new law took effect (Ross and Katzenelson 1999).

But a corresponding increase in the percentage of active prison terms for violent felonies has not occurred. The proportion for violent crimes in 1993–94 was 66 percent, and remained near that level under the new law, ranging between 60 and 65 percent. The proportion of

[10] Unless indicated otherwise, all the tables in this part of the essay draw on the annual "Monitoring Reports" issued by the commission. The figures for 1993–94 derive from a commission study of felony sentencing before structured sentencing (NCSPAC 1994). They do not include Mecklenburg County because of incompatibility of the computer systems for Charlotte.

TABLE 5

Mean Length of Active Terms Served or Minimum Term Imposed
for Felony Convictions (Months)

	1993–94	1995–96	1996–97	1997–98	1998–99	1999–2000
Violent crimes	21.0	59.6	59.4	62.2	64.8	67.0
Property crimes	6.5	12.3	11.2	11.9	11.2	12.0

SOURCE.—North Carolina Sentencing and Policy Advisory Commission 1994, 1996, 1998, 1999, 2000, 2001b.

active prison sentences for some particular violent crimes did move up or down. The proportion of active prison terms for common law robbery went from 70 percent to 50 percent; three forms of rape (those other than first degree) went from the 60–86 percent range in 1993–94 to 100 percent under the new law. But these changes in particular violent crimes canceled each other out; the rate for the group of crimes remained about the same.

The changes in the use of prison for violent crimes came not in the proportion of felons going to prison, but in the length of the prison terms actually served. (The increase in the length of prison terms actually served in North Carolina is consistent with a national trend [Blumstein and Beck 1999].) As table 5 shows, the average time served for active prison terms imposed in fiscal year 1993–94 for personal injury crimes was twenty-one months.[11] The minimum term imposed for personal injury crimes under structured sentencing ranged from 59.4 to 67 months. The average time served for property crimes also increased. Although fewer property felons received prison terms under structured sentencing, those who did go to prison served longer terms.

As the inmates sentenced under the new laws filled up the system, the overall makeup of the prison population changed. Since 1995, the population has shifted toward those who committed assaultive crimes—from 46 percent in 1995 to 52 percent in 2000—and away from those who committed property crimes—from 27 percent in 1995

[11] The Department of Correction calculated in 2001 the mean time served for sentences imposed in FY 1993–94 for violent felonies and property felonies. As a result, the figure does not include those whose sentence is not yet complete. Ultimately, the figure for violent crime sentences imposed in 1993–94 will rise higher than twenty-one months. But given the large proportion of cases with a maximum term imposed of seven years or less (those whose sentences were complete by 2001), it is clear that the time served for 1995–96 sentences will remain higher.

to 18 percent in 2000 (North Carolina Department of Correction 2001, p. 12). The changes in the makeup of the population will make it more difficult over time for the state to use minimum- and medium-security prison facilities, another source of increased costs.

Thus, the system delivered on the feature that produced its broad political appeal. It directed prison resources to longer sentences for violent offenders. This did not occur quite as predicted, since the proportion of violent felons receiving an active term remained about the same. But the violent criminals who did go to prison received longer active terms. These outcomes make North Carolina a bit different from other sentencing guidelines states, where the proportion of violent offenders receiving active prison terms went up markedly, along with increases in sentence length (Knapp 1984, p. 31; Washington State Sentencing Guidelines Commission 1986, fig. 1; Gebelein 1997, pp. 89–90).

Although the system managed to redirect prison resources, it has not succeeded so clearly in slowing the growth of the prison system, one of the major concerns of the legislators who started this process in 1988. The prison system added (and used) lots of new beds during the 1990s. The legislature added prison capacity with the proceeds from the 1990 referendum bonds, and the construction from those funds was largely in place by 1994. The general assembly also provided for construction needed to handle the influx of new prisoners under the 1994 and 1995 increases in sentences, along with the anticipated natural growth in convictions, bringing the current system capacity to about 34,000. This is almost twice the size of the system in 1989. Local governments have also added jail capacity. The number of persons held in jails increased from 8,939 in 1993 to 10,122 in 1995 (Community Corrections Coalition 1996, pp. 4–5). With no further changes to the system, between 5,000 and 8,000 new prison beds will be needed over the next ten years (Katzenelson 2001).

Table 2 shows trends in the prison population in the state. A deluge occurred the first year that structured sentencing took effect: the population went from about 24,000 in 1994 to 29,000 in 1995. This increase, however, was the result of prisoners first admitted under the Fair Sentencing Act. The parole commission drastically slowed the rate of releases for prisoners sentenced under the old law in 1995, so the population grew more quickly than anticipated. Indeed, until the last of the new prison construction was ready for use, North Carolina had to rent prison space out of state (Neff 1996).

The prison population remained almost unchanged between 1996 and 1999, hovering around 31,000 inmates. As North Carolina's general population increased, this meant a declining imprisonment rate for the state—from 379 to 345—during a time when the national average rate for the states was still climbing, from 394 to 434. In sum, while the prison system did grow during the 1990s, there were reasons to expect even faster growth.

After the increased spending and growth during the mid-1990s, the legislature has now adopted a system with almost the same prison capacity that the sentencing commission originally proposed in 1993. The commission at that time endorsed a system that would have increased prison space to just under 40,000 beds by 2004. The legislature adopted instead the less expensive "standard operating capacity" proposal, which would have resulted in a prison capacity of about 31,000 by 2004. With its 1994 and 1995 increases in prison usage, the legislature has split the difference between the SOC proposal and the commission's original plan.

Did the legislature accomplish anything in 1993 by insisting on the lighter use of prison, only to add to the system again over the next few years? Perhaps the way things happened, prison growth occurred later and gave the state more time to pay for the expansion. The commission's 1993 proposal would have required growth right away, while the increments added in 1994 and 1995 took longer to show their effects. It is also possible that even if the Democrat-dominated legislature in 1993 had opted for a more expansive program, the 1995 Republican-dominated legislature still would have left its own mark on the system by adding onto the existing population base.

But it is also plausible, after reviewing this history, to conclude that the new system did not control prison growth. Structured sentencing in North Carolina surely allowed for planned growth, but planning does not necessarily mean moderation. A system that monitors sentencing practices carefully also keeps criminal justice closer to the top of the public agenda. Growth might be built into this system.

In the end, we cannot know whether structured sentencing in North Carolina controlled the growth of the prison system. The fact that North Carolina's rate of imprisonment grew more slowly than the national average (see table 2) is suggestive, but that trend was happening before the commission was born. It may be that prison rates reach equilibrium through forces other than sentencing policy. The movement toward the national average rates may be driven by demograph-

TABLE 6

Use of Intermediate and Community Punishments in Felony Cases
(Percent)

	1993–94	1995–96	1996–97	1997–98	1998–99	1999–2000
Intermediate		46	42	40	41	44
	52					
Community		26	26	27	25	23
Total felons	21,192	17,871	20,531	20,495	20,536	24,146

SOURCE.—North Carolina Sentencing and Policy Advisory Commission 1994, 1996, 1998, 1999, 2000, 2001*b*.

ics—the influx of so many newcomers to North Carolina from other regions and nations. As Zimring and Hawkins (1991) have demonstrated, there is no clear relationship over the long haul between the scale of imprisonment and particular sentencing policies or social conditions. We have much to learn about what causes the stops and starts of massive prison growth.

B. Community and Intermediate Sanctions

The availability of more nonprison sanctions was necessary for the system to remain in balance. Local governments and state agencies developed enough programs overall. The sentencing commission also made efforts to educate sentencing judges about the programs available. Its annual "Compendium of Community Corrections Resources" listed the programs operating and described the types of offenders best suited for each (NCSPAC 2001*a*). But some types of programs—especially residential treatment programs—remained underdeveloped, and judges too often had to select a community or intermediate punishment that was not their first choice.

The overall use of community and intermediate punishments did grow as intended under structured sentencing. As table 6 shows, judges during fiscal year 1993–94 sentenced about 11,000 felony offenders to nonprison sanctions. By fiscal year 1998–99, those nonprison sentences had increased to over 16,000.

Most of the increase came in the use of intermediate sanctions. The largest single intermediate punishment, year in and year out, has been the split sentence (called "special probation"), under which the offender serves some fraction of the term—no more than a quarter of the maximum term, with a six-month cap—in prison or jail, and the remainder of the term on probation. Intensively supervised probation has become almost as important as special probation, growing from 2,528 felons in 1992–93 to 10,362 felons admitted in 1999–2000. Day reporting centers, which did not exist before the advent of structured sentencing, now admit close to 4,000 felons each year.

Unfortunately, the supposed distinction between community sanctions and intermediate sanctions is not apparent to many of those working in the system. For many sentencing judges, intermediate punishments do not seem significantly different from community punishments (Drennan 2001).

The offenders in the intermediate programs are now more chronic and serious offenders than in the past. They present special challenges because they are less likely to comply with program rules and more likely to abscond (Pearce 2001). The number of offenders violating program requirements also could be a consequence of better monitoring rather than different behavior by the offenders. More intrusive supervision will inevitably uncover more violations of the program conditions (Tonry 1996, pp. 108–21).

The partnership between state and local authorities also hindered some of the newer intermediate programs. Local governments and agencies had experience providing mental health services, but they had no experience keeping tight controls on people outside the local jail. Thus, the intermediate programs meant to provide strict controls on offenders have operated more like the training and service-oriented community sanctions. It was perhaps asking too much of local agencies to design new programs so different from the ones they had known in the past. The Department of Correction may need to get more involved in setting standards or in operating intermediate programs, to assure judges that offenders sentenced to these programs will be properly monitored.

C. Trial Judge Signals about Proportionality

It is clear enough that the growth of prisons and intermediate punishments has occurred on a scale that legislators and commissioners intended from the start. But judges, prosecutors, and defense attorneys do not concern themselves with the overall scope of the corrections system. They ask whether the punishment in the case at hand is proportional—that is, whether it is appropriate in light of the facts about the offense and the offender that everyone considers relevant. If they believe that the sentencing structure is not distributing the available punishments fairly and proportionately, they will change their charging and sentencing practices. The ability of the North Carolina system in the future to recognize changing practices and to adjust as needed is still in doubt.

Any changes to the structure, whether large or small, must go through the legislative process. The commission does not have authority to accomplish these amendments by itself, through an administrative rule-making process. This process slows the reaction time when changes occur (Wright 1994).

Furthermore, because of the emphasis on control of resources in North Carolina, the system has a weakened ability to recognize changes in practice as they develop. Because its judges cannot "depart" from the prescribed sentence ranges, it is difficult for the commission to notice and respond to developing problems. In an ordinary "departure" jurisdiction, a pattern of departures in particular types of cases, including the explanations of the trial and appellate judges in such cases, is a rich source of information to a sentencing commission. It can signal the cases where judges are most unhappy with the operation of the sentencing rules and can suggest potential amendments to the rules (Wright 1991; Berman 2000).

In North Carolina, sentencing judges do not depart and do not give enlightening explanations for their decisions to choose a sentence in the "mitigated" or "aggravated" range. This leaves little room for appellate courts to create a common law of sentencing that could reinforce or redirect the statutes. Moreover, North Carolina's appellate courts have been reluctant to use their limited authority. The court of appeals and supreme court have made it plain that they will overturn a sentence only based on legal error in calculating prior criminal record or for a failure to select one of the readily available grounds for an aggravated sentence. The government cannot appeal a sentencing judge's decision to select a mitigated sentence.

It is true that appellate courts expect sentencing judges to make minimal factual findings to support an aggravating factor. For example, in *State v. Ballard* (349 N.C. 286 [1998]), the defendant was convicted of second degree murder after wrecking the car he was driving while impaired, killing the passenger, who was the son of his former girlfriend. The judge at sentencing found "abuse of a position of trust" as an aggravating factor, sending the sentence into the aggravated range. But the supreme court reversed, because the sentencing judge made no factual findings about whether the child's trust in the defendant caused him to get into the car.

The courts also hear many appeals complaining about trial judges who rely on nonstatutory aggravating factors. The appellate courts typically uphold the sentence. When they do overturn the use of an aggravating factor in the case, they stress that it is relatively easy for the sentencing judge to avoid trouble. Because the appellate courts have developed no limits on the weight that sentencing judges must put on a factor, any finding of a statutory aggravating factor will legitimize a sentence outside the presumed range. There is no reason for the sentencing judge in that situation to take the legal risk of creating a nonstatutory factor to test on appellate review. As the court advised in *State v. Rollins* (131 N.C. App. 601, 607 [1998]), "trial judges may wish to exercise restraint when considering nonstatutory aggravating factors after having found statutory factors."

Because it is so easy for sentencing judges to avoid trouble on appeal, the appellate courts in North Carolina have played almost no role in shaping sentencing policy. In other jurisdictions, such as Minnesota, the appellate courts became central players (Frase 1993*a*; Reitz 1997). In Alaska, appellate courts created "benchmark" sentences for various types of offenses. In the federal system, the U.S. sentencing commission relies on "circuit splits" to identify many potential trouble spots in the federal guidelines. The North Carolina sentencing commission cannot count on this sort of reasoned feedback from judges.

Instead of statements from trial and appellate judges, the North Carolina commission must rely on more subtle clues. In border boxes, the commission can watch for shifts over time from intermediate sanctions to active prison terms, or from community sanctions to intermediate sanctions (Wright 2001). They can also look for changes over the years in judges' choices between concurrent and consecutive sentences when there are multiple convictions. There are now some anecdotal reports that the use of consecutive sentences is increasing, especially for Class H and Class I felonies.

More telling are the proportions of cases that judges sentence outside the presumptive range for each grid box. Although these decisions are not accompanied by a full explanation and appellate review, the simple fact that many judges are moving outside the presumptive range says something about a potential problem spot.

Overall, the number of cases falling within the presumptive range has stayed fairly steady, moving between 79 and 83 percent. Table 7

TABLE 7

Range Locations of Felony Sentences (Percent)

	1995–96	1996–97	1997–98	1998–99	1999–2000	Total
Aggravated, all	8.4	7.4	8.2	8.3	7.9	8.0
Level I only	12.8	9.5	11.3	12.2	11.6	11.4
Levels V–VI	9.1	7.7	7.0	7.3	6.4	7.4
Presumptive, all	82.1	83.0	80.7	78.5	75.0	79.5
Level I only	70.7	75.7	72.5	70.2	68.3	71.5
Levels V–VI	84.8	84.1	84.2	81.7	78.7	82.2
Mitigated, all	9.5	9.6	11.1	13.2	17.1	12.4
Level I only	16.5	14.8	16.3	17.6	20.1	17.0
Levels V–VI	6.2	8.1	8.7	11.0	14.9	10.4

SOURCE.—North Carolina Sentencing and Policy Advisory Commission 1994, 1996, 1998, 1999, 2000, 2001b.

shows the presumptive, mitigated, and aggravated sentences imposed for each fiscal year since the start of structured sentencing. Aggravated and mitigated sentences were imposed in North Carolina about as often as judges in other states departed from the prescribed durations in their guidelines (Frase 1993a; Austin et al. 1996). But sentencing judges are now showing the first signs of discomfort with the sentencing structure as a whole. The most noteworthy change in the combined numbers is a near doubling of mitigated range cases, from 9.5 percent to 17.1 percent over the first five years.

The sentencing judges are not signaling any strong unhappiness with the role of prior criminal record in setting durations in the grid. If judges believed that the structure placed too much weight overall on prior record, Prior Record Levels V and VI (the most serious) would show the most mitigated sentences and the fewest aggravated sentences. That pattern has not appeared. Instead, Prior Record Level I (offenders with little or no criminal record) shows the highest proportions of both mitigated and aggravated sentences. The judges have responded in more diverse ways to offenders with less experience in the system, those at Level I.

It is also interesting that the aggravated range sentences have grown less quickly than the mitigated range. This holds true for all the levels of criminal record. The faster growth for mitigated sentences could mean that judges, on the whole, find the structure too severe to fit the cases they see from day to day. Alternatively, the faster growth in the mitigated-range sentences may simply reflect the asymmetrical grounds for appellate review. Defendants may appeal aggravated-range cases, but the prosecution usually cannot appeal a judge's decision to impose a mitigated sentence (N.C. Gen. Stat., secs. 15A-1441, 1444, 1445).

There are also a few particular felony classes that are attracting more than the usual share of mitigated or aggravated sentences. Judges are choosing mitigated sentences more often than usual for Class D felonies—such as first degree burglary or armed robbery—and are choosing aggravated sentences more frequently for Class F felonies—such as assault inflicting serious injury, embezzlement, or some lesser forms of arson (Wright 1999).

Although the judges do not offer meaningful statements of reasons for their mitigated and aggravated sentences, the pattern of sentences has something to say. By breaking down the felony classes into particular crimes, the commission can discover which crimes are the source of judicial discontent. If judges are too often unhappy with the normal choices available to them for a given crime, some change in the structure might be necessary. The commission must inquire at this level of detail if it hopes to hear what judges are saying about the workability of its presumptive sentencing ranges over time.

Now that the sentencing structure has settled into place, the commission can begin to address questions about racial disparity that have always remained in the background under structured sentencing. The race of all felons taken together has not changed much since the start of structured sentencing. According to sentencing commission calculations, the proportion of blacks convicted of felonies has ranged between 59.4 percent and 63.1 percent since 1995–96, and the numbers do not show any particular trend. The proportion of whites convicted of felonies has stayed between 33 and 37 percent, again showing no trend over time. The percentage of Hispanics, although small, has grown steadily from 0.5 percent in 1995–96 to 1.9 percent in 1999–2000.

A study of structured sentencing in North Carolina by the Research Triangle Institute (Collins et al. 1999) found almost no shift in the racial mix of convicted felons after structured sentencing took effect. The percentage of blacks changed from 56.7 percent in 1994 to 55.7 percent in 1996.

The stability in the aggregate numbers does not mean that racial disparity is missing from North Carolina sentencing. The figures reported above compare unfavorably to the overall population of North Carolina, which the 2000 Census identified as follows: 70.2 percent white, 21.6 percent black, 4.7 percent Hispanic, and 1.2 percent American Indian. Nobody has yet investigated whether the disproportionate number of blacks in the prison population is explained by different levels of participation in crime, or racial differences at arrest, charging, conviction, and sentencing, or some combination of them all. The commission stopped publishing demographics for particular crimes or types of sentences after its first two full years of statistical reports, so it is difficult to delve any further into the influence of race at sentencing. The commission is currently researching this subject and will soon issue a report.

D. Shifts in Charging Decisions

A system that makes the charge of conviction one of the two major factors in selecting the proper range for a sentence gives enormous power to the prosecutor. The high volume of work in state court makes it difficult for a prosecutor's office to take full advantage of this power by systematically changing its charging practices (Miethe 1987). Momentum plays a huge role in a busy state system.

Despite the press of time, however, North Carolina prosecutors do appear to be adjusting their charging habits over time. There is some evidence of "bracket creep." If prosecutors were systematically choosing charges that take full advantage of the sentencing structure, then one would expect over time to notice higher numbers of crimes being charged in the higher felony classes, and higher numbers in the more serious criminal history categories on the right side of the grid. According to table 8, both of these shifts are taking place to a limited degree, both for felonies and for misdemeanors.

For felonies, the proportions of low-level (Classes H and I) felonies have gone down slightly throughout the first five years of structured sentencing. Meanwhile, the percentages of some midlevel felonies (Classes F and G) have gone up during the same period. Unless criminal behavior has become more serious in North Carolina during this period of falling crime rates, this trend indicates that prosecutors are becoming more aggressive about selecting felony charges. The numbers are similar for misdemeanors. The most serious category, Class A1, has increased in about the same amount that Class 1 has decreased. The small increase in the seriousness of felonies charged marks a distinction between North Carolina and some other states, where prose-

TABLE 8

Offense Class, 1995–2000 (Percent)

	1995–96	1996–97	1997–98	1998–99	1999–2000
Felony class:					
A	.2	.3	.3	.4	.2
B1	.4	.3	.5	.5	.5
B2	1.1	1.0	1.2	1.4	1.0
C	2.2	2.1	2.6	2.9	2.6
D	3.0	2.9	3.0	3.1	3.0
E	4.9	5.1	5.4	4.8	4.1
F	3.5	4.1	4.8	5.4	6.8
G	7.0	7.5	8.3	10.6	11.6
H	46.6	44.1	41.5	40.7	40.0
I	31.2	32.5	32.5	30.3	30.2
Misdemeanor class:					
A1	3.4	7.8	10.6	10.7	9.8
1	60.7	54.6	51.0	51.9	53.7
2	21.4	22.9	23.4	22.8	20.6
3	14.5	14.7	15.0	14.6	15.9

SOURCE.—North Carolina Sentencing and Policy Advisory Commission 1994, 1996, 1998, 1999, 2000, 2001b.

cutors charged fewer serious crimes after new sentencing guidelines took effect (Tonry 1988). Table 9 shows similar changes happening in the level of criminal history points that defendants are accumulating.

Both for felonies and misdemeanors, the least serious category (Level I) is becoming less common over time, while each of the higher levels is growing slightly over time. Perhaps prosecutors are searching more thoroughly for prior criminal convictions or are finding ways to structure charges—by filing multiple charges, for instance—to escalate criminal history more quickly. Frase (1993a) described efforts by prosecutors in Minnesota along these lines.

Collins et al. (1999) found evidence that prosecutors are now filing more charges than they did before 1995. The number of single-charge felony cases stayed flat between 1994 and 1996 (about 31 percent). However, in multiple-charge felony cases, there was a slight shift from cases with two charges up to cases with three or more charges, as table 10 shows.

The Collins study found clearer signs of changes in charging and plea negotiations by looking at the number of cases dismissed and the cases where the defendant was convicted of fewer or less serious crimes

TABLE 9

Changes over Time in Criminal History Level (Percent)

	1995–96	1996–97	1997–98	1998–99	1999–2000
Felony level:					
I	33.3	33.5	33.2	30.6	27.3
II	35.3	35.7	36.1	36.5	36.0
III	18.3	17.9	17.7	18.4	19.5
IV	9.9	9.8	9.6	10.6	12.6
V	1.8	1.9	2.2	2.3	2.9
VI	1.3	1.1	1.1	1.5	1.7
Misdemeanor level:					
I	47.9	50.0	47.8	45.8	45.7
II	39.7	38.3	39.6	40.7	41.2
III	12.4	11.7	12.6	13.5	13.1

Source.—North Carolina Sentencing and Policy Advisory Commission 1994, 1996, 1998, 1999, 2000, 2001b.

than the prosecutor originally filed. As summarized in table 10, there were increases in all these areas.

Taken together, tables 8–10 reveal a bit of a paradox. On the one hand, prosecutors appear to be obtaining convictions for more serious offenses and more extensive criminal records. On the other hand, they are dismissing and discounting more felony charges. Perhaps prosecutors are charging more aggressively for many felonies and then are dis-

TABLE 10

Indications of Changes in Felony Charging Practices (Percent)

Felony Defendants with . . .	January–June 1994	January–June 1996
Single charge filed	31.2	31.4
Two charges filed	25.1	23.9
Three or more charges filed	43.7	44.7
Multiple charges, most serious dismissed	46.3	48.5
Reduction in number of offenses between charge and conviction	74.3	76.5
Single offense charged, reduction in offense class at conviction	59.7	64.2
Multiple offenses charged, reduction in offense class for most serious offense	59.3	63.3

Source.—Collins et al. 1999, tables 2.4, 2.6, 2.7, 2.8, 2.9.

Table 11

Habitual Felon Convictions, with Class of Most Serious Previous Felony (Percent)

	1995–96	1996–97	1997–98	1998–99	1999–2000
Total	213	248	342	460	560
Class D	7.0	4.0	5.8	5.2	5.7
Class E	6.6	3.6	3.5	3.7	2.3
Class F	1.4	3.2	2.6	2.4	4.1
Class G	9.4	9.7	12.6	12.8	19.8
Class H	54.5	55.2	46.8	50.9	43.8
Class I	19.7	23.8	24.3	20.9	16.6

SOURCE.—North Carolina Sentencing and Policy Advisory Commission 1994, 1996, 1998, 1999, 2000, 2001b.

missing or discounting more heavily only in those cases where the defense has more negotiating leverage.

There is one particular area that is contributing to the increase both in felony levels and to the importance of prior criminal records. The "habitual felon" provisions, as expanded in 1994, allow prosecutors to target any felony defendant who was convicted of any three previous felonies. This could include relatively minor crimes such as failure to appear. The habitual felon is then convicted of a Class C felony, even if the underlying offense was a much less serious class (N.C. Gen. Stat., sec. 14-7.1). This provision gives prosecutors the power to ignore the sentencing structure for most defendants who would normally land in the lower right-hand quarter of the sentencing grid.

Before structured sentencing arrived, prosecutors did not often invoke the habitual felon law. Prosecutors obtained convictions on 82 habitual felony charges in 1991, 136 in 1992, 164 in 1993, and 230 in 1994. But after the passage of structured sentencing, the small annual increases started to mount. As table 11 shows, the previous felonies committed by those who are later convicted as habitual felons shifted away from highest and lowest classes (D, E, H, and I), and toward the middle classes (F and G).

Given the length of sentences involved for Class C felonies (up to 210 months for those with enough prior convictions), the increase is now significant. Habitual felon has become by far the most common charge in Class C (560 of the 618 convictions for Class C in 1999–2000).

Why are prosecutors turning more often to habitual felon charges? The increase may reflect general objections by prosecutors to the weight that the structure gives to prior record. A habitual felon charge dramatically increases the importance of prior record. But it seems more likely that the habitual felon laws reflect a prosecutorial strategy for a special type of case. Under the old law, if the prosecutor encountered a defendant who seemed especially dangerous even though the crime charged was not very serious, the judge still had enough discretion to impose a long prison term. Under structured sentencing, the constraints are tighter and it becomes more worthwhile for the prosecutor to do the extra paperwork needed to move the defendant up into Class C.

Prosecutors in different districts have different approaches to the habitual felon law. Some make it a priority to increase the use of this law, while others ignore it (Cunningham 2000). In those districts most actively pursuing habitual felon cases, prosecutors use a few techniques to expand the reach of the law. The Governor's Crime Commission, under the "Bull's Eye Project," funded extra prosecutors in selected offices around the state to complete the extra paperwork necessary (verification of prior convictions) to increase habitual felon prosecutions. Some offices also found ways to convert multiple misdemeanor convictions into a habitual felon case. Under North Carolina's chaotic criminal code, multiple convictions for some misdemeanors—such as breaking into coin-operated machines—can be charged as a felony (N.C. Gen. Stat., sec. 14-56.1). These charges combine with other felonies to create the necessary prior convictions (Spence and Boyum 2000).

Such a systematic effort to exploit a weak point in the sentencing structure is a real danger for the future. What is happening with habitual felon crimes could just as easily happen with assault crimes and others that give the prosecutor a choice among related crimes within different felony classes (Wright 2001). This is a blind spot in the North Carolina sentencing scheme. While the effects of shifting charging decisions have not been large so far, prosecutors could throw the system into serious imbalance before the commission and the legislature could react.[12]

---

[12] The sentencing commission recommended new restrictions on the habitual felon provision as part of a legislative package that the general assembly will debate during 2002.

VI. Conclusion

North Carolina sentencing is approaching another transition point. The initial period of guideline development and the creation of a working relationship with the legislature is ending. After about five years of routine operation, favorable attention in the national press cast a positive light on this first phase. Both Robin Lubitz and Judge Tom Ross received national recognition for their work and made speeches to national public policy groups. In October 1997, the commission was one of ten programs nationwide to receive the Innovations in American Government award from the Ford Foundation. Newspaper articles in states with troubled sentencing systems sometimes turned to North Carolina as a possible solution (Hall 1999; *Atlanta Journal-Constitution* 2000). Although other states were operating systems similar to North Carolina's—and indeed had pioneered the basic features of the system—the conservative political culture of this southern state made North Carolina an appealing model. The optimistic view of the North Carolina experience was that better targeting of prisons and expansion of community punishments were possible in many places and not just in a handful of more liberal states such as Minnesota, Washington, and Massachusetts.

More difficult times for the sentencing commission will likely arrive in the near future. The commission has new leadership: Robin Lubitz left in 1997, and the commission hired Susan Katzenelson as the new executive director. Tom Ross, who was considered synonymous with structured sentencing, left in 1999 and was replaced by superior court judge Erwin Spainhour. Katzenelson has meaningful experience at other sentencing commissions; she served as staff director at the federal sentencing commission. Spainhour also brings credibility to the job; he had served on the sentencing commission since 1998. But neither has yet faced the sort of intense political testing that was a daily reality for the commission during the first half of the 1990s.

Such intense moments will occur within the next few years. If the commission's population projections hold true, then by 2002 the state's expanded prison capacity will be full again. The legislature will have to decide whether to expand prisons again to meet the next few years of growth or keep the prison capacity steady and shift more offenders into other punishments. Or another more insidious possibility could occur: the legislature could do nothing at all, and allow the strong linkage between sentencing rules and corrections resources to atrophy, inviting another crisis down the road.

Whatever the future holds, it is already possible to reach some judgments about the recent past. The second phase of sentencing redesign in North Carolina sustained its promise longer than the first did. Structured sentencing appears to be more successful and stable today than was true after the first five years under the FSA. Perhaps this is because the FSA endured a more severe test early on. Violent crime rates and numbers of convictions were rising when the FSA took effect, while structured sentencing began to operate about the time that violent crime rates began to fall.

But there were also important differences in the design of the two statutes. Structured sentencing fared better than the FSA for one overarching reason: the legislature viewed structured sentencing as a long-term management process rather than a one-time change to the sentencing rules. The decision to fund the sentencing commission permanently reflects this view. Steadier investment in both prison space and credible alternatives also reveals this ongoing management mentality and distinguishes the current system from the early 1980s. Neglect of corrections resources, alternating with haphazard growth, led to the downfall of the FSA. Thus far, the corrections resources for structured sentencing have kept pace with growth in the state's population. There is reason to hope, therefore, that no pressure is building beneath the surface among judges for greatly expanded sentencing options.

The legislature has maintained some self-discipline in the form of routine fiscal notes; this is a sign that the state's elected leaders think of sentencing as an ongoing management process. The commission has also acted with an awareness of its long-term place in system management. Among its highest priorities was its reputation among lawmakers as an apolitical source of technical information. It devoted careful attention to its routine projections for prison populations and use of other corrections resources. The executive director and chair of the sentencing commission have become two of the most influential policy makers in the state on matters of criminal justice, yet they operate within political boundaries set by others.

This approach to sentencing policy, emphasizing fiscal planning, has benefited North Carolina. Perhaps it was the only viable way to convince a politically fractured commission—in a politically fractious state—to endorse a plan. If the legislature had instructed the commission to address unequal distribution of punishment among defendants, the commission might have foundered. The members were not going to agree on how to apply general sentencing purposes to concrete sentencing rules. Because of the legislature's impatience with more prison spending during a stretch of tight state budgets, the commissioners never had to resolve for themselves the ideal use of prison as a sanction. It was easy to agree on the best use for prison—directing it toward violent offenders—and to leave the rest unanswered.

But there are losses to go along with the gains for managerial sentencing. Important questions about sentencing have gone unasked and unanswered in North Carolina. Some relate to crime control. Is the structure selecting those defendants who are most likely to commit truly harmful crimes and using the state's prison space to incapacitate criminals and reduce crime in a targeted way? Some questions relate to the scope of the criminal code. North Carolina has one of the most vague, disjointed, and duplicative substantive criminal codes in the nation (Robinson, Cahill, and Mohammad 2000). Would a revision of the code prove more effective than election of prosecutors as a way for the public to control the criminal sanction?

Some of the most urgent questions—as always in American life—relate to race. What explains the racial differences in the sentences that North Carolina courts impose? Is it possible to isolate the most important causes and to change practices? Other states have pursued these questions more aggressively than North Carolina (Dailey 1993).

Thus, designers of sentencing systems elsewhere might look to North Carolina for guidance on some questions, even while appreciating that the state has not yet progressed much on some other crucial dimensions of sentencing policy. North Carolina offers the most when it comes to the connections between prison and other punishments. The structure not only determines the "in-out" disposition for most sentences but also designates which of two categories—intermediate or community punishments—the judge should select for nonprison sentences. The structure also controls to a limited degree the overall length of the nonprison punishment. The legislature understands the linkage between funding for community punishments and longer prison terms for violent offenders, and the commission monitors the number of available program slots.

Other places might also take note of the state's handling of misdemeanors. The North Carolina structure was one of the first to cover misdemeanors as well as felonies. The coverage was crucial for the system to prevent misdemeanants from overwhelming the prisons and jails, not to mention the intermediate punishment programs. Much of the prison overcrowding under the FSA grew from the fact that many misdemeanants were assigned to the prison system rather than to local jails. The new system would have failed if it had ignored misdemeanors. North Carolina's system demonstrates that it is possible to construct a misdemeanor grid that is workable in the busy, high-volume atmosphere of misdemeanor court.

The limited role for judges—especially appellate judges—in the North Carolina system is also noteworthy. The aggravated and mitigated ranges function much like durational departures in other states; the "border boxes" offer judges some of the freedom of a dispositional departure. But North Carolina judges are still confined more closely than their colleagues elsewhere. This leaves few opportunities for appellate courts to shape the system, and the appellate decisions thus far have declined the few opportunities that have appeared. Such a system does make it easier to predict judicial behavior and to plan correctional resources. North Carolina has demonstrated that tight limits on judges will not necessarily create major opposition from the judges during the legislative debate. Whether the commission can adjust the system over time with only muted feedback from judges remains to be seen.

Some of these lessons are transferable to other places, because they resulted from the structure of the institutions involved. The legislature thought carefully about the groups that sent representatives to the commission. Although the initial legislation was not explicit on the question of prison capacity, later signals made it plain that the commission would have to remain within current prison resources. The commission staff highlighted for everyone the connections between felons and misdemeanants, between prison and nonprison sanctions. All of these structural features of the North Carolina system might work in other settings.

There are other parts of the North Carolina experience, however, that might not transplant so easily. The political savvy of figures such as Jim Coman, Gregg Stahl, Ann Barnes, Tom Ross, and Robin Lubitz might be difficult to duplicate. And part of the story in North Carolina turned on a working habit—incrementalism—that developed for reasons now hard to reconstruct. The state's leaders have shown, over the last ten years, an ability to give routine attention to sentencing matters without allowing themselves to unravel their earlier work. If this incrementalism continues, the next twenty years of sentencing policy could (with a little luck) prove far less interesting than the previous twenty.

106   Ronald F. Wright

REFERENCES

American Bar Association. 1994. *Standards for Criminal Justice, Sentencing Alternatives and Procedures,* 3d ed. Project of the Criminal Justice Standards Committee. Washington, D.C.: American Bar Association.
Ashford, Kathryn, and Craig Mosbaek. 1991. *First Year Report on Implementation of Sentencing Guidelines, November 1989 to January 1991.* Portland: Oregon Criminal Justice Council.
Atlanta Journal-Constitution. 2000. "Editorial: Sentencing Guidelines 'Win-Win.'" (January 30), p. 4D.
Austin, James, Charles Jones, John Kramer, and Phil Renninger. 1996. *National Assessment of Structured Sentencing.* NCJ 153853. Washington, D.C.: U.S. Department of Justice, Office of Justice Programs, Bureau of Justice Assistance.
Bennett, Amanda. 1994. "State Tailors Sentences to Cost of Prison Space with Computer's Help." *Wall Street Journal* (August 5), pp. A1, A5.
Berman, Douglas A. 2000. "Balanced and Purposeful Departures: Fixing a Jurisprudence That Undermines the Federal Sentencing Guidelines." *Notre Dame Law Review* 76:21–108.
Blumstein, Alfred, and Allen J. Beck. 1999. "Factors Contributing to the Growth in U.S. Prison Populations." In *Prisons,* edited by Michael Tonry and Joan Petersilia. Vol. 26 of *Crime and Justice: A Review of Research,* edited by Michael Tonry. Chicago: University of Chicago Press.
Bogan, Kathleen M. 1990. "Constructing Felony Sentencing Guidelines in an Already Crowded State: Oregon Breaks New Ground." *Crime and Delinquency* 36(4):467–87.
Boyd, Sam. 1992. North Carolina Parole Commission. Interview with author, December 9.
Bureau of Justice Statistics. 1992. *Sourcebook of Criminal Justice Statistics—1991.* Washington, D.C.: U.S. Department of Justice, Office of Justice Programs.
———. 1999. "Truth in Sentencing in State Prisons." NCJ 170032. Washington, D.C.: U.S. Department of Justice, Office of Justice Programs.
———. 2000. *Sourcebook of Criminal Justice Statistics—1999.* Washington, D.C.: U.S. Department of Justice, Office of Justice Programs.
Case, Cathy. 1990. "Martin, Legislature Reach Prison Deal." *United Press International* (June 27, 1990).
Citizens Commission on Alternatives to Incarceration. 1982. *Report.* Durham, N.C.: Citizens Commission on Alternatives to Incarceration.
Clarke, Stevens H. 1984. "North Carolina's Determinate Sentencing Legislation." *Judicature* 68:140–52.
———. 1987. *Felony Sentencing in North Carolina, 1976–1986: Effects of Presumptive Sentencing Legislation.* Chapel Hill: Institute of Government, University of North Carolina at Chapel Hill.
———. 1991. *Law of Sentencing, Probation and Parole in North Carolina.* Chapel Hill: Institute of Government, University of North Carolina at Chapel Hill.
———. 1997. "North Carolina Prisons Are Growing." In *Sentencing Reform in*

Overcrowded Times: A Comparative Perspective, edited by Michael Tonry and Kathleen Hatlestad. New York: Oxford University Press.

Clarke, Stevens H., Susan Turner Kurtz, Glenn F. Lang, Kenneth L. Parker, Elizabeth W. Rubinsky, and Donna J. Schleicher. 1983. *North Carolina's Determinate Sentencing Legislation: An Evaluation of the First Year's Experience.* Report submitted to the Governor's Crime Commission and the National Institute of Justice. Chapel Hill: Institute of Government, University of North Carolina at Chapel Hill.

Clarke, Stevens H., and Carl Pope. 1982. "Recent Developments in North Carolina's Prison Population." *Popular Government* 48:1–7.

Collins, James J., Donna L. Spencer, George H. Dunteman, Harlene C. Gogan, Peter H. Siegel, Brad A. Lessler, Kenneth Parker, and Thomas Sutton. 1999. *Final Report: Evaluation of North Carolina's Structured Sentencing Law.* Study supported by U.S. Department of Justice, National Institute of Justice. Research Triangle Park, N.C.: Research Triangle Institute.

Coman, James. 1992. North Carolina Department of Justice, Criminal Division. Interview with author, August 6.

Community Corrections Coalition. 1996. *Rebuilding the Future.* Raleigh, N.C.: Community Corrections Coalition.

Corrigan, Mark D. 1989*a*. "Corrections Strategic Planning: Corrections Population Analysis." Phase I consultant report to the North Carolina Special Committee on Prisons, North Carolina General Assembly. National Institute of Sentencing Alternatives, Waltham, Mass.

———. 1989*b*. "Corrections Strategic Planning: Implementation Strategies." Phase II consultant report to the North Carolina Special Committee on Prisons, North Carolina General Assembly. National Institute of Sentencing Alternatives, Waltham, Mass.

———. 1990. *Corrections Strategic Planning: Working Papers.* Prepared for the North Carolina Special Committee on Prisons, North Carolina General Assembly. Duxbury, Mass.: National Institute of Sentencing Alternatives.

Cunningham, Bruce. 2000. Criminal defense attorney, Southern Pines, North Carolina. Interview with author, December 15.

Dailey, Debra L. 1993. "Prison and Race in Minnesota." *University of Colorado Law Review* 64:761–80.

Denton, Van. 1992. "Martin Seeks Last $87.5 Million in Prison Bonds." *Raleigh News and Observer* (June 19), p. B2.

Drennan, James. 1992. North Carolina Institute of Government. Interview with author, August 6.

———. 2001. Interview with author, March 14.

Eubank, Jay. 1993. "Lawsuit Aims to Overturn Prison Cap." *Greensboro News and Record* (September 9), p. B1.

Frankel, Marvin E. 1973. *Criminal Sentences: Law without Order.* New York: Hill & Wang.

Frankel, Marvin E., and Leonard Orland. 1984. "Sentencing Commissions and Guidelines." *Georgetown Law Journal* 73:225–47.

Frase, Richard S. 1993*a*. "Implementing Commission-Based Sentencing

108   Ronald F. Wright

Guidelines: The Lessons of the First Ten Years in Minnesota." *Cornell Journal of Law and Public Policy* 2:279–337.

———. 1993*b*. "Sentencing Guidelines in the States: Lessons for State and Federal Reformers." *Federal Sentencing Reporter* 6(3):123–25.

———. 1995. "State Sentencing Guidelines: Still Going Strong." *Judicature* 78(4):173–79.

———. 1999. "Sentencing Guidelines in Minnesota, Other States, and the Federal Courts: A Twenty-Year Retrospective." *Federal Sentencing Reporter* 12(2):69–82.

Gebelein, Richard S. 1997. "Sentencing Reform in Delaware." In *Sentencing Reform in Overcrowded Times: A Comparative Perspective*, edited by Michael Tonry and Kathleen Hatlestad. New York: Oxford University Press.

Governor's Advisory Board on Prisons and Punishment. 1990. *A Report to the Governor: North Carolina's Prison Crisis*. Raleigh, N.C.: Governor's Advisory Board on Prisons and Punishment.

Governor's Crime Commission. 1987. *Truth in Sentencing: A Report to the Governor*. Raleigh, N.C.: Governor's Crime Commission.

Hall, Andy. 1999. "Expert Says Key Is Deciding Who Must Be Locked Up." *Wisconsin State Journal* (March 21), p. 1B.

Handberg, Roger, and N. Gary Holten. 1993. *Reforming Florida's Sentencing Guidelines: Balancing Equity, Justice, and Public Safety*. Dubuque, Iowa: Kendall/Hunt.

Hunt, James. 1992. *A North Carolina Agenda for Action*. Publication of the Hunt for Governor Campaign.

Joost, Robert. 1994. "Guidelines as Code: Viewing the Sentencing Guidelines as a Product of the Federal Criminal Code Effort." *Federal Sentencing Reporter* 7(3):118–21.

Katzenelson, Susan. 2001. Executive Director, North Carolina Sentencing and Policy Advisory Commission. Interview with author, March 6.

Knapp, Kay A. 1984. *The Impact of the Minnesota Sentencing Guidelines: Three-Year Evaluation*. St. Paul: Minnesota Sentencing Guidelines Commission.

———. 1993. "Allocation of Discretion and Accountability within Sentencing Structures." *University of Colorado Law Review* 64:679–705.

Kramer, John. 1997. "The Evolution of Pennsylvania's Sentencing Guidelines." In *Sentencing Reform in Overcrowded Times: A Comparative Perspective*, edited by Michael Tonry and Kathleen Hatlestad. New York: Oxford University Press.

Legislative Commission on Correctional Programs. 1977. "Final Report." Presented to the North Carolina General Assembly, February 1977. Legislative Commission on Correctional Programs, Raleigh, N.C. Photocopy.

Lewandowski, Denis. 1992. *An Advisory Discussion Regarding Structured Sentencing without Discretionary Release*. Raleigh: North Carolina Parole Commission.

Lubitz, Robin. 1994. Director, North Carolina Sentencing and Policy Advisory Commission. Interview with author, November 8.

———. 1996. Interview with author, February 29.

———. 2001. "Sentencing Changes in North Carolina." In *Penal Reform in*

Overcrowded Times, edited by Michael Tonry. New York: Oxford University Press.

Lubitz, Robin, and Thomas W. Ross. 2001. "Sentencing Guidelines: Reflections on the Future." *Sentencing and Corrections: Issues for the 21st Century.* Papers from the Executive Sessions on Sentencing and Corrections, No. 10. NCJ 186480. Washington, D.C.: U.S. Department of Justice, Office of Justice Programs.

Martin, Susan E. 1984. "Interests and Politics in Sentencing Reform: The Development of Sentencing Guidelines in Minnesota and Pennsylvania." *Villanova Law Review* 29:21–113.

McFadyen, David. 1993. District Attorney for Craven County; Member of Sentencing Commission representing North Carolina Conference of District Attorneys. Interview with author, February 3.

Meyer, Louis B. 1993. "North Carolina's Fair Sentencing Act: An Ineffective Scarecrow." *Wake Forest Law Review* 28:519–70.

Miethe, Terance D. 1987. "Charging and Plea Bargaining Practices under Determinate Sentencing: An Investigation of the Hydraulic Displacement of Discretion." *Journal of Criminal Law and Criminology* 78(1):155–76.

Miller, Marc. 1997. "Cells vs. Classrooms vs. Cops." In *The Crime Conundrum: Essays on Criminal Justice*, edited by Lawrence M. Friedman and George Fisher. Boulder: Westview.

Moore, Luther. 1992. Appointee to the North Carolina Sentencing and Policy Advisory Commission from the business community. Interview with author, December 30.

Morris, Norval, and Michael Tonry. 1990. *Between Prison and Probation: Intermediate Punishments in a Rational Sentencing System.* Oxford: Oxford University Press.

Neff, Joseph. 1996. "State Prisoners Burden County Jails." *Raleigh News and Observer* (May 26).

North Carolina Bar Association. 1971. "North Carolina Penal System Study Committee: Interim Report." Submitted to Governor Robert Scott; Ralph N. Strayhorn, committee chair. North Carolina Bar Association, Raleigh. Photocopy.

———. 1972. "North Carolina Penal System Study Committee, Second Interim Report." Submitted to Governor Robert Scott; Isaac T. Avery, Jr., committee chair. North Carolina Bar Association, Raleigh. Photocopy.

North Carolina Bar Association, Criminal Justice Section. 1993. "Report on Guidelines Sentencing." Submitted to the North Carolina Bar Association, Raleigh. Photocopy.

North Carolina Department of Correction. 2001. "Report on Trends in North Carolina Probation and Parole Populations after the Structured Sentencing Act." Prepared by Charles C. Stokes of the Office of Research and Planning. North Carolina Department of Correction, Raleigh. Photocopy.

North Carolina Public Television (NCPTV). 1991. *Search for Justice.* First episode of a three-part series produced by NCPTV and the North Carolina Center for Crime and Punishment. Aired December 1991.

————. 1992*a*. *Search for Justice*. Second episode of a three-part series produced by NCPTV and the North Carolina Center for Crime and Punishment, aired January 1992.

————. 1992*b*. *Search for Justice*. Third episode of a three-part series produced by NCPTV and the North Carolina Center for Crime and Punishment, aired June and July 1992.

North Carolina Sentencing and Policy Advisory Commission (NCSPAC). 1990. Minutes of commission meetings. North Carolina Sentencing and Policy Advisory Commission, Raleigh.

————. 1991*a*. Minutes of commission meetings. North Carolina Sentencing and Policy Advisory Commission, Raleigh.

————. 1991*b*. Minutes of commission subcommittee meetings. North Carolina Sentencing and Policy Advisory Commission, Raleigh.

————. 1992*a*. Minutes of commission meetings. North Carolina Sentencing and Policy Advisory Commission, Raleigh.

————. 1992*b*. Minutes of commission subcommittee meetings. North Carolina Sentencing and Policy Advisory Commission, Raleigh.

————. 1992*c*. "Report to the 1991 General Assembly of North Carolina, 1992 Session." North Carolina Sentencing and Policy Advisory Commission, Raleigh.

————. 1992*d*. "Report to the 1991 General Assembly of North Carolina, Minority Report." December 4, 1992. North Carolina Sentencing and Policy Advisory Commission, Raleigh.

————. 1993*a*. "Report to the 1993 Session of the North Carolina General Assembly." North Carolina Sentencing and Policy Advisory Commission, Raleigh.

————. 1993*b*. "Summary of New Sentencing Laws and the State-County Criminal Justice Partnership Act." North Carolina Sentencing and Policy Advisory Commission, Raleigh.

————. 1994. "FY 1993/94 Felony Sentencing Practices in North Carolina: A Report of the North Carolina Sentencing and Policy Advisory Commission." Prepared by Kitty B. Herrin. North Carolina Sentencing and Policy Advisory Commission, Raleigh.

————. 1996. "Structured Sentencing Monitoring System Report for Felons: July 1995 through June 1996." Prepared by Deborah Meagher, Kitty B. Herrin, and Robin L. Lubitz. North Carolina Sentencing and Policy Advisory Commission, Raleigh.

————. 1998. "Structured Sentencing Monitoring System Report for Felonies: July 1996 through June 1997." Prepared by Deborah Meagher, Kitty B. Herrin, and Susan Katzenelson. North Carolina Sentencing and Policy Advisory Commission, Raleigh.

————. 1999. "Structured Sentencing Statistical Report for Felonies and Misdemeanors: Fiscal Year 1997/98 (July 1, 1997–June 30, 1998)." Prepared by Ginny M. Hevener, Kitty B. Herrin, and Susan Katzenelson. North Carolina Sentencing and Policy Advisory Commission, Raleigh.

————. 2000. "Structured Sentencing Statistical Report for Felonies and Misdemeanors: Fiscal Year 1998/99 (July 1, 1998–June 30, 1999)." Prepared by Ginny M. Hevener and Susan Katzenelson. North Carolina Sentencing and Policy Advisory Commission, Raleigh.

———. 2001a. "Compendium of Community Corrections Programs in North Carolina: Fiscal Year 1999–2000." North Carolina Sentencing and Policy Advisory Commission, Raleigh.

———. 2001b. "Structured Sentencing Statistical Report for Felonies and Misdemeanors: Fiscal Year 1999/00 (July 1, 1999–June 30, 2000)." Prepared by Ginny M. Hevener and Susan Katzenelson. North Carolina Sentencing and Policy Advisory Commission, Raleigh.

North Carolina Special Committee on Prisons. 1987. "Report to the 1987 General Assembly of North Carolina." North Carolina Special Committee on Prisons, Raleigh.

———. 1990. *Final Report to the 1989 General Assembly of North Carolina, 1990 Session.* Raleigh: North Carolina Special Committee on Prisons.

Orland, Leonard, and Kevin R. Reitz. 1993. "Epilogue: A Gathering of State Sentencing Commissions." *University of Colorado Law Review* 64:837–45.

Parent, Dale G. 1988. *Structuring Criminal Sentences: The Evolution of Minnesota's Sentencing Guidelines.* Stoneham, Mass.: Butterworth Legal Publishers.

Pearce, Sandy. 2001. North Carolina Department of Correction, Office of Research and Planning. Interview with author, March 25.

Peek, Charlie. 1992. "N. C. Prison Isn't Fair, Predictable—or All That Tough, Many Say." *Winston-Salem Journal* (July 26), p. A10.

Reitz, Kevin. 1997. "Sentencing Guideline Systems and Sentence Appeals: A Comparison of Federal and State Experiences." *Northwestern University Law Review* 91:1441–1506.

Robinson, Paul H., Michael T. Cahill, and Usman Mohammad. 2000. "The Five Worst (and Five Best) American Criminal Codes." *Northwestern University Law Review* 95:1–89.

Ross, Thomas W. 1992. Superior Court Judge; Chair, North Carolina Sentencing and Policy Advisory Commission, 1990–1997. Interview with author, August 11.

Ross, Thomas W., and Susan Katzenelson. 1999. "Crime and Punishment in North Carolina: Severity and Costs under Structured Sentencing." *Federal Sentencing Reporter* 11:207–14.

Spelman, William. 2000. "What Recent Studies Do (and Don't) Tell Us about Imprisonment and Crime." In *Crime and Justice: A Review of Research*, vol. 27, edited by Michael Tonry. Chicago: University of Chicago Press.

Spence, David L., and William Boyum. 2000. "Prosecuting Habitual Felons: A Practical Approach." North Carolina District Attorneys Association. Presentation to the Association, October 20.

Stahl, Gregg C. 1992. Assistant Secretary, North Carolina Department of Correction. Interview with author, February 10.

———. 2001. Interview with author, August 28.

Stith, Kate, and José A. Cabranes. 1998. *Fear of Judging: Sentencing Guidelines in the Federal Courts.* Chicago: University of Chicago Press.

Tonry, Michael H. 1979. "The Sentencing Commission in Sentencing Reform." *Hofstra Law Review* 7:315–53.

———. 1988. "Structuring Sentencing." In *Crime and Justice: A Review of Research*, vol. 10, edited by Michael Tonry and Norval Morris. Chicago: University of Chicago Press.

———. 1991. "The Politics and Processes of Sentencing Commissions." *Crime and Delinquency* 37:307–29.

———. 1996. *Sentencing Matters*. New York: Oxford University Press.

Twentieth Century Fund Task Force on Criminal Sentencing. 1976. *Fair and Certain Punishment: Report on Criminal Sentencing*. New York: McGraw-Hill.

von Hirsch, Andrew. 1987. "The Enabling Legislation." In *The Sentencing Commission and Its Guidelines*, edited by Andrew von Hirsch, Kay Knapp, and Michael Tonry. Boston: Northeastern University Press.

Washington State Sentencing Guidelines Commission. 1986. *Preliminary Evaluation of Washington State's Sentencing Reform Act*. Olympia: Washington State Sentencing Guidelines Commission.

Wright, Ronald F. 1991. "Sentencers, Bureaucrats, and the Administrative Law Perspective on the Federal Sentencing Commission." *California Law Review* 79:1–90.

———. 1994. "Amendments in the Route to Sentencing Reform." *Criminal Justice Ethics* 13:58–66.

———. 1998a. "Managing Prison Growth in North Carolina through Structured Sentencing." Research in Brief, NCJ 168944. Washington, D.C.: National Institute of Justice, U.S. Department of Justice.

———. 1998b. "Three Strikes Legislation and Sentencing Commission Objectives." *Law and Policy* 20:429–63.

———. 1999. "The Future of Responsive Sentencing in North Carolina." *Federal Sentencing Reporter* 11:215–18.

———. 2001. "Flexibility in North Carolina Structured Sentencing, 1995–1997." In *Penal Reform in Overcrowded Times*, edited by Michael Tonry. New York: Oxford University Press.

Wright, Ronald F., and Susan P. Ellis. 1993. "A Progress Report on the North Carolina Sentencing and Policy Advisory Commission." *Wake Forest Law Review* 28:421–61.

Yacoe, Donald. 1990. "North Carolina Assembly Expected to Pass $275 Million Prison GO Bond Package." *Bond Buyer* (July 13, 1990), p. 4.

Zimring, Franklin E., and Gordon Hawkins. 1991. *The Scale of Imprisonment*. Chicago: University of Chicago Press.

Nadine Lanctôt and Marc Le Blanc

Explaining Deviance by Adolescent Females

ABSTRACT

The gender gap in deviance is well known. Why women's offending levels
are much lower than men's is less evident. Three theoretical perspectives
are influential. The first perspective applies mainstream criminological
theories, typically based on male offenders, to female samples. The second
perspective focuses on gender differences to explain differences in deviant
behaviors of adolescent females and males. The third perspective
emphasizes male-dominated constructions of knowledge. Each offers
theoretical insights and generates numerous empirical studies. For better
understanding of deviant behavior of adolescent females, constructs from
all three theoretical perspectives should be integrated into comprehensive
models.

The literature dealing with adolescent female problem and delinquent
behaviors is often described as scant. This observation was offered during the 1970s (Smart 1976; Harris 1977; Bertrand 1979), maintained
during the 1980s (Naffine 1987; Daly and Chesney-Lind 1988), and
reiterated in the 1990s (Chesney-Lind and Shelden 1998). Things have
changed, however, and this description is no longer true. Hannon and
Dufour (1998) observed that studies in the 1990s often include mixed-
gender samples rather than only males samples. Although females
have increasingly been included in empirical studies, their representa-

Nadine Lanctôt is assistant professor, School of Criminology, University of Montreal. Marc Le Blanc is professor, School of Psychoeducation and School of Criminology, University of Montreal. The Conseil Québécois de la Recherche Sociale, the Fonds
pour la Formation des Chercheurs et l'Action Concertée du Québec, and the Conseil
de Recherches en Sciences Humaines du Canada supported preparation of this essay.
Special thanks to Karl Thomassin and Sylvie Beaulieu for translation assistance.

113

tion remains limited. Instead of focusing on the factors responsible for adolescent females' participation in deviance, for example, most studies with mixed samples use gender only as a control variable (Hannon and Dufour 1998). Such empirical weaknesses no doubt contribute to superficial understanding of adolescent females' deviance. The paucity of knowledge stems also from theoretical fragmentation.

Three different theoretical discussions have developed separately. First, some researchers assert that mainstream criminological theories can explain adolescent females' deviance even if these theories derive from work on males (Simons, Miller, and Aigner 1980; Smith and Paternoster 1987). Second, other researchers focus on gender differences, whether biological or social, to understand the disparities (Heimer 1996; Steffensmeier and Allan 1996). Third, still other researchers argue that the male-dominated construction of knowledge should be challenged from feminist perspectives (Smart 1976; Leonard 1982; Daly and Chesney-Lind 1988).

Which perspective offers the best understanding of adolescent females' deviant behavior? Each perspective possesses its own strengths and weaknesses, so this cannot easily be answered. Each aims at different objectives and defends specific interests. For example, the first, criminological, perspective identifies individual factors that explain deviance. Concepts such as differential-association or social bonding are frequently used. The second perspective, gender differences, is concerned with explaining why girls are less involved than boys in deviance. Differential socialization according to gender, or gender roles, becomes the central explanation. The feminist perspective relies mostly on sociopolitical explanations, such as patriarchal attitudes, which modulate women's roles and women's oppression. We examine these three theoretical perspectives in the hopes that promising avenues for future inquiry can be identified. Integration of the main constructs of these theoretical perspectives is the most promising way forward.

We use the term "deviance" to refer to behaviors that violate consensual social norms that apply to adolescents. Deviant behavior includes "delinquent behaviors," which are violations of a criminal code. Deviant behavior also includes "problem behavior" that is considered by adults to be reckless or risky for adolescents. These behaviors include such things as substance abuse, family rebellion, dangerous driving, and school drop out. In consequence, when we use the term "deviance" we refer to all these behaviors, and we employ the terms "delinquent" or "problem" behaviors according to criteria used in the publications we discuss.

This terminology is supported by a vast empirical literature (see Le Blanc and Loeber 1998). The mainstream, gender-differences, and feminist perspectives employ our broad definition of deviance and recognize the distinction between problem and delinquent behaviors.

We mostly limit ourselves in this essay to theoretical and empirical works that address adolescence, from twelve to eighteen years of age, although sometimes we discuss works that spill over into the last few years of childhood and the first few years of youth. Finally, we restrict our coverage to adolescent female deviance. Our analysis and conclusions do not apply to female deviance in general. To avoid overgeneralizing, we often use the expression "adolescent female" even though it makes the text denser.

The three theoretical perspectives rely on a variety of methods, data sources, and definitions of adolescent female deviance. Each, however, relies primarily on specific methods, data sources, and operational definitions. Mainstream criminological theories are most often tested with large, mainly representative, samples but occasionally with purposive, such as adjudicated, samples. This research uses increasingly sophisticated statistical techniques, and the measure of the dependent variable is most often self-reported problem or delinquent behavior. At the opposite pole, the feminist perspective relies mostly on qualitative methods and aggregate data such as official delinquency. The gender-differences perspective relies on a mix of quantitative and qualitative methods and on operational definitions of deviance that include either self-reported or official behavior. Our challenge is to make sense of all these data sources and definitions and to propose an integration of the main concepts of these theoretical perspectives at a specific level of explanation—the behavior of individuals.

Before we examine the three theoretical perspectives and propose avenues for theoretical integration, we review existing knowledge on the gender gap. We first present the synthesis of the literature on the development of deviance among females. We argue that the deviance syndrome is composed of the same types of problem and delinquent behaviors for females and males and that the gender gap is more a difference in degree than in kind. The development of adolescent female deviance appears to be explained by the same mechanisms and processes as males' deviance. Girls, however, have fewer tendencies to get involved in delinquency on a long-term basis; in consequence, their careers are shorter and start later.

Although the mainstream, gender-differences, and feminist theoretical perspectives all recognize the existence of the gender gap, they offer different answers to the following questions: What are the causes of adolescent females' involvement in deviance? Are the causes of adolescent females' deviant behavior similar or dissimilar to those of adolescent males?

We are convinced that mainstream theories, though mostly developed in reference to males, are relevant to understanding adolescent females' deviance. An increasing number of researchers have examined the application of mainstream and integrative theories to samples composed of females. In consequence, we can answer the following questions: Do common social factors encourage the participation of both male and female adolescents in deviant behavior? Are exposure to deviant influences and weak bonds to society among the most prominent of these factors? Both answers are yes. Consequently, these concepts help explain adolescent girls' deviance. However, the use of these concepts with female samples is not without limits. Even if these factors, taken separately, influence girls' and boys' deviance in the same direction and at a somewhat similar force, boys remain more involved than girls in deviance. Thus, the inability of mainstream concepts to explain the gender gap is one of the strongest limits of these theories. This points at another explanation—that is, differences in the way girls and boys are socialized or in the ways they learn to conform to social standards. Mainstream theories and integrative models often invoke this explanation for the gender gap. However, empirical studies do not measure that concept of differential socialization. The gender-differences perspective does.

Gender-differences studies look at biological or sociological differences distinguishing girls and boys that affect the nature and the extent of their deviant behavior. In this context, the first question to be investigated is the influence of biological factors. These factors, such as sexual maturity, interact with some social influences, for instance, increased parental expectations and older peers. Although these studies might contribute to an understanding of adolescent female deviant behavior, resort to biological factors remains highly controversial. The second question to be discussed is the impact of gender roles or differential socialization. Studies on this question have become numerous and sophisticated. They suggest that the identification to gender roles is an important mediator of gender differences in deviance. Finally, a third question to be investigated is the importance of the context in which adolescent girls commit deviant acts. Studies in this area have mostly been conducted through participant observation and interviewing and by identification of gender-specific situational factors that seem to influence the nature of adolescent female deviant behavior— for example, adolescent girls' roles in gangs. How can the knowledge of biological, differential socialization, or situational differences be used? Researchers can attempt to elaborate new models that take account of these influences that have differential impact on females' and males' deviance. Gender differences highlighted in these studies can also be employed in sophisticated models already being used to explain boys' involvement in deviant behavior.

Feminist researchers, concerned about the lack of attention to female offenders, concluded that mainstream theories reflect males' androcentric character. The feminist perspective (especially in more radical versions) also tended to be in conflict with the gender-differences perspective. This conflict arose from the tendency of the gender-differences perspective to adopt positivist approaches or to compare females' deviance to males'. From the feminist point of view, this demonstrates that males are considered as being the norm. The most significant work within the feminist perspective in recent years concerns females' pathways to deviance, typically explained as a survival strategy to escape from an abusive environment. A comprehensive explanation of adolescent females' deviance cannot avoid some of the factors highlighted by the feminist perspective, particularly past and present victimization.

This essay would be incomplete if we did not explore the possibility of integrating the concepts and the constructs of the mainstream, gender-differences, and feminist perspectives. There has been a considerable debate in criminology about the possibility of theoretical integration. Recognizing that substantive integration is extremely difficult, even impossible, we propose that empirical models can import constructs from various theories and test their relative usefulness. Mainstream theories and integrative models can serve as a reference frame for the choice of constructs. Adjustments can be made to reflect knowledge pertaining to gender differences. Finally, feminist constructs are necessary because of their emphasis on social institutions rather than on individual factors and particular life experiences of females. Refinements of theoretical concepts, juxtaposed with the elaboration of integrative and developmental theories, lead to improved understanding of boys' misconduct (Thornberry 1997). Why would these developments not be as promising for adolescent females?

This essay is organized as follows. Section I reviews the literature on the gender gap in deviant behavior through three frames: patterns of deviant behavior of girls and boys, characteristics of the developmental process of deviant behavior for adolescent females, and identification of pathways into deviance. Sections II, III, and IV review theories and empirical research from the three main theoretical perspectives. Section V suggests challenges for the criminology of adolescent females deviance and delineates an integrative model for heuristic purposes. Finally, concluding remarks are presented in Section VI.

I. The Gender Gap

The gender gap in deviance, a pervasive phenomenon, is the low level of female offending in relation to that of males. Steffensmeier and Allan (1996) assert that criminologists agree that the gender gap in crime is universal. Psychiatrists concur that antisocial behavior is more prevalent among boys than girls (Silverthorn and Frick 1999). In consequence, three fundamental questions must be considered. What are the patterns of adolescent females' involvement in deviant behavior? Is there a deviance syndrome for adolescent females? What are the characteristics of the development of females' deviant behavior? Studies analyzed in this section demonstrate that self-reported data attenuate the gender gap observed with official statistics and that it is more a difference of degree than of type of behavior. In addition, for females as for males, all forms of deviant behaviors are part of a latent construct, which is the deviance syndrome. The analysis of females' deviant careers indicates that girls have fewer tendencies than boys to display a persistent involvement in delinquency and that they start their careers later. However, the development of their deviant behavior seems to be governed by the same mechanisms of activation and aggravation as for males. Finally, as with boys, the development of deviance in adolescent females follows many trajectories.

A. Adolescent Females' Involvement in Deviance

Adolescent females' involvement in deviant behavior has been described by many authors (Glueck and Glueck 1934; Cernkovich and Giordano 1979a; Bowker 1981; Feyerherm 1981; Canter 1982b;

Ageton 1983; Campbell 1984*a;* Figueira-McDonough 1985; Cario 1992; Chesney-Lind and Shelden 1992; Sommers and Baskin 1993). An exhaustive review of the literature would be redundant. Instead, we summarize main observations and report data from a recently recruited adjudicated sample.

Official statistics, confirmed by victimization surveys, have long indicated that adolescent females are less likely than boys to commit delinquent acts, particularly most serious property and violent crimes (Steffensmeier and Allan 1996; DeKeseredy 2000). Conduct disorder, as defined by the DSM-IV (American Psychiatric Association 1994) criteria of violations of rules, destruction of property, and physical aggression, are more prevalent, more severe, and more precocious among boys than among girls (Keenan, Loeber, and Green 1999). Official data indicate that girls mainly find their way into juvenile justice because of status offenses or minor thefts. Federal Bureau of Investigation data reveal that arrests for status offenses represented a quarter (25 percent) of all girls' arrests in 1986 but only 8 percent of boys' (Chesney-Lind 1989). In 1995, those statistics remained quite similar: 27 percent of girls' arrests and 10 percent of boys' were for status offenses (Chesney-Lind 2001).

However, since Canter's (1982*b*) landmark analysis, it has repeatedly been documented that self-report data attenuate the gender gap in official statistics (Chesney-Lind and Shelden 1992). Self-reports show that the proportions of girls and boys involved in problem behavior (e.g., running away from home, sexual intercourse, drug and alcohol use, etc.) are similar. This could mean that girls charged with status offenses are significantly overrepresented in the juvenile justice system (Chesney-Lind 1989, 2001). However, there are clear differences in participation and frequency for all forms of delinquency for different waves of the National Youth Survey (Elliott, Huizinga, and Menard 1989). Thus, even while using self-report measures, some differences between girls and boys remain: girls are less involved than boys in serious property and violent crimes. For example, self-reported data from a national sample indicate that the male/female ratio was under 2:1 for minor thefts, but almost 4:1 for fights causing injuries to others (Bureau of Justice Statistics 1999). Liu and Kaplan (1999) compared 3,100 girls and boys from Houston on measures of aggression, theft, drug use, and school violation. Boys displayed significantly higher scores on the first three scales in seventh and ninth grades, while girls and boys were similar on school violations only in seventh grade. Jang and Krohn (1995) report longitudinal data on the continuity of the gender gap. Their sample, 534 African Americans between ages thirteen and seventeen, lived in the region of Rochester, New York. Male and female adolescents were interviewed nine times with six-month intervals between interviews. Self-reported questionnaires were completed at each interview allowing analysis of gender differences from the beginning to the end of adolescence. Differences between male and female adolescents were highest at the age of fifteen. The gender gap for participating in public disturbances, crimes against property, and crimes against the person increased between ages thirteen and fifteen. From ages fifteen to seventeen, the gap diminished. Parental supervision partly explained gender differences up to fifteen years of age. That predictor lost its strength until the end of adolescence.

Some behaviors are more prevalent among girls than among boys. These behaviors have an internalized mode of expression. Girls are more prone to show psychological distress (Robins 1986; Ge, Conger, and Elder 1996), suicidal ideas (Chesney-Lind and Shelden 1998), somatization (Timmons-Mitchell et al. 1997), and eating disorders (Timmons-Mitchell et al. 1997). In addition, adolescent pregnancy confronts many high-risk girls. Each year in the United States, 1 million adolescent girls are pregnant (Schellenbah, Whitman, and Borkowski 1992). These internalized problems often co-occur with externalized problem behaviors and delinquency and are especially prevalent among girls handled by the juvenile justice system (Office of Juvenile Justice and Delinquency Prevention 1998).

Although the gender gap is well documented on population and representative samples, there are no comparable self-reported data on adjudicated adolescent females. The use of self-reported measures among adjudicated samples has some advantages. First, participation rates for all forms of problem and delinquent behavior are high. Second, the definition of deviance can encompass a large variety of acts, including serious delinquency. The sample we discuss, recruited in the early 1990s at the Montreal juvenile court (see Le Blanc and Bouthillier 2002), is composed of 505 males and 150 females between thirteen and seventeen years of age (average 15.6 years) adjudicated for a criminal offense under the Young Offender Act or for problem behavior under the Youth Protection Act. The sample includes nearly all adolescents adjudicated in that court over two years. All were sentenced to probation or placed in a correctional institution with a treatment philosophy. The majority (83 percent) of the girls were adjudicated under the

Youth Protection Act, compared with only 43 percent of the boys. These proportions are consistent with the existence of paternalistic attitudes in the juvenile justice system toward adolescent females (Chesney-Lind 1989, 2001). The girls were slightly younger, 15 years old on average, than the males, 15.7 years old. The proportion of immigrant parents was 9 percent for girls compared with 19 percent for males.

A self-report card-sorting interview on sixty-three deviant behaviors was administered in private settings. Results are presented in table 1. For each behavior, three descriptors are listed. "Variety" refers to the number of different acts ever committed. "Age of onset" is the age at which the conduct was first perpetrated. "Frequency" is an indication of the intensity of involvement in problem and delinquent activities during the year before the interview. This component does not measure the exact number of times an act was committed since an ordinal scale was used for every behavior (never, once or twice, seldom, and very often). The numbers in parentheses after the scales' names identify the number of behaviors in the scale.

Results reveal more differences between genders than similarities. These relate to the variety and the frequency of problem and delinquent behaviors rather than to ages of onset. Adjudicated adolescent females tend to rebel more against their families and against schooling than males do. These girls are also more engaged in prostitution. These results suggest that the high proportion of girls facing justice for status offenses should not be interpreted as a unique result of paternalistic reactions toward girls' misbehavior. These data indicate that girls participate more in problem behaviors than do boys. However, the existence of a patriarchal juvenile justice system should not be disregarded since involvement in sexual intercourse does not significantly differentiate adjudicated girls and boys; this is also the case for alcohol and drug use.

However, consistent with data from nonadjudicated samples, males more than females are engaged in a myriad of delinquent behaviors. These include physical violence expressed in fights, minor and serious thefts, and thefts of motor vehicles. Adjudicated adolescent males also committed a greater variety of acts of vandalism than girls did. Threats, however, which imply more verbal or relational violence than physical violence, are self-reported as much by girls as by boys. Similar results were observed by Crick and Grotpeter (1995) in a sample of 490 third-through-sixth-grade youth from four public schools, includ-

TABLE 1

Self-Report Deviance, Adjudicated Adolescents
from Montreal, 1992–93

	Males		Females		
	Mean	S.D.	Mean	S.D.	t-Test
Problem behavior (11):					
Variety	6.41	(2.50)	7.14	(2.30)	−3.18**
Age of onset	9.71	(2.88)	9.74	(2.99)	−.12
Frequency	22.62	(6.63)	25.16	(7.34)	−4.02***
Family rebellion (3):					
Variety	1.68	(.94)	1.99	(.89)	−3.64***
Age of onset	10.24	(3.23)	10.29	(3.19)	−.17
Frequency	5.03	(2.03)	6.35	(2.33)	−6.70***
School rebellion (6):					
Variety	3.83	(1.28)	3.99	(1.20)	−1.41
Age of onset	8.79	(2.97)	9.32	(2.84)	−1.91
Frequency	10.95	(4.51)	12.67	(4.24)	−2.95**
Sexual intercourse (2):					
Variety	.95	(.33)	1.00	(.36)	−1.73
Age of onset	12.62	(1.98)	12.96	(1.76)	−1.83
Frequency	4.31	(1.10)	4.25	(1.14)	.61
Prostitution (2):					
Variety	.11	(.35)	.31	(.57)	−5.22***
Age of onset	14.47	(2.06)	13.40	(1.89)	2.45*
Frequency	2.16	(.64)	2.51	(1.10)	−4.84***
Drug and alcohol use (5):					
Variety	2.66	(1.79)	2.87	(1.62)	−1.26
Age of onset	12.55	(2.37)	12.45	(1.95)	.40
Frequency	10.19	(4.53)	10.85	(4.62)	−1.57
Deliquent behavior (21):					
Variety	11.21	(5.27)	7.35	(5.01)	7.96***
Age of onset	9.03	(2.79)	9.48	(2.79)	−1.71
Frequency	35.79	(12.38)	30.23	(10.15)	5.02***
Aggression toward family (2):					
Variety	.50	(.67)	.73	(.69)	−3.69***
Age of onset	11.64	(3.49)	11.28	(3.02)	.85
Frequency	2.40	(.85)	2.81	(1.23)	−4.69***
Threat (5):					
Variety	1.47	(1.65)	1.31	(1.47)	1.09
Age of onset	12.29	(2.87)	11.41	(2.84)	2.55**
Frequency	6.87	(3.01)	6.63	(2.64)	.88
Fight (8):					
Variety	4.51	(2.25)	3.35	(2.53)	5.40***
Age of onset	10.02	(2.99)	11.09	(2.73)	−3.64
Frequency	14.24	(5.77)	12.51	(5.05)	3.32***
Vandalism (4):					
Variety	1.57	(1.39)	1.07	(1.30)	3.95***
Age of onset	11.44	(2.93)	11.26	(2.38)	.51
Frequency	5.33	(2.01)	5.08	(2.10)	1.31

TABLE 1 (*Continued*)

	Males		Females		
	Mean	S.D.	Mean	S.D.	*t*-Test
Minor thefts (3):					
Variety	1.84	(1.13)	1.37	(1.17)	4.45***
Age of onset	10.39	(3.02)	10.67	(2.82)	−.85
Frequencies	5.43	(2.76)	4.75	(2.62)	2.71**
Stolen motor vehicle (4):					
Variety	1.81	(1.36)	.79	(1.01)	8.52***
Age of onset	13.65	(1.94)	13.85	(1.71)	−.83
Frequencies	6.74	(3.17)	4.99	(1.72)	6.45***
Serious thefts (3):					
Variety	1.58	(1.21)	.62	(.93)	8.95
Age of onset	13.36	(2.07)	13.51	(1.93)	−.52
Frequencies	5.40	(2.81)	3.79	(1.67)	6.64***

NOTE.—Numbers in parentheses after the scales' names identify the number of behaviors in the scale. S.D. = standard deviation.
* $p < .05$.
** $p < .01$.
*** $p < .001$.

ing 235 girls and 256 boys. In addition, girls had started to use threats at an earlier age than boys. However, girls got involved in fights at later ages than boys. The Montreal self-report survey also showed that adjudicated adolescent females tend to use violence against their parents more than males do.

The mainstream, gender-differences, and feminist perspectives cannot focus exclusively on delinquent behavior or one of its forms, or on problem behavior or one of its varieties. The gender gap for most deviant behaviors is such that explanations for its emergence and development must apply to deviant behavior in general. The three theoretical perspectives must explain what some criminologists have called the general deviance syndrome (Osgood et al. 1988). Is this syndrome composed of the same behaviors for adolescent females and males? This question becomes fundamental because it concerns the content of the dependent variable in the explanation of adolescent females' deviance.

B. The Deviance Syndrome

Empiricists proposed, after Nye and Short (1957), omnibus scales of self-reported delinquency for adolescents. These scales were frequently misnamed. For example, Nye and Short's twenty-one-item questionnaire was composed of a large array of deviant behavior. It included theft, vandalism, sex, alcohol and drug use, fighting, aggression, joyriding, driving, and misbehavior at school and in the family. Since then, most criminologists have continued to misname their measures of adolescent deviance as self-reported delinquency. Most delinquency scales in published papers involve delinquent acts that are more serious, but they also include many types of delinquency, substance use, and other problem behavior. Elliott, Huizinga, and Ageton (1985) have partly avoided that pitfall. Their scale is composed mainly of various forms of self-reported delinquency. Their twenty-four-item scale of general delinquency has only four questions that are not clearly criminal offenses: runaway, joyriding, gang fights, and sexual intercourse. Most researchers, however, have followed the omnibus route indicated by Nye and Short.

General theorists support this perspective. Gottfredson and Hirschi (1990) argue that all forms of deviant behavior are analogous phenomena. Using various methods, they showed that a large variety of deviant behaviors represent the notion of deviance. The idea of a latent construct is supported for officially recorded crimes (Parker and McDowell 1986). In addition, numerous empirical studies of self-reported deviance have reached the same conclusion since Jessor and Jessor (1977) identified a general deviance factor. Replications have taken place with children under twelve years of age (Capaldi and Patterson 1989; Gillmore et al. 1991), with adolescents of various ages (Johnston, O'Malley, and Eveland 1978; Donovan and Jessor 1985; Brownfield and Sorenson 1987; Donovan, Jessor, and Costa 1988; McGee and Newcomb 1992; Bartusch et al. 1997; Benda and Corwyn 1998; Ary et al. 1999), and with young adults (Donovan and Jessor 1985; Osgood et al. 1988; McGee and Newcomb 1992). Only Dembo et al. (1992) and Le Blanc and Girard (1997) have replicated the general deviance model with samples of high-risk adolescents.

Le Blanc and Bouthillier (2002) showed that eleven forms of deviant behavior are investigated in the studies just mentioned, even if all are not used in each study: theft, vandalism, interpersonal violence, sexual violence, school problems, parental defiance, sexual intercourse, forms of acting out, use and traffic of a large array of drugs, use of alcohol, and use of tobacco. In addition, all sixteen studies used measures of theft and interpersonal violence; most used measures of drug use or traffic; fourteen included vandalism; twelve employed alcohol use; and nine studies involved school problems. Sex and parental defiance were present in seven studies. Sexual violence, dangerous driving, and smoking were very rarely considered. Some studies included measures that are not intrinsically deviant, such as academic results, going to church, grade point average, and so on. A general deviance factor is always found. Le Blanc and Bouthillier concluded that this result is independent of the measures of deviance, the statistical method, the nature of the sample, the historical period, and the site of the study. The replicability of the deviance syndrome is undisputed because of the diversity of the studies. The omnibus route indicated by Nye and Short was appropriate. One question still to be resolved is its applicability to adolescent females.

Thirteen of the sixteen studies used mixed gender samples. However, only three studies tested the general deviance model by gender, and it was on the same group of representative samples (Jessor and Jessor 1977; Donovan and Jessor 1985; Donovan, Jessor, and Costa 1988). Le Blanc and Bouthillier (2002) tested the deviance syndrome with the adjudicated sample described earlier. They performed confirmatory factor analysis on a hierarchical measurement model of deviance composed of sixty-three behaviors, ten types of problem and delinquent behaviors, four forms of deviance, and the latent construct. The data used to test the models were the frequencies of these behaviors rather than participation in deviant and criminal behavior, as in many studies with representative samples, and they tested the model with the onset of these behaviors. They tested their deviance model independently for females and males and in a group comparison. In all their tests, the statistical indices were in the range of the standards for such analysis. However, as in the Donovan and Jessor studies, Le Blanc and Bouthillier showed statistical indices a little lower for adolescent females than for males.

Le Blanc and Bouthillier (2002) suggest that the deviance syndrome for adolescent females is composed of four major forms of behaviors (see fig. 1), the first three of which were proposed by Loeber et al. (1993). The first form is overt or confronting behaviors; it is the dimension of deviance that is composed of interpersonal violence (threats and physical aggression) and vandalism. The second category is covert or concealing behaviors; it is composed of three forms of property crimes: common theft, motor vehicle theft, and fraud. The third category is concerned with authority conflict or rebellion; it consists of stubborn, defiant, and avoidant behaviors at home and in

General deviance

Reckless behavior	**Motor vehicle use**	Driving without a permit Dangerous driving
	Sexual activity	Relations of various kinds Homosexual Heterosexual Prostitution Pregnancy (self or someone else) Pornographic material
	Substance use	Smoking Alcohol Drugs (soft, chemical, hard) Dealing
	Disorderly conducts	Trespassing Panhandling or loitering Disturbing the peace
Authority conflict	**In school**	Defying authority Truancy Thrown out (class or school) Hit or intimidate teachers
	At home	Defying, disobedience Staying out late Running away Hit or intimidate parents
Covert	**Theft**	Minor (shoplifting ...) Major (burglary, car, robbery ...) Bought or sell stolen goods
	Fraud	False ID Lying Entering without paying Monetary frauds
Overt	**Vandalism**	Vandalism (public, school ...) Fire setting
	Violence	Intimidation Fighting (physical, gang) Assault (attack, strong-arm) Sexual

FIG. 1.—A comprehensive hierarchical model of adolescent general deviance

school, and we use that type of deviant behavior in our model. The fourth category is reckless or risky deviant behaviors. These include substance use, sexual activity, and disorderly conduct; they were not part of Loeber et al.'s taxonomy (1993).

We conclude that the deviance syndrome is composed of the same types of problem and delinquent behaviors for females and males. The gender gap is then more a question of differences in the degree of participation, frequency, and variety than in types of behavior. In addition, we expect that the development of general deviance is supported by the same mechanisms and processes as Loeber and Le Blanc described for males' offending ([1990], updated by Le Blanc and Loeber [1998]).

C. Developmental Processes

Glueck and Glueck (1934) conducted the first longitudinal study of female delinquency. Among the 500 women met in penal institutions and interviewed during the following five years, 62 percent were not brought to justice again. However, 76 percent self-reported criminal acts that could have led to an arrest. More precisely, 24 percent of females reported no illegal conduct following their release, 24 percent committed illegal acts but ceased before the end of the observation period, and half (52 percent) were involved in criminality throughout the five years. The persistent offenders were those who became involved in crime at the earliest age. With these data, Glueck and Glueck were addressing two questions of the developmental criminology paradigm. What is the level of continuity in deviant behavior? How is deviant behavior activated?

Concerning continuity, recent studies concur with the Gluecks' finding that only a small proportion of females are recidivists (see Dunford and Elliott 1984; Lewis 1989; Ayers et al. 1999). For example, Lewis (1989) gathered official data for fifteen years following the first arrest in 1973 of 17,842 females. The majority (59 percent) of females had been in contact with the justice system only once, whereas 30 percent had been arrested two to four times, and a minority (11 percent) had been arrested more than ten times. Females who committed criminal activities in a chronic fashion were mostly arrested for drug possession, drug sale, and prostitution. When Lewis compared proportions of females and males who persisted, he observed that six times more males than females became deeply involved in crime over the years. However, Lewis noticed important similarities since, for both females and males, a small proportion of individuals were responsible for a great number of crimes. Eleven percent of females were responsible for almost half (48 percent) of the charges against females, and 22 percent of males were responsible for 61 percent of the charges against males. Others' findings are comparable (Warren and Rosenbaum 1986; Stattin and Magnusson 1989; English 1993).

Tracy and Kempf-Leonard (1996) examined the link between teenage delinquency and persistence in crime during adulthood with official data for 13,160 males and 14,000 females born in Philadelphia in 1958. Data were collected through age twenty-six. Table 2 summarizes the results. First, as studies with adult female samples have shown, persistence was less common for females than for males. Among females who had been in contact with the justice system during their teenage years, 12 percent were rearrested once at age eighteen or after compared with 42 percent for males. Furthermore, very few females who had not been arrested during adolescence were arrested during adulthood. This pattern was less pronounced for males. Only 3 percent of females who were not arrested during adolescence had been in contact with the justice system during adulthood compared with 14 percent for males.

However, important things remain hidden when analyzing data this way. The proportion of subjects facing the justice system during adulthood inevitably is lower for females than for males, since, regardless of their behavior during adolescence, the proportion of males facing the justice system is continuously higher than for females. Only 4 percent of females possessed a judicial record during adulthood compared with 23 percent for their male counterparts. Instead of comparing the female proportion of persisters in criminality with the male proportion (12 percent vs. 42 percent), it is interesting to compare females among themselves and males among themselves. A vertical reading of table 2 shows that a majority of females arrested during adulthood were not arrested during adolescence (56 percent). Hence, the proportion of girls who offended from adolescence into adulthood is lower than the proportion of females who faced the justice system for the first time during adulthood. These results are inverted for males, since the majority of those arrested during adulthood had also been arrested during adolescence (59 percent).

Viewed this way, these results concur with those of Stattin and Magnusson (1989). Their analysis of official data of a representative sample of 1,393 Swedish males and females showed that girls had their first court appearance at a later average age than males. Females mostly

TABLE 2

Synthesis of Table 5.3 of Tracy and Kempf-Leonard (1996)

	Not Arrested in Adulthood			Arrested in Adulthood					
	n	H (%)	V (%)	n	H (%)	V (%)	Total	H (%)	V (%)
Females:									
Not arrested in adolescence	11,724	97	87	304	3	56	12,028	100	86
Arrested in adolescence	1,736	88	13	236	12	44	1,972	100	14
Total females	13,460	96	100	540	4	100	14,000	100	100
Males:									
Not arrested in adolescence	7,573	86	76	1,272	14	41	8,845	100	67
Arrested in adolescence	2,510	58	24	1,805	42	59	4,315	100	33
Total males	10,083	77	100	3,077	23	100	13,160	100	100

tended to face the justice system between ages twenty-one to twenty-three, while the majority of males did so at age fifteen. In the literature, however, the relationship between age, delinquency, and gender is not clearly distinguished. Some assert that the relationship between gender and delinquency is stable throughout adolescence and adulthood. Gottfredson and Hirschi (1990) argued that the causes leading to participation in criminal behavior settle early in the development of the individual, and, consequently, gender differences remain stable once reaching adolescence. Steffensmeier and Streifel (1991) observed that the age curves of arrests were almost identical for boys and girls.

Official data on continuity of offending during the life course supports the view that there is a gender gap in the development of official delinquency: continuity in delinquency is more frequent among males than females. Self-report data are scarce but point to a similar conclusion. For example, using data from the National Youth Survey, a representative sample of the eleven-to-seventeen-years-old population in the United States, Elliott (1994) reported that continuity in violent offending between the adolescent and the adult years was slightly higher for males (22 percent) than for females (18 percent). Ageton (1983) used data gathered on a five-year period (1977–81). She found that participation of female adolescents in thefts decreased over time from 17 percent to 10 percent, while the proportion of female adolescents involved in crimes against the person dropped from 36 percent to 12 percent. Talbot and Thiede (1999) evaluated continuity in girls' participation in antisocial behavioral pathways during adolescence. Their sample was also drawn from the National Youth Survey; self-reported data from interviews with 763 girls in the first and third waves were considered. They observed that there is continuity for disruptive acts, vandalism, and fighting but not for stealing and school troubles. They also reported that the only risk factor that was related to the continuity of these behaviors was association with deviant peers.

The gender gap in continuity has mostly been analyzed regarding delinquency. Hence, data are scarce concerning continuity of problem behaviors such as substance use, risky driving, and sexual activities. The hypothesis of continuity in problem behavior seems sound, but we do not know the levels of continuity for all types of problem behavior. This lack of data is evident for males but is even more evident for females. The few studies that evaluated the gender gap in continuity of problem behaviors were mostly conducted in the field of substance abuse. These studies indicate that early onset of substance use is predictive for both genders of continued use (Jessor, Donovan, and Widmer 1980; Fleming, Kellam, and Brown 1982; Robins and Przybeck 1985).

Some studies analyzed the heterotypic continuity of self-reported deviant behavior among females. Deviance manifests itself under different forms from one period to another. For example, in a study of a large sample of Montreal kindergarten children, Tremblay and colleagues (1992) showed that aggression exhibited by girls in early elementary school and delinquency during adolescence were highly correlated; similar results were observed for boys with correlations being 0.76 and 0.79, respectively. The Swedish Project Metropolitan found that girls' aggression at age thirteen is predictive of adult criminality and substance abuse (Wängby, Bergman, and Magnusson 1999), as has repeatedly been shown for boys (see Le Blanc and Loeber 1998). Krohn, Lizotte, and Perez (1997) observed that experiencing precocious life transitions, such as dropping out of school or having a teenage pregnancy, increased the likelihood of substance use among girls during the early adult years. They analyzed data from the Rochester Youth Development Study (see Thornberry, Bjerregaard, and Miles [1993] for a complete description of this study), a multiwave panel study designed to oversample youth at high risk for serious delinquency and drug use. Bardone et al. (1996) also noted that conduct-disordered girls are more at risk to accumulate adverse outcomes at the beginning of adulthood than girls without such a diagnosis. Study data came from the Dunedin Multidisciplinary Health and Development Research Unit, a longitudinal investigation of a complete birth cohort of children born between 1972 and 1973 in Dunedin, New Zealand. The findings were obtained from assessments at ages fifteen and twenty-one. In the final followup, data were collected for 470 girls (94 percent of the original cohort). These results indicated that many conduct-disordered girls were, when reaching adulthood, single mothers with little education and low-income jobs, and some had partners who were physically abusive. Pajer (1998) confirmed these adult adverse consequences of antisociality during adolescence through a review of research. Finally, Wängby, Bergman, and Magnusson (1999), for their part, followed 683 females from early adolescence through adulthood. The females who showed conduct and school problems had the highest rates of adult criminality and drug use. Internalizing problems during adolescence did not predict any of these outcomes during adulthood, nor did mental health problems.

The study of developmental processes implies the analysis of dynamic mechanisms that support deviant behavior. Do the mechanisms of activation and aggravation operate differently according to gender? Activation refers to the process by which the development of deviant behavior is stimulated (Le Blanc and Loeber 1998). This happens when an early onset produces an increase of seriousness, frequency, and variety of deviant behavior along the life course. This relationship between precocious involvement and persistence has been observed in recent studies with adolescent (Lanctôt and Le Blanc 2000) and adult females (Lewis 1989; Sommers and Baskin 1994). The influence of an early onset of drug use on its persistence was also evaluated, and the effect was somewhat stronger for males than for females (Jessor, Donovan, and Widmer 1980; Fleming, Kellam, and Brown 1982; Robins and Przybeck 1985). Early onset also influences the seriousness of acts committed. Sommers and Baskin (1994) found that women who committed the most serious crimes became involved in delinquency at the youngest ages. This qualitative study was conducted with eighty-five women sentenced for nondomestic violence. Finally, the influence of activation on the subsequent frequency of the involvement of females in delinquency remains unobserved. Using the second cohort of the Philadelphia study, Tracy, Wolfgang, and Figlio (1985) did not find a relationship between age of onset and frequency of official offending for females; this relationship was observed for males. The official nature of those data may explain this result, rates of official delinquency being much lower among females than among males.

In sum, few data are available on the manifestation of the mechanism of activation for females. Nevertheless, it is reasonable to suppose that this mechanism contributes to the development of adolescent females' deviant behavior. However, and once again, a gender gap is perceptible. Even if the activation mechanism seems to influence the development of deviant behavior in the same way regardless of gender, its impact may be more pronounced for males than for females. Early onset of conduct problems and delinquency appears to be more predictive of later offending for males than for females (Block and van der Werff 1987; Wikström 1987; Loeber and Snyder 1988).

There is also urgent need for more research on aggravation. The main feature is escalation, the shift to increasingly serious deviant behaviors. To analyze this mechanism, an identification of a developmental sequence of behaviors is required. Le Blanc and Loeber (1998) indicate that knowledge of the developmental sequences of males' conduct problems, substance use, delinquency, and other forms of deviance is vast but not without controversy. Le Blanc and Loeber could not find studies identifying developmental sequences of females' conduct problems and delinquent activities. However, they concluded that the developmental stages of drug use (successively using tobacco; alcohol; soft, chemical, and hard drugs) are robust and are similar for female and male adolescents. They also reported that early use of drugs increased the probability of early sexual intercourse for both sexes.

The only data available on escalation of females' deviant behaviors concerns women who start committing illegal activities at a later age. Their involvement in violence coincides with when they become more dependent on drugs (Sommers and Baskin 1994). Fagan (1995) discussed the criminal careers of women who became involved in drug markets. He wanted to identify the deviant and delinquent trajectories of 311 women following their initiation to the use or sale of cocaine, or both. The study revealed that initiation to cocaine led to an intensification of the criminal career. Although these women had already committed illegal acts, their involvement in deviance and in delinquency leaped once they started using cocaine. Hence, initiation to cocaine did not reflect an initiation to deviant and delinquent activities; it produced an aggravation of offending. Fagan (1995) described two trajectories for women involved in the cocaine market. Women who used cocaine without involvement in trafficking or sale of cocaine mostly met their financial needs by prostituting themselves; this was much less common for women who took advantage of the gains to be obtained from selling cocaine.

It is possible to explore the process of escalation with Lanctôt, Bernard, and Le Blanc's (2002) sample of adjudicated adolescents (505 males and 150 females). They reported the cumulative proportion of females involved in four major forms of deviant behaviors—overt, covert, authority-conflict, and reckless—from birth to age twenty-one. Figure 2 presents these results and broadens their scope by juxtaposing the curves of the cumulative age of onset for each gender. Figure 2 clearly illustrates that males' and females' deviant behaviors develop through a similar sequence of aggravation. The curves are almost identical for all forms of behaviors. The only difference takes place in overt violent acts, which emerge earlier for boys than for girls. This confirms the escalation process proposed by Loeber et al. (1993), since the authority-conflict behaviors appeared first, followed by covert delinquent acts and overt violent acts. Reckless behaviors, which in first appearance might be evaluated as less serious, come last. This could be ex-

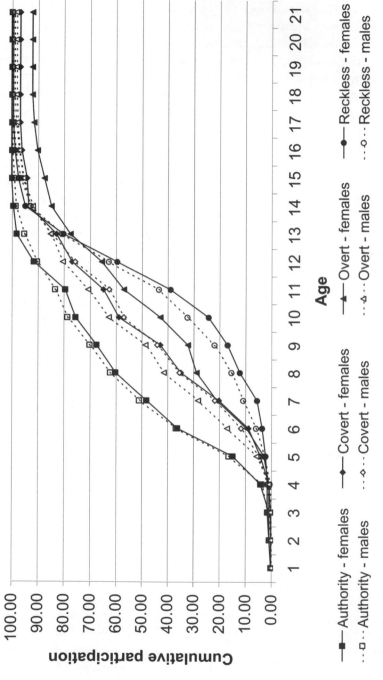

Fig. 2.—Cumulative age of onset of deviance by sex

Authority - females ■——— Covert - females ◆——— Overt - females ▲——— Reckless - females ●———
Authority - males □·· Covert - males ◇·· Overt - males △·· Reckless - males ○··

plained by the inclusion of dangerous driving and prostitution in this form of behavior. Authority-conflict behaviors were initiated by age seven for half of the adjudicated adolescent females, and this increased to 75 percent at age ten and to 100 percent at age fifteen. The covert delinquent acts such as theft were initiated at a median age of nine. By age twelve, 75 percent had already committed these acts, and 94 percent had committed covert acts by age fifteen. Overt, or violent, behaviors were initiated at a median age of eleven; by age thirteen, 75 percent of the adjudicated females were involved in these delinquent acts. By age eighteen, 92 percent had participated in violent activities. Finally, reckless behaviors, such as drug use, dangerous driving, and sexual promiscuity were initiated by half of the adjudicated females before age thirteen; by age seventeen, 99 percent were involved. Results for males are almost identical, so they are not described in detail. The median age of onset of overt violent acts among boys, however, is almost two years lower than that of girls.

In summary, the mechanisms of continuity, activation, and aggravation seem to govern the development of adolescent female deviant behavior as they do for males. The gender gap, however, continues to manifest itself, particularly in the degree of continuity in deviant behavior. Females, compared with males, have fewer tendencies to become involved in delinquency on a long-term basis. Thus, on average, they have a shorter delinquency career. However, it is more common for females than for males to have their first contact with the justice system after reaching age eighteen. The extent to which girls become involved in delinquency when they have a delayed onset is unknown. Leaving continuity aside, we conclude that there are fewer robust facts about the gender gap in activation. Finally, the literature contains no comparisons of females and males on aggravation of deviant conduct. However, exploratory data presented here support the hypothesis that the development of adolescent females' deviant behavior escalates in the same manner as for males'.

D. Developmental Trajectories

The last approach in analysis of the development of deviant behavior is identification of trajectories or pathways. A trajectory is the behavioral development of a group of individuals that differs across the life cycle from the behavioral development of other groups of individuals (Le Blanc and Loeber 1998). Pathways have been identified through various methods. Le Blanc (2002) reviews crime-switching, empirical cross-classification, group-detection, and theoretical meta-trajectories studies. Very few of the major studies involved females.

Rojek and Erickson (1982) analyzed crime switching using data on official delinquency for 1,180 boys and girls from Arizona. They concluded that switching was significantly different for adolescent males and females; females were much more likely than males to desist from official delinquency or to shift to runaway offenses. These switches represented 73 percent of offense transitions for females and only 36 percent for males. This study is limited, however, by its reliance on official statistics. Many girls find their way into juvenile justice because they commit status offenses. Data from the Federal Bureau of Investigation reveal that arrests for status offenses represented 27 percent of all girls' arrests in 1995 but only 10 percent for boys (Chesney-Lind 2001).

Two studies have explored ad hoc empirical cross classifications of adolescent females' self-reported delinquency. First, Dunford and Elliott (1984) constructed a typology of career offenders with frequency of crimes, grouped according to three categories of seriousness (the crimes of the Uniform Crime Report, Part 1) and with five waves of National Youth Survey data. Dunford and Elliott (1984) identified three trajectories. Five percent of adolescent females adopted the serious persistent career compared with 14 percent of males. Adolescents in this trajectory committed at least two serious crimes each year for at least two consecutive years. These persistent adolescents were also frequently involved in other crimes. The second study was conducted by Ayers and colleagues (1999), using self-reported measures of delinquency at two periods separated by a two-year interval. The classification was made according to the most serious act committed. Girls who engaged in serious delinquency did so for a shorter period compared with boys who committed serious acts. These two studies indicated that the majority of adolescent females' careers were characterized by transitory delinquency, a form of offending that is limited to a specific time period. A consequence was that there were few adolescent females engaged in persistent careers. This conclusion also applied to males; however, more males than females were in the persistent trajectory. Twenty percent of boys and 14 percent of girls were classified as escalators from one time to the other. Also, 28 percent of boys and 19 percent of girls persisted in delinquency at a moderate or at a high level.

A more recent study (Lanctôt and Le Blanc 2000) identified trajectories using the Montreal adjudicated sample described earlier and identified the within-individual pathways of girls' participation in deviance during adolescence. Results demonstrated that adolescent females' deviant behavior evolved through three different trajectories. First, for 39 percent of the girls, involvement in deviance was benign throughout adolescence. Girls from this benign deviance trajectory initiated deviant activities latest. They showed their first misconduct around the age of ten, and their first delinquent activities toward the age of eleven. Drug use was typically initiated toward the age of fourteen. These adolescents showed the least diversification of deviant activities. Problem behavior and delinquent activities were manifested under forms that were less varied compared with the activities of the girls in the other trajectories. Finally, the deviance of these adolescents remained less diversified at the end of adolescence.

The second trajectory (42 percent of the sample) had relatively high involvement in deviance until midadolescence. Thereafter, involvement declined significantly. The third trajectory included 19 percent of the sample. These girls had high and persistent involvement in deviance throughout adolescence. The adolescent girls of the declining and persistent trajectories share many similarities until midadolescence. These girls have made a precocious entry into deviance—about three years earlier than the girls who follow the benign trajectory. As early as age seven, acts of rebellion toward family or school were evident. Initiation to delinquent activities followed quickly; on average, these girls committed their first offenses when they were eight years old. The use of drugs was also typically precocious, beginning around eleven-and-a-half years old. The adolescents of these two trajectories are similar in the variety of their deviant activities in the middle of adolescence. However, their pathways are different as they reach the end of adolescence, when only the persistent girls maintain high levels of deviant activities.

The psychosocial profiles of the girls in each trajectory were assessed. Differences in degree of the quality of social and personal adaptations of girls in each trajectory were observed. The more the trajectory denotes a persistent involvement in deviance, the more the personal and social deficits increase. A pronounced gap was observed between the benign and persistent trajectories throughout adolescence. Girls from the persistent trajectory were characterized by important personal and social deficits, and these difficulties persisted throughout adolescence. The profile of the girls from the declining trajectory changed. By the end of adolescence, girls from the declining trajectory had become more attached to their parents, associated less with delinquent peers, had more respect toward individuals in positions of authority, and had interpersonal relationships that were less tinged with mistrust and toughness.

This study (Lanctôt and Le Blanc 2000) observed that such life events as school dropout and maternity influenced the resumption of deviant behaviors. However, the quality of those transitions and their future consequences, particularly during youth and adulthood, were not evaluated. Giordano, Cernkovich, and Rudolph (2002) provide important insights. Data were gathered from questionnaires ($n = 109$) and open-ended life-history narratives (97) from women (mean age = 29.6) who were in a state-level institution for delinquent girls in Ohio during adolescence. The very few women whose lives included average or better levels of marital happiness, stable employment, and household income above poverty level were more likely than others to be desisters. Motherhood created possibilities for changes in self-conception, but the internalization of this status was far from automatic. This transition was successful when the women focused on positive attributes of parenting; however, for some, narratives on mothering were dominated by negative themes. This study merits replication to better understand desistance among females. Bottcher's (2001) qualitative study showed that females, compared with their delinquent brothers, assumed adult responsibilities at younger ages than males. This transition to adulthood accelerates the process of desistance.

Another group detection method, a semiparametric statistical model, has been proposed by Land and Nagin (1996). One analysis was conducted with a sample of 885 French-speaking girls from Quebec; they were six to twelve years old, and their disruptive behaviors (a scale composed of three fighting behaviors and eight oppositional behaviors) were measured through teachers' rating (Côté et al. 2001). Four trajectories were obtained. The lowest group comprised most of the sample (57 percent), the medium group 36 percent, the medium-high group 10 percent, and the high group only 1 percent. These last three groups had a significantly higher number of conduct disorder symptoms (DSM-III-R), and the medium-high and high groups were significantly more at risk of a conduct disorder diagnosis during adolescence. Similar trajectories have been observed for males' delinquency (Nagin, Farrington, and Moffitt 1995) and aggression (Nagin and Tremblay 1999).

The last method used to identify pathways is Moffitt's (1993) theoretically based typology. Two antisocial trajectories are proposed, adolescence-limited and life-course persistent, based respectively on adolescent and childhood initiation of deviant behavior. This theoretical classification was the subject of numerous studies over the following eight years (Moffitt and Caspi 2001). These authors tested this taxonomy on involvement of both females and males in deviant behavior.

The Dunedin Multidisciplinary Health and Development sample serves for this test. This sample consists of 1,037 three-year-old children followed until age eighteen. Moffitt and Caspi (2001) observed that 10 percent of the males and 1 percent of the females manifested a life-course persistent pathway, and 26 percent of the males and 18 percent of the females displayed an adolescence-limited pathway. Their taxonomy thus applies only to 36 percent of the males and 19 percent of the females. These prevalence rates are disappointing because the vast majority of adolescents are not classified. In contrast, there is much evidence that the vast majority of adolescents are involved in deviance (see, e.g., the international comparison of Junger-Tas, Terlouw, and Klein [1994]). If there are a good proportion of nonantisocial individuals among the 64 percent of unclassified males and the 81 percent of unclassified females, there remains room for other types of antisocial individuals. Elaborating on the profiles of adolescence-limited and life-course persistent individuals, Moffitt and Caspi (2001) reported that females and males of the same subtype share the same background risk factors (a variety of social and personal characteristics measured at different ages). They also observed that, regardless of gender, the background of the adolescence-limited pathway differs significantly from that of the life-course persistent pathway. Moffitt and Caspi (2001) concluded their analysis by arguing that the childhood backgrounds of life-course persistent delinquents are typically pathological, while those of adolescence-limited delinquents are more normative.

Silverthorn and Frick (1999) argued that this two-trajectory model is not consistent with evidence on antisocial girls. They claim that girls' deviance tends to follow a singular trajectory, which they label the delay-onset pathway. Their data, gathered from thirty-two boys and forty girls incarcerated in a juvenile detention facility, confirmed this unique pathway for girls (Silverthorn and Frick 2001). Ninety-four percent of the sample had an adolescent onset of antisocial behavior; this proportion was 54 percent for boys, with the remaining portion having a childhood onset. This delayed-onset pathway merits more attention since other studies have reported that girls tend to start their involvement in deviance at later ages as compared with boys (Stattin and Magnusson 1989). However, consideration of more than one pathway seems essential since some studies have reported that girls' deviant activities evolve within different pathways. For example, a recent study (Lanctôt and Le Blanc 2000) identified more than one pathway to explain girls' antisocial behavior; in addition, for many adjudicated girls, problem behavior emerged before adolescence.

Sommers and Baskin (1994) tried to understand the entry of women into violent street crimes. This qualitative study of the life history was conducted with eighty-five women sentenced for nondomestic violent crimes. Two trajectories were identified. The first trajectory characterizes women who became involved in deviance at an early age. These women represent 60 percent of their sample. The second trajectory distinguishes women who manifested very few deviant behaviors during adolescence but who started committing violent acts after having a problem of substance abuse. Sommers and Baskin (1994) assert that for a certain proportion of women, violence represents the expression of a dysfunctional adaptation to society that persists from early adolescence. However, for another proportion of women, violence seems supported more by a situational context, often involving drug use.

In summary, the study of adolescent female developmental trajectories in deviant behavior has mostly emerged recently. Knowledge is limited. Nonetheless, the data from these studies, using various methodologies and statistical techniques, are converging to suggest that there are at least three major pathways into deviant behavior: occasional, transitory or adolescence-limited, and persistent. From the sparse data that we reported, we can hypothesize these pathways for various problem behaviors as well as for various forms of delinquency.

II. Mainstream Criminological Theories Applied to Females

Criminological theories are mostly based on the experiences of males. Few theoretical writings comment on female-related issues. Most observations on girls deal with the protective influence of roles given by society to female adolescents. Thus, few explanations shed light on the involvement of girls in deviant behavior. Mainstream theories nonetheless are relevant to the study of participation of adolescent females in deviance. During the 1980s, researchers began to examine the possible applications of mainstream theories to female samples. Some studies evaluated the predictive power of integrative theoretical models built from concepts found in different mainstream theories.

Common social factors encourage the participation of male and female adolescents in deviant behavior. Exposure to deviant influences and the establishment of weak ties with society and its members are prominent among these factors. Consequently, those results confirm that concepts from mainstream criminology are useful in explaining girls' involvement in deviance. However, the application of these concepts to female samples has some limits. Even if concepts from mainstream criminology, taken separately, influence the participation of girls and boys in deviant activities in the same direction and to a somewhat similar degree, boys remain more involved in deviance than do girls. The incapacity to explain gender differences, or the gender gap, is one of the strongest limits of mainstream theories. A review of mainstream theories underlines their tendency to consider only the isolated effects of a specific factor instead of evaluating the interaction effects between many factors. Interaction effects are important since the ordering of various criminogenic predictors of deviance may not be different for adolescent males and females.

A. Mainstream Theories

Mainstream theories propose that the socialization process for adolescent females reduces their risks of exposure to deviant opportunities. Thrasher (1927), in his study of Chicago gangs, asserted that girls, regardless of their background, were exposed to social habits and traditions that limited the availability of deviant opportunities. Whether they lived in a disorganized environment or not, girls were subjected to stricter parental control than boys. Cloward and Ohlin (1960) argued that criminal and violent opportunities were less accessible to girls and that girls tended more to engage in subcultures that led them to take drugs and to take part in deviant cultural movements. The idea that adolescent females have a lesser degree of liberty is also found in Sutherland and Cressey's (1978) formulation of differential-association theory. According to them, girls are given social roles that often restrain them to stay home. Hence, the types of social status conferred upon females limit their chances to learn delinquent behavior.

These propositions suggest that adolescent females are not often involved in delinquency because they are mostly exposed to prosocial influences. However, empirical studies show that girls are not immune from deviant influences. Gottfredson, McNeil, and Gottfredson (1999) revealed that girls living in disorganized areas, as well as boys, are at a greater risk of being exposed to negative peer influence. Furthermore, female adolescents deemed at risk of participating in deviant conduct, and those handled by the justice system, participate in gangs as much as boys (Bjerregaard and Smith 1993; Lanctôt and Le Blanc 1996). A representative survey of Montreal females adjudicated for criminal code violations or conduct problems shows that 69 percent of them had already been members of a gang (Lanctôt and Le Blanc 1997). This percentage is very close to that for boys (62 percent) in the same situation (Lanctôt and Le Blanc 1996). In another study targeting students at high risk for deviant behavior, 22 percent of female respondents reported being a gang member in the past twelve-month period compared with 18 percent for males (Bjerregaard and Smith 1993). In addition, by associating with peer groups made up of both genders, adolescent females are confronted with values and attitudes supporting the violation of laws and social norms (Giordano 1978). Undoubtedly, then, peer attitudes promoting the violation of social rules encourage adolescent females to commit deviant acts (Hindelang 1973; Simons, Miller, and Aigner 1980; Bjerregaard and Smith 1993; Lanctôt and Le Blanc 1997).

Moreover, mainstream criminological theories dealing with low social status families and communities assert that girls commit fewer unlawful acts than boys since the gap between their aspirations and their expectations is almost nonexistent. Cohen (1955) argued that lower-class boys have difficulties reaching the objectives set out by middle-class standards. These difficulties lead them to a reactive formation process, which encourages them to commit violent and criminal acts in order to reach a higher social status. Cohen thought that did not apply to girls, because adolescent females do not have to perpetrate criminal conducts in order to gain a higher social status. Instead, their chances of higher status depend upon the quality of relationships they develop with men. Consequently, for a better future, girls would have to respect social norms. Cloward and Ohlin (1960) also acknowledged that girls did not have to turn to deviant subcultures in order to achieve higher status. They argued that while boys longed for financial success, adolescent females mainly wished to get married. Consequently, the difficulties of pursuing middle-class objectives were not as pervasive for girls as for boys.

Since the end of the 1970s, empirical studies of adolescent female deviant behavior using strain theory have ceased to propose a dichotomous view of the aspirations of boys and girls. The evolution of the women's movement made researchers aware that marriage did not constitute the single objective of girls in social life. Hence, the occupational status aimed at by women became a growing focus of attention. Empirical studies showed that, compared with their counterparts who had not been in contact with the justice system, female adolescents in contact with that system were more prone to believe their access to legitimate opportunities was limited. Datesman, Scarpitti, and Stephenson (1975) observed that 60 percent of delinquent female adolescents considered themselves to have restricted academic and professional opportunities, in contrast to 21 percent of nondelinquent girls. Moreover, Cernkovich and Giordano (1979b) reported that involvement of girls in delinquency was partly explained by their perception of limited academic and occupational opportunities. Data were derived from self-reported questionnaires administered to samples of girls in three high schools ($n = 740$) or in two state institutions ($n = 187$) in a Midwestern state. They also pointed out that involvement of girls in delinquent conduct had a stronger association with their assessment of their individual opportunity than with their assessment of their social opportunities as women (explained variance of 9.6 percent vs. 0.7 percent). Female adolescents who were most involved in delinquency were those who believed they would probably not complete their studies or find a suitable job. Compared with their nondelinquent counterparts, however, these female adolescents were not more inclined to think that women face discrimination when trying to find a job. Gagnon, Biron, and Bertrand (1980) reported that, in a representative sample recruited in Montreal, the gap separating academic, professional, and family aspirations of female adolescents from their perception of being able to fulfill these aspirations was not a strong predictor that influenced them to commit deviant acts. This factor explained barely 10 percent of delinquent behavior and 11 percent of problem behavior. These results came close to those of Cernkovich and Giordano (1979b).

Compared with other theories, the explanatory power of strain theory was trivial (Simons, Miller, and Aigner 1980), nonsignificant (Smith and Paternoster 1987), or indirect (Liu and Kaplan 1999). Compared with the explanatory power of variables dealing with deviant peers, stigmatization, or social bonding, having a pessimistic view about the chances of finishing school or getting a fulfilling job does not constitute a strong predictor of adolescent female deviance.

Hoffmann and Su (1997) analyzed the applicability of strain theory following Agnew's (1992) update. Instead of focusing on the strain stemming from the consideration of future projects, current stressful situations were the focus of attention. These situations included parental affective disorders, parental drug or alcohol consumption problems, and uneasiness following changes in family structure or school environment. The self-report data were from two years (1992–94) of the High Risk Study, a longitudinal study designed to assess how parental risk factors affect adolescents. The sample of adolescents included 393 females and 410 males. The authors conclude that the correlation between strain-inducing life events and delinquency was the same for both girls and boys ($r = 0.40$). Moreover, the uneasiness originating from these troubling life events weakened the ties bonding adolescents and their parents ($r = -0.25$). However, Hoffmann and Su (1997) did not evaluate the correlation between parental attachment and delinquency. Therefore, it is impossible to know whether the relationship between strain and delinquency might be explained by an interaction effect involving family attachment.

Becker (1963) does not mention the possible applications of labeling theory to adolescent females. Furthermore, few studies have discussed the causal link between stigmatization of adolescent females and their participation in deviant behavior. Most studies based on labeling theory consider girls' behavior on a normative rather than on an empirical level. In work on stigmatization of women, for example, Schur (1983, p. 11) indicated: "We are going to focus primarily on gender as a normative system, a pervasive network of interrelated norms and sanctions through which female (and male) behavior is evaluated and controlled." Feminist writers have used labeling theory to observe that female adolescents become stigmatized in a patriarchal society not so much because of their delinquent activities but because of problem behaviors such as those related to their sexual conduct (Chesney-Lind and Shelden 1992).

A few empirical studies using labeling theory have included females. Simons, Miller, and Aigner (1980) observed, in a sample of 2,012 boys and 1,913 girls attending grades seven through twelve in Iowa public schools in the fall of 1976, that the stigmatization of male and female adolescents by their parents and teachers was positively correlated with delinquency. These statistical associations were of similar strength. However, one limitation is that the stigmatizing process was not recorded from its true sources—parents and teachers. Instead, the variables originated from adolescents' perceptions of what these authority figures might be thinking about them. Bartusch and Matsueda's (1996) analysis was more sophisticated since constructs from Matsueda's (1992) symbolic-interactionist approach were included. The data were drawn from the first three annual waves of the National Youth Survey, a sample of 1,725 youths initially interviewed in 1977. The effects of stigmatization on delinquency were similar and different according to gender. When parents label their child as delinquent, both male and female adolescents tend to view themselves as delinquent. Contrary to what the authors expected, girls were no more affected than boys when their parents judged them in a negative way. In return, this negative self-appraisal prompted adolescents to commit delinquent acts. The link between stigmatization and delinquency represented more than a direct causal relationship, since self-evaluations of male and female adolescents must also be taken into account. Bartusch and Matsueda (1996) showed the importance of adding this variable in the study of adolescent female deviant behavior, because the direct relationship between stigmatization by parents and delinquency was significant only for boys (the correlation was not significant for girls).

Hirschi's (1969) social-bonding theory also focused mainly on boys. This was not inherent in the formulation of the theory, which postulates that strong social ties facilitate conformity to conventional standards of conduct, but concerned its empirical verification. Hirschi's analysis could have dealt with adolescent females (the sample was drawn as part of the Richmond Youth Project and was stratified according to race, gender, schools, and grades), but only adolescent males were used in the analysis. Hirschi admitted difficulty in justifying the absence of female adolescents. In a footnote, Hirschi (1969, p. 35) mentioned, "since girls have been neglected for too long by students of delinquency, the exclusion of them is difficult to justify. I hope to return to them soon." Many other researchers have evaluated the applicability of social-bonding theory to adolescent females (Hindelang 1973; Burkett and Jensen 1975; Jensen and Eve 1976; Krohn and Massey 1980; Simons, Miller, and Aigner 1980; Canter 1982a; Figueira-McDonough 1985; Segrave and Hastad 1985; Campbell 1987; Cernkovich and Giordano 1987; Smith and Paternoster 1987; Friedman and Rosenbaum 1988; Le Blanc, Ouimet, and Tremblay 1988; LeGrande and Shoemaker 1989; Mak 1990; Torstensson 1990; Shoemaker 1994; Sommers and Baskin 1994).

Results concur with those reported by Hirschi for males. Male and female adolescents forming the strongest social bonds were less involved in deviant behavior. Only in one study was the relationship between loosening of social bonds and adolescent female delinquency not found (Shoemaker 1994). While the theory applied suitably to boys in Shoemaker's sample (22 percent of explained variance), for female delinquent behavior a variance of only 5 percent was explained. For girls, the nonsignificant results might be explained by the sample composition. Shoemaker (1994) conducted his study with male and female Filipino adolescents. Only a slight proportion of girls reported committing any delinquent acts. Furthermore, women in that country might be confronted with traditions that strongly limit their possibilities to deviate from social rules.

Most of these studies show that social-bonding theory is applicable to female samples. However, knowledge pertaining to the specific influence of social bonding on adolescent female deviance remains scarce. Most studies do not distinguish girls from boys when presenting results; thus, the relative importance of each predictor according to gender cannot be known. However, studies distinguishing results of girls and boys are generally limited to discussing the influence of the family on deviant behavior. For example, Canter (1982a) examined the influence of familial controls on the conduct of 1,725 male and female adolescents in the National Youth Survey. In bivariate analyses, she first found that girls were a little more attached to their families than were boys. Multivariate analyses showed that the loosening of family ties, and the disintegration of the family structure, prompted boys to commit delinquent acts to a greater extent than girls. Canter (1982a) also specified that the differences between genders were more visible for the most serious delinquent acts. Campbell (1987) was inspired by Hirschi's (1969) questionnaire to examine the influence of the quality of family interactions on adolescent female delinquency. She administered questionnaires to sixty-four British girls aged fifteen and sixteen. Twenty-nine girls were drawn from an assessment center and thirty-five from a secondary school in a working-class area. The strongest factor predicting the involvement of girls in delinquency was their lack of emotional attachment to their mother. This variable explained 24 percent of the variance, which represented almost all of the observed variance.

Cernkovich and Giordano (1987) considered parental attachment to be an important factor preventing either adolescent male or female deviant behavior. However, the many dimensions composing this type of bond operated differently according to gender. The authors refined the concept of parental attachment by including new elements to the usual control, supervision, and conflict dimensions. The analysis, based on a sample of 401 adolescent males and 423 adolescent females living in private households, led to specification of six distinct interactions: control and supervision, identity support, caring and trust, intimate communication, instrumental communication, parental disapproval of peers, and conflicts. The modified scale of parental attachment explained 14 percent of adolescent female involvement in deviance, compared with 12 percent for males. Although the explanatory power was similar, the relative importance of predictors varied according to gender. For boys, lack of parental supervision and lack of communication with parents constituted the major factors predicting both problem behavior and delinquency. However, for girls, the strongest predictors were weak parental support concerning the adolescent's identity, conflicts, weak instrumental communication, and disapproval of peers by parents. Heimer and De Coster (1999) confirmed these results when they observed that familial controls leading adolescent females into delinquency are more subtle than those encouraging adolescent males to commit delinquent activities. Their results indicated that girls are more affected by deficient emotional bonds with parents while boys are more affected by the lack of direct parental controls such as supervision (see Le Blanc and Ouimet [1988] for a cross-cultural replication of these results).

According to Figueira-McDonough (1985), resorting primarily to variables related to family might stem from the belief that this institution explains adolescent female deviance most adequately, whereas the quality of school adaptation and peer influence would best predict adolescent male deviance. However, Krohn and Massey (1980) cast some doubts on this explanation, since they reached different conclusions from a sample of 3,065 adolescents in grades seven through twelve in six school districts in three Midwestern states. Their analysis showed that engaging in academic, cultural, or sports projects, and believing in social norms were the most powerful factors preventing adolescent female involvement in delinquency. For boys, weak attachment to the mother was the main predictor. These findings indicated that a thorough examination of the role played by the different social institutions is necessary for a better understanding of their respective influences on adolescent male and female deviant behavior. Social-bonding theory, then, offers a predictive power that could help explain adolescent female deviant behavior.

In summary, empirical studies for many types of samples, locations, and decades identify common social factors influencing the involvement of both male and female adolescents in deviant behavior. Exposure to deviant influences, support from a deviant subculture, negative self-appraisal, and the establishment of weak ties with society and its members all constitute factors encouraging the emergence of deviant behaviors for both male and female adolescents. However, testing mainstream criminological theories with female samples does not come without problems. One important limit has to do with the explanation of gender differences. Although the predictive power of each concept taken independently varies little according to gender, the gender gap in the extent of deviant behavior continues unexplained. The involvement of male adolescents in deviant behavior is always greater than for females, even when a given predictor is statistically controlled—whether it is the exposure to delinquent peers, perceptions of blocked opportunities, stigmatization, or the quality of social bonds.

This difficulty may result from the tendency of researchers to consider only the isolated effects of a few theoretical concepts when studying adolescent female deviant behavior. Kruttschnitt (1996) and Anderson, Holmes, and Ostresh (1999) assert that researchers tend to examine only a few concepts belonging to a theoretical perspective instead of evaluating the applicability of a theory in its entirety. Moreover, the studies are generally conducted within the scope of only one mainstream theory. Among the studies discussed above, those that considered more than one theory tended to evaluate only the isolated effect of each construct. Interaction effects were then left out (see, e.g., Simons, Miller, and Aigner [1980]). Integrative models, which bring an increasingly sophisticated understanding of male deviance, are thus rarely discussed or tested. This comes as a surprise, since the studies by Krohn and Massey (1980), Biron, Gagnon, and Le Blanc (1980), Le Blanc, Ouimet, and Tremblay (1988), and Heimer and De Coster (1999) suggested that the ordering of criminogenic factors or the magnitude of their effects could vary according to gender. Use of integrative models might help solve this problem.

B. Integrative Models

Integrative models, which have been tested mostly with male adolescents, rely on constructs found in the social-bonding and social-learning theories. Constructs belonging to strain theory were included in the first attempts at integration but have since been left out.

Johnson (1979) analyzed interactions among occupational expectations, academic performance, social ties, association with delinquent
peers, and attitudes encouraging delinquent behavior. Data were obtained from self-administered questionnaires completed by 734 high
school students in Washington state during April 1975. The interactions identified were pretty much the same for male and female adolescents. Academic failure encouraged the perpetration of delinquent acts
to a greater extent for boys than for girls, but otherwise the influence
of the other variables on delinquency was similar. Association with delinquent peers had the most important direct effects. The quality of
ties with parents did not generate more delinquency for girls than for
boys.

Elliott, Huizinga, and Ageton (1985) proposed an integrative model
that included constructs belonging to strain, social-bonding, and social-learning theories. The first two waves of the National Youth Survey were used in their analysis. The model explained male and female
delinquency and drug use with significant results. Interactive effects
were the same for both groups. Thus, the strain felt at home and at
school hindered the development of ties in the family or at school.
Those weak ties were positively associated with the attachment to delinquent peers. Having delinquent peers, combined with having negative attitudes toward the law, directly led to the perpetration of delinquent acts and drug use. Apart from previous involvement in deviance,
these two variables were the only ones directly linked with deviant behavior. Even though the observed relationships were similar regardless
of gender, the predictive capacity of the model was greater for male
than for female adolescents, particularly for serious delinquency (R^2 =
37 percent for boys vs. 11 percent for girls) and for the use of hard
drugs (R^2 = 50 percent vs. 14 percent). However, the explained vari-
ances were more alike for minor thefts (R^2 = 41 percent vs. 33 percent)
and marijuana use (R^2 = 62 percent vs. 55 percent).

Segrave and Hastad (1985) evaluated a similar model. Their data
were obtained from self-reported questionnaires administered to a
sample of 1,776 students from eight selected high schools within the
metropolitan area of a major east coast U.S. city. The subjects ranged
in age from fourteen to eighteen years old, and females composed 49
percent of the sample. The correlations between predictors and delinquent activities went the same way for both male and female adolescents. However, the magnitude of coefficients varied somewhat according to gender. While the percentages of variance explained by

strain ($R^2 = 7$ percent) and social-bonding variables ($R^2 = 13$ percent) were identical for girls and boys, associating with delinquent peers had a greater influence on male than on female delinquency (25 percent vs. 15 percent). Combining all variables related to the three theoretical perspectives explained 30 percent of male delinquency compared to 22 percent of female delinquency. The interaction effects examined by Segrave and Hastad (1985) were similar to those observed by Elliott, Huizinga, and Ageton (1985). Perceived blocked opportunities lessened adhesion to conventional norms of conduct, which, in turn, encouraged association with delinquent peers. Delinquent peers then facilitated delinquent behavior.

Le Blanc, Ouimet, and Tremblay (1988) tested their integrative model with two representative samples of Montreal male and female adolescents. The first sample was recruited in 1976 and consisted of 825 adolescents age fourteen to eighteen (367 girls and 458 boys). The second sample was recruited in 1985 and consisted of 797 fourteen- and fifteen-year-old adolescents (438 boys and 359 girls). All responded to a self-administered questionnaire. The model adopted Hirschi's (1969) social-bonding theory as its main frame of reference. It included the construct of attachment and involvement, as well as external and internal constraints. The model also took into account affiliation with delinquent peers and quality of school adaptation. Those two last variables were combined to create the construct of adolescent role. Finally, a distinguishing feature was the model's inclusion of personality-related variables. The dependent variable represented a general index of delinquency. The structure of the model did not vary according to gender. Again, however, the model had higher explanatory power for males than for females ($R^2 = 59$ percent vs. 49 percent). Deficiencies related to the imposition of social constraints and adolescent role constituted the predictors that showed the most direct impact on delinquency. Psychological functioning marked by egocentrism, and weakness of social ties, came second. Le Blanc (1997b) tested a more sophisticated version of this integrative model with an adjudicated sample but did not apply it specifically to female counterparts.

By combining concepts of different theoretical perspectives, researchers were able to examine the ordering of criminogenic factors that prompt female adolescents to commit deviant acts. Overall, interactions were of the same nature for both genders. This conclusion supports the necessity of the integration of different concepts from mainstream theories to explain adolescent females' deviance adequately.

However, applying integrative models to female samples does not resolve the problems surrounding the explanation of the gender gap. The integrative models display a greater capacity to explain males' participation in deviant behavior than females' participation. The difference of explained variance according to gender could vary up to 26 percent when serious delinquency is considered (see Elliott, Huizinga, and Ageton 1985). This might occur because adolescent females commit fewer serious offenses. It might also be because empirical studies conducted with female adolescents do not pay enough attention to differences distinguishing both sexes. In studies dealing with adolescent female delinquency, for example, the dependent variable generally turns out to be composed of the same indicator as is used for boys. This is odd, since girls rarely commit serious offenses compared with boys. Elliott, Huizinga, and Ageton (1985) showed that the capacity to predict adolescent females' delinquency was at its lowest when differences in offending between girls and boys were at their highest, that is, when serious offenses were considered. In consequence, the measure of deviant behavior may need to be adjusted to capture more accurately the behaviors that are committed by female adolescents. For example, Crick and Grotpeter (1995) observed that girls tend to rely more on relational violence, which is intended to harm others through their peer relationships or their reputation, than on physical violence. However, since the overall structure of deviant behavior is similar for girls and boys, resorting to a specific measure of deviance is not a strategy supported by empirical data. In consequence, the explanation of the gender gap in the explanatory power of integrative models must be found elsewhere.

Whether we consider classic theories or integrative models, two conclusions are warranted. First, criminologists have always entertained a certain level of confusion concerning the dependent variable. The theories generally used the term "delinquency" without precisely defining it, and the frontier between delinquency and deviance is thereby blurred. Empirical tests of these theories encouraged that confusion because their measure of self-reported delinquency is very often a measure of various forms of deviance. This confusion is perilous for criminological theories. They must explain girls' involvement in deviance and the gender gap. Second, even if the same integrated set of constructs is useful in understanding adolescent females' and males' deviance, understanding of the gender gap remains limited. This points to another source of explanation: differences in the way girls and boys are socialized or in the ways they learn to conform to social standards according to their gender. Mainstream theories and integrative models often explain the gender gap in involvement in deviant behavior by resorting to this notion. However, empirical studies that tested these theories and models do not measure differential socialization.

III. Gender Differences and Deviant Behavior

Studies pertaining to gender differences do not attempt to examine the applicability of specific concepts to female populations. The main objective is to show that biological or sociological differences distinguishing adolescent females and males affect the nature and the extent of their respective deviant behavior.

This section discusses knowledge about gender differences in order to enrich models elaborated by mainstream criminology. The analysis of biological factors relates mostly to the influence of sexual maturation on girls' involvement in deviance. Findings suggest that girls' early sexual development contributes to greater involvement in deviance because it encourages girls to interact with older peers. However, these biological explanations are controversial. Many authors believe that gender differences should be considered more as social and cultural constructs than as biological traits. Hence, both gender roles and differences in socialization processes are key concepts that explain girls' deviance and the gender gap. Empirical studies highlight the importance that young women devote to the well-being of others and demonstrate that deviance is at odds with females' gender roles. Adherence to so-called female gender roles may be an important mediator of gender differences in deviance and explain why girls are less involved than boys in acts that cause serious harm to others. However, the state of knowledge about gender roles and the differential impact of socialization according to gender is still incomplete. This is due to the difficulty of operationalizing the concept of gender roles. Finally, gender differences are examined by analyzing the contexts in which adolescent females commit deviant acts. These studies present qualitative information, which allows identification of situational factors and motivations that influence the forms deviant behavior takes for females. Most studies in this area concern violence and gang membership.

A. Biological and Physical Influences

Researchers have discussed for more than a century the possible roles of biological differences in influencing girls' and boys' behavior.

Early studies were controversial notably because young women were described negatively and because statements were made without empirical testing. Recent studies are sounder. They mostly investigate whether girls' early sexual maturation has an effect on their involvement in deviance. Findings demonstrate that early sexual development contributes to greater involvement in deviant behavior when this factor interacts with social influences. An example of such social influence is the tendency of precocious girls to join older peers, particularly older boys.

The first study attempting to demonstrate that biological and physical factors prevented women from getting involved in delinquency was conducted by Lombroso and Ferrero (1895). They asserted that women were generally characterized by a lack of sensitivity to others and feelings of revenge, jealousy, and weak morals. However, the feebleness of women's physical and mental capacities were said to neutralize these characteristics. Hence, Lombroso and Ferrero argued that women could commit only a few delinquent acts since their weaknesses prevented their possessing the characteristics of criminal men. Thomas (1923), Freud (1933), and Pollak (1950) also asserted the biological inferiority of women. They argued that the passive sexual functions of women explained their lesser involvement in crime. Sexual dysfunction has been said to encourage girls to commit some types of deviant acts (Freud 1933; Konopka 1966). The development of girls' sexual maturity was considered by others to be a triggering factor that prompted misconduct. Thomas (1923) indicated that girls quickly learn that manipulating their sexual capital allows them to have new and exciting experiences. Pollak (1950) also argued that reaching sexual maturity offered new deviant opportunities to female adolescents.

Recently, researchers have shown renewed interest in the influence of biological and physical factors on deviant behavior. For example, Bottcher (1995) and Steffensmeier and Allan (1996) acknowledged that gender differences regarding physical strength limit the involvement of young women in delinquency. Their real or perceived vulnerability restrains them from acting alone or committing crimes that might require physical altercations (Steffensmeier and Allan 1996).

The influence of sexual maturity has been the subject of renewed attention. Pubertal development is now treated in terms of its "social-stimulus value" (Caspi et al. 1993). Although all adolescents experience sexual maturation, there are important individual differences in timing. Magnusson, Stattin, and Allen (1986) suggested that sexual development of girls should be examined, since chronological age is not the only reference point relating to individual development. They found that the gap between early and late maturation could be as much as five or six years. Magnusson and his colleagues (1986) hypothesized that these differences might affect the social and psychological development of female adolescents and that early puberty might cause social maladjustment because girls' sexual maturity might not correspond with psychological maturity. Late puberty onset might, by contrast, allow girls more time to prepare for new situations and demands. Caspi and Moffitt (1991) reasoned that girls who reach sexual maturity prematurely may not possess social skills for coping with new responsibilities and demands of adolescence.

Besides the hypothesis predicting the negative effects of girls' early sexual development, two hypotheses concerning the relationship between menarcheal timing and deviance have been put forward. One hypothesis is that, regardless of the age of onset, the discomfort brought by the first menstrual period encourages girls to perpetrate deviant acts (Simmons and Blyth 1987; Caspi and Moffitt 1991; Ge, Conger, and Elder 1996). The second hypothesis is that the most maladjusted girls occupy marginal positions in comparison with other girls of their age. Hence, girls who have menstruated by the end of the latency period would be predicted to be the most maladjusted because of their minority status. Similarly, girls who have not reached sexual maturity by the middle or end of adolescence might also be at high risk of deviating from social norms (Simmons and Blyth 1987; Caspi and Moffitt 1991; Ge, Conger, and Elder 1996).

Empirical research showed that the first hypothesis is the most plausible and refuted both versions of the second hypothesis. The involvement of girls in deviance does not tend to increase following the onset of the first menstrual period. Nor does the minority status conferred upon girls who reach sexual maturity late result in disproportionate misconduct on their part. By contrast, Caspi and Moffitt (1991) and Ge, Conger, and Elder (1996) showed that late menstruation is a preventive factor. Even though female adolescents who had not had their first menstruation by fifteen were a minority compared with those who had, they were less involved in problem and delinquent behavior.

However, an early first menstruation significantly affects levels of participation in deviant activities (Caspi and Moffitt 1991). Girls who have had their menstruation during the latency period tend to participate in a greater amount of problem and delinquent conduct than do others. Simmons and Blyth (1987) showed that early onset of puberty significantly influenced perpetration of deviant acts. This study involved a representative sample of 924 students from public schools in a large Midwestern U.S. city in the mid-1970s. There were two waves: students were first contacted in sixth grade and again during ninth and tenth grades. Girls who began their menstruations during the latency period rebelled most against schooling. They were more likely to be expelled frequently from school and to commit truancy during high school. Their academic results were typically lower. Simmons and Blyth (1987) showed that the association between school rebellion and precocious physical development was not found for boys. They also learned that adults expected more from girls who had reached sexual maturity at an early age. For example, parents tended to encourage their autonomy by allowing them to stay home alone, take the bus alone, and baby-sit a few hours per week during the school year. Although these parental behaviors may enhance the personal development of precocious girls, they also expose them to deviant opportunities.

Magnusson, Stattin, and Allen (1986) reached similar conclusions using data from the Swedish Project Metropolitan that followed subjects from early school years through adulthood. The sample consisted of 466 girls for whom complete menarcheal data were obtained when they were in eighth grade. The earlier the onset of first menstruation, the more frequent were a variety of problem behaviors directed against school or family. Compared with nonprecocious girls, a larger proportion had drunk alcohol, used soft drugs, stayed out at night when they were supposed to be home, and shoplifted. The frequency of these behaviors was an indicator of maladjustment of girls who had developed early sexually. Twenty-seven percent of girls who had their first menstruation before age eleven frequently ignored the curfew set by their parents, compared with only 4.5 percent of girls who had their first period after age thirteen who disobeyed their curfew more than four times.

Girls who matured during the latency period were also more likely to associate with older peers (Magnusson, Stattin, and Allen 1986). Seventy-four percent associated with older friends, 83 percent had a boyfriend, and 45 percent had sexual relationships. For girls who developed later, these percentages were 39 percent, 52 percent, and 11 percent, respectively. Magnusson and his colleagues (1986) concluded that the deviant behaviors of precocious girls were explained mostly by their tendency to associate with older friends. Their differential involvement in deviance, however, occurred only when they associated with older peers. It seems the association with older peers was the triggering factor prompting precocious girls to deviate from social norms. These girls expected their peers to judge them less harshly when deviating from standard codes of conduct.

Does the enhanced vulnerability of girls who develop physically and sexually at an early age persist until the end of adolescence, even during adulthood? Current knowledge is too limited to answer this question. However, some clues are available. According to Simmons and Blyth (1987), differences found between the school adaptations of precocious and nonprecocious girls vanish by the tenth grade. Precocious girls, then, are only more deviant than other girls from the latency period to the beginning of adolescence. Similar results were observed by Caspi et al. (1993). Those results indicate that at age fifteen on-time maturers had caught up with their early maturer peers regarding involvement in deviant behavior. However, longitudinal data gathered by Magnusson, Stattin, and Allen (1986) indicate that precocious girls seem to have persistent difficulties of adaptation. Early sexual maturation had an enduring effect on hard drug use. Differences were also found concerning educational levels. Only 2 percent of girls who had their first periods during latency entered college, compared with 15 percent of girls who developed later. The inferior educational level of precocious girls might be explained by their stronger desire, during mid-teenage years, to have children than to care about their education. More than two-thirds of precocious girls wished to start a home and family compared with less than half of nonprecocious girls. This desire had been fulfilled for many girls who reached sexual maturity at an early age. Magnusson (1988) observed that up to the mid-twenties in age, precocious girls were more likely to have a child. Concerning adult criminality, Magnusson, Stattin, and Allen (1986) cautiously stated that girls who reached sexual maturity early had more contact with the justice system. This assertion was offered cautiously because very few girls received a criminal record during adulthood.

In summary, recent empirical studies examining the influence of biological factors on deviant behavior show the impact of these factors to be mediated by social influences facing female adolescents. These include the higher parental expectations toward girls who reached sexual maturity; the tendency of precocious girls to associate with older peers, particularly boys; and the desire felt by many precocious girls to be-

come mothers. Although these studies contribute to understanding adolescent females' deviant behavior, biological factors remain highly
controversial.

B. From Sex Differences to Gender Differences

Smart (1976) and Daly and Chesney-Lind (1988) vigorously denounced biological explanations, arguing that sex differences, or,
rather, gender differences, should be considered as social and cultural
constructs rather than as natural facts. Hence, gender roles and differences in the socialization processes of girls and boys became key concepts that could explain the disparities existing between adolescent female and male behaviors. A meta-analysis of 172 studies challenges the
idea that parents make systematic differences in rearing girls and boys
(Lytton and Romney 1991). It concluded that the effect sizes for most
socialization domains were not significant for genders and generally
were very small, even fluctuating in direction across studies. This
meta-analysis challenges the basic assumption of the theoretical perspective that underlies gender differences. However, a review of research by Keenan and Shaw (1997) indicates that it would be wrong to
conclude that there are no differences in the socialization processes of
girls and boys. Keenan and Shaw (1997) reported that parents tend to
devote more energy to teaching and modeling skills with girls, such
as empathic responding, than with boys. Thus, studies evaluating the
influence of differential socialization on girls' deviant behavior seem
warranted.

Examination of concepts pertaining to differential socialization is a
promising avenue that must be pursued. Theoretical work and empirical studies highlight the importance that young women devote to the
well-being of others and demonstrate that delinquency is at odds with
females' gender roles. Adhesion to so-called female gender roles might
explain why girls become more involved than boys in acts that put their
security at risk rather than in acts that risk serious harm to others.
However, knowledge about gender roles and the differential socialization effect is still insufficient. This might be due to the persistent difficulty in operationalizing the concept of gender roles. Although consideration of this concept became more popular when the women's
liberation movement started, this way of analyzing sex differences to
explain deviance was proposed by Parsons as early as 1947.

Parsons (1947) attempted to show that gender differences in socialization processes model the behavior of girls and boys. The distribu-

tion of roles in the family, he argued, favors the conformity of girls. Girls, he maintained, face less anxiety than boys during their process of forming a sexual identity. Unlike boys, girls do not have to dissociate themselves from the feminine image with which they daily evolve. While the positive identification of girls with their mother would facilitate conformity, the absence of a father at home would predispose boys to express aggressive behaviors in order to dissociate themselves from female roles. Passive attributes acquired by maternal education would also explain the conformity of girls. In short, Parsons (1947) argued that girls were encouraged to be passive and dependent whereas boys had to fight and be assertive in order to reach a higher social status. Miller (1958) argued that female adolescents do not have to be rebellious since their sexual identification process was made easier by the presence of the mother at home. These hypotheses have not been tested empirically.

This discourse has been transformed in feminist writings. For example, Adler (1975) argued that the conformity of girls was ensured by their passive roles until the women's liberation movement appeared. Adler predicted that the situation would change with the emergence of the women's movement because, from that time onward, girls could be compared with boys regarding aggressiveness, competition, and access to opportunities. In other words, girls would come to adopt masculine behavioral patterns to the detriment of femininity. Since Adler asserted that the involvement into delinquency necessitates masculine attributes, she predicted that crime would be more widespread among liberated women.

However, Adler's prediction is flawed by methodological and theoretical weaknesses. First, official data revealed that the rise of female delinquency mostly represented a statistical illusion caused by the limited number of criminal women. A slight increase in absolute numbers produced disproportionate increases in percentages. Furthermore, violent conduct by women had not increased significantly in numbers. The increase was in minor property crimes (Simon 1979). Adler's thesis was also challenged because female offenders tend not to come from social groups that benefited from improvements in women's conditions (Pollock 1999; DeKeseredy 2000).

The relationship between deviant behavior and the adoption of so-called masculine attitudes remains ambiguous. Cullen, Golden, and Cullen (1979) concluded that there was a significant relationship between delinquency and masculinity. This study used a nonrandom sample of ninety-nine young men and eighty-three young women (mean age = 18.8 years) drawn from the student body of a Midwestern U.S. university. Although the reported correlations were stronger for boys than for girls, the so-called masculine features were positively and directly related to both violent and property crimes. However, this study suffered from an important methodological weakness regarding temporality. The masculinity scale measured current attitudes of male and female students about gender roles, but the self-reported delinquency questionnaire referred to earlier conduct during adolescence. How can researchers be sure that attitudes prevailing at the beginning of adulthood reflect those during adolescence? Hence, these results must be interpreted cautiously. In addition, adhesion to gender roles appears to decline as female adolescents grow older (Heimer 1996), and the influence of liberal attitudes on conduct increases with time (Horwitz and White 1987).

Other studies have shown that girls' adhesion to typically masculine conduct does not necessarily lead to delinquency. Thornton and James (1979) observed that female adolescents who frequently committed delinquent acts were neither more prone than others to endorse typically masculine attitudes nor to reject them. Of the most delinquent female adolescents, 28 percent asserted that they could repair a car, invite a boy, pay the bill on a date with a boy, or contribute to family income, while 29 percent did not endorse such conducts. The sample consisted of 1,002 students from the Nashville Metropolitan School System; ages ranged from thirteen to nineteen years. Wilkinson (1985), by contrast, investigated whether the statistical control of so-called masculine personality traits (self-confidence, independence, taste for adventure, and aggressiveness) weakened the correlation between sex and delinquency. Her data were drawn from a survey conducted in six southern Arizona high schools in the fall of 1975. Questionnaires were collected from 3,257 students. She concluded that control of masculine traits did not modify the correlation; it went from −0.23 to −0.22. These ways of conceptualizing masculinity seem inappropriate, as is explained below.

We conclude that the absence of a clear relationship between masculinity and deviant behavior is the result of conceptual and methodological weaknesses. Many theoretical statements suggest that social roles have a protective function on girls' deviant behavior (Heidensohn 1968; Leonard 1982; Chesney-Lind and Shelden 1992). It would be surprising to find that gender roles have no influence on deviant behavior. To understand this influence, gender roles should be conceptualized differently.

According to Messerschmidt (1993), use of masculinity scales leads too often to a polarization of genders. The roles attributed to girls and boys are strictly considered from a normative standpoint in which differences between same-sex individuals are ignored. Individual differences are thus discarded, giving place to stereotyped images of men and women. Instead of being considered on a continuum, femininity and masculinity tend to be conceptualized as poles. Hence, the results presented above often hide an important misinterpretation that assumes that girls who endorse so-called masculine attitudes reject typically feminine social roles. That a girl perceives herself as being independent and competitive, however, does not necessarily mean that she will reject other roles such as those of mother and wife.

When analyzing the influence of feminine roles on deviant behavior, attitudes toward the women's liberation movement and personal aspirations of female adolescents must not be confounded. According to Giordano and Cernkovich (1979), opinions of female adolescents regarding positions women should occupy at work, for example, might differ from their own personal aspirations: "The simple 'liberation-causes-crime' argument ignores the fact that gender roles must be conceptualized as multidimensional, and further that there can be important differences between an actor's attitudes about women in general and herself in particular" (p. 479).

Giordano and Cernkovich (1979) observed that liberal attitudes of female adolescents concerning women's family roles are not a significant predictor of participation in delinquent behavior. The data derived from self-reported questionnaires administered to samples of girls who were either in one of three high schools ($n = 740$) or in one of two state institutions ($n = 187$). The mean age for the high school sample was 16.3 years and for the institutionalized sample, 16.1 years. On an individual basis, adolescent females who attached less importance to family roles turned out to be the most delinquent. Giordano and Cernkovich specified that liberal attitudes that best predicted involvement in delinquency were those that implied a greater sense of behavioral autonomy. Female adolescents who set themselves fewer normative restrictions were more likely to engage in delinquency. For example, female adolescents who thought it appropriate for a girl to go alone to a drinking establishment showed higher results on the delinquency scale.

Deviant behavior is a complex phenomenon, and gender roles alone cannot explain it (Shover et al. 1979; Messerschmidt 1993; Heimer 1996; Heimer and De Coster 1999). Study of gender roles cannot be done apart from the study of social interactions and social bonds. Shover and his colleagues (1979) showed the relevance of including these constructs. Their study, which was conducted with 1,002 male and female students, revealed that female adolescents involved in delinquency were more likely than nondelinquent girls to reject constraints related to their future roles as mother and wife (being responsible for domestic chores and for the education of their children instead of occupying a paid job). However, they observed that the relationship between the dismissal of so-called feminine roles and delinquency was indirect. Thus, if female students displayed fewer expectations directed toward traditional definitions of femininity, they also showed less attachment to others, less belief in social norms, and more access to delinquent opportunities. These interactions facilitated the commission of delinquent acts.

Some researchers suggest that greater attention should be paid to values and attitudes (e.g., empathy, moral evaluation) than to stereotyped behaviors (paying on a date, fixing a car, staying at home with children, etc.) when conceptualizing gender roles. Beutel and Marini (1995) suggest that female gender roles might be defined as a propensity to care and to feel responsible for the well-being of others. Mears, Ploeger, and Warr (1998, p. 253) similarly posit that "females ordinarily possess something that acts as a barrier to inhibit or block the influence of delinquent peers." They argue that females seem to be socialized in such ways that they are more constrained by moral evaluations of conduct than are males. Multivariate analyses (Mears, Ploeger, and Warr 1998) indicated that moral evaluations regulate the effects of delinquent peers for females and males, but these evaluations protect females more than males from negative peer influences. The most comprehensive study of the influence of gender roles on deviant behavior (Heimer 1996) emphasizes the importance of conceptualizing adhesion to gender roles as the product of internalized sets of values. Using a symbolic-interactionist perspective, Heimer asserts that gender roles modulate social interactions and that individuals evaluate themselves according to the gender standards they have internalized. Hence, gender roles are internalized in the same way as are attitudes toward social norms: "Building on symbolic interactionist work on gender, I argue that gender definitions—or beliefs about femininity and masculinity—are acquired and incorporated into the self (the 'me') through role-taking and then serve to regulate behavior, just as do attitudes about rules/laws and other types of attitudes and values" (Heimer 1996, p. 56).

Social control is thus transformed into personal control, since individuals who have internalized gender-related standards are motivated to act according to them. Heimer (1996) formulated the following hypothesis: internalization of so-called feminine gender roles would direct female adolescents toward conformity, whereas internalization of so-called masculine roles would encourage delinquency for boys. Girls would be less delinquent than boys, since the roles conferred upon them would not encourage them to commit delinquent acts. Heimer (1996) postulated that the internalization of gender roles and social norms allowed adolescents to anticipate reactions of others. Referring to Chodorow (1978) and Gilligan (1982), Heimer opined that girls are more sensitive than boys to others' evaluations of them. Hence, girls would be deterred from committing delinquent acts by their anticipation of the reactions of others.

Heimer (1996) tested these hypotheses with data from the National Youth Study (and more recently for violent delinquency, see Heimer and De Coster [1999]). That these hypotheses have been evaluated with data gathered twenty years ago is unfortunate. Today's female adolescents may have different attitudes about gender roles than those of female adolescents in the 1970s. The model explained 40 percent of the variance of delinquent behavior for adolescent females and 47 percent for adolescent males. The proportions are satisfactory even if previous delinquency explained the greatest part of the variance. Adherence of adolescent females to feminine gender roles constituted, as was predicted, an inhibitor to delinquency whereas, for boys, endorsement of masculine roles led to delinquent behavior. Adolescent females who considered delinquency as inappropriate for their gender and incompatible with the traditional feminine image were less likely to participate in delinquent behavior. Bottcher (2001), in his qualitative study of twenty-nine male wards and their brothers and sisters on the social practices of gender, produced similar results: female adolescents were more sensitive to the anticipated reactions of peers, and males were significantly less sensitive. Richards and Tittle (1981) showed that potential sanctions had a greater deterrent effect on girls than on boys. Tibbetts (1999) demonstrated that young women tend to display a higher propensity to feelings of shame when committing deviant acts than do young men.

Heimer thus showed that socialization into so-called feminine gender roles can prevent adolescent female delinquency. Female adolescents tend to set different internal constraints for themselves. For example, they anticipate negative reactions of peers if they violate social rules. They are motivated to act in concordance with feminine roles, thus showing conformity. Heimer reported that internal constraints acted in concordance with the strength of ties with family as well as those with peers.

Although the symbolic-interactionist perspective contributes to the understanding of gender differences, some dimensions of social control are left out. To understand the gender gap in deviance, the development of allocentrism, the ability to consider others' interests, should also be taken into account (Le Blanc 1997*a*). This dimension may be essential, since an egocentric personality structure would not prompt adolescent females to anticipate consequences from others' reactions nor encourage them to set internal constraints for themselves. In addition, the influence of social class on attitudes toward gender roles deserves attention. Heimer (1996) observed that identification with traditional feminine roles was less pronounced for girls in upper-economic classes, since they were exposed to less traditional maternal models. This is consistent with analyses of Hagan, Simpson, and Gillis, who tried to explain the participation of girls and boys in petty crimes (Hagan, Gillis, and Simpson 1985; Hagan, Simpson, and Gillis 1987; see also McCarthy, Hagan, and Woodward 1999).

Power control theory predicts that the gender gap in deviance will be smaller in less patriarchal family structures, in which male and female positions in the workplace are similar, than in households that are more patriarchal. In these latter families, mothers are the primary socialization agents. The lesser involvement of girls in deviance results from the stratification of social control: girls face stricter controls and are less free to deviate from norms of conduct. Girls are not encouraged to take risks. Hagan, Gillis, and Simpson (1985) and Hagan, Simpson, and Gillis (1987) assert that this differential control should be less common in balanced families than in patriarchal families. Girls in balanced families would be encouraged to take risks at almost the same level as boys. Mothers with power in the workplace would be likelier to allow daughters to adopt risky behaviors, which might help daughters free themselves from traditional feminine roles and obtain promising jobs. McCarthy, Hagan, and Woodward (1999) further noted that mothers in less patriarchal families also intensify the control exerted upon their sons by giving them less freedom and more family responsibilities.

Although Hagan and his colleagues concluded that their hypothesis was confirmed (that gender differences are greater in patriarchal families than in more egalitarian families), the results were not convincing, particularly in later analyses of their data. In the more recent study (McCarthy, Hagan, and Woodward 1999), almost no significant differences were reported within genders across family types. The power control theory was tested with data collected in 1987 from 562 students in grades nine through twelve who attended one of three randomly selected schools in Toronto. Information on mothers' and fathers' employment status, authority within the workplace, and business ownership was used to classify each parent's class position. Patriarchal families were those in which males had higher-class positions than females. Less patriarchal families were those in which men's and women's class positions were similar. There were too few matriarchal households (families in which women's class position was superior) to include this type of family in their analysis. A strong confirmation of the theory would have been that girls in less patriarchal families are less controlled, have a stronger preference for risk taking, and are more engaged in minor delinquency compared with girls from more patriarchal families. None of the results reached statistical significance.

Power control theory has been the subject of much criticism. One important difficulty is other researchers' inability to replicate Hagan and his colleagues' results (Hagan, Gillis, and Simpson 1985). Singer and Levine's (1988) findings, for example, do not concur. Results indicated that patriarchal families, more than balanced families, showed the greatest gender differences regarding control, risk taking, and deviant behavior. Their study, in the spring of 1987, concerned a representative sample of 705 adolescents in public and private senior high schools and 560 of their parents. Morash and Chesney-Lind (1991) collected data on this question in 1981 through interviews with 1,423 adolescents and with an adult responsible for each child. They showed that gender differences were present regardless of family types and that stricter control of girls affected only their sexual behavior.

Operationalization of "risk taking" has been criticized. Morash and Chesney-Lind (1991) thought this concept confusing because it can take different meanings according to gender. Morasch and Chesney-Lind, and Leiber and Wacker (1997), criticized the treatment given to single-headed families. Hagan, Gillis, and Simpson (1985) regarded single-parent families with woman-headed households as egalitarian families because youths in such families do not face a power imbalance between the father and the mother. Leiber and Wacker (1997) believed this weakness cast serious doubt on the validity of power control theory: "The inconsistent application of a central tenet of the theory (single mother's authority in the workplace) has major implications for the theory's overall validity. If the power component, as it is conceptualized by Hagan and colleagues, is not an essential factor in explaining delinquency of children of single mothers, then it is difficult to understand why it is important for those of two-parent families" (p. 321).

Jensen (1993) questioned the legitimacy of the power concept. He argued that the demonstration of the influence of parental power on girls' and boys' conduct was weak. He urged that the theory be evaluated according to the unique contribution of the concept of power, regardless of the variables related to control. The absence of this demonstration, he suggested, resulted from the redundancy of the concept of power, a concept that Hagan, Simpson, and Gillis (1987) associated with parental control. Jensen (1993) argued that theoretical propositions of power control theory and of social-bonding theory are incompatible. Why is it that youths with the best potential to reach a high social status would be the likeliest to perpetrate delinquent acts? Jensen argued that male and female adolescents who have high aspirations are less likely to engage in problem and delinquent behaviors. Furthermore, why would high-status parents with power not encourage conformity more than risk taking? Many questions about power control theory are thus left unanswered.

In summary, empirical studies about gender roles and the differential impact of socialization according to gender have not reached conclusive results. However, studies are becoming increasingly sophisticated and offer interesting leads to follow. Additional research would be beneficial because identification with gender roles is a phenomenon that may be an important mediator of gender differences in deviance (Eagly and Steffen 1986; Beutel and Marini 1995). Broidy and Agnew (1997) argue that the importance females attach to the well-being of others may explain their lesser propensity to commit acts that cause serious harm to others. It may be difficult for females to commit serious crimes while feeling responsible for the well-being of their children and the people surrounding them or when high expectations are set upon them as mothers and wives. Hence, Heimer (1996) and Heimer and De Coster (1999) suggest that adhesion to so-called female gender roles may transform itself into internal barriers. Broidy and Agnew (1997) argue that the social pressures related to female gender roles may explain why girls are more involved than boys in acts that put their security at risk rather than in acts which cause serious harm to others. Escape attempts such as running away, and self-destructive behaviors like drug use, would help girls manage negative emotions without directly harming others (Broidy and Agnew 1997).

C. The Gendered Context of Deviance

Gender differences can also be examined by analyzing the contexts in which adolescent females commit deviant acts. These studies are mostly ethnomethodological and do not attempt to establish causal relationships between females' status or roles and their behavior. Rather, they allow identification of situational factors and motivations that influence the ways deviant behavior is manifested. Most studies concern violence and gang membership.

Better understanding of the complex relationship between violence and gender requires analysis of the different experiences to which females and males are exposed (Chesney-Lind and Shelden 1998; Heimer and De Coster 1999; Artz and Nicholson 2001; Kruttschnitt 2001). Moretti and Odgers (2001) proposed a bilateral model of violence: "gender differences in aggression arise because of fundamental differences between females' and males' social goals: males' social goals emphasize instrumentality and physical dominance, while females' goals are more focused on interpersonal issues. The bilateral model of aggression captures gender differences in aggressive behavior, according to the specific focus or goal to which aggressive acts are directed" (p. 7).

The bilateral model is supported by research that evaluates females' and males' perceptions of violence. Adolescent females interviewed by Crick, Bigbee, and Howes (1996) reported that verbal threats and insults cause more prejudice to others than does physical violence. Adolescent males were more prone to cite physical violence than indirect forms of violence as a way to cause prejudice to others. The sample consisted of 245 children (106 girls and 139 boys) from two elementary schools. These differences reflect the modes of expression of violence characteristic of each gender: violence tends to be more indirect or relational among females than among males (Crick and Grotpeter 1995). In addition, these differences might be explained by the stronger emphasis given by females, compared with males, to the preservation of harmonious interpersonal relationships (Broidy and Agnew 1997). Damaging someone's relationships thus becomes an effective way for girls to harm someone.

Campbell (1993) pointed out that females and males may have different perceptions regarding their involvement in violence. Young women whom she interviewed perceived their involvement in violence as a loosening of self-control, especially in situations of interpersonal conflicts. By contrast, young men tended to believe that violence was a legitimate means to manifest their authority or to exercise control over someone else.

Campbell (1984a) also investigated motives leading adolescent females to participate in fights. The data were collected as part of a two-year study of three New York City gangs; the girl members ranged in age from fifteen to thirty years old. Girls fought mostly after attacks on their integrity or in response to rumors that had been spread about them. Fights frequently originated from sexual jealousy. Artz (1998) offered similar results. In interviews with six violent schoolgirls, females' sexual and seductive behavior seemed to be the main reasons for physical assaults on females. Campbell (1984a) observed, in contrast, that adolescent males were mostly involved in fights to preserve the solidarity of their group or to maintain their tough-guy reputations. Some studies have shown that females are more likely to victimize people in their surroundings while males tend more to attack acquaintances or strangers (Sommers and Baskin 1993). In addition, when women commit crimes against the person, homicides in particular, immediate family members tend to be the victims (Simon 1979; Young 1981; Silverman and Kennedy 1987; Cario 1992). Study of offending contexts also shows that girls' deviant activities are typically less harmful to victims than are boys' (Triplett and Myers 1995).

The position of girls in gangs is a topic of high recent interest. Female gang members involved in deviant activities mostly occupy secondary roles (Steffensmeier and Allan 1996). Adolescent female gang members, for the most part, revolve around the hard core of the gang (Sarnecki 1986; Taylor 1990). This positioning results in formation of feminine versions of boys' gangs (Welfare Council of New York City 1950; Short 1968; Miller 1975; Campbell 1984b; Taylor 1993; Joe and Chesney-Lind 1995). Miller (1975) gathered data on gangs from different sources in twelve major North American cities and showed that few female gangs had developed independently. Female gang members defined themselves according to the male gang with which they were involved. "Vice Queens," for example, a well-known U.S. female gang, is an extension of the "Vice Kings" (Fishman 1988). Once the "Bo-gars" (which means handsome boys) appeared in Montreal, the "Belles" (which means cute girls) soon emerged (Roy 1993). The male-composed gang determines the reputation of its female division. When male gangs are highly antisocial, the female gang also is highly antisocial (Spergel 1990).

These extensions of male gangs were composed mainly of female adolescents from the immediate surroundings of the boys (Campbell 1984*a*; Sarnecki 1986). Campbell (1984*b*) found, in a qualitative research involving participant observations and interviews with female gang members, that the status of female gang members varied according to the relative positions of the boys who introduced them into the gang. However, girls rarely occupied a high-status position among hard-core gang members (Campbell 1984*b*). Although leaders are boys, the girl who occupies the highest position can be the emotional center of the gang. Campbell (1984*b*) compared this role to the one of a mother who provides affection as well as support to her children. The auxiliary role of female gang members often makes them sexually promiscuous. From the first studies to the latest, data have shown that those girls had to be sexually accessible (Thrasher 1927; Welfare Council of New York City 1950; Ackley and Fliegel 1960; Haskins 1974; Campbell 1984*b*; Brunson and Miller 2001). Girls who join gangs are often described as sexual objects. Boys exploit them, and they make many sexual compromises, which often lead to adolescent pregnancies. Female gang members must maintain the prestige of the gang's boys by being sexually promiscuous (Short 1968). Another role commonly assigned to girls is the carrying of weapons (Ackley and Fliegel 1960; Haskins 1974; Adler 1975; Brown 1977; Campbell 1984*b*). Brown (1977) explained that girls assume this role to reduce arrest risks for boys, since girls are less likely to be noticed by police.

Exploration of the contexts of adolescent females' deviant activities aids understanding of the gender gap. These mostly qualitative studies suggest that adolescent females' deviant behavior is modulated in large part by the importance girls attach to interpersonal relationships. Investigation of the motives precipitating fights indicates that females' sexual and seductive behavior is often implicated.

D. Integrating Concepts Relevant to Gender Differences

Contextual factors explain the gender gap, at least in part. Knowledge concerning biological, social, and situational differences may be used in two different ways. Some researchers have attempted to elaborate models that take account of these influences (e.g., Steffensmeier and Allan 1996). These predictors had never before been analyzed simultaneously. Steffensmeier and Allan (1996) proposed a model to examine interactional effects among biological and physical differences, gender roles, differential socialization, motivations, and contexts. Their model has not been verified empirically.

The second option in considering gender differences is to refine models already in use in relation to adolescent males (e.g., Broidy and Agnew 1997). This approach investigates the gender gap and the emergence and development of adolescent female deviant behavior. The gender gap observed in the explained variance of mainstream integrative models (Elliott, Huizinga, and Ageton 1985; Segrave and Hastad 1985; Le Blanc, Ouimet, and Tremblay 1988) reflects the relevance of proceeding this way. These models highlight different factors that prompt girls and boys to become involved in deviant behavior, although the predictive capacity is weaker for females.

This gap could be filled by adjusting the dependent variable to make it more representative of behaviors specific to girls. For example, Shoemaker (1994) and Crick and Grotpeter (1995) emphasized the importance of gender differences. They argue that indicators of violence may vary between genders because girls are more likely to be abusive verbally or in a relational context than physically abusive. This does not mean that the dependent variable in studying adolescent females' deviant behavior cannot be the same as is used for adolescent males. The use of a dependent variable specific to females is not warranted because the structure of girls' and boys' deviant behavior is similar, and the gender gap is a question more of level than of type of behavior.

Nonetheless, when testing the applicability of mainstream theories to female samples, adjustments to the measures should be made according to knowledge of gender differences. The dependent variable would then refer to a myriad of deviant activities. Another way to fill this gap is to integrate new concepts that are emerging from studies on gender differences into mainstream integrative models. Adherence to gender roles merits more precise conceptualization and operationalization if it is to be included in a general model of adolescent females' deviant behavior.

This second option is more promising. Identifying factors that account for gender differences is certainly important. However, restricting analyses to differences between girls and boys has some limitations. Studies that apply mainstream theories to female samples show that adolescent females' and males' deviant behavior is related to similar social influences. Hence, many similarities between girls and boys might not be considered if models were based solely on gender differences. At the same time, resorting only to mainstream criminological theories is insufficient. Concepts emerging from the gender-differences perspective are valuable in understanding girls' deviance. Consideration of both perspectives is essential.

IV. A Critical Stand toward Male Criminology

Lack of concern for girls in the development of mainstream criminological theories provoked strong dissatisfaction. Feminist researchers criticized mainstream theories regarding their permeability to values and sexist judgments (Heidensohn 1968; Smart 1976; Harris 1977; Bertrand 1979; Leonard 1982; Naffine 1987; Daly and Chesney-Lind 1988; Chesney-Lind 1989; Chesney-Lind and Shelden 1992; Parent 1998). From the feminist point of view, criminology was based, like other human and social sciences, on male standards, and mainstream theories reflected males' androcentric character. Theories elaborated by males, it was argued, cannot accurately reflect women's experiences. Consequently, mainstream theories were of limited use. For example, Chesney-Lind (1989, p. 10) asserted: "The extensive focus on male delinquency and the inattention to the role played by patriarchal arrangements in the generation of adolescent delinquency and conformity has rendered the major delinquency theories fundamentally inadequate to the task of explaining female behavior. There is, in short, an urgent need to rethink current models in light of girls' situation in a patriarchal society."

Harris (1977), Naffine (1987), and Chesney-Lind and Shelden (1992) discussed the impact of research paradigms created by men and the validity of different criminological theories. Many criticisms were addressed to strain theory. These authors argued that, according to theoretical propositions of Cohen (1955) and Cloward and Ohlin (1960), women should participate more frequently in deviance than men. Chesney-Lind and Shelden (1992) asserted that the various forms of discrimination with which females were confronted should create feelings of frustration. Harris (1977) argued that women should turn more to illegitimate opportunities than men since women's status limits their access to legitimate opportunities. Naffine (1987) argued that feelings of frustration should be more acute for females than for males since females usually find themselves in subordinate positions in the labor market, while males enjoy superior status.

However, these criticisms have not been supported by empirical evidence. Instead, these authors adopted a normative discourse by assuming that women felt limited in their opportunities and that their female status provoked feelings of frustration. Naffine (1987) deplored the fact that middle-class values, referred to by strain theory, were strictly associated with men. She pointed out that ambition, performance, and assertion were values that Cohen (1955) associated with men while inactivity and sensibility characterized women. However, Naffine did not take note of the historic context surrounding the conception of strain theory. The places of women in modern society are not the same as in the 1950s. For instance, Datesman, Scarpitti, and Stephenson (1975) illustrated that females of the seventies were as much preoccupied as males with education and work.

Moreover, showing that theories have been conceived by men and for males is not the main task if the objective is to understand factors that prompt females' deviance. This type of discourse is ubiquitous in the feminist literature. For example, the demonstration of the male construction of knowledge is one way Chesney-Lind and Shelden (1992) try to show that differential-association theory (Sutherland and Cressey 1978) is inappropriate to understanding adolescent females' behavior.

Simons, Miller, and Aigner (1980), however, point out that a theory's elaboration by a man, or its testing on male samples only, does not necessarily imply that it is inapt to understanding female deviance. Females and males interact with each other and live in the same society. Why would they not be vulnerable to similar social influences? Recent empirical studies, discussed above, show that many common social factors encourage the participation of both male and female adolescents in deviant behavior. Exposure to deviant influences is among these factors. Of course, the influence of girls' adhesion to gendered social roles should not be dismissed. For example, even if exposure to delinquent peers leads adolescent females and males to deviance, it may be experienced differently, as discussed earlier in describing adolescent females' roles in gangs.

Criticism has also targeted labeling theory. Harris (1977) questioned the validity of this theory when applied to females. Since it proposes that deviance results from a lack of power of social actors, why do males more than females commit crimes? Harris (1977) reasoned that men are in a better position than women because they enjoy more power. The limited potential of labeling theory to explain female deviance, according to Harris (1977), is the emphasis given to secondary deviance over primary deviance; that few females become involved in deviance is explained not by their capacity to escape formal social control but by the intensity of informal social controls they face.

Naffine (1987) agreed. She relied on Harris (1977) and Schur (1983) to demonstrate that females' conformity is related to social expectations. Naffine asserted that girls and women conform because of the societal message that delinquency is inconsistent with femininity. Social values discourage them from misconduct. Females, therefore, are not stigmatized by the formal agencies of social control but by the values that are daily conveyed in society. This is similar to the explanation suggested by Heimer (1996) and by Heimer and De Coster (1999). Heimer showed that, while identifying with so-called feminine roles, female adolescents tend to set different internal constraints on themselves. They anticipate peer attitudes in a negative way when they violate social rules. Adolescent females are less deviant than boys because their social roles do not encourage deviant acts.

Finally, Hirschi's (1969) social bond theory has been criticized. Naffine (1987) argued that Hirschi did not respect his original logic. Given that he wanted to study conformity, Hirschi should have focused on girls instead of on boys. Naffine pretended that Hirschi's decision must have been modulated by the intellectual conventions of his time when few studies included girls. Naffine also argued that exclusion of adolescent females in the verification of Hirschi's theory showed how much emphasis was put on adolescent males. According to Naffine, this exclusion occurred even when theoreticians pretended that their theories apply to girls and boys. Harris (1977) argued that social bonding theory was incomplete in reference to female delinquency because, controlling for commitment and attachment to social institutions, boys were more delinquent than girls. The empirical tests of control theory with adolescent females, however, although not numerous, show that it applies also to adolescent females (Kempf 1993).

Feminist studies therefore denounced the male construction of knowledge and use of the male experience as a norm. The implicit male point of view, it was said, falsified females' reality. From this perspective, the values and experiences of men cannot accurately represent the realities of women. However, these criticisms relied more on ideological and normative discourse than on empirical evidence. Only a few studies have empirically verified the application of mainstream criminological theories with samples composed of female adolescents, and their applicability for females remains an empirical question (Smith 1979; Simons, Miller, and Aigner 1980; Figueira-McDonough 1985; Smith and Paternoster 1987; Kruttschnitt 1996; Liu and Kaplan 1999). It is premature to reject mainstream theories even if the results for females remain largely unknown: "While acknowledging that the literature on female deviance is both limited and crude, the conclusion that gender-specific theories should be formulated is premature. Since most empirical tests of deviance theories have been conducted with male samples, the applicability of these theories to females is largely unknown. Moreover, the fact that most theories of deviance were constructed to account for male deviance does not mean that they cannot account for female deviance. Before proceeding to develop gender-specific theories, an empirical assessment of the applicability of traditional theories of deviance to explain patterns of female misconduct would be useful" (Smith and Paternoster 1987, p. 142).

Interests defended by feminists explain why little interest is shown in empirical verification of mainstream theories. Most feminist studies are not interested in identifying the individual causes of deviant behavior. Much work instead pays attention to social and penal reactions to females' deviance and to historical and sociopolitical factors that modulated women's roles and oppression. The feminist approach tries to demonstrate that deviant behavior of female adolescents results from their status in patriarchal and capitalist societies (Smart 1976; Daly and Chesney-Lind 1988; Chesney-Lind and Shelden 1992; Parent 1998; DeKeseredy 2000). For example, Artz (1998) maintained that girls' violence is an expression of anger that is provoked by sexist oppression. Violence is then represented as a means to gain power. The main points of the feminist approach were summarized by Daly and Chesney-Lind:

—gender is not a natural fact but a complex social, historical, and cultural product, related to, but not simply derived from, biological sex differences and reproductive capacities;
—gender and gender relations order social life and social institutions in fundamental ways;

—gender relations and constructs of masculinity and femininity are not symmetrical but are based on an organizing principle of men's superiority and social and political-economic dominance over women;

—systems of knowledge reflect men's views of the natural and social world; the production of knowledge is gendered;

—women should be at the center of intellectual inquiry, not peripheral, invisible, or appendages to men. (1988, p. 504)

Pollock (1999) asserted that one main contribution of feminist criminology is the importance given to subjective, qualitative methods of research. The feminist approach considered females in social, economic, and political contexts. Part of the explanation of females' involvement in deviant behavior can be found in the marginal positions occupied by many females in patriarchal societies. Van Wormer and Bartollas (2000, p. 32) go further: the feminist perspective "places the theory in the context of the gender roles of girls in patriarchal society and includes class (poverty) and race (minority status) as part of the oppression and victimization of girls." Pollock (1999) argues that the feminist approach, with its emphasis on life histories and contextual realities, has helped expand knowledge of female deviance.

The most significant recent work within the feminist perspective is identification of females' pathways to deviance (Belknap and Holsinger 1998). During the last decade, some empirical studies have identified a pattern of female deviance that begins with their victimization and eventually results in their involvement in deviant activities (Chesney-Lind and Shelden 1992; Gilfus 1992; Belknap and Holsinger 1998; Pollock 1999). From the feminist standpoint, females' participation in deviance is often seen as a survival strategy to escape from an abusive environment. Gilfus's (1992) qualitative study clearly delineates this pathway. In-depth interviews with twenty incarcerated women produced life histories that were analyzed in an attempt to understand their pathways into street crime. Many of these women were sexually or physically abused during childhood. This prompted women to run away from home during adolescence. Their lack of resources triggered the commission of illicit acts as gang members or in prostitution.

There remains controversy about the nature and the force of links between childhood maltreatment and subsequent deviance, but that childhood abuse increases girls' risk of deviance cannot be denied (Alfaro 1981; Widom 1991; Smith and Thornberry 1995; Belknap and

Holsinger 1998; Dougherty 1998). A literature review by Chesney-Lind and Shelden (1992) showed that prevalence rates of physical and sexual abuse among delinquent girls in the juvenile justice system varied between 40 percent and 73 percent. A history of childhood maltreatment, especially sexual abuse, seems to be a significant experience in the lives of many prostitutes (Silbert and Pines 1981; O'Neill 1996; Widom 1996). Silbert and Pines (1981), examining the relation between childhood sexual abuse and prostitution, interviewed 200 current and former prostitutes ages ten to forty-six years old in the San Francisco Bay area. Sixty percent reported sexual abuse before age sixteen.

Rates of teenage pregnancy are also higher among adolescent females with a history of childhood maltreatment. Lanctôt and Smith's (2001) multivariate analysis revealed an official report of child maltreatment to be among the significant predictors of adolescent pregnancy. The data were from the Rochester Youth Development Study based on an analysis of 196 African-American adolescent female seventh and eighth graders in public schools in Rochester, New York, in the spring of 1988.

The existence of a relationship between child abuse and juvenile delinquency is not a new idea. Despite this link, Belknap and Holsinger (1998, p. 32) asserted that "it is interesting and somewhat disturbing, however, how little attention the child-abuse-victim-to-offender link has received and how it has often focused on boys." Consideration of the risk of abuse appears to be essential in order to improve our understanding of females' involvement in deviance. This link between victimization and deviance has been nearly invisible in mainstream and gender-differences criminological theories.

Feminist works attempted to highlight females' values, perceptions, and experiences. Control of men's violence, domination, and oppression toward women represented a main concern. Any comprehensive explanation of adolescent females' involvement in deviant behavior must take account of past and present victimization.

V. Challenges and Prospects

The raison d'être of this essay is to assess knowledge about adolescent females' involvement in deviance. This knowledge has rapidly grown during the last decade. The growth is observable in the number of publications and in the diversity of methodologies and theoretical advances. Mainstream, gender-differences, and feminist points of view produced this knowledge. Each perspective has produced a large number of quantitative and qualitative studies. Concepts and methodologies emerging from each perspective have contributed to understanding adolescent females' deviance. The three perspectives proposed a large array of theoretical concepts to explain adolescent females' deviance. What are the gaps in this knowledge? It is impossible to answer completely this question. We limit ourselves to analysis of the behavior of adolescent females as individuals and to questions that can be investigated by use of longitudinal and cross-sectional designs.

A. The Initiation and Development of Adolescent Females' Deviance

Our assessment of current knowledge was dominated by one question: Is there a gender gap? First, we demonstrated that there is a clear and undoubted gender gap. Second, we concluded that the deviance syndrome applies to females even if not with the same robustness as for males. Third, we suggest that preliminary observations support the existence of the same developmental processes for both sexes. Fourth and finally, we showed that females' developmental trajectories can be identified and that they are comparable to the main male trajectories. In sum, we concluded that the gender gap takes the form of differences in degree rather than in differences in types of behavior. Overall, adolescent females are more or less involved than males in deviant behavior, depending on the behaviors under analysis. Equivalent structures of the latent deviance construct can be elaborated for adolescent females and males. Continuity in deviant behavior characterizes females as well as males but with less durability. However, the development of deviance seems to be governed by the same mechanisms of activation and aggravation as for males. Finally, although adolescent females are less deviant than males, a certain proportion follow similar pathways, such as occasional, adolescence-limited, and life-course persistent deviance.

These observations lead to the following objectives for future research. Researchers should focus on in-depth understanding of females' deviance rather than on the gender gap. Leschied and colleagues (2000) arrive at the same conclusion in their review of adolescent females' violence. This means that comparisons of females and males should no longer be a priority. Researchers should focus on representative samples of females and especially on high-risk samples.

High-risk samples are essential because all forms of deviant behaviors will display much higher prevalence rates compared with representative samples. Prevalence rates for most forms of deviant behavior are low for adolescent females, and statistical analyses are much more robust with higher prevalence rates. Moretti and Odgers (2001) argue that research from representative and clinical samples can produce knowledge if researchers will devote careful thought to divergent results from different types of samples. Purposive samples can serve as microscopes to enlarge our view of the emergence and development of female deviance.

There have been few longitudinal studies of females. More such studies are needed to assess continuities in deviance between phases of the life course. Some scant data exist between childhood and adolescence and between adolescence and adulthood. However, we found no data connecting these three phases of the life course. Longitudinal data are needed on deviant behavior in general, but also on each dimension of problem behavior and of delinquency across the life span. Particularly, it is essential to assess the developmental comorbidity between forms of deviance. Another challenge is to analyze the heterotypic hypothesis, that deviance manifests itself under different forms of behavior at each phase of the life course, and the homeotypic hypothesis, that deviance can be assessed by the same measures during each phase of the life course. Thus, we need to measure deviance in the same way and in different ways during different phases of the life course to assess the proportion of the development that is heterotypic or homeotypic.

Continuity of deviant behavior is only one of its aspects that should be analyzed according to the developmental criminology paradigm (Le Blanc and Loeber 1998). We also need to assess the developmental processes that support females' deviant behaviors. Empirical evidence remains lacking that would allow us with confidence to state that early onset of delinquency activates adolescent females' offending or increases its frequency, duration, and variety over time. Some data show these hypotheses to be tenable, but there are no data concerning specific types of deviant behavior (e.g., drug use or violence). In addition, developmental sequences and the processes of escalation are well established for some specific types of females' deviant activities, such as drug use. The challenge is to learn if this type of sequence, or escalation, can be observed for other problem behaviors and delinquent activities.

Analysis of adolescent females' deviant behavioral continuity and developmental processes leads to another challenge: the identification of females' pathways through deviance. Some preliminary data support the hypothesis that there are multiple trajectories and that the three main pathways long known in criminology apply to females. These pathways are occasional, temporary, and persistent deviant behavior. However, data on pathways are insufficient because they concern mainly childhood and adolescence and leave out adulthood. Available data do not evaluate offending in depth nor do they consider specific forms of deviant behavior. Consequently, the domain of research surrounding adolescent females' deviant pathways is wide open for explorations and replications.

Concerning desistance, current knowledge indicates that adolescent females end their official criminal careers earlier than do adolescent males. However, we do not know if this conclusion holds for all types of deviant activities. The dynamic process leading to the desistance of adolescent females' from deviance is also largely unknown. Many questions remain unanswered. One challenge is to establish whether females' desistance from deviance is accompanied by a reduction in the frequency of offending (de-escalation), by a decrease in seriousness of offending, and by increased specialization of offending. In addition, to our knowledge there are no data on females' desistance from drug use and from other problem behaviors. Another challenge is to analyze desistance from specific behaviors.

In summary, the initiation and development of females' deviance is a wide-open domain for empirical research. Descriptive data concerning the entire life course and various manifestations of deviance should be collected and analyzed. More important, these descriptive analyses should be replicated across samples and over time. The research agenda should not focus primarily on gathering descriptive data from cross-sectional explanatory research, since we already know how to measure females' deviant behavior during various life-course phases, particularly adolescence. Description of the developmental mechanisms of females' deviant behavior is, however, essential and preliminary to the formulation and verification of developmental theories.

B. Integrative Models: A Promising Avenue

The literature on development of knowledge concerning explanations of adolescent females' deviant behavior permits identification of strengths and weaknesses particular to each of the mainstream, gender-differences, and feminist theoretical perspectives. Even if some studies conducted within the gender-differences perspective use concepts from mainstream theories, there is a deficiency that is common to all three perspectives: an absence of theoretical integration.

In criminology, there is considerable debate about the potential of theoretical integration (e.g., Messner, Krohn, and Liska 1989). We accept, as do some contributors to that book, that substantive integration is extremely difficult, even impossible. Many axioms of various theories are incompatible. However, we agree with other contributors that integration is possible via the elaboration of models. Le Blanc (1997a) proposed such a model. Models can import constructs from various theories and test their relative usefulness. Evidence from our literature review supports that view.

First, studies conducted to test mainstream criminological theories showed that involvement of girls and boys in deviance is partly explained by the same factors. Correlations between explanatory variables of mainstream theories and deviant behaviors are usually similar for adolescent females and males. Weakness of social bonds and exposure to delinquent peers received strong and consistent empirical support. However, although application of mainstream theories seems appropriate to study of females, these theories do not consider gender differences.

Second, studies solely focusing on gender differences identified several dissimilarities between girls and boys concerning biological capacities, social roles, or contexts in which deviant activities are performed. These studies show that explanatory factors of deviance must be qualified according to their differential effects in relation to gender. However, the identification of factors of differentiation, such as sex role identification and socialization, is insufficient for understanding of the emergence and development of girls' deviant behavior.

Third, the feminist approach is much less interested in explaining individual conduct than in identifying structural factors that modulate interactions between gender and the influence of penal reactions on girls' misbehaviors. However, the feminist perspective has recently identified a pathway toward deviance. This pathway, that aims to explain girls' individual conducts, defines girls' involvement in deviance as a survival strategy. Several studies have pointed to important determinants of females' adolescent deviance, notably a history of victimization.

Because this essay is concerned with explanation of adolescent females' involvement in deviant behavior, combination of the three perspectives appears particularly promising. Mainstream criminological theories can act as a reference frame for the choice of construct, with adjustments based on knowledge pertaining to gender differences. Finally, integration into models of constructs developed by the feminist approach may prove essential because of their specificity to females' issues. This integrative effort should not be limited to combination of different constructs used to explain female adolescents' deviant behavior. Concepts used to explain males' deviance should also be considered. According to Thornberry (1997), refinement of theoretical concepts and the elaboration of integrative and developmental theories have improved our understanding of boys' misconduct. Such developments are promising for girls.

It is now time to propose a model that could guide future research. First, Magnusson (1988) demonstrated the importance of considering individuals not as static human beings but as beings in constant evolution. The first criterion that the integrative model must meet is its capacity to analyze the individual factors that influence deviant behavior longitudinally. Second, Magnusson (1988) argued that relations between the individual components that influence behavior must not be analyzed unidirectionally since these components interact. The integrative model must be able to evaluate the reciprocity of relations of interacting explanatory factors. Third, Magnusson (1988) suggested that the individual interacts continuously with his or her environment. Consequently, the integrative model should display the different domains of life surrounding and influencing the development of female adolescents. Family, school, and peers must then be included. Fourth, and finally, Magnusson (1988) indicated that the quality of interactions with the social environment cannot be analyzed independently from the biological and personal capacities of individuals. The integrative model has to combine these components. Moretti and Odgers (2001) plead for proposals and tests of such developmental and interactional models for females.

Le Blanc's (1997a) integrative model meets these criteria. It formulates interaction effects among biological, personal, and social components of the individual in a developmental perspective in order to explain the emergence and development of deviant behavior. Six major constructs are proposed: social status, biological capacity, bonds, self-control, constraints, and prosocial influences. Thornberry (1997) has acknowledged the model's scientific value, and it has been tested with male samples (Le Blanc, Ouimet, and Tremblay 1988; Le Blanc 1997b). The model we propose for explanation of adolescent females' deviant behavior is therefore constructed around this framework. It is inspired mainly by social control theory. This theory stipulates that deviant behavior results from deficiencies in control mechanisms. This perspective blends easily with explanations of female adolescent's deviant behavior; the literature gives great importance to social control of girls and has done so since Parsons's (1947) initial writing on this subject. This model posits that conformity to conventional standards of behavior occurs and persists if an appropriate level of self-control exists and the bond to society is firm, and if external and internal constraints are appropriate and models of behavior are prosocial. The personal and social regulation of conformity is conditioned by the biological capacities of the person and his or her position in the social structure.

Mainstream theories stress the importance of social status, that is, the position of the individual in the social structure. This constitutes the first contextual condition that affects the development of bonds to society and exposure to prosocial influences. Whether social status is operationalized in terms of social class or socioeconomic strain, it will be a remote explanation of adolescent females' deviance. This construct should be maintained in an integrative model even if researchers have to change its operationalization as society changes. In addition, if high-risk samples are used, measures of welfare dependency may be more efficient than measures of social class.

Gender difference studies demonstrate the usefulness of the biological construct. This construct, operationalized in terms of physical and sexual maturity, should be tested in relation to other constructs to explain adolescent females' deviance. Le Blanc's model posits that precocity in this domain will affect the appropriate development of self-control and of bonding and limit peers' prosocial influences. In consequence, adolescent females will be more likely to be deviant and more likely to persist in deviance.

We could add a concept from the feminist perspective to the model: females' experiences of victimization. One of the most significant weaknesses of mainstream theories is their lack of concern for the oppressions some females experience. It would then be necessary to adjust Le Blanc's model to evaluate the influence of this set of factors on deviant behavior. A component related to troubling life events that might influence the development of female adolescents will allow the reconciliation of the interests of feminist works with those of mainstream criminology. Broidy and Agnew (1997) enumerated different situations that might affect the development of female adolescents: physical or sexual victimization, abortion, single parenthood, and requirements related to the roles of spouse and mother. This fits nicely with Le Blanc's model because Broidy and Agnew (1997) specify that the relation between these difficult life events and deviant behavior is mediated by a variety of factors such as social bonds, attitudes toward social rules, and exposure to delinquent peers.

Social bonds are an inescapable concept in modeling adolescent females' deviant behavior. An individual's bond to society manifests itself toward several institutions constituting the different spheres of a person's world (Hirschi 1969; Kempf 1993; Le Blanc and Caplan 1993). Three institutions receive particular emphasis for adolescents: family, school, and peers. Adolescents relate to these institutions through two avenues: attachment to persons and commitment to institutions. There are at least three categories of attachment figures: parents, peers, and persons in positions of informal authority.

An individual's level of attachment to conventional individuals determines his level of attachment to peers and to persons in positions of informal authority. The cumulative effect of these bonds protects the individual against criminal influences and discourages occasional and persistent deviance.

The second element of the bond is commitment to institutions. An individual's commitment to institutions develops toward school, religion, work, or success, and so on. Commitment refers to acceptance of an institution, an affective investment. Conversely, deviant behavior is costly for that investment. When a person faces the temptation to deviate, she must evaluate the costs of her behavior relative to the investment she has made. The proposed model posits that development of bonds with society may be more difficult when the adolescent female lives in adverse socioeconomic conditions, experiences an inharmonious physical and sexual development, was victimized, and displays low self-control. Contrarily, the strength of the bond should protect adolescent females against deviant peers' influence and deviant behavior.

The criminological literature documents the importance of individual differences in the emergence and development of individual deviant behavior. Social control theorists are now considering psychological dimensions more explicitly. Gottfredson and Hirschi (1990) proposed a construct of low self-control as an integral part of control theory. In our view, this construct is too narrow to represent the various psychological traits that are associated with individual offending. It refers only to vulnerability to the temptation of the moment and assumes that individuals with low self-control are impulsive, insensible, physical, risk taking, shortsighted, and nonverbal. If criminologists want to replace concepts such as criminal personality or antisocial personality with the concept of self-control, they should enlarge the construct of low self-control. It should include all dimensions of personality that refer to its social, affective, moral, relational, and cognitive components. Using a more comprehensive concept of self-control that includes these components, Le Blanc's model posits that normal development of self-control favors the establishment of strong bonds with society, receptivity to social constraints, and preference for prosocial influences, and, in turn, encourages conformity to conventional standards of behavior. However, the level of self-control is dependent on individual biological capacity and varies with victimization experiences.

Le Blanc's model integrates internal and external constraints following Durkheim's (1934) classic distinction between norms and discipline. Norms are defined as rules that come from law and from moral values, while discipline is characterized by monitoring and punishment.

External constraints are of two categories, formal and informal. Labeling theory proponents fully elaborate on the dimension of formal external constraints, particularly through the impact of the official label of delinquent (a position supported by the feminist perspective), while bonding theory supporters develop the dimension of informal external constraints, particularly through parental monitoring and discipline.

Internal constraints are of two categories: beliefs and perceptions of sanctions. Social control theorists elaborate the notion of internal constraint under the concept of beliefs in social norms and under the concept of perceived certainty and severity of sanctions, a notion borrowed from deterrence theorists. Le Blanc's model posits that the adolescent's internalization of external constraints depends on the quality of his or her bond to society, his or her level of self-control, and his or her exposure to strong prosocial influences. Internal constraints are one of the most proximal barriers against deviant behavior. When constraints are inappropriate to the age of the person, erratic, or absent, they constitute direct and proximal causes of deviant behavior.

An adequate explanation of adolescent females' deviant behavior must take into account internal and external constraints. Heimer (1996) confirms that for females the influence of internal constraints on deviance is greater than the influence of external constraints. Le Blanc (1995) observed similar results for males. Heimer shows that

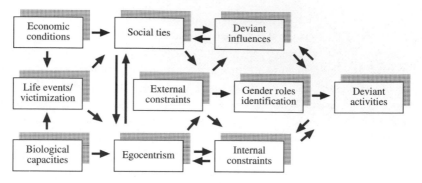

Fɪɢ. 3.—Personal and social regulation of female adolescents' deviance

participation of females in deviant behavior is largely governed by the values and attitudes they have internalized. In this regard, the gender difference literature proposes an interesting link between internalization of social norms and adherence to so-called feminine gender roles. Heimer (1996) points out that the internalization of gender roles is made in a similar fashion as the internalization of attitudes about other rules and social standards. We propose to include an independent component to the constraints construct: beliefs related to gender roles. In consequence, female adolescents' beliefs in gender roles act as a moral obstacle to deviant behavior. The less adolescent females believe they should obey the gendered rules of society, the greater the probability they will deviate from social norms.

Our literature review makes clear the importance of concepts and measures proposed by differential association theory. Le Blanc's model is broader. It posits that an adolescent is exposed to deviant influences not only through affiliation with delinquent peers but through the nature of the deviant subcultures that are present in his community, through television and video viewing, through parental deviance and criminality, and through routine activities. Many empirical studies of adolescent females have demonstrated that exposure to deviant influences is a direct and proximal cause of their deviant behavior.

Figure 3 schematizes the proposed model. Figure 3 also hypothesizes cross-sectional and longitudinal relations between the nine proposed constructs: economic conditions, biological capacities, difficult life events/victimization, social ties, egocentrism, external constraints, internal constraints, gender roles identification, and deviant influences.

Figure 3 predicts that precarious economic conditions may produce more difficult life events for adolescent females. These life events can be sexual or physical abuse, parental negligence, dropping out of school, adolescent pregnancy, or single parenthood. Adolescent females living in such situations would be expected to display more difficulties bonding to social institutions and their members. For example, a girl abused in her family would likely maintain weaker bonds with her parents, or a young female single parent would be less committed to her schooling. Confrontation with possible troubling life events would also affect the adolescent female's capacity to solve problems with socially approved means. This characteristic could be transposed into a low level of self-control. For example, an abused girl could maintain feelings of mistrust toward others, or she could have cognitive deficits prompting her to use violence to solve her interpersonal problems. Self-control would then also be affected by problematic biological conditions, whether cognitive or physical. These biological conditions can lead to specific life events. For example, conventional peers might tend to reject girls who reach their sexual maturity at an early age, and these girls might be more at risk of sexual victimization.

The seven components at the center of the model interact directly and indirectly with one another. We list only a few of these interactions because criminologists can imagine all the others. The model predicts that the adolescent female's deficient social bonds facilitate her exposure to deviant influences and weaken her receptivity to external constraints. Hence, the bonds adolescent females form with their school, peers, or boyfriends should be analyzed in greater depth. Adolescent females' low self-control hinders establishment of solid relationships with others and reduces their receptivity to rules and social standards. Insufficient formal and informal controls facilitate adolescent females' association with negative social peers and do not favor development of internal barriers to deviance. Rejection of beliefs surrounding feminine gender roles would increase receptivity to antisocial influences, weaken prosocial bonds, hinder development of self-control, and favor emergence and aggravation of deviant behavior.

Finally, the shadowed boxes hiding behind each of the components of figure 3 represent ages or phases of the life course. These boxes illustrate the possibility of evaluating the behaviors of girls in a longitudinal standpoint. This remains virtually unexplored in scientific works on female adolescents. Only Thornberry and his collaborators (1991) and Heimer (1996) verified the influence of females' social adaptation at more than one period during adolescence. These studies concluded that social influences strengthen one another as years go by. Thornberry and colleagues (1991) also evaluated the effects of delinquent behavior on the quality of individuals' social adaptation. However, these researchers used gender only as a control variable. The impact of girls' deviant behavior on personal and social development has thus never been evaluated specifically for female adolescents. Furthermore, a developmental analysis would not only specify factors that predispose to deviance but would also identify factors that favor withdrawal from these activities. For example, if the commitment to maladjusted behavior decreases at the end of the teenage years or at the beginning of adulthood, it might be because new life events are experienced in such a way that social and personal controls get stronger. Numerous life events can happen during the last part of adolescence (living in couples, pregnancy, entering the labor market, or choosing a career), and their influence deserves to be analyzed. This model in whole or part can guide empirical research or help in the revision of theories. Resort to this model may be interesting for many researchers interested in females' involvement in deviance since all the constructs composing the model have been used in studies concerning female adolescent deviance.

VI. Conclusion

Female adolescents' involvement in deviance should be discussed within three theoretical perspectives. The first perspective relies on the applicability of mainstream criminological theories. The second perspective focuses on gender differences. The third perspective adopts a critical perspective by emphasizing the male-dominated construction of knowledge. Instead of trying to determine which perspective offers the most comprehensive understanding of adolescent female deviant behavior, we address the question differently: Which main explanatory concepts can we retain from each theoretical perspective?

Before answering this question, we investigated the gender gap in deviant behavior. Four themes were reviewed: the comparison of female and male patterns of involvement in deviance, the applicability of the deviance syndrome to female adolescents, the existence of the same developmental processes for both sexes, and the identification of females' developmental trajectories in deviance. The gender gap exists and takes the form of differences in degree rather than differences in types of behavior. Adolescent females are more or less involved in deviant behavior depending on the nature of deviant behavior. The structure of the deviance construct is comparable for both sexes. Even if there is less continuity and often a later onset of deviant behavior for adolescent females, stability is important. This continuity seems to be governed, as it is for males, by the mechanisms of activation and aggravation. Finally, comparable pathways into deviance are observed for females and males.

These observations lead to the following question: Do theories have to be different for females and males? Mainstream theories assert that the same theoretical concepts and operational definitions can be used for the explanation of adolescent deviance for both genders. The feminist perspective takes the opposite position: criminology needs to create a specific explanation for an adequate understanding of female deviance. The gender difference perspective takes an in-between position. Some of the concepts of the mainstream theories have to be supplemented by concepts of the gender difference tradition.

The best solution consists of integrating the main concepts of the three perspectives into a single theoretical model. These perspectives have contributed to the development of knowledge concerning female adolescents' deviance. Why not go beyond the level of confrontation and take advantage of the knowledge represented by these different perspectives? This is what the integrative model we proposed envisages. Mainstream criminological theories could be used as a reference frame in order to choose concepts for construction of the model. Adjustments should be made according to knowledge pertaining to gender differences and to experiences to which females are vulnerable, like victimization. The model we suggest is heuristic. Many researchers can build models with some, if not all, of the constructs that we propose, and test them. Even if all the constructs are not available in their data bank, there will be a buildup of knowledge explaining adolescent females' deviance. Comparison of these models will be as fruitful as it was for explanations of adolescent males' deviance.

The principal feature of this guiding model is methodological. The empirical tests are multivariate and longitudinal. This strategy is incompatible with the feminist epistemology. This epistemology holds that researchers must stand up for the well-being of females (Harding 1987, 1991). Even if this objective is legitimate, the feminist methodology has been exposed to many criticisms. From the feminist standpoint, doing research becomes a political commitment. The feminist approach, mostly transposed into qualitative methodology, has often been characterized as being more ideological than scientific (Parent

1998; Oakley 2000). When considering the main criticism addressed by feminists to mainstream criminology, that males' values represent an obstacle to the comprehension of females' realities, how can feminists pretend not to bias the realities of females if they stand up unconditionally for them? This strategy has led feminists on to slippery ground.

The strategy we propose is different since it relies on the solid empirical tradition of criminology. In our opinion, using the positivist standards allows, as does the feminist strategy, an opening to the complexity of human beings. However, the methodology we favor aims at conducting studies with quantitative methods—more precisely, multivariate methods. This methodology has recently received support from the feminist perspective (Oakley 2000). These methods will not only allow the identification of girls' risk factors but also a better understanding of how these factors interact. Longitudinal analyses will offer opportunities to improve criminological knowledge on the continuity and consequences of participating in deviant behavior. The explanation of adolescent females' deviance is characterized by complexity. There is a large gap between our perception of the complexities of these interactions, our discursive statements of these phenomena, our operational models describing them, and the results of empirical tests.

The factors explaining that gap between these levels of apprehension of reality are numerous. They include insufficiency of empirical knowledge about female deviance and its possible explanatory factors, researchers' cognitive capacities to consider simultaneously many factors from different levels of explanation in continuous interactions, researchers' abilities to communicate their perceptions of these interactions, availability of an appropriate technology to model the interactions, and researchers' difficulty communicating intelligibly the complexity of the interactions between explanatory factors.

In this essay, we consider and manage the complexity of females' deviance rather than simplify this reality. In doing so we are relatively inefficient for at least four categories of reasons: the proposed explanatory model is incomplete, its constructs are difficult to operationalize, its measures may be deficient, and researchers' strategies and methods of analysis may be inadequate. Independent of these reasons, we think that we are inefficient because our theories and models are linear, even if they are sometimes interactional and recursive (see, e.g., Thornberry 1996) or if they consider multiple levels of explanations (Le Blanc 1997*a*). Even these models do not take completely into account numerous and complex interactions and the random component that is part of development. These theories and models suffer from two difficulties: considering the maximum possible number of perceived interactions and integrating a random component in the development of deviance and explanatory factors.

In this essay, we explore a new way of overcoming these difficulties. This approach, from both theoretical and methodological points of view, necessitates an integration of the different perspectives used to explain girls' involvement in deviant activities. Thus, confrontation between these perspectives should be put aside. This way of studying female adolescents' deviance also necessitates an examination of the evolution of the literature dealing with boys' involvement in deviance.

Does dissatisfaction regarding the masculine construction of knowledge justify the literature on adolescent female deviance's ignoring the progress made in mainstream criminology? Our proposed new way of analyzing females' deviance implies the use of multivariate statistics in order to evaluate more precisely the interactions between different concepts or, stated differently, the complexity of adolescent females' involvement in deviance. The feminist discourse may have to be renewed: rather than staying away from mainstream criminology and from quantitative criminology and modeling, it would be better, in our opinion, if that perspective could recognize the benefits that the mainstream approach can have for understanding females' lives and experiences. The maintenance of a critical stance is a substantial contribution of feminist perspective. This is why we believe that these approaches should be better integrated in further studies on deviance among adolescent females.

REFERENCES

Ackley, E. G., and B. R. Fliegel. 1960. "A Social Work Approach to Street-Corner Girls." *Social Work* 5(4):27–36.

Adler, F. 1975. *Sisters in Crime: The Rise of the New Female Criminal.* New York: McGraw-Hill.

Ageton, S. S. 1983. "The Dynamics of Female Delinquency, 1976–1980." *Criminology* 21(4):555–84.

Agnew, R. 1992. "Foundation for a General Strain Theory of Crime and Delinquency." *Criminology* 30(1):47–87.

Alfaro, J. D. 1981. "Report on the Relationship between Child Abuse and Neglect and Later Socially Deviant Behavior." In *Exploring the Relationship between Child Abuse and Delinquency*, edited by R. J. Hunner and Y. E. Walker. Montclair, N.J.: Allanheld, Osmun.

American Psychiatric Association. 1994. *Diagnostic and Statistical Manuals for Mental Disorders*. 4th ed. Washington, D.C.: American Psychiatric Association.

Anderson, B. J., M. D. Holmes, and E. Ostresh. 1999. "Male and Female Delinquents' Attachments and Effects of Attachments on Severity of Self-Reported Delinquency." *Criminal Justice and Behavior* 26(4):435–52.

Artz, S. 1998. *Sex, Power, and the Violent School Girl*. Toronto: Trifolium.

Artz, S., and D. Nicholson. 2001. "Understanding Aggressive Girls in Canada: A Literature Review." Report prepared for the National Clearinghouse on Family Violence, Health Canada, Vancouver.

Ary, D. V., T. E. Duncan, A. Biglan, C. W. Metzler, J. W. Noell, and K. Smolkowski. 1999. "Development of Adolescent Problem Behavior." *Journal of Abnormal Child Psychology* 27:141–50.

Ayers, C. D., H. Williams, J. D. Hawkins, P. L. Peterson, R. F. Catalano, and R. D. Abbott. 1999. "Assessing Correlates of Onset, Escalation, and Desistance of Delinquent Behavior." *Journal of Quantitative Criminology* 15: 277–305.

Bardone, A. M., T. E. Moffitt, A. Caspi, N. Dickson, and P. A. Silva. 1996. "Adult Mental Health and Social Outcomes of Adolescent Girls with Depression and Conduct Disorder." *Development and Psychopathology* 8:811–29.

Bartusch, D. J., and R. L. Matsueda. 1996. "Gender, Reflected Appraisals, and Labeling: A Cross-Group Test of an Interactionist Theory of Delinquency." *Social Forces* 75(1):145–77.

Bartusch, D. R. J., D. R. Lynam, T. E. Moffitt, and P. A. Silva. 1997. "Is Age Important? Testing a General versus a Developmental Theory of Antisocial Behavior." *Criminology* 35:13–48.

Becker, H. S. 1963. *Outsiders: Studies in the Sociology of Deviance*. London: Collier-Macmillan.

Belknap, J., and K. Holsinger. 1998. "An Overview of Delinquent Girls: How Theory and Practice Have Failed and the Need for Innovative Changes." In *Female Offenders: Critical Perspectives and Effective Interventions*, edited by R. T. Zaplin. Gaithersburg, Md.: Aspen.

Benda, B. B., and R. F. Corwyn. 1998. "Adolescent Deviant Behavior: Multiple Contingency Table Analyses of Overlap between Behaviors." *Journal of Social Service Review* 24(1):29–59.

Bertrand, M. A. 1979. *La femme et le crime*. Montreal: Editions L'univers.

Beutel, A. M., and M. M. Marini. 1995. "Gender and Values." *American Sociological Review* 60(3):436–48.

Biron, L., R. Gagnon, and M. Le Blanc. 1980. *La délinquance des filles*. Groupe de Recherche sur l'Inadaptation Juvénile. Montreal: University of Montreal.

Bjerregaard, B., and C. Smith. 1993. "Gender Differences in Gang Participation and Delinquency." *Journal of Quantitative Criminology* 9(4):329–55.

Block, C. R., and C. van der Werff. 1987. "Career Criminals in the Netherlands." Paper presented at the meeting of the American Society of Criminology, Montreal, November, 1987.

Bottcher, J. 1995. "Gender as Social Control: A Qualitative Study of Incarcerated Youths and Their Siblings in Greater Sacramento." *Justice Quarterly* 12:33–57.

———. 2001. "Social Practices of Gender: How Gender Relates to Delinquency in the Everyday Lives of High-Risk Youths." *Criminology* 39(4): 893–931.

Bowker, L. H. 1981. *Women and Crime in America*. New York: Macmillan.

Broidy, L., and R. Agnew. 1997. "Gender and Crime: A General Strain Theory Perspective." *Journal of Research in Crime and Delinquency* 34(3):275–306.

Brown, W. K. 1977. "Black Female Gangs in Philadelphia." *International Journal of Offender Therapy and Comparative Criminology* 21(3):221–28.

Brownfield, D., and A. M. Sorenson. 1987. "A Latent Structure Analysis of Delinquency." *Journal of Quantitative Criminology* 3(1):103–24.

Brunson, R. K., and J. Miller. 2001. "Girls and Gangs." In *Women, Crime, and Criminal Justice: Original Feminist Readings*, edited by C. M. Renzetti and L. Goodstein. Los Angeles: Roxbury.

Bureau of Justice Statistics. 1999. *Sourcebook of Criminal Justice Statistics*. Washington, D.C.: U.S. Government Publishing Office.

Burkett, S. R., and E. L. Jensen. 1975. "Conventional Ties, Peer Influence, and the Fear of Apprehension: A Study of Adolescent Marijuana Use." *Sociological Quarterly* 16(4):522–33.

Campbell, A. 1984a. "Girl's Talk: The Social Representation of Aggression by Female Gang Members." *Criminal Justice and Behavior* 11(2):139–56.

———. 1984b. *The Girls in the Gangs*. Oxford: Blackwell.

———. 1987. "Self-Reported Delinquency and Home Life: Evidence from a Sample of British Girls." *Journal of Youth and Adolescence* 16(2):167–77.

———. 1993. *Men, Women, and Aggression*. New York: Basic.

Canter, R. J. 1982a. "Family Correlates of Male and Female Delinquency." *Criminology* 20(2):149–67.

———. 1982b. "Sex Differences in Self-Report Delinquency." *Criminology* 20(3):373–93.

Capaldi, D. M., and G. R. Patterson. 1989. *Psychometric Properties of Fourteen Latent Constructs from the Oregon Youth Study*. New York: Springer.

Cario, R. 1992. *Femmes et criminelles*. Toulouse: Erès.

Caspi, A., D. Lynam, T. E. Moffit, and P. A. Silva. 1993. "Unraveling Girl's Delinquency: Biological, Dispositional, and Contextual Contributions to Adolescent Misbehavior." *Developmental Psychology* 29(1):19–30.

Caspi, A., and T. E. Moffitt. 1991. "Individual Differences Are Accentuated during Periods of Social Change: The Sample Case of Girls at Puberty." *Journal of Personality and Social Psychology* 61(1):157–68.

Cernkovich, S. A., and P. C. Giordano. 1979a. "A Comparative Analysis of Male and Female Delinquency." *Sociological Quarterly* 20(1):131–45.

———. 1979b. "Delinquency, Opportunity, and Gender." *Journal of Criminal Law and Criminology* 70(2):145–51.

———. 1987. "Family Relationships and Delinquency." *Criminology* 25(2): 295–321.

Chesney-Lind, M. 1989. "Girls' Crime and Woman's Place: Toward a Feminist Model of Female Delinquency." *Crime and Delinquency* 35:5–29.

———. 2001. " 'Out of Sight, Out of Mind': Girls in the Juvenile Justice System." In *Women, Crime, and Criminal Justice: Original Feminist Readings*, edited by C. M. Renzetti and L. Goodstein. Los Angeles: Roxbury.

Chesney-Lind, M., and R. G. Shelden. 1992. *Girls, Delinquency and Juvenile Justice.* Pacific Grove, Calif.: Brooks/Cole.

———. 1998. *Girls, Delinquency and Juvenile Justice.* 2d ed. Belmont, Calif.: West/Wadsworth.

Chodorow, N. 1978. *The Reproduction of Mothering: Psychoanalysis and the Sociology of Gender.* Berkeley: University of California Press.

Cloward, R. A., and L. E. Ohlin. 1960. *Delinquency and Opportunity: A Theory of Delinquent Gangs.* Glencoe, Ill.: Free Press.

Cohen, A. K. 1955. *Delinquent Boys: The Culture of the Gang.* Glencoe, Ill.: Free Press.

Côté, S., M. Zoccolillo, R. E. Tremblay, and D. Nagin. 2001. "Predicting Girls' Conduct Disorder in Adolescence from Childhood Trajectories of Disruptive Behaviors." *Journal of the American Academy of Child and Adolescent Psychiatry* 40:678–84.

Crick, N. R., M. A. Bigbee, and C. Howes. 1996. "Gender Differences in Children's Normative Beliefs about Aggression: How Do I Hurt Thee? Let Me Count the Ways." *Child Development* 67:1003–14.

Crick, N. R., and J. K. Grotpeter. 1995. "Relational Aggression, Gender, and Social-Psychological Adjustment." *Child Development* 66:710–22.

Cullen, F. T., K. M. Golden, and J. B. Cullen. 1979. "Sex and Delinquency: A Partial Test of the Masculinity Hypothesis." *Criminology* 17(3):301–10.

Daly, K., and M. Chesney-Lind. 1988. "Feminism and Criminology." *Justice Quarterly* 5:497–535.

Datesman, S. K., F. R. Scarpitti, and R. M. Stephenson. 1975. "Female Delinquency: An Application of Self and Opportunity Theories." *Journal of Research in Crime and Delinquency* 12(2):107–23.

DeKeseredy, W. S. 2000. *Women, Crime and the Canadian Criminal Justice System.* Cincinnati: Anderson.

Dembo, R., L. Williams, W. Wothke, J. Schmeidler, A. Getreu, E. Berry, and E. D. Wish. 1992. "The Generality of Deviance: Replication of a Structural Model among High-Risk Youths." *Journal of Research in Crime and Delinquency* 29(2):200–216.

Donovan, J. E., and R. Jessor. 1985. "Structure of Problem Behavior in Adolescence and Young Adulthood." *Journal of Consulting and Clinical Psychology* 53(6):890–904.

Donovan, J. E., R. Jessor, and F. M. Costa. 1988. "Structure of Problem Behavior in Adolescents: A Replication." *Journal of Consulting and Clinical Psychology* 56(5):762–65.

Dougherty, J. 1998. "Female Offenders and Childhood Maltreatment: Understanding the Connections." In *Female Offenders: Critical Perspectives and Effective Interventions*, edited by R. T. Zaplin. Gaithersburg, Md.: Aspen Publishers.

Dunford, F. W., and D. S. Elliott. 1984. "Identifying Career Offenders Using Self-Reported Data." *Journal of Research in Crime and Delinquency* 21(1):57–86.

Durkheim, E. 1934. *L'éducation morale*. Paris: Universitaires de France.

Eagly, A. H., and V. J. Steffen. 1986. "Gender and Aggressive Behavior: A Meta-Analytic Review of the Social Psychological Literature." *Psychological Bulletin* 100(3):309–30.

Elliott, D. S. 1994. "Serious Violent Offenders: Onset, Developmental Course, and Termination—the American Society of Criminology 1993 Presidential Address." *Criminology* 32:1–21.

Elliott, D. S., D. Huizinga, and S. S. Ageton. 1985. *Explaining Delinquency and Drug Use*. Beverly Hills, Calif.: Sage Publications.

Elliott, D. S., D. Huizinga, and S. Menard. 1989. *Multiple Problem Youth: Delinquency, Substance Use, and Mental Health Problems*. New York: Springer.

English, K. 1993. "Self-Reported Crime Rates of Women Prisoners." *Journal of Quantitative Criminology* 9(4):357–82.

Fagan, J. 1995. "Women's Careers in Drug Use and Drug Selling." *Current Perspectives on Aging and the Life Cycle* 4:155–90.

Feyerherm, W. 1981. "Gender Differences in Delinquency: Quantity and Quality." In *Women and Crime in America*, edited by L. H. Bowker. New York: Macmillan.

Figueira-McDonough, J. 1985. "Are Girls Different?: Gender Discrepancies between Delinquent Behavior and Control." *Child Welfare* 64(3):273–89.

Fishman, L. T. 1988. "The Vice Queens: An Ethnographic Study of Black Female Gang Behavior." Paper presented at the annual meeting of the American Society of Criminology, Chicago, November 1988.

Fleming, J. P., S. G. Kellam, and C. H. Brown. 1982. "Early Predictors of Age at First Use of Alcohol, Marijuana, and Cigarettes." *Drug and Alcohol Dependence* 9:285–303.

Freud, S. 1933. *Sexuality and the Psychology of Love*. New York: Collier Books.

Friedman, J., and D. P. Rosenbaum. 1988. "Social Control Theory: The Salience of Components by Age, Gender, and Type of Crime." *Journal of Quantitative Criminology* 4(4):363–81.

Gagnon, R., L. Biron, and M. A. Bertrand. 1980. *Aspirations et délinquance révélée chez les adolescentes: Comparaison entre un groupe institutionnalisé et un groupe non-institutionnalisé*. Groupe de Recherche sur l'Inadaptation Juvénile. Report no. 3. Montreal: University of Montreal.

Ge, X., R. D. Conger, and G. H. Elder. 1996. "Coming of Age Too Early: Pubertal Influences on Girls' Vulnerability to Psychological Distress." *Child Development* 67(6):3386–400.

Gilfus, M. E. 1992. "From Victims to Survivors to Offenders: Women's Route of Entry and Immersion in Street Crime." *Women and Criminal Justice* 4(1): 63–89.

Gilligan, C. 1982. *In a Different Voice: Psychological Theory and Women's Development.* Cambridge, Mass.: Harvard University Press.

Gillmore, M. R., J. D. Hawkins, R. F. Catalano, L. E. Day, M. Moore, and R. Abbott. 1991. "Structure of Problem Behaviors in Preadolescence." *Journal of Consulting and Clinical Psychology* 59(4):499–506.

Giordano, P. C. 1978. "Girls, Guys and Gangs: The Changing Social Context of the Female Delinquency." *Journal of Criminal Law and Criminology* 69(1): 126–32.

Giordano, P. C., and S. A. Cernkovich. 1979. "On Complicating the Relationship between Liberation and Delinquency." *Social Problems* 26(4):467–81.

Giordano P. C., S. A. Cernkovich, and J. L. Rudolph. 2002. "Gender, Crime, and Desistance: Toward a Theory of Cognitive Transformation." *American Journal of Sociology* (forthcoming).

Glueck, S., and E. Glueck. 1934. *One Thousand Juvenile Delinquents.* Cambridge, Mass.: Harvard University Press.

Gottfredson, D. C., R. J. McNeil III, and G. D. Gottfredson. 1999. "Social Area Influences on Delinquency: A Multilevel Analysis." *Journal of Research in Crime and Delinquency* 28(2):197–226.

Gottfredson, M. R., and T. Hirschi. 1990. *A General Theory of Crime.* Stanford, Calif.: Stanford University Press.

Hagan, J., A. R. Gillis, and J. Simpson. 1985. "The Class Structure of Gender and Delinquency: Toward a Power-Control Theory of Common Delinquent Behavior." *American Journal of Sociology* 90:1151–78.

Hagan, J., J. Simpson, and A. R. Gillis. 1987. "Class in the Household: A Power Control Theory of Gender and Delinquency." *American Journal of Sociology* 92(4):788–860.

Hannon, L., and L. R. Dufour. 1998. "Still Just the Study of Men and Crime? A Content Analysis." *Sex Roles* 38(1):63–71.

Harding, S. 1991. *Whose Science? Whose Knowledge?: Thinking from Women's Lives.* Ithaca, N.Y.: Cornell University Press.

Harding, S., ed. 1987. *Feminism and Methodology: Social Science Issues.* Bloomington: Indiana University Press; Milton Keynes (Buckinghamshire): Open University Press.

Harris, A. R. 1977. "Sex and Theories of Deviance: Toward a Functional Theory of Type-Scripts." *American Sociological Review* 42(1):3–16.

Haskins, J. 1974. *Street Gangs: Yesterday and Today.* New York: Hastings House.

Heidensohn, F. M. 1968. "The Deviance of Women: A Critique and an Enquiry." *British Journal of Sociology* 19(2):160–76.

Heimer, K. 1996. "Gender, Interaction, and Delinquency: Testing a Theory of Differential Social Control." *Social Psychology Quarterly* 59(1):36–91.

Heimer, K., and S. De Coster. 1999. "The Gendering of Violent Delinquency." *Criminology* 37:277–317.

Hindelang, M. J. 1973. "Causes of Delinquency: A Partial Replication and Extension." *Social Problems* 21:471–87.

Hirschi, T. 1969. *Causes of Delinquency*. Berkeley: University of California Press.

Hoffmann, J. P., and S. S. Su. 1997. "The Conditional Effects of Stress on Delinquency and Drug Use: A Strain Theory Assessment of Sex Differences." *Journal of Research in Crime and Delinquency* 34(1):46–78.

Horwitz, A. V., and H. R. White. 1987. "Gender Role Orientations and Styles of Pathology among Adolescents." *Journal of Health and Social Behavior* 28(2):158–70.

Jang, S. J., and M. D. Krohn. 1995. "Developmental Patterns of Sex Differences in Delinquency among African American Adolescents: A Test of the Sex-Invariance Hypothesis." *Journal of Quantitative Criminology* 11(2):195–222.

Jensen, G. F. 1993. "Power-Control vs. Social Control Theories of Common Delinquency: A Comparative Analysis." In *New Directions in Criminological Theory: Advances in Criminological Theory*, vol. 4, edited by Freda Adler and William S. Laufer. New Brunswick, N.J.: Transaction Publishers.

Jensen, G. F., and R. Eve. 1976. "Sex Differences in Delinquency." *Criminology* 13:427–48.

Jessor, R., J. E. Donovan, and K. Widmer. 1980. "Psychosocial Factors in Adolescent Alcohol and Drug Use: The 1978 National Sample Study, and the 1974–1978 Panel Study." Unpublished final report. Institute of Behavioral Science. Boulder: University of Colorado.

Jessor, R., and S. L. Jessor. 1977. *Problem Behavior and Psychosocial Development: A Longitudinal Study of Youth*. New York: Academic Press.

Joe, K. A., and M. Chesney-Lind. 1995. "Just Every Mother's Angel: An Analysis of Gender and Ethnic Variations in Youth Gang Membership." *Gender and Society* 9(4):408–31.

Johnson, R. E. 1979. *Juvenile Delinquency and Its Origins: An Integrated Theoretical Approach*. Cambridge: Cambridge University Press.

Johnston, L. D., P. M. O'Malley, and L. K. Eveland. 1978. "Drugs and Delinquency: A Search for Causal Connections." In *Longitudinal Research on Drug Use: Empirical Finding and Methodological Issues*, edited by D. B. Kandel. Washington, D.C.: Hemisphere.

Junger-Tas, J., G. J. Terlouw, and M. W. Klein, eds. 1994. *Delinquent Behavior among Young People in the Western World: First Results of the International Self-Report Delinquency Study*. Amsterdam: Kugler.

Keenan, K., R. Loeber, and S. Green. 1999. "Conduct Disorder in Girls: A Review of the Literature." *Clinical Child and Family Psychology Review* 2:3–19.

Keenan, K., and D. Shaw. 1997. "Developmental and Social Influences on Young Girls' Early Problem Behavior." *Psychological Bulletin* 121(1):95–113.

Kempf, K. L. 1993. "Hirschi's Theory of Social Control: Is It Fecund but Not Yet Fertile?" *Advances in Theoretical Criminology* 4:143–86.

Konopka, G. 1966. *The Adolescent Girl in Conflict*. Englewood Cliffs, N.J.: Prentice-Hall.

Krohn, M. D., A. J. Lizotte, and C. M. Perez. 1997. "The Interrelationships between Substance Use and Precocious Transitions to Adult Statuses." *Journal of Health and Social Behavior* 38(1):87–103.

Krohn, M. D., and J. L. Massey. 1980. "Social Control and Delinquent Behavior: An Examination of the Elements of the Social Bond." *Sociological Quarterly* 21(4):529–43.

Kruttschnitt, C. 1996. "Contributions of Quantitative Methods to the Study of Gender and Crime, or Bootstrapping Our Way into the Theoretical Thicket." *Journal of Quantitative Criminology* 12(2):135–61.

———. 2001. "Gender and Violence." In *Women, Crime, and Criminal Justice: Original Feminist Readings,* edited by C. M. Renzetti and L. Goodstein. Los Angeles: Roxbury.

Lanctôt, N., M. Bernard, and M. Le Blanc. 2002. "Le début de l'adolescence: Une période critique pour l'éclosion des conduites déviantes des adolescents." *Criminologie* (forthcoming).

Lanctôt, N., and M. Le Blanc. 1996. "La participation des garçons aux bandes marginales: Un phénomène de sélection et d'opportunités." *Revue Canadienne de Criminologie* 38(4):375–400.

———. 1997. "Les adolescentes membres des bandes marginales: Un potentiel antisocial atténué par la dynamique de la bande?" *Criminologie* 30(1): 111–30.

———. 2000. "Les trajectoires marginales chez les adolescentes judiciarisées: Continuité et changement." *Revue Internationale de Criminologie et de Police Technique et Scientifique* 53(1):46–68.

Lanctôt, N., and C. Smith. 2001. "Sexual Activity, Pregnancy and Deviance in a Representative Urban Sample of African American Girls." *Journal of Youth and Adolescence* 30(3):349–72.

Land, K. C., and D. S. Nagin. 1996. "Micro-Models of Criminal Careers: A Synthesis of the Criminal Careers and Life Course Approaches via Semiparametric Mixed Poisson Regression Models, with Empirical Applications." *Journal of Quantitative Criminology* 12(2):163–91.

Le Blanc, M. 1995. "The Relative Importance of Internal and External Direct Constraints in the Explanation of Late Adolescent Delinquency and Adult Criminality." In *Coercion and Punishment in Long-Term Perspectives,* edited by J. McCord. Cambridge: Cambridge University Press.

———. 1997a. "A Generic Control Theory of the Criminal Phenomenon, the Structural and the Dynamical Statements of an Integrative Multilayered Control Theory." In *Developmental Theories of Crime and Delinquency: Advances in Theoretical Criminology,* vol. 7, edited by T. P. Thornberry. New Brunswick, N.J.: Transaction Publishers.

———. 1997b. "Socialization or Propensity: A Test of an Integrative Control Theory with Adjudicated Boys." *Studies in Crime and Crime Prevention* 6(2): 200–224.

———. 2002. "The Offending Cycle, Escalation and De-escalation in Delinquent Behavior: A Challenge for Criminology." *International Journal of Comparative and Applied Criminal Justice* (forthcoming).

Le Blanc, M., and C. Bouthillier. 2002. "A Developmental Test of the General Deviance Syndrome with Adjudicated Girls and Boys Using Confirmatory

Factor Analysis." Unpublished manuscript, University of Montréal, Montréal.

Le Blanc, M., and A. Caplan. 1993. "Theoretical Formalization, a Necessity: The Example of Hirschi's Bonding Theory." *Advances in Theoretical Criminology* 4:239–343.

Le Blanc, M., and S. Girard. 1997. "The Generality of Deviance: Replication over Two Decades with a Canadian Sample of Adjudicated Boys." *Canadian Journal of Criminology* 39(2):171–83.

Le Blanc, M., and R. Loeber. 1998. "Developmental Criminology Upgraded." In *Crime and Justice: A Review of Research*, vol. 23, edited by Michael Tonry. Chicago: University of Chicago Press.

Le Blanc, M., and G. Ouimet. 1988. "Système familial et conduite délinquante au cours de l'adolescence à Montréal en 1985." *Santé Mentale au Québec* 13(2):119–34.

Le Blanc, M., M. Ouimet, and R. E. Tremblay. 1988. "An Integrative Control Theory of Delinquent Behavior: A Validation 1976–1985." *Psychiatry* 51: 164–76.

LeGrande, G., and D. J. Shoemaker. 1989. "Social Bonding and Delinquency: A Comparative Analysis." *Sociological Quarterly* 30(3):481–99.

Leiber, M. J., and M. E. E. Wacker. 1997. "A Theoretical and Empirical Assessment of Power-Control Theory and Single-Mother Families." *Youth and Society* 28(3):317–50.

Leonard, E. B. 1982. *Women, Crime and Society: A Critique of Criminology Theory*. New York: Longman.

Leschied, A. W., A. Cummings, M. V. Brunschot, A. Cunningham, and A. Saunders. 2000. *La violence chez les adolescentes: Etude documentaire et corrélations*. Provided to the Solicitor General of Canada under contract no. 9914-UNI-587. Ottawa: Solliciteur Général du Canada.

Lewis, R. V. 1989. "Does There Exist an Adult Female Chronic Offender?" Paper presented at the forty-first meeting of the American Society of Criminology, Reno, Nevada, November.

Liu, X., and H. B. Kaplan. 1999. "Explaining the Gender Difference in Adolescent Delinquent Behavior: A Longitudinal Test of Mediating Mechanisms." *Criminology* 37:195–214.

Loeber, R., and M. Le Blanc. 1990. "Toward a Developmental Criminology." In *Crime and Justice: A Review of Research*, vol. 12, edited by Michael Tonry and Norval Morris. Chicago: University of Chicago Press.

Loeber, R., and H. Snyder. 1988. "Age at First Arrest and Rate of Offending: Findings on the Constancy and Change of Lambda." Unpublished manuscript. Pittsburgh: University of Pittsburgh.

Loeber, R., P. Wung, K. Keenan, B. Giroux, M. Stouthamer-Loeber, W. B. Van Kammen, and B. Maughan. 1993. "Developmental Pathways in Disruptive Child Behavior." *Development and Psychopathology* 5:101–33.

Lombroso, C., and W. Ferrero. 1895. *The Female Offender*. New York: Philosophical Library.

Lytton, H., and D. M. Romney. 1991. "Parents' Differential Socialization of Girls and Boys: A Meta-Analysis." *Psychological Bulletin* 109:267–96.

Magnusson, D., H. Stattin, and V. L. Allen. 1986. "Differential Maturation among Girls and Its Relations to Social Adjustment: A Longitudinal Perspective." *Life-Span Development and Behavior* 7:135–72.

Magnusson, D., ed. 1988. *Individual Development in an Interactional Perspective: A Longitudinal Study.* Hillsdale, N.J.: Erlbaum.

Mak, A. S. 1990. "Testing a Psychological Control Theory of Delinquency." *Criminal Justice and Behavior* 17(2):215–30.

Matsueda, R. L. 1992. "Reflected Appraisals, Parental Labeling, and Delinquency: Specifying a Symbolic Interactionist Theory." *American Journal of Sociology* 97:1577–611.

McCarthy, B., J. Hagan, and T. S. Woodward. 1999. "In the Company of Women: Structure and Agency in a Revised Power-Control Theory of Gender and Delinquency." *Criminology* 37(4):761–88.

McGee, L., and M. D. Newcomb. 1992. "General Deviance Syndrome: Expanded Hierarchical Evaluations at Four Ages from Early Adolescence to Adulthood." *Journal of Consulting and Clinical Psychology* 60(5):766–76.

Mears, D. P., M. Ploeger, and M. Warr. 1998. "Explaining the Gender Gap in Delinquency: Peer Influence and Moral Evaluations of Behavior." *Journal of Research in Crime and Delinquency* 35(3):251–66.

Messerschmidt, J. W. 1993. *Masculinities and Crime: Critique and Reconceptualization of Theory.* Lanham, Md.: Rowman & Littlefield.

Messner, S. F., M. D. Krohn, and A. E. Liska, eds. 1989. *Theoretical Integration in the Study of Deviance and Crime: Problems and Prospects.* Albany: State University of New York Press.

Miller, W. B. 1958. "Lower-Class Culture as a Generating Milieu of Gang Delinquency." *Journal of Social Issues* 14:5–19.

———. 1975. *Violence by Youth Gangs and Youth Groups as a Crime Problem in Major American Cities.* Monograph. Cambridge, Mass.: Center for Criminal Justice, Harvard Law School.

Moffitt, T. E. 1993. "Life-Course-Persistent and Adolescence-Limited Antisocial Behavior: A Developmental Taxonomy." *Psychological Review* 100: 674–701.

Moffitt, T. E., and A. Caspi. 2001. "Childhood Predictors Differentiate Life-Course Persistent and Adolescence-Limited Antisocial Pathways among Males and Females." *Development and Psychopathology* 13:355–75.

Morash, M., and M. Chesney-Lind. 1991. "A Reformulation and Partial Test of the Power Control Theory of Delinquency." *Justice Quarterly* 8:347–77.

Moretti, M., and C. Odgers. 2001. "Aggressive and Violent Girls: Prevalence, Profiles and Contributing Factors." In *Multi-problem and Violent Youth: A Foundation for Comparative Research,* edited by R. Roesch, R. Corrado, and S. Hart. Amsterdam: IOS Press.

Naffine, N. 1987. *Female Crime: The Construction of Women in Criminology.* Sydney: Allen & Unwin.

Nagin, D., D. P. Farrington, and T. Moffitt. 1995. "Life-Course Trajectories of Different Types of Offenders." *Criminology* 33:111–39.

Nagin, D., and R. E. Tremblay. 1999. "Trajectories of Boys' Physical Aggression, Opposition, and Hyperactivity on the Path to Physically Violent and Nonviolent Juvenile Delinquency." *Child Development* 70:1181–96.

Nye, F. I., and J. F. Short. 1957. "Scaling Delinquent Behavior." *American Journal of Sociology* 63:381–89.

Oakley, A. 2000. *Experiments in Knowing: Gender and Method in the Social Sciences.* New York: New Press.

Office of Juvenile Justice and Delinquency Prevention. 1998. *Guiding Principles for Promising Female Programming: An Inventory of Best Practices.* Washington, D.C.: Office of Juvenile Justice and Delinquency Prevention, U.S. Department of Justice.

O'Neill, M. 1996. "Researching Prostitution and Violence: Towards a Feminist Praxis." In *Women, Violence, and Male Power: Feminist Activism, Research, and Practice,* edited by M. Hester, L. Kelly and J. Radford. Philadelphia: Open University Press.

Osgood, D. W., L. D. Johnston, P. M. O'Malley, and J. G. Bachman. 1988. "The Generality of Deviance in Late Adolescence and Early Adulthood." *American Sociological Review* 53(1):81–93.

Pajer, K. A. 1998. "What Happens to Bad Girls? A Review of Adult Outcomes of Antisocial Adolescent Girls." *American Journal of Psychiatry* 155:862–70.

Parent, C. 1998. *Féminismes et criminologie.* Montreal: University of Montreal Press.

Parker, R. N., and D. McDowell. 1986. "Constructing an Index of Officially Recorded Crime: The Use of Confirmatory Factor Analysis." *Journal of Quantitative Criminology* 2(3):237–50.

Parsons, T. 1947. "Certain Primary Source and Patterns of Aggression in the Social Structure of the Western World." *Psychiatry* 10:167–81.

Pollak, O. 1950. *The Criminality of Women.* Philadelphia: University of Pennsylvania Press.

Pollock, J. M. 1999. *Criminal Women.* Cincinnati: Anderson.

Richards, P., and C. R. Tittle. 1981. "Gender and Perceived Chances of Arrest." *Social Forces* 59(4):1182–99.

Robins, L. N. 1986. "The Consequences of Conduct Disorder in Girls." In *Risk in Intellectual and Psychosocial Development,* edited by D. C. Farran and J. C. McKinney. Orlando, Fla.: Academic Press.

Robins L. N., and T. R. Przybeck. 1985. "Age of Onset of Drug Use as a Factor in Drug and Other Disorders." *National Institute of Drug Abuse Research Monograph Series* 56:178–92.

Rojek, D. G., and M. O. Erickson. 1982. "Delinquent Careers: A Test of the Career Escalation Model." *Criminology* 20:5–28.

Roy, J. H. 1993. "Les gangs et la violence chez les jeunes: Kidz n the hood." *Voir* (August 12–18), pp. 6–8.

Sarnecki, J. 1986. *Delinquent Networks.* Stockholm: National Council for Crime Prevention, Research Division.

Schellenbah, C. J., T. L. Whitman, and J. G. Borkowski. 1992. "Toward an Integrative Model of Adolescent Parenting." *Human Development* 35(2):81–99.

Schur, E. 1983. *Labeling Women Deviant: Gender, Stigma, and Social Control.* Philadelphia: Temple University Press.

Segrave, J. O., and D. N. Hastad. 1985. "Evaluating Three Models of Delinquency Causation for Females and Males: Strain Theory, Subculture Theory, and Control Theory." *Sociological Focus* 18(1):1–17.

Shoemaker, D. J. 1994. "Male-Female Delinquency in the Philippines: A Comparative Analysis." *Youth and Society* 25(3):299–329.

Short, J. F., Jr., ed. 1968. *Gang Delinquency and Delinquent Subcultures.* New York: Harper & Row.

Shover, N., S. Norland, J. James, and W. E. Thornton. 1979. "Gender Roles and Delinquency." *Social Forces* 58(1):162–75.

Silbert, M. H., and A. M. Pines. 1981. "Sexual Child Abuse as an Antecedent to Prostitution." *Child Abuse and Neglect* 5:407–11.

Silverman, R. A., and L. W. Kennedy. 1987. *The Female Perpetrator of Homicide in Canada.* Edmonton: University of Alberta, Center for Criminological Research.

Silverthorn, P., and P. J. Frick. 1999. "Developmental Pathways to Antisocial Behavior: The Delayed-Onset Pathway in Girls." *Development and Psychopathology* 11:101–26.

Silverthorn, P., and P. J. Frick. 2001. "Timing of Onset and Correlates of Severe Conduct Problems in Adjudicated Girls and Boys." *Journal of Psychopathology and Behavioral Assessment* 23(3):171–81.

Simmons, R. G., and D. A. Blyth. 1987. *Moving into Adolescence: The Impact of Pubertal Change and School Context.* New York: Aldine de Gruyter.

Simon, R. J. 1979. "Arrest Statistics." In *The Criminology of Deviant Women,* edited by F. Adler and R. J. Simon. Boston: Houghton Mifflin.

Simons, R. L., M. G. Miller, and S. M. Aigner. 1980. "Contemporary Theories of Deviance and Female Delinquency: An Empirical Test." *Journal of Research in Crime and Delinquency* 17(1):42–57.

Singer, S. I., and M. Levine. 1988. "Power-Control Theory, Gender, and Delinquency: A Partial Replication with Additional Evidence on the Effects of Peers." *Criminology* 26:627–47.

Smart, C. 1976. *Women, Crime and Criminology: A Feminist Critique.* London: Routledge & Kegan Paul.

Smith, C., and T. P. Thornberry. 1995. "The Relationship between Childhood Maltreatment and Adolescent Involvement in Delinquency." *Criminology* 33:451–82.

Smith, D. A. 1979. "Sex and Deviance: An Assessment of Major Sociological Variables." *Sociological Quarterly* 20(2):183–86.

Smith, D. A., and R. Paternoster. 1987. "The Gender Gap in Theories of Deviance: Issues and Evidence." *Journal of Research in Crime and Delinquency* 24(2):140–72.

Sommers, I., and D. R. Baskin. 1993. "The Situational Context of Violent Female Offending." *Journal of Research in Crime and Delinquency* 30(2):136–62.

———. 1994. "Factors Related to Female Adolescent Initiation into Violent Street Crime." *Youth and Society* 25(3):468–89.

Spergel, I. A. 1990. "Youth Gangs: Continuity and Change." In *Crime and*

Justice: A Review of Research, vol. 12, edited by Michael Tonry and Norval Morris. Chicago: University of Chicago Press.

Stattin, H., and D. Magnusson. 1989. "The Role of Early Aggressive Behavior in the Frequency, Seriousness and Types of Later Crime." *Journal of Consulting and Clinical Psychology* 57(6):710–18.

Steffensmeier, D., and E. Allan. 1996. "Gender and Crime: Toward a Gendered Theory of Female Offending." *Annual Review of Sociology* 22:459–87.

Steffensmeier, D., and C. Streifel. 1991. "Age, Gender and Crime across Three Historical Periods: 1935, 1960 and 1985." *Social Forces* 69(3):869–94.

Sutherland, E., and D. Cressey. 1978. *Criminology*. 10th ed. Philadelphia: Lippincott.

Talbot, E., and K. Thiede. 1999. "Pathways to Antisocial Behavior among Adolescent Girls." *Journal of Emotional and Behavioral Disorders* 7:31–39.

Taylor, C. S. 1990. *Dangerous Society*. East Lansing: Michigan State University Press.

———. 1993. *Girls, Gangs, Women and Drugs*. East Lansing: Michigan State University Press.

Thomas, W. I. 1923. *The Unadjusted Girl: With Cases and Standpoint for Behavior Analysis*. Boston: Little Brown.

Thornberry, T. P. 1996. "Empirical Support for Interactional Theory: A Review of the Literature." In *Delinquency and Crime: Current Theories*, edited by J. D. Hawkins. New York: Cambridge University Press.

———. 1997. "Developmental Theories of Crime and Delinquency." *Advances in Criminological Theory* 7:1–10.

Thornberry, T. P., B. Bjerregaard, and W. Miles. 1993. "The Consequences of Respondent Attrition in Panel Studies: A Simulation Based on the Rochester Youth Development Study." *Journal of Quantitative Criminology* 9: 127–58.

Thornberry, T. P., A. J. Lizotte, M. D. Krohn, M. Farnworth, and S. J. Jang. 1991. "Testing Interactional Theory: An Examination of Reciprocal Causal Relationships among Family, School, and Delinquency." *Journal of Criminal Law and Criminology* 82(1):3–35.

Thornton, W. E., and J. James. 1979. "Masculinity and Delinquency Revisited." *British Journal of Criminology* 19(3):225–41.

Thrasher, F. 1927. *The Gangs*. Chicago: University of Chicago Press.

Tibbetts, S. G. 1999. "Differences between Women and Men regarding Decisions to Commit Test Cheating." *Research in Higher Education* 40(3):323–42.

Timmons-Mitchell, J., C. Brown, C. Schulz, S. E. Webster, L. A. Underwood, and W. E. Semple. 1997. "Comparing the Mental Health Needs of Female and Male Incarcerated Juvenile Delinquents." *Behavioral Sciences and the Law* 15(2):195–202.

Torstensson, M. 1990. "Female Delinquents in a Birth Cohort: Tests of Some Aspects of Control Theory." *Journal of Quantitative Criminology* 6(1):101–15.

Tracy, P. E., and K. Kempf-Leonard. 1996. *Continuity and Discontinuity in Criminal Careers*. New York: Plenum.

Tracy, P. E., M. E. Wolfgang, and R. M. Figlio. 1985. *Delinquency in Two Birth Cohorts.* Executive summary. Washington, D.C.: Office of Juvenile Justice and Delinquency Prevention, U.S. Department of Justice.

Tremblay, R. E., B. Masse, D. Perron, M. Le Blanc, A. E. Schwartzman, and J. E. Ledingham. 1992. "Early Disruptive Behavior, Poor School Achievement, Delinquent Behavior and Antisocial Personality: Longitudinal Data for Male and Female Samples." *Journal of Consulting and Clinical Psychology* 6(1):64–72.

Triplett, R. A., and L. B. Myers. 1995. "Evaluating Contextual Patterns of Delinquency: Gender-Based Differences." *Justice Quarterly* 12(1):59–84.

Van Wormer, K. S., and C. Bartollas. 2000. *Women and the Criminal Justice System.* Boston: Allyn & Bacon.

Wängby, M., L. R. Bergman, and D. Magnusson. 1999. "Development of Adjustment Problems in Girls: What Syndrome Emerge?" *Child Development* 70:678–99.

Warren, M. O., and J. L. Rosenbaum. 1986. "Criminal Careers and Female Offenders." *Criminal Justice and Behavior* 13(4):398–418.

Welfare Council of New York City. 1950. *Working with Teen-Age Gangs: A Report on the Central Harlem Street Clubs Project.* New York: Welfare Council of New York City, Central Harlem Street Clubs Project.

Widom, C. S. 1991. "Avoidance of Criminality in Abused and Neglected Children." *Psychiatry* 54(2):162–74.

———. 1996. "Childhood Sexual Abuse and Its Criminal Consequences." *Society* 33:47–53.

Wikström, P-O. 1987. "Patterns of Crime in a Birth Cohort: Age, Sex and Class Differences." Project Metropolitan: A Longitudinal Study of a Stockholm Cohort, no. 24. Stockholm: Department of Sociology, University of Stockholm.

Wilkinson, K. 1985. "An Investigation of the Contribution of Masculinity to Delinquent Behavior." *Sociological Focus* 18(3):249–63.

Young, V. D. 1981. *Patterns of Female Criminality.* Albany: State University of New York Press.

George C. Thomas III and Richard A. Leo

The Effects of *Miranda v. Arizona*: "Embedded" in Our National Culture?

> You have the right to remain silent. Anything you say can
> be used against you in court. You have the right to the pres-
> ence of an attorney. If you cannot afford an attorney, one
> will be appointed for you prior to any questioning. (*Mi-
> randa v. Arizona*, 384 U.S. 436 [1966])

ABSTRACT

Miranda v. Arizona required that police inform suspects, prior to custodial
interrogation, of their constitutional rights to silence and appointed
counsel. It also required that suspects voluntarily, knowingly, and
intelligently waive these rights in order for any resulting confession to be
admitted into evidence at trial. The rationale of *Miranda* as elaborated by
the Supreme Court has evolved from encouraging suspects to resist police
interrogation to informing suspects that they have a right to resist.
Reflecting a fundamental tenet in American culture and law, *Miranda*
today seeks to protect the "free choice" of a suspect to decide whether to
answer police questions during interrogation. Two generations of
empirical scholarship on *Miranda* suggest that the *Miranda* requirements
have exerted a negligible effect on the ability of the police to elicit
confessions and on the ability of prosecutors to win convictions. There is
no good evidence that *Miranda* has substantially depressed confession
rates or imposed significant costs on the American criminal justice system.
The practical benefits of *Miranda* to custodial suspects may also be
negligible. Police have developed multiple strategies to avoid, circumvent,
nullify, or simply violate *Miranda* and its invocation rules.

We thank Michael Tonry, Charles Weisselberg, Welsh White, and three anonymous
reviewers for helpful comments. We thank John Douard and Mike Mulligan for research
assistance and helpful comments.

In 1966, the Supreme Court sought to revolutionize the judicial oversight of police interrogation. Prior to *Miranda v. Arizona*, 384 U.S. 436 (1966), the Court had typically examined the facts of individual cases to determine whether police pressure had rendered the confession "involuntary" and thus inadmissible as a violation of the Fourteenth Amendment Due Process Clause. A confession was deemed involuntary when the "will" of the suspect was "overborne" by police interrogators' use of coercion or compulsion. The classic example is the deputy sheriff in *Brown v. Mississippi*, 297 U.S. 278 (1936), who used physical torture (beatings with studded belts, hanging one suspect from a tree) to obtain confessions. But coercion analysis is more difficult when the pressure is simply the length and intensity of the interrogation. Does thirty-two hours of sustained interrogation, followed a few days later by another ten hours, coerce the defendant's confession as a matter of law? No, the Court held in *Lisenba v. California*, 314 U.S. 219 (1941). But three years later in *Ashcraft v. Tennessee*, 322 U.S. 143 (1944), the Court held that thirty-six continuous hours of interrogation did coerce the confession in that case. A thin distinction can be made between the facts of the two cases, but drawing such a fine line does not provide much guidance for lower courts faced with a steady stream of confession cases, each of which has facts at least a little different from all the others.[1]

Eschewing this case-by-case method, *Miranda* created a presumption of compulsion that can be dispelled only if the suspect receives a set of warnings, as set out above. *Miranda* was a bold stroke, one that sent shock waves throughout the United States. Police and prosecutors claimed that few would confess in the face of these warnings and that many crimes would go unsolved (Baker 1983, pp. 243–44). As a result, dangerous criminals would be freed to prey upon the innocent. Congress viewed the crime rate in 1966 as already too high, and the prospect of *Miranda* pushing it higher caused grave concern (Kamisar 2000, pp. 894–99). On the floor of the United States Senate, Senator John McClellan pointed to a graph of the crime rate and said, "Look at it and weep for your country" (Cong. Rec. 114:14,146 [1968]). Even normally staid Supreme Court Justices came close to outrage in their dissenting opinions in *Miranda*. For example, Justice Byron White wrote near the end of his dissent: "In some unknown number of cases the

---

[1] Indeed, a distinction between internal preferences and external acts that seek to shape preferences might always be elusive (Seidman 1990), suggesting that legal coercion may almost be impossible to discern in many individual cases.

Court's rule will return a killer, a rapist or other criminal to the streets and to the environment which produced him, to repeat his crime whenever it pleases him. As a consequence, there will not be a gain, but a loss, in human dignity. . . . There is, of course, a saving factor: the next victims are uncertain, unnamed and unrepresented in this case" (*Miranda*, pp. 542–43 [White, J., dissenting]).

The political reaction was swift and clear. By the spring of 1968, Congress passed the Omnibus Crime Control and Safe Streets Act of 1968 (18 U.S.C. sec. 3501 *et seq.* [1968]). Robert Burt characterized this legislation as "a gesture of defiance at a Court which protected criminals and Communists, and attacked traditional religious, political, and social institutions" (Burt 1969, p. 127). Part of the act, section 3501, created a protocol for federal judges to use to evaluate the admissibility of confessions. The statute, explained in more detail in Section V of this essay, required judges to admit all voluntary confessions and set out a series of factors to use in deciding whether a confession is voluntary. While providing *Miranda*-like warnings is one way to show that the suspect voluntarily answered questions, the statute is clear that the absence of warnings "need not be conclusive on the issue of voluntariness" (18 U.S.C. sec. 3501[b]). The net effect of section 3501 was to abrogate *Miranda*'s conclusive presumption by congressional action.

The bill became law on June 19, 1968. Thirty-two years would pass before the Supreme Court ruled on its constitutionality in *Dickerson v. United States*, 120 S.Ct. 2326 (2000). The case was on appeal from a decision of the Fourth Circuit Court of Appeals holding that the prescribed warnings were not themselves required by the Constitution. In effect, the Fourth Circuit held, the Constitution does not specify precisely how a suspect is protected from being compelled to be a witness against himself, and *Miranda* simply filled that gap in the Constitution. But this kind of gap filling might be simply a placeholder until Congress acts (Monaghan 1975). Indeed, one paragraph in the *Miranda* opinion "encourage[d] Congress and the States to continue their laudable search for increasingly effective ways of protecting the rights of the individual while promoting efficient enforcement of our criminal laws" (*Miranda*, p. 467). As section 3501 was a specific regime for evaluating the admissibility of confessions, the Fourth Circuit held that Congress had rendered unnecessary *Miranda*'s remedy for the interrogation gap in the Constitution.

Dickerson rejected this distinction between what is specifically in the Constitution and what might be viewed as filling a gap in the Constitution. The Court noted that *Miranda*'s core holding was to require a procedure "that will warn a suspect of his right to remain silent and which will assure the suspect that the exercise of that right will be honored" (*Dickerson*, p. 2335). Because section 3501 does not require warnings, but makes them only one factor in the analysis, it failed to meet *Miranda*'s minimum requirement. And because *Miranda* is based on the Constitution, the Court held that Congress lacked the authority to prescribe a remedy that fell below the *Miranda* threshold. It reversed the Fourth Circuit and held section 3501 unconstitutional.

The Supreme Court itself, of course, has the authority to overrule *Miranda*. Though the Court dislikes overruling precedent, it has done so many times.[2] It was not impossible that the current Court would overrule *Miranda*. The Court invited Paul Cassell, a zealous critic of *Miranda* (Cassell 1996a, 1996b, 1996c, 1997; Cassell and Fowles 1998), to write a brief supporting the Fourth Circuit's decision. Chief Justice Rehnquist had written several opinions that manifested a skeptical view of *Miranda* and had been joined on occasion by Justices O'Connor, Kennedy, Scalia, and Thomas.[3] Five votes would overrule *Miranda*, and those five looked plausible.

The Court explicitly considered whether to overrule *Miranda* but, by a vote of seven to two, "decline[d] to do so" (*Dickerson*, p. 2336). Chief Justice Rehnquist wrote the opinion for the Court, joined by Justices O'Connor and Kennedy (as well as by Justices Stevens, Souter, Breyer, and Ginsburg). Only Justices Scalia and Thomas dissented. What happened to the distaste of *Miranda* that often pervaded the opinions of Rehnquist and O'Connor? The Court's response to the re-

---

[2] In the three-year period from 1961 to 1964, e.g., the Court overruled three major criminal procedure precedents. Malloy v. Hogan, 378 U.S. 1 (1964), required states to follow the Fifth Amendment privilege against compelled self-incrimination, overruling Twining v. New Jersey, 211 U.S. 78 (1908). Gideon v. Wainwright, 372 U.S. 335 (1963) required states to make lawyers available to all indigent felony defendants, overruling Betts v. Brady, 316 U.S. 455 (1942). Mapp v. Ohio, 367 U.S. 643 (1961) required states to suppress evidence found in violation of the Fourth Amendment, overruling Wolf v. Colorado, 338 U.S. 25 (1949).

[3] Four members of the *Dickerson* Court—Chief Justice Rehnquist and Justices O'Connor, Scalia, and Thomas—dissented in 1993 when the Court held that *Miranda* claims were constitutional for purposes of federal habeas review (Withrow v. Williams, 507 U.S. 680 [1993]). Though Justice Kennedy joined the *Withrow* majority, he has on occasion joined an opinion expressing a somewhat narrow view of *Miranda*. See, e.g., Davis v. United States, 512 U.S. 452 (1994) (rejecting the view that an ambiguous request for counsel triggers a duty for police to inquire into whether accused wants counsel); McNeil v. Wisconsin, 501 U.S. 171 (1991) (holding that an invocation of the right to counsel for Sixth Amendment counsel purposes is not, at the same time, an invocation of the right to counsel under *Miranda*).

quest to overrule *Miranda* is illuminating. Chief Justice Rehnquist wrote, "*Miranda* has become embedded in routine police practice to the point where the warnings have become part of our national culture." Moreover, and perhaps more important, "our subsequent cases have reduced the impact of the *Miranda* rule on legitimate law enforcement while reaffirming the decision's core ruling" (*Dickerson*, p. 2335).

Translated: *Miranda* does not cause much harm to "legitimate law enforcement," and the core ruling manifests important enough values to justify what harm it causes. In this essay, we investigate both halves of that claim. What are the values in the "core ruling" that justify even limited harm to law enforcement? And is it true that the Court's "subsequent cases have reduced the impact of the *Miranda* rule on legitimate law enforcement"? The latter claim has a doctrinal and empirical dimension. In Section I we discuss the original and subsequent doctrinal rationales for *Miranda*. After discussing the initial negative reaction to *Miranda* in Section II, we investigate in Section III the effect of subsequent cases on the *Miranda* doctrine and its underlying analytical foundation. In Section IV, we examine how *Miranda* has affected the police interrogation process and the rate at which police secure incriminating statements. Ultimately, in Section V, we ask whether *Miranda* is acceptable today because it has become, through television and the movies, "part of our national culture," or is it part of our national culture because it stands for something our society thinks important? Though this question is impossible to answer with certainty, it provides a useful framework within which to consider how the culture might understand *Miranda* today.

Today's *Miranda* is subtly but importantly different from the *Miranda* that the Supreme Court decided in 1966. The rationale has evolved from encouraging suspects to resist police interrogation to informing suspects that they have a right to resist. The Warren Court saw *Miranda* as an active participant in the interrogation room, a regime that changes the psychology of the encounter between suspect and interrogator. Today's version is closer to a passive administrative requirement to be gotten out of the way so that the suspect can "tell his side of the story" to the police. This evolution resulted in part from the Court tilting more toward the law enforcement side of the balance in the 1970s and 1980s, relaxing the *Miranda* doctrine in some key ways. In addition, the police adjusted to *Miranda* and learned how to comply in a way that minimizes the chance that the suspect will resist interrogation. As *Miranda* became increasingly passive, a piece of furniture in the interrogation room, police became less hostile to its strictures. Though it is unclear why the *Dickerson* challenge arose when it did, the Court's ultimate judgment was unsurprising (Kamisar 2000; Thomas 2000): as it now exists, the *Miranda* rule does not seriously obstruct law enforcement interests. Indeed, in operation *Miranda* might further law enforcement interests more than it does the interests of suspects.

I. Doctrinal Puzzles

For a case that has been as thoroughly debated and discussed as *Miranda*, it remains curiously opaque as an opinion. The first step is easy enough. The Fifth Amendment forbids the government from compelling anyone to be a witness against himself. The paradigm application of this right is to prevent the prosecution from requiring a defendant to testify in his own criminal case. Consequently, the Fifth Amendment right is often called a privilege not to be compelled to incriminate oneself. The *Miranda* Court applied the Fifth Amendment privilege to the police interrogation room by presuming that all custodial interrogation is, in the absence of warnings, inherently compelling. The next step is trickier: Did the Court hold that all responses to the inherently compelling pressures of police interrogation are, as a result, compelled? Justice White in his *Miranda* dissent described the Court's holding along these lines. But he noted an alternative understanding—perhaps the Court held only that the risk of Fifth Amendment compulsion is unacceptably high unless warnings are given. This understanding of *Miranda*'s holding presupposes that there can be noncompelled responses to the inherently compelling pressures. How might this be? A suspect might have decided to confess prior to the beginning of interrogation or might decide to confess during interrogation to gain some perceived advantage rather than in response to the compelling pressures. To say that compelling pressures exist is not to entail that every response is compelled.

But the more likely reading of *Miranda*'s holding is that "any answers to any interrogation [are] compelled regardless of the content and course of examination" (*Miranda*, p. 536 [White, J., dissenting]). The Court spoke about the "cherished" principle "that the individual may not be compelled to incriminate himself" and then said: "Unless adequate protective devices are employed to dispel the compulsion inherent in custodial surroundings, no statement obtained from the defendant can be the product of his free choice" (*Miranda*, p. 458). Here, "free choice" seems to operate as "noncompelled," thus allowing the following "translation": "no statement . . . is anything but compelled" if taken without "adequate protective devices."

This understanding of *Miranda*'s holding provoked much criticism, on the ground that it was ahistorical, bad philosophy, and bad policy. The Fifth Amendment provides that no person "shall be compelled in any criminal case to be a witness against himself." This language strongly implies a protection intended to be limited to formal hearings, a protection that might be out of place in the context of police interrogation. Moreover, it is not easy to defend the philosophical premise that every response to custodial police interrogation is compelled. Imagine a guilt-ridden husband who is asked by a police detective why he is sobbing into his hands. He responds, "I killed my wife." Compelled? Only on an exquisite account of compulsion,[4] or on Seidman's account of *Miranda* that denies the individualism implicit in the whole notion of voluntary acts of confession (Seidman 1992).

The policy question concerns the social value of police interrogation. The Due Process Clause protects against coerced confessions. As long as the police do not use coercion to get confessions, we should not discourage them from attempting to persuade guilty suspects to confess. After all, a freely given confession from a guilty suspect has two significant benefits—it helps convict the guilty person and reduces the risk that an innocent person will be arrested or convicted. But whether *Miranda*'s conclusive presumption of Fifth Amendment compulsion is good history, good philosophy, or good policy, it was a coherent interpretation of the Fifth Amendment.

As we describe in more detail in Section III, the Court soon began to seek ways to permit limited use of evidence taken in violation of *Miranda*. The conceptual mechanism to accomplish this goal was to view the rights created in *Miranda* as "not themselves rights protected by the Constitution but . . . instead measures to insure that the right

---

[4] Stephen Schulhofer offers the best defense of this premise, drawing on cases applying the Fifth Amendment privilege in contexts different from police interrogation (Schulhofer 1987). On Seidman's account, *Miranda* was concerned with the compulsion of preferences, that the police by clever use of various strategies could "change what the suspect wanted, at least for a brief period" (Seidman 1990, p. 174). *Miranda* thus rejected atomistic individualized choice in favor of "a contextual and communal idea of choice" that resulted from the social interaction of custodial police interrogation (Seidman 1992, p. 739). "Statements resulting from such interrogation were never the product of isolated choice. It was always true that statements were preceded by a form of social interaction with the police" (Seidman 1992, p. 739). This interaction that compels preferences is, on Seidman's account, *Miranda*-style compulsion.

against compulsory self-incrimination was protected" (*Michigan v. Tucker*, 417 U.S. 433 [1974], p. 444). This is consistent with Justice White's alternative interpretation that requires warnings to reduce the risk that police interrogation might compel a response. A prophylactic understanding is different from claiming that every answer to every question is compelled unless the suspect is warned.

Understood as a prophylaxis that protects the Fifth Amendment privilege, *Miranda* is a coherent approach to the problem of police interrogation. An earlier Supreme Court doctrine, limited to federal cases, presumed the involuntariness of any confession made after the police failed to take the suspect before a magistrate as required by the federal rules of evidence.[5] This presumption freed federal courts from having to inquire into the voluntariness of confessions when the police isolated the suspect and deprived him of the warnings that the judge is required to give. Similarly, *Miranda* presumes that a statement is compelled if no warnings are given prior to custodial interrogation as a way of simplifying the task of determining voluntariness. Implicit in both of these presumptions is that sometimes courts will suppress statements that are not compelled. The Court has explicitly admitted as much when limiting the extent to which *Miranda* causes the prosecution to lose evidence.[6]

For decades, *Miranda* has been caught between two fires represented by these conflicting justifications for its holding. On the one hand, *Miranda* needs to be seen as a straightforward application of the Fifth Amendment privilege to justify the basic holding that excludes all statements taken without warnings. On the other hand, it needs to be seen as not quite the same as the Fifth Amendment to justify the rules qualifying and limiting the original doctrine that we describe in Section III. The hydraulic tension produced by these conflicting doctrinal imperatives has produced a doctrine that is broader than the Fifth Amendment privilege, because it sometimes suppresses statements that

---

[5] See Mallory v. United States, 378 U.S. 1 (1964); McNabb v. United States, 318 U.S. 332 (1943). The key difference between these presumptions is that *McNabb-Mallory* is a nonconstitutional rule that applies only in federal court, while *Miranda* applies in federal and state courts. While the Court has no authority to impose nonconstitutional rules like *McNabb-Mallory* on the states, *Dickerson* makes plain that the Court views the *Miranda* prophylactic presumption as a constitutional rule.

[6] In Oregon v. Elstad, 470 U.S. 298 (1985), p. 307, the Court said that "unwarned statements that are otherwise voluntary within the meaning of the Fifth Amendment must nevertheless be excluded from evidence under *Miranda*. Thus, in the individual case, *Miranda*'s preventive medicine provides a remedy even to the defendant who has suffered no identifiable constitutional harm."

are not compelled, and yet narrower than the privilege, because it does not apply in some contexts when the privilege would suppress a statement.

To justify this somewhat oddly shaped rule, the Court needs an account of how and why the *Miranda* rule is different from the Fifth Amendment privilege. What the Court has offered instead of an explanation is a series of ad hoc cases usually limiting, though sometimes expanding, the original *Miranda* holding. When the *Miranda* opinion is read in light of these later cases, an account of the relationship between *Miranda* and the Constitution emerges. Moreover, the empirical data on the effect of *Miranda* suggests that the rule operates to achieve at least a formal version of what this account contemplates.

In sum, our view is that *Miranda* sought a mechanism to protect the "free choice" of the suspect to decide whether to answer police questions during interrogation. The use of the Fifth Amendment privilege against compelled self-incrimination was just a convenient doctrinal "home" for a right that, the Court must have hoped, would produce self-regulating interrogations (Stuntz 2001). If the suspect was afraid of the police, or nervous, or drunk, or guilty, he would (in most cases) simply invoke the right to silence and the interrogation would be over before it began. If he agreed to answer questions, and the police applied too much pressure, the suspect could terminate the interrogation at any time and without giving a reason. Providing a mechanism to protect this free choice must have seemed to the Court like a tidy solution to the very difficult problem of regulating police interrogation.

The concern with "free choice" can be seen in the due process confession cases that preceded *Miranda*. As Kamisar put it, "There is nothing very new or unusual about the problem which confronted the Court in *Miranda*; there is nothing really startling or inventive about the solution" (Kamisar 1966, p. 66). In 1961, the Court found a due process violation and suppressed a confession because the particular police interrogation did not permit the suspect to act on "a rational intellect and a free will" (*Blackburn v. Alabama*, 361 U.S. 199, 201 [1960]). In 1963, the Court noted the "effect of psychologically coercive pressures and inducements on the mind and will of an accused" created by police interrogation in general and not just the one in the case before the Court (*Haynes v. Washington*, 373 U.S. 503, 514 [1963]). The Court found the confession inadmissible on due process grounds largely because of this background coercive pressure; the police made no threats except to keep the suspect from talking to his wife until he answered their questions. Thus, nothing much turns on whether the "free choice" protected by *Miranda* is found in the Fifth Amendment privilege or in the more spacious protections of the Due Process Clause.

We want to be clear about our claim. To say that *Miranda* protects "free choice" is not the end of our task, because different kinds of choice exist in the police interrogation room. Moreover, we are not claiming that the Supreme Court created a general right to a fully informed choice whenever the government seeks information, or even a right to a fully informed choice every time the police seek information or evidence from a suspect in a criminal case. For example, the Court has permitted the police to put an undercover agent in a cell and question an inmate without providing the quite relevant information that the "cell mate" is an agent (*Illinois v. Perkins*, 496 U.S. 292 [1990]). The Court has also held that a consent search is constitutional even if the suspect does not know that he has the right to refuse consent. (*Schneckloth v. Bustamonte*, 412 U.S. 218 [1973]).[7] We do not suggest that the Court should reevaluate those cases based on our understanding of *Miranda*. The only free choice that *Miranda* protects is the choice to decide whether to answer police questions posed in a custodial setting by those known to be police officers.

Narrow though our claim is, it manifests a fundamentally important choice. Understood as a right to relevant information when faced with compelling pressures in the interrogation room, *Miranda* reflects a fundamental tenet in American culture and law—that individuals should receive notice that they have certain rights before they face official pressure that causes the rights to be lost. This obvious, yet profound, principle is the best explanation of *Miranda* and also best explains its staying power. The original decision could marshal only five votes on the Court that invented it as a solution to a perplexing problem,[8] while the reaffirmation of *Miranda* garnered seven votes on the

[7] The defendant in Schneckloth v. Bustamonte relied on *Miranda* to support his claim that he had a right to notice, but the Court rejected the analogy.

[8] Justice Clark dissented in *Miranda* even though he had earlier written the majority opinion in Mapp v. Ohio, 367 U.S. 643 (1961), forcing the states to suppress evidence found in violation of the Fourth Amendment. Justice Stewart dissented in *Miranda* even though he had earlier written the majority opinion in *Massiah v. United States*, 377 U.S. 201 (1964), requiring suppression of confessions taken after indictment and without a lawyer present. Justices White and Harlan dissented in *Miranda* even though both joined the Court's opinion in Gideon v. Wainwright, 372 U.S. 335 (1963), forcing the states to provide free lawyers for indigent defendants. It seems clear that *Miranda* was among the Court's most controversial criminal procedure cases. That controversy is far more muted in *Dickerson*, though Scalia's dissent is, as usual, quite barbed.

Court that has cut back on *Miranda*'s scope. This says something quite remarkable about *Miranda*'s staying power. That Chief Justice Rehnquist, an early critic of *Miranda*,[9] wrote the opinion in *Dickerson* perhaps says even more.

But while *Miranda* seems like a safe middle-of-the-road solution to police interrogation today (Seidman 1992, p. 743), it was not always perceived in that way. The next section discusses what seemed so dangerous about *Miranda* in 1966.

II. In the Early Days: Storm and Fury

Detailing the negative reaction to *Miranda* in the first months and years after it was decided is beyond the scope of this essay,[10] though we attempt to provide a taste. During the debates on the confessions provision in the Omnibus Crime Control Act, Senator Sam Ervin accused the *Miranda* majority of ruling the land as a "judicial oligarchy." He said that a vote against the act expressed a belief "that self-confessed murderers, rapists, robbers, arsonists, burglars, and thieves ought to go unpunished," while a vote for the act expressed a belief "that something ought to be done for those who do not wish to be murdered or raped or robbed" (114 Cong. Rec. 14,155 [1968]). Senator McClellan said, "If this confessions provision . . . is defeated, every gangster and overlord of the underworld; every syndicate chief, racketeer, captain, lieutenant, sergeant, private, punk, and hoodlum in organized crime; every murderer, rapist, robber, burglar, arsonist, thief, and conman will have cause to rejoice and celebrate [but] every innocent, law-abiding, and God-fearing citizen in this land will have cause to weep and despair" (114 Cong. Rec. 14,155 [1968]).

Both Republican Richard Nixon and independent candidate George Wallace ran against the Warren Court in the 1968 presidential election. Wallace said the Supreme Court was a "sorry, lousy, no-account outfit," and he promised that if he were elected president "you wouldn't get raped or stabbed in the shadow of the White House even if we had to call out 30,000 troops and equip them with two-foot-long bayonets and station them every few feet apart" (Baker 1983, p. 243). Richard Nixon campaigned on a "law and order" theme during the 1968 election, offering a velvet glove alternative to George Wallace's

---

[9] He wrote the Court's opinion in Michigan v. Tucker, 417 U.S. 433 (1974), that first characterized *Miranda* as a prophylactic protection, rather than one firmly anchored in the Fifth Amendment.

[10] Liva Baker's excellent book provides a thorough, engrossing account (Baker 1983).

mailed fist (Baker 1983, p. 244). Not even Democratic presidential candidate Hubert Humphrey defended the Supreme Court's criminal procedure decisions, the most controversial of which was *Miranda* (Graham 1970, p. 158).

The Omnibus Crime Control and Safe Streets Act of 1968 had already passed and been signed into law by the time the presidential campaigns began. One mystery is why President Lyndon Johnson, a liberal, signed the bill. Johnson had declined to run for a second term and thus was insulated from any political fallout that would have accompanied vetoing the bill. In signing the bill, he expressed his view that it did not overrule *Miranda* (Baker 1983, pp. 207–8; Dallek 1998, pp. 516–17), but it is very difficult to read section 3501 any other way, as the Supreme Court concluded in *Dickerson*. Perhaps Johnson chose not to veto the legislation to deprive Nixon of an additional weapon to use against Humphrey, Johnson's vice president.

Miranda was controversial because of what it did instrumentally and also for what it said about society and criminals. The instrumental fear was that warning suspects of a "right to remain silent" and then promising a free lawyer to stand between them and the police would cause the rate of successful interrogations to plummet and the crime rate to soar. Any Court decision that portended more crime was a natural target of conservatives and moderates, the "law and order" constituency that Nixon sought to build. Why would the Court create a doctrine that seemed to have, as its most likely effect, an increase in the crime rate?

At one level, that of doctrine and the Court's responsibility to set standards for lower courts to follow, the answer is easy. The "voluntariness" test used for centuries to determine whether to admit confessions required inquiry into metaphysical states of mind that, by the 1960s, were believed to be inherently unknowable. Consider *Lisenba v. California*, 314 U.S. 219 (1941). The police interrogated Lisenba for about forty hours over two sessions, separated by several days. Prior to the second session, police confronted him with the confession of his alleged partner in crime. After a midnight dinner and cigars in a café with a group that included two deputy sheriffs, Lisenba discussed the crime, shifting much of the blame to the "partner." Was he confessing because of the relentless interrogation, or because he knew that his partner's confession would hurt his case and it was thus his "will" to offer his own, more exculpatory, version of events? Or did he confess because of some complex combination of those reasons along with guilt and other deeply hidden psychological forces acting on him? How would a court—indeed how would anyone, including the suspect—know the "thick" answer to that question?[11]

While this is a metaphysical conundrum of the first order, the law had already "solved" the problem of locating human "will" in this context. If a suspect confessed without the police using or threatening force, or making promises, there was a strong presumption that it was his will. In *Lisenba*, the Court held, seven to two, that the confession was admissible, noting that the defendant "exhibited a self-possession, a coolness, and an acumen throughout his questioning, and at his trial, which negatives the view that he had so lost his freedom of action that the statements were not his but were the result of the deprivation of his free choice to admit, to deny, or to refuse to answer" (*Lisenba*, p. 241). Lower courts followed the Supreme Court's robust view of human will, admitting confessions routinely in the absence of physical coercion or promises of leniency.[12] This stable judicial doctrine indicates that the law had a solution to the problem of locating human will in the interrogation room. But the *Miranda* majority did not think the *Lisenba* solution fully captured the ways in which police interrogation sapped the will of the suspect. Indeed, the two Justices who dissented in *Lisenba* in 1941 (Justices Hugo Black and William O. Douglas) were still on the Court in 1966 and constituted two-fifths of the *Miranda* majority.

The road from the *Lisenba* presumption of voluntariness to *Miranda*'s concern with free choice was not completely smooth, but it did lead only in one direction. Through the 1950s and early 1960s, the Court began to change its mind about how much pressure would turn a confession from voluntary to involuntary. The lower courts did not change as quickly, leading to a series of cases in which the Supreme Court reviewed, and reversed, state court decisions to admit confessions (Leo and Thomas 1998, p. 24, n. 61). In these cases, the Court seemed to be trying to send a message to the lower courts that they should be more discerning in their review of confessions, that involun-

---

[11] We do not doubt that humans offer reasons for their acts, but these accounts are likely to be a "thin" description of complex human motivation that can never be fully described.

[12] See, e.g., Davis v. North Carolina, 384 U.S. 737 (1966), in which two state courts and two federal courts had held voluntary a confession obtained after sixteen days of incommunicado interrogation. The Supreme Court reversed, noting that it "had never sustained the use of a confession obtained after such a lengthy period of detention and interrogation" (*Davis*, p. 752).

tariness can result from fatigue and the relentless pressure of the interrogation as well as from threats and promises. In reversing one state court, the Supreme Court pointedly remarked that "the blood of the accused is not the only hallmark of an unconstitutional inquisition" (*Blackburn v. Alabama*, 361 U.S. 199, 206 [1960]).

The message did not get through to the state courts. The Supreme Court hears only about 120 cases a year, involving a wide range of issues. The Court interprets federal statutes and regulations in areas as disparate as patents, employment discrimination, and environmental law. It also reviews cases from state and federal courts involving myriad constitutional issues, choosing from among thousands of petitions. The Court simply lacks the resources to review all, or even an appreciable fraction, of state cases on the single issue of confessions.[13] To get the state courts to change their ways would take a bold, new approach. *Miranda* was that approach. The concern with official pressure, fatigue, and various techniques designed to persuade or cajole the suspect into confessing could be addressed by letting the suspect control the interrogation. To accomplish that goal, why not simply require the police to tell the suspect that he can refuse to answer and that he can insert a lawyer (paid for by the state) between himself and the interrogators? In short, the *Miranda* solution was to require notice that the suspect has "rights" against the police with the purpose of ensuring that any decision he makes is his free choice.

Why did the Court change its attitude toward confessions? What was wrong with the approach in *Lisenba* that presumed suspects confessed because they saw an advantage in confessing? The answer is found in the deep premise of the *Miranda* opinion—that the suspect deserves at least some measure of sympathy when faced with relentless police interrogation. The *Miranda* Court seemed to see the police as the ones engaged in a morally dubious endeavor when trying to trick, cajole, or persuade suspects to incriminate themselves. The Court in *Lisenba* described in great detail the crime for which the defendant was convicted. He plotted to kill his wife for the double indemnity insurance proceeds and first attempted to kill her by tying her to a table and letting a poisonous snake bite her. Her leg swelled horribly but she did not die from the snakebite. After she had suffered for hours, Lisenba took her to a pond in the back yard and drowned her. He then filed

---

[13] A Westlaw search of state cases for the year 1999 that mentioned "*Miranda*" produced 1,843 cases.

for the insurance proceeds. It is difficult to feel sympathy for Lisenba when he faced his interrogators.

In *Miranda*, by contrast, the Court barely mentions the crimes that the four defendants committed (the Court had granted review in four different cases, consolidated for purposes of the oral argument and decision; it is merely coincidental that *Miranda*'s name came first). The crimes are not mentioned until more than fifty pages into the majority opinion. Instead, the Court discusses at length how police trickery, deception, and manipulation act to deprive suspects of their "free choice" (a locution that, with its variants, appears several times in the *Miranda* opinion) to decide whether to answer police questions.[14] Somehow, suspects gained a measure of the Court's sympathy between *Lisenba* and *Miranda*. Somehow, the police had become authoritarian rather than simply overzealous. How did this happen?

Identifying the causes of human conduct or attitudes risks reductionism. It is wise to remember Kant's view that our causal knowledge of the world is structured by the human mind: the concept of causality is imposed on experience by thought (Kant 1998, p. 115). We nonetheless note some ways the society was changing. The United States in the 1950s and 1960s grew more concerned about incipient racism. One manifestation of racism was in police practices, especially in the South. And one flagrant form of racism was when white police used their power and authority to intimidate black suspects into confessing. Rather than a cocky, self-assured Lisenba facing police interrogators in California, the cases from the 1950s often had poor black suspects facing white police in a Southern police station.[15]

The 1960s also brought a heightened concern about fairness and distributive justice. A few suspects knew they did not have to answer questions and routinely insisted on seeing their lawyers (Kamisar 1965). This group, probably disproportionately white and middle class, was privileged compared to the rest of the suspects. Why not level the playing field by providing that information to all suspects? Yale Kami-

[14] See 384 U.S. at 457 ("free choice"), id. at 458 ("free choice"), id. at 474 ("free choice"), id. at 465 ("free and rational choice"), id. at 467 ("compel him to speak where he would not otherwise do so freely"), id. at 478 (statements are admissible when "given freely and voluntarily without any compelling influences"), id. at 460 ("unfettered exercise of his own will").

[15] The Court reversed state convictions in cases involving a claim of coercive police interrogation in five cases from 1954–60. The suspect was black in three of the cases, and all cases took place in the South (Blackburn v. Alabama, 361 U.S. 199 [1960]; Payne v. Arkansas, 356 U.S. 560 [1958]); Fikes v. Alabama, 352 U.S. 191 [1957]).

sar's classic study of confession law paved the way for *Miranda* and drew heavily on this principle of equal treatment (Kamisar 1965, pp. 4–11 and 64–81).[16] He argued that "respect for the individual and securing equal treatment in law enforcement" require the state to make counsel available to suspects who face police interrogation and to warn them that they need not answer (Kamisar 1965, pp. 79–80). He concluded: "To the extent the Constitution permits the wealthy and educated to 'defeat justice,' if you will, *why shouldn't* all defendants be given a like opportunity?" (Kamisar 1965, p. 80).

At a more general level, 1960s thinking about the causes of crime and delinquency minimized the individual's responsibility for his actions. Was crime really the fault of the lower class citizen or a failure of the larger society to provide him the right environment, education, and job opportunities? President Johnson's War on Poverty was "fought" not just because poverty is bad but also because providing education and jobs to lower class citizens will reduce crime rates. If the war on poverty has not been won, whose fault is that? It is certainly not the fault of the inner city resident huddled in the interrogation room being badgered by police officers. Gerald Caplan put it this way: "When *Miranda* was decided in 1966, it was popular to see the criminal as a type of victim; he was caught in the role assigned to persons in his circumstances, a member of the underclass. One spoke not of volition but of status or condition. The idea of individual guilt and remorse for wrongful deeds was out of fashion. The causal factors of criminality were thought to lie outside the individual, in the deeper, corrupt foundations of society—the so-called root causes" (Caplan 1985, p. 1472).

Some combination of these cultural changes might explain *Miranda*'s sympathy for the suspect who is undergoing interrogation. The Court portrayed the police officer as manipulative, as taking advantage of a frightened, confused individual. In describing some of the cases decided in the 1963 term under the old voluntariness analysis, the *Miranda* Court remarked, "In other settings, these individuals might have exercised their constitutional rights. In the incommunicado police-dominated atmosphere, they succumbed" (*Miranda*, p. 456). In the next paragraph, the Court described the four cases it was deciding: "In each of the cases, the defendant was thrust into an unfamiliar atmo-

---

[16] Kamisar's paper laid out the theory that the privilege against self-incrimination should apply to the police interrogation room and that notions of equal protection required providing suspects notice that they did not have to answer questions.

sphere and run through menacing police interrogation" (*Miranda*, p. 457). A few lines below, the Court remarked: "It is obvious that such an interrogation environment is created for no purpose other than to subjugate the individual to the will of his examiner. This atmosphere carries its own badge of intimidation" (*Miranda*, p. 457).

This is a seismic shift from the attitude the Court displayed toward the suspect in *Lisenba* when the opinion stressed his "self-possession," his "coolness," his "acumen." Instead of assessing the individual's capacity to resist police interrogators, *Miranda* "opted for a theory of group rather than individual rights . . . subsum[ing] the claims of individuals in an effort to restructure the police-citizen interaction" (Seidman 1992, p. 738). The Court's new view of interrogation also explains why it created the remedy it did—warnings that, in theory at least, gave control of the interrogation to the suspect. Because the Court relied on the Fifth Amendment privilege to justify its holding, it could have created greater rights in suspects. It could have made the suspect's situation more analogous to that of defendants in court. The prosecutor is not permitted to ask the defendant at trial whether he wants to answer questions. The defendant must affirmatively put himself on the stand and tell his story, aided by his lawyer. If the Court was serious about making the privilege not to testify applicable to the police interrogation room, it could have forbidden police interrogation unless the suspect stated, through his lawyer, that he wanted to make a statement. That remedy was not only politically more risky but also, given *Miranda*'s premises, excessive. If the problem was the unfair advantage in knowledge and power possessed by the police, the remedy should be to turn control of the interrogation over to the suspect. The solution should be to give the suspect the free choice to answer or to refuse to answer.

The Court's change in attitude, perhaps as much as the pragmatic concern about the rise in crime rates, outraged *Miranda*'s critics. No longer did the Court talk about criminals as evil actors who are responsible for the consequences of their actions, whatever their other misfortunes in life. No longer did the Court seem concerned about victims. Miranda's rape victim did not get the Court's sympathy. Instead, the Court worried about the plight of her rapist. Custodial interrogation, the Court tells the reader, "exacts a heavy toll on individual liberty and trades on the weakness of individuals" (*Miranda*, p. 454). Custodial interrogation fails to accord sufficient weight "to the dignity and integrity" of citizens, fails "to respect the inviolability of the human personality" (*Miranda*, p. 460). Finding the right balance between rights of suspects and the protection of victims has divided philosophers, criminologists, and politicians for centuries. Anger flared in the post-*Miranda* period because rarely does one side "win" quite so decisively or obviously as did the view of the sympathetic criminal suspect in *Miranda*.

The seismic shift in the Court's attitude toward suspects is the most satisfying explanation of the Court's opinion in *Miranda*. The Court could have justified giving control of the interrogation to the suspect by focusing on the formal presumption of innocence and the state's burden of proving defendants guilty. While the opinion mentions these coolly logical principles (*Miranda*, pp. 460–61), it spends much more time and energy describing the strategies in the interrogation manuals for inducing reluctant suspects to answer questions (*Miranda*, pp. 448–55). This discussion, as well as the Court's oft-repeated conclusion that police interrogation is inherently compelling and destructive of human dignity, humanizes the suspect in a way that a reliance on a presumption of innocence could never achieve.

Nor is *Miranda* about police manipulating innocent people to confess. There is a single reference in the opinion, in a footnote, to the problem of innocent suspects being coerced to confess (*Miranda*, p. 455, n. 24). The Court cites as authority three stories in the *New York Times*. Nor is *Miranda* about police denying a request to talk to counsel, as was true two years earlier in a landmark case that foreshadowed *Miranda* (*Escobedo v. Illinois*, 378 U.S. 478 [1964]). None of the four defendants in *Miranda* had asked to speak to a lawyer.

Nor is *Miranda* really about police using the third degree to coerce confessions from unwilling suspects. There is a reference early in the opinion to the role a "proper limitation upon custodial interrogation" might play in eradicating the third degree (*Miranda*, p. 447), but a warnings requirement plays this role only if the police respect an invocation of the *Miranda* rights. It is not clear why police willing to use the third degree would be deterred by a suspect asking for interrogation to stop, or that these police would even give the warnings in the first place. Police willing to use coercion could always lie in court about whether they gave warnings and about what the suspect said. Justice Harlan made this point in his *Miranda* dissent: "The new rules are not designed to guard against police brutality or other unmistakably banned forms of coercion. Those who use third-degree tactics and deny them in court are equally able and destined to lie as skillfully about warnings and waiver" (*Miranda*, p. 505 [Harlan, J., dissenting]).

No, *Miranda* was simply about police taking advantage of suspects who were poor, ignorant, frightened, and thus no match for police interrogators. They talked to police without making a robust choice to do so. Part of their lack of robust choice, *Miranda* seemed to say, resulted from a belief that they had a formal or informal duty to answer police questions. The warnings, which include a right to consult with a lawyer, should dispel that notion. After *Miranda*, the playing field appeared more level. The suspects were, in theory at least, more in control of the interrogation.

But as *Miranda* critics liked to ask in the aftermath—What is wrong with an uneven playing field against guilty suspects? Joseph Grano made this critique forcefully and often (Grano 1979*a*, 1979*b*, 1986, 1988, 1989, 1992, 1993, 1996). What is wrong with taking advantage of whatever the police need to use (short of coercion or threats of coercion) to get confessions from guilty suspects? As a society, let us do what it takes to improve the conditions in the cities, eradicate poverty, provide jobs, and protect innocent defendants from conviction, but what do those goals have to do with whether Ernest Miranda raped his victim? If he did, why should we care that he was not told of a right to remain silent or to have a lawyer present before he confessed? That has always been the ethical Achilles heel of *Miranda*. As long as a guilty suspect makes a choice to answer police questions, even if it is not the robust choice made by a defendant to take the witness stand, it might be that society is better served by using that statement against him.

To be sure, that ethical balance is inconsistent with what appears to be *Miranda*'s core value of enhancing the "free choice"—the autonomy—of suspects. But, as the Court began to tinker with *Miranda* in the 1970s and 1980s, the core value shifted to protecting a different kind of choice. Various kinds of choice are available in the interrogation room, some more free than others (Thomas 1993). Wigmore's famous aphorism on this point captures an important truth: "As between the rack and a false confession, the latter would usually be considered the less disagreeable; but it is nonetheless voluntary" (Wigmore 1923, sec. 824).[17] To say that the suspect knew, at some level of cognition,

---

[17] Wigmore used this truism to demonstrate what he believed to be the unhelpful nature of the voluntary test. He preferred a test that asked whether the interrogation methods were likely to produce an unreliable confession.

that he had no obligation to answer police questions is not necessarily to say that he made the kind of robust "free choice" that *Miranda* seems to contemplate.

The current version of *Miranda* choice seems to require only that the suspect understand the warnings and that the police do not use coercion. It does not matter if the suspect fails to understand why he might be better off not to confess or why he should consult a lawyer or how the state might use his statement. In effect, the Court has clarified and diminished what *Miranda* seemed to mean by "free choice." The "free choice" that the *Miranda* Court had in mind turned into a formalized, devalued choice that the state can easily show by merely showing the fact of the warnings. Devaluing the choice that is at stake was, in effect, a response to the ethical critique of *Miranda*. Ironically, by devaluing the relevant choice, the Court made *Miranda* a more difficult target for those who wanted it overruled. The current version of *Miranda* no longer limits the police the way the original version seemed likely to do. Indeed, the new *Miranda* might not limit police in any meaningful way. Perhaps *Miranda* "traded the promise of substantial reform implicit in prior doctrine for a political symbol" (Seidman 1992, p. 746).

III. The Middle Period: Refining *Miranda*

By 1971, two members of the *Miranda* majority had resigned from the Court, and President Nixon had replaced them with judges thought to be conservative on criminal justice issues. In 1969, Warren Burger took the seat of Chief Justice Earl Warren, author of *Miranda*, and in 1970 Harry Blackmun took the seat of Justice Abe Fortas. On the other side of the ledger, before leaving office, President Johnson appointed Thurgood Marshall to take the seat of Justice Tom Clark, who dissented in *Miranda*.[18] The net effect was to leave the *Miranda* majority one vote short. And the vote in the next *Miranda* case was indeed five to four against applying *Miranda*. But it was not a vote to overrule *Miranda*. Instead, in *Harris v. New York*, 401 U.S. 222 (1971), the Court limited the reach of the original decision and, we think, shifted its conceptual foundation.

Harris represents the intersection of *Miranda* with the law of evidence. Under the standard law of evidence, a party can introduce evi-

---

[18] Clark concurred in this result in one of the cases but used the traditional voluntariness test to reach that result. He dissented from the holding in *Miranda* that substituted warnings and waiver for the voluntariness test.

dence of prior inconsistent statements made by a witness to impeach his credibility. The point is not to show that the impeaching statements are true but, rather, to show that the witness has told more than one story and may not be completely credible in his in-court testimony. Could prosecutors use statements taken in violation of *Miranda* for this purpose? On the robust view of *Miranda*'s holding—that custodial police interrogation unmediated by warnings always produces compelled statements—Harris should have won. Compelled statements cannot be used in court for any purpose.[19] But the purpose of *Miranda* might be narrower than its apparent doctrinal reach. If the purpose is to equalize the suspect with his crafty interrogators, to enhance the suspect's autonomy, the calculus perhaps shifts when we realize that the suspect is now insisting on his right to tell an exculpatory story in court and have *Miranda* hide his inconsistent statements from the jury. The Court held the statements admissible, albeit only to impeach the defendant's credibility.

The Court offered little explanation for its holding in *Harris*. It first explained that, having taken the witness stand, Harris had an obligation to speak truthfully. Then the Court claimed that had Harris made inconsistent statements to third persons (not the police), "it could hardly be contended that the conflict could not be laid before the jury by way of cross-examination and impeachment" (*Harris*, p. 226). But the analogy to statements made outside police interrogation ignores *Miranda*'s premise that custodial police interrogation compels all responses. The Court ultimately retreated to metaphor: "The shield provided by *Miranda* cannot be perverted into a license to use perjury by way of a defense, free from the risk of confrontation with prior inconsistent utterances" (*Harris*, p. 226).

Limiting the use to impeachment might seem to manifest a rather fanciful notion of how juries make decisions. If a jury hears the defendant's confession, it will likely consider it directly on the issue of guilt despite the judge's admonition to consider it only on credibility. Indeed, three years prior to *Harris*, the Court had taken that very approach to jury decision making in the context of joint trials. In *Bruton v. United States*, 391 U.S. 123 (1968), two defendants were tried together. One had confessed, implicating the other. The issue was whether the confession could be introduced in the joint trial if the

<hr/>

[19] That proposition had yet to be decided when *Harris* reached the Court, but it was ultimately decided in favor of defendants. See Portash v. New Jersey, 440 U.S. 450 (1979); Mincey v. Arizona, 437 U.S. 385 (1978).

judge instructed the jury to disregard the confession as to the guilt of the nonconfessing defendant.[20] The Court held that this instruction was insufficient to "cleanse" the mind of the jury: "Too often such admonition against misuse is intrinsically ineffective in that the effect of such a nonadmissible declaration cannot be wiped from the brains of the jurors" (*Bruton*, p. 129, quoting *Delli Paoli v. United States*, 352 U.S. 232, 247 [1957] [Frankfurter, J., dissenting]). This is true even though juries are likely to be somewhat skeptical of the confession of one defendant that shifts most or all of the blame to the other defendant.

But if an already skeptical jury cannot follow the judge's instruction to ignore a codefendant's confession, why would the Court assume that the jury would follow the judge's instructions to disregard, as to guilt, the defendant's very own confession? Juries presumably know that suspects have no incentive to lie in ways that make them seem more culpable, unlike codefendants who have plenty of incentive to lie to shift blame to someone else. The *Harris* Court not only did not follow *Bruton*, it did not even mention the case. The Court mentioned, but disregarded, language in the *Miranda* opinion forbidding the impeachment use of statements taken in violation of *Miranda*.[21] *Miranda* was already shrinking in 1971, only five years after it was decided.

In 1979, the Court made clear that the Fifth Amendment privilege is not as easily ignored as the *Miranda* prophylaxis. In *Portash v. New Jersey*, 440 U.S. 450 (1979), the defendant claimed the privilege not to testify but was compelled to testify by the threat of contempt of court. This, the Court held, was a violation of the Fifth Amendment privilege, and Portash's testimony could not be used to impeach his later testimony. The Court distinguished *Harris* on the ground that it involved a violation of the Fifth Amendment privilege presumed by failure to follow *Miranda*, rather than a violation of the privilege in its "most pristine form" (*Portash*, p. 459). In the latter situation "a defendant's compelled statements, as opposed to statements taken in viola-

---

[20] The case was decided under the Confrontation Clause right for defendants to be confronted with the witnesses against them. U.S. Const., amend. VI. *Bruton* involved a case where the confessing defendant did not testify. Had he testified, then the confession could be introduced because the other defendant would have a chance to confront the confessor.

[21] See *Miranda*, pp. 476–77: "Statements merely intended to be exculpatory by the defendant are often used to impeach his testimony at trial. . . . These statements are incriminating in any meaningful sense of the word and may not be used without the full warnings and effective waiver required for any other statement."

tion of *Miranda,* may not be put to any testimonial use against him in a criminal trial" (*Portash,* p. 459). The net effect of *Harris* and *Portash* is that the prophylaxis purportedly designed to protect the Fifth Amendment privilege sometimes does not apply when the privilege itself would suppress evidence. Nor is the same analytical structure used to analyze "real" violations of the Fifth Amendment privilege as opposed to *Miranda* violations. In distinguishing *Harris,* the Court in *Portash* wrote: "Balancing of interests was thought to be necessary in *Harris* . . . when the attempt to deter unlawful police conduct collided with the need to prevent perjury. Here, by contrast, we deal with the constitutional privilege against compulsory self-incrimination in its most pristine form. Balancing, therefore, is not simply unnecessary. It is impermissible" (*Portash,* p. 459).

Portash makes clear that *Miranda* is not necessarily connected to the Fifth Amendment privilege. *Miranda* does not protect the same set of choices that the privilege protects but, instead, creates a right to notice that can be balanced against other worthy goals and thus sometimes lost. Perhaps the Court full well realized that impeachment use effectively means that the jury will consider the statement on guilt but found this use permissible as long as the defendant is trying to turn his lack of choice about answering police questions into a wedge that facilitates perjury. By telling an exculpatory story on the witness stand that is different from what he told the police, Harris lost his right to complain that he did not know he could keep quiet in the interrogation room.

If *Harris* is best viewed as balancing the interest in making an informed choice to answer police questions, rather than the interest in not being compelled to answer questions, it fits neatly with *New York v. Quarles,* 467 U.S. 649 (1984). There, the police arrested a rape suspect in a store late at night and, without providing warnings, asked him where the gun was that he had used to commit the rape. On the traditional view of *Miranda* as required to rebut the compulsion of custodial interrogation, the answer to that question should be inadmissible. As Justice Marshall's dissent pointed out, Quarles was in the presence of four police officers, at least one of whom had drawn his weapon and ordered Quarles to stop just prior to asking him the location of the gun. This situation creates far more compulsion to answer than typical police interrogation.

The Court explained *Quarles* as a broad-gauged exception to the original *Miranda* rule based on a balancing of the interests at stake. But the balance is pretty close if one uses the traditional understanding of *Miranda* as presuming compulsion. Four members of the *Quarles* Court dissented, including Justice O'Connor, who often takes conservative positions in criminal cases but who here accused the Court of an unprincipled application of *Miranda*. The *Quarles* balance is ostensibly between public safety and the interest of the suspect in not being compelled to answer questions. *Harris* implicitly used the same kind of balancing: the interest of the criminal justice system in accurate fact finding goes on one side of the balance, and the interest in not being compelled to answer police questions on the other. But if we are really serious that the *Miranda* prophylaxis presumes compulsion, it is not clear how this balance comes out. Our whole criminal law system, after all, is premised on autonomous actors making noncompelled choices.

It is easier to justify *Quarles* and *Harris* if one views *Miranda* as permitting choice in the police interrogation room, rather than as presuming compulsion. One can recognize the pressure of police interrogation, and the necessity to give the suspect information that he need not answer, without at the same time finding every answer compelled and always inadmissible. To say that choice is valuable is not to say that it is equally valuable in every case. The value of choice can be balanced against other goals of the justice system. So Quarles did not make a free choice? Perhaps he forfeited that right when he hid the gun in a public place. So Harris did not make a free choice? Perhaps he forfeited the right to suppress his statements when he took the witness stand and told a different story.

One could explain *Harris* and *Quarles* by asserting that *Miranda* conclusively presumes that every answer is compelled but that the Court should sometimes admit into evidence compelled confessions. It is not a very satisfying explanation. Why would a system of justice rely on compelled testimony in any context? Our system does not use compelled testimony at all when the compulsion is "real" as opposed to "presumed" *Miranda* compulsion. It is thus more satisfying to say that *Miranda* enhances choice but that sometimes the value of that choice is outweighed by other goals. Without using the "choice" locution, the Court effectively adopted this analytical structure in *Harris* and *Quarles*.

But the *Miranda* evolution toward protecting choice did not always reduce the scope of the protection against police interrogation. In *Arizona v. Edwards*, 451 U.S. 477 (1981), the police gave warnings and the suspect requested counsel. The police followed the letter of *Miranda* and ceased interrogation. The next day, without counsel present, the police again gave warnings and asked Edwards if he was willing to waive his *Miranda* rights. He agreed. The issue was whether the second set of warnings and the waiver satisfied *Miranda*—did the waiver permit the police to continue even though they had not provided counsel as Edwards had requested? The outcome, in the conservative Burger Court, did not seem automatic. One could quite plausibly take the position that Edwards had simply changed his mind. Asking for a waiver again the next day hardly seems the kind of abusive interrogation that should create a presumption of compulsion.[22]

But the Court followed *Miranda*'s "choice" purpose and ruled, unanimously, that the statement had to be suppressed.[23] If the goal of *Miranda* is to prevent police from taking advantage of suspects who lack the information and skills to make free choices in the interrogation room, the suspect who admits his disadvantage by requesting counsel perhaps should be absolutely protected from further pressure to answer police questions. The "waiver" that the police got in the second attempt must therefore be ignored because it came from someone who had already admitted that, without counsel, he was not able to make robust choices about whether to answer police questions.

It is instructive to compare *Edwards* with *Michigan v. Mosley*, 423 U.S. 96 (1975), a case decided six years earlier. *Mosley* presented the analogous question of whether a suspect who has invoked the *Miranda* right to silence can be asked later if he wishes to talk. The Court reached the opposite answer here. If a suspect indicates that he wishes to remain silent, this does not insulate him from all later efforts to get him to waive his rights. The police must respect the invocation but can reapproach the suspect later and provide the warnings again. The difference between invoking the right to silence and the right to counsel makes sense, understood as a manifestation of choice. If you say you

[22] The facts of *Edwards* suggest more compulsion than we described in the text. When approached the next day, Edwards told the jail guard he did not want to talk to the detectives, but the guard told him he had to talk. Moreover, Edwards waived his *Miranda* rights only after listening to a tape recording of his accomplice that implicated him. The Court could have issued a narrow ruling, holding that on these facts the waiver was no good. It instead issued a very broad ruling—that once a request for counsel has been made, no further interrogation can occur unless counsel has been provided or the suspect "himself initiates further communications, exchanges, or conversations with the police" (*Edwards*, pp. 484–85). Indeed, it was the breadth of the ruling that caused Justices Powell and Rehnquist to concur in the judgment rather than join the majority opinion.

[23] Justices Powell and Rehnquist concurred in the result because they were concerned about the scope of the majority opinion but they, too, were in favor of suppressing the statement in the case before the Court.

do not want to talk to me, it does not mean you never want to talk to me, and I can ask again later without denying your free choice to say "no" again. The request for a lawyer is different because it admits a structural disadvantage, the very disadvantage at the heart of *Miranda*'s desire for a level playing field that permits free choices in the interrogation room. In short, the suspect's autonomy is undermined more when the right to counsel is ignored. *Mosley* makes less sense if the role of the warnings is to rebut compulsion. The suspect who has had his request to remain silent ignored seems likely to perceive as much compulsion as the suspect who has had his request for counsel ignored.

By the 1980s it was clear that the presumption of compulsion no longer answered all questions about how best to apply *Miranda*. The post-*Miranda* Court has consistently rejected a mechanical application based on a doctrinal presumption of compulsion in favor of tailoring *Miranda* to fit the purpose of promoting suspect choice about whether to answer police questions. As the doctrine evolved toward protecting choice, the choice being protected also changed. This can be seen most clearly in the waiver standard that the Court adopted. *Miranda* seemed to require a high standard for waiver. "If the interrogation continues without the presence of an attorney and a statement is taken, a heavy burden rests on the government to demonstrate that the defendant knowingly and intelligently waived his privilege against self-incrimination and his right to retained or appointed counsel" (*Miranda*, p. 475). But the Court ultimately held that waiver requires only that the suspect state that he understands the warnings and is willing to answer police questions (*North Carolina v. Butler*, 441 U.S. 369 [1979]).

That holding makes little sense if the point of *Miranda* is to protect the suspect from the inherent compulsion of the police interrogation room. To ameliorate inherent compulsion would seem to require more than just the suspect's agreement to talk to the creators of that inherent compulsion. Similarly, if *Miranda* is best understood as empowering suspects by giving them a robust "free choice," a court might want to require more than a mere statement from the suspect that he understands the warnings and is willing to talk. Part of the "heavy burden" of demonstrating waiver that *Miranda* contemplated could be to require a specific waiver of each right, perhaps in writing, rather than permitting a single statement to waive everything. This might seem like an inconsequential difference, but in practice it is probably very important. A more involved waiver process, particularly one that requires writing, would be more likely to impress upon the suspect the gravity of the rights he is surrendering.

If this process were followed, it would increase the likelihood that the choice being protected manifested the suspect's autonomy. It would increase the likelihood that the suspect would refuse to waive his rights. Under the Court's current standard, however, a formalized, legalistic choice is all that is necessary. This is clear under the facts of *Butler*. When asked if he understood his rights, Butler said that he did. But he refused to sign the waiver form. The agents told him he did not have to sign the waiver form or talk to them. He responded, "I will talk to you but I am not signing any form" (*Butler*, p. 371). Was Butler making a fully informed free choice to talk to the agents? It seems unlikely that he would talk to the agents after refusing to sign the form if he truly understood the consequences of what he was doing. He did make a choice, of sorts, after hearing the warnings and stating that he understood them, and this choice is enough to satisfy the Court. The *Butler* waiver standard makes the life of the interrogator much easier.

Miranda's choice rationale is consistent with the way the Court has analyzed the *Miranda* "poisoned fruit" issue—whether evidence found because of a *Miranda* violation should also be suppressed. To take a classic example from another context, if a search violates the Fourth Amendment and leads police to other evidence, this "derivative" evidence is presumed to be fruit of the poisonous tree (the Fourth Amendment violation) and thus generally cannot be admitted into evidence.[24] Should a *Miranda* violation also be viewed as a poisoned tree? Perhaps not. To correct a Fourth Amendment violation, courts can do little but to pretend that the search or seizure did not take place. How else can a court put the defendant back in the position he was in prior to the violation?

But a violation of *Miranda* does not produce evidence in the same way that a Fourth Amendment violation produces evidence. Rather than the police putting their hands on the evidence by virtue of an un-

---

[24] The Court has carved out three exceptions to the Fourth Amendment derivative evidence rule. Evidence is not suppressed when the taint is attenuated by passage of time or an exercise of volition by the person who surrenders the evidence (Wong Sun v. United States, 371 U.S. 471 [1963]), when the evidence is not really derivative because found from an independent source (Murray v. United States, 487 U.S. 533 [1988]), or when the evidence would have been discovered anyway by lawful means (Nix v. Williams, 467 U.S. 431 [1984]).

constitutional search, the harm in the *Miranda* violation is that the suspect did not have a sufficient choice to decide whether to answer police questions. But the causal link between the violation—the lack of choice—and the evidence is weaker than in the Fourth Amendment context. The answer that the suspect gives, the Court has now told us clearly, is not actually compelled, and the suspect might have given the same statement had the police complied with *Miranda*.

Because the causal link between the violation and the statement is more tenuous in the *Miranda* context, the violation might be sufficiently remedied by suppressing, at trial, the statement that we presume was taken without adequate choice. Courts need not, on this view, suppress the other evidence found by means of the statement. Once again, this doctrinal move is better explained if *Miranda* is viewed as protecting choice and not as presuming compulsion. The causal link between a presumptively compelled statement and derivative evidence is more solid than the link between a denial of choice in the interrogation room and derivative evidence.

The current *Miranda* doctrine contemplates that choice in the interrogation room is a valuable goal that is subject to being outweighed by other goals in a justice system. A statement taken without warnings is suppressed except when the police are protecting public safety (*Quarles*) or when the defendant tells a different story at trial (*Harris*). In addition, the *Miranda* violation is fully remedied by suppressing the statement. There is no need to suppress other evidence found by means of the statement, such as other witnesses (*Michigan v. Tucker*, 417 U.S. 433 [1974]) or later statements that the suspect makes after receiving warnings (*Oregon v. Elstad*, 470 U.S. 298 [1985]). Suspects waive *Miranda* by agreeing to talk to police (*Butler*). While this is not the only coherent doctrine that could have evolved from *Miranda*, it is the one the Supreme Court developed during the 1970s and 1980s.

In a sense, then, later Courts were creating, and endorsing, a slimmed-down *Miranda*. If *Miranda* in 1966 had the potential to change the psychology of the interaction between the suspect and the interrogator, if the warnings ever had the power to "restructure preferences" to make cooperation less likely (Seidman 1990, p. 174), that possibility was undermined by the cases in the 1970s and 1980s. *Miranda* was still about leveling the playing field in the interrogation room, but the leveling was limited to providing suspects with information about their rights, rather than empowering them to resist the police interrogation. Refining *Miranda* in the 1970s and 1980s meant being true to this narrower purpose of *Miranda*, rather than simply indulging a knee-jerk application of the doctrinal rule that *Miranda* violations presume compulsion.

If these later Courts saw themselves as continually rewriting *Miranda*, it should come as no surprise that in the year 2000, the current Court refused to overrule its own creation. *Miranda* in the year 2000 was perhaps seen more as the product of thirty-four years of moderate-to-conservative Court labor than that of the Warren Court of 1966. That seems the import of the statement in *Dickerson* that "our subsequent cases have reduced the impact of the *Miranda* rule on legitimate law enforcement while reaffirming the decision's core ruling that unwarned statements may not be used as evidence in the prosecution's case in chief" (*Dickerson*, p. 2335).

Davis v. United States, 512 U.S. 452 (1994), is an example of the reduced impact on "legitimate law enforcement" and the narrowing of the relevant choice from autonomy enhancing to formal. Davis waived his *Miranda* rights but about an hour and a half into the interview said, "Maybe I should talk to a lawyer." Is this an invocation of the right to counsel that should terminate the interview? It is not a wholly unambiguous invocation, as the Court concluded. But is it close enough to create an obligation for police to inquire into what the accused meant? A Court concerned with the substance of "free choice," with enhancing the suspect's autonomy, would have adopted that rule. A bright line rule could require police to respond to any statement with the word "lawyer" in it by asking whether the accused wanted to speak with a lawyer. That is not a difficult burden. But five members of the *Davis* Court refused to go that far, insisting that if the suspect's words fall short of an unambiguous request for counsel, police can simply disregard what was said and continue the interrogation. Choice is still protected here, perhaps, but it is a formalized kind of choice that lawyers, but few others, would recognize.

Protecting only a formal choice in the interrogation room accomplishes less than *Miranda* seemed to contemplate. Suspects who understand the warnings might nonetheless choose to talk to police, to persuade the police to release them, or to take advantage of a better "deal" than the prosecutor will offer later, or just because in other contexts in life one does not stand silent in the face of an accusation (Kamisar 1974, p. 35). That these suspects are almost always making a mistake does not, of course, diminish the formal freedom they have to talk or not. Even if one views police tactics that encourage these misapprehensions as inappropriate—even if the tactics exert compelling pressure on suspects—it remains true that as a formal matter, the suspect who understands the warnings should know that he can talk or not as he sees fit. Perhaps the studies showing little *Miranda* effect on police interrogation (see, e.g., Wald et al. 1967; Witt 1973) are consistent with the way the Court has shaped *Miranda*. The crown jewel of the Warren Court's protection of suspects now provides formal notice of the right to control the interrogation and, after that notice is given, the suspect is pretty much on his own. The psychology of the encounter between interrogator and suspect is little changed.

IV. The *Miranda* Impact Studies

In the three decades prior to *Miranda*, there had been relatively little field research on police interrogation practices in America (see Leo [1996*b*] for a review). It was thus hardly surprising that the Warren Court in 1966 relied on police training manuals—rather than empirical studies—to describe the techniques and methods of police interrogation in America. Emphasizing the absence of firsthand knowledge of actual police interrogation practices at the time, the Warren Court in *Miranda* noted that "interrogation still takes place in privacy. Privacy results in secrecy and this in turn results in a gap in our knowledge as to what in fact goes on in the interrogation room" (*Miranda*, p. 448).

A. First Generation Studies, 1966–73

In the years immediately following the *Miranda* decision, scholars published approximately a dozen empirical studies that sought to fill this gap (Younger 1966*a*, 1966*b*; Griffiths and Ayres 1967; Seeburger and Wettick 1967; Wald et al. 1967; Medalie, Zeitz, and Alexander 1968; Robinson 1968; Leiken 1970; Milner 1971; Schaefer 1971; Stephens, Flanders, and Cannon 1972; Witt 1973; Neubauer 1974). Undertaken in a variety of locations (e.g., Pittsburgh; New Haven, Conn.; Washington, D.C.; Los Angeles; Denver; Madison, Wisc.; and elsewhere), these studies sought to identify and analyze police implementation of, and compliance with, the new *Miranda* requirements; police attitudes toward *Miranda*; the effect of the *Miranda* warning and waiver regime on police and suspect behavior during interrogation; and the impact of *Miranda* on confession, clearance, and conviction rates.

These first-generation *Miranda* impact studies relied on a variety of methodologies (participant observation, surveys, interviews, analysis of case files), each with its own strengths, weaknesses, and limitations.

One of the earliest and most widely cited studies was conducted by Yale law students, who observed 127 live interrogations inside the New Haven Police Department during the summer of 1966 (Wald et al. 1967) and then compared their observations to data they reviewed from approximately 200 cases from 1960 to 1965 in the New Haven Police Department. The researchers found that while the detectives failed to read all or part of the required warnings to custodial suspects in the immediate aftermath of *Miranda*, they eventually began to comply with the letter (but not the spirit) of the new *Miranda* requirements. The quality of the warnings varied inversely with the strength of the evidence (the stronger the evidence, the worse the warnings) and directly with the seriousness of the offense, suggesting that detectives delivered more adequate warnings when failure to do so might jeopardize the admissibility of a highly valued confession.

Most of the suspects appeared unable to grasp the significance of their *Miranda* rights, thus undermining *Miranda*'s effect on a suspect's decision to answer police questions. Only a few suspects refused to speak to police or requested counsel prior to questioning, and in only 5 percent of the cases did the *Miranda* requirements adversely affect the ability of police to obtain a confession that the researchers judged necessary for conviction. In addition, the researchers noted that *Miranda* appeared to have little impact on police behavior during interrogation, since detectives continued to employ many of the psychological tactics of persuasion and manipulation that the Warren Court had deplored in *Miranda*. Wald and colleagues (1967) concluded that the interrogation process had become "considerably less hostile" from 1960 to 1966 and that *Miranda* does not substantially impede successful law enforcement.

In addition to participant observation, several of the early *Miranda* researchers relied on broad surveys of existing police practices to assess the impact of *Miranda* on the apprehension and prosecution of criminal suspects. Less than a month after *Miranda* was decided, Evelle Younger (1966a, 1966b) administered a survey to the members of the Los Angeles County District Attorneys' Office. In the previous year (1965), the same office had compiled a similar survey to gauge the effect of *People v. Dorado*, 398 P.2d 361 (Cal. 1965), a California Supreme Court case that anticipated *Miranda* because it required California law enforcement officers to warn custodial suspects of their rights to counsel and to remain silent. Comparing the results of these two surveys, Younger concluded that police officers began complying with *Miranda* immediately after it became law; that the required warnings did not reduce the percentage of admissions and confessions made to officers in cases that reached the complaint stage; and that *Miranda* requirements did not decrease the percentage of felony complaints issued by prosecutors or their success in prosecuting cases at the preliminary stage. As Younger pointed out, the confession rate—in cases in which police requested that felony complaints be issued—rose approximately 10 percent (from 40 percent to 50 percent) after *Miranda*!

In addition to participant observation, field research, and surveys of police practices, some early researchers attempted to study *Miranda*'s impact on the processes and outcomes of custodial interrogation by interviewing custodial suspects, detectives, and lawyers. In one such study, Lawrence Leiken (1970) interviewed fifty suspects inside the Denver County jail in 1968. Leiken found that Denver police typically read the *Miranda* warnings to each suspect from a standard advisement form that the suspect was then asked to sign twice (to acknowledge that he understood his rights and to indicate the he wished to waive them). Nevertheless, Leiken argued that a large percentage of the suspects in his sample inadequately understood their rights because they could not recall the right to silence or counsel warnings and did not know that oral statements could be used against them in court or that their signatures on waiver forms had any legal effect in their cases. Paradoxically, however, those suspects who best understood their rights were most likely to speak to detectives. In addition, Leiken reported that the Denver police used the very psychological pressures deplored by the *Miranda* Court (including the use of promises and threats to obtain waivers and to elicit statements and confessions). Leiken concluded that the *Miranda* rights did not effectively achieve the Supreme Court's goal of dispelling the inherent pressures of interrogation because suspects could not make a meaningful, knowing waiver of their rights. Instead, police interrogators used the warnings to their advantage to create the appearance that a voluntary statement had been obtained.

The fourth method used in the first-generation of *Miranda* impact research was the analysis of case files and documents. In one study, for example, Witt (1973) analyzed 478 felony case files from 1964 to 1968 in an unidentified Southern California police department in a city with over 80,000 residents, which he dubbed "Seaside City." Witt found that although police officers believed they were receiving far fewer admissions and confessions as a result of the *Miranda* requirements, their confession rate declined only 2 percent, and the clearance rate only 3 percent, from the pre-*Miranda* period to the post-*Miranda* period. The conviction rate, however, declined almost 10 percent from the pre-*Miranda* to the post-*Miranda* period. Witt argued that *Miranda* had little impact on the effectiveness of police interrogations in the cases he studied, but that *Miranda* did have an impact on the collateral functions of interrogation: the police interrogated fewer suspects, implicated fewer accomplices, cleared fewer crimes, and recovered less stolen property through interrogation than prior to *Miranda*.

These four studies (Younger 1966*a*, 1966*b*; Wald et al. 1967; Leiken 1970; Witt 1973) exemplify the range, as well as the strengths and weaknesses, of the various methodologies employed in the first round of *Miranda* impact research. Wald et al.'s (1967) participant observation study broke new ground because these researchers directly witnessed and analyzed the interrogation process that, to that time, had been rarely observed. The downside of Wald et al.'s study, however, is that the researchers could never be certain whether their presence in the interrogation room altered the behavior of the detectives or the suspects, and, as with so many other *Miranda* impact studies, their focus on one jurisdiction limited the generalizability of their study. The *Miranda* impact studies that relied on interviews were able to ask probing questions to suspects, detectives, and other actors in the criminal justice system to better understand the perceptions, attitudes, and motivations of those who give and receive *Miranda* warnings. But these interview studies suffered from a different type of bias: the researcher never knew whether the subjects were distorting information—either intentionally or unintentionally—to portray themselves in a favorable light or to hide wrongdoing or perhaps simply due to ordinary errors of memory or recall. The problem of respondent bias inherent in the interviewing method is, of course, magnified by the adversarial context of American criminal justice. In the Leiken's study, for example, one may justifiably treat the statements of his incarcerated subjects with some skepticism (Thomas 1996*a*, pp. 828–29).

The two other methods of data gathering used in the first round of studies—surveys and documentary analysis—also provided researchers with useful information about *Miranda*'s impact on the process and outcomes of interrogation. The survey studies like Younger's allowed researchers to quantify and compare large numbers of case outcomes at different stages of the criminal process. The weakness of Younger's (and other survey studies of *Miranda*'s impact), of course, was that what they gained in coverage they sacrificed in depth: survey studies may provide useful information about trends and outcomes but do not tell us the "why's" that lay behind those trends and outcomes. The analysis of documents and case files to assess the processes and outcomes of police interrogation, as in the Witt (1973) study, proved to be among the most useful methods in parsing out *Miranda*'s impact, especially where pre- and post-*Miranda* data were available. As with Witt's study, the strengths and weaknesses of any documentary analysis depend primarily on the quality of the documents themselves—which tell a story that cannot be distorted (since the documents have been memorialized), but which may be incomplete or inaccurate. Regrettably, the problem with Witt's study of *Miranda*'s impact—as with several other first-generation studies—was that he failed to employ even the most elementary statistical techniques to evaluate whether any of the pre-*Miranda* versus post-*Miranda* differences that he observed were statistically significant.

The methodological problem of inferring the precise causal effects of a judicial decision on case outcomes goes beyond any particular data-gathering approach. Impact studies have been premised on a quasi-experimental model in which the impact of a single decision is evaluated as if all other factors could be held constant. But this assumption is rarely achieved since controlled experimentation is rarely, if ever, possible in the study of naturally occurring data. As a result, social scientists have traditionally relied on two positive strategies to measure judicial impact: before/after studies, and comparison-with-excluded-jurisdiction designs. While the latter method suffers from a lack of statistical comparability among jurisdictions (and in the case of *Miranda* there are no excluded jurisdictions—since all jurisdictions are required to follow the *Miranda* rules), the former suffers from the problem of intervening factors. Thus, our inability to hold constant extraneous and potentially confounding (independent) variables undermines our ability to draw precise causal inferences in the study of judicial impact. Though often imperfect, the best research designs in the study of *Miranda*'s impact have employed multiple approaches so that the strengths of one method may compensate for the weaknesses of another and the findings from one method may be triangulated against (and better understood by) the findings from another.

Several scholars have cataloged and analyzed the findings of the first-generation *Miranda* studies (Cassell 1996*b*; Leo 1996*a*; Schulhofer 1996*b*; Thomas 1996*a*). Although an in-depth discussion of these studies is beyond the scope of this essay, several general patterns are worth noting. First, in the initial aftermath of *Miranda* some police immediately began complying with *Miranda* (Younger 1966*b*), while others ignored the decision or failed to recite part or all of the required warnings to suspects in custody (Wald et al. 1967). After a brief adjustment period, virtually all police began to comply regularly with the letter, though not always the spirit, of the fourfold warning and waiver requirements (Wald et al. 1967; Leiken 1970). Despite their compliance, however, many detectives resented the new *Miranda* requirements (Wald et al. 1967; Stephens, Flanders, and Cannon 1972).

Second, despite the fourfold warnings, suspects frequently waived their *Miranda* rights and chose to speak to their interrogators. Some researchers attributed this largely unexpected finding to the manner in which detectives delivered the *Miranda* warnings, while others attributed it to the failure of suspects to understand the meaning or significance of their *Miranda* rights (Wald et al. 1967; Medalie, Zeitz, and Alexander 1968; Leiken 1970).

Third, once a waiver of rights had been obtained, the tactics and techniques of police interrogation did not appear to change as a result of *Miranda*. For example, Wald et al. (1967) observed in New Haven that *Miranda* appeared to have little impact on police behavior during interrogation, since detectives continued to employ many of the psychological tactics of persuasion and manipulation that the Warren Court had deplored in *Miranda*. Stephens and colleagues (1972) reported that while most detectives in Knoxville, Tennessee, and Macon, Georgia, issued formalized warnings, *Miranda* did not change the nature and role of the interrogation process.

Fourth, suspects continued to provide detectives with confessions and incriminating statements. In some studies, however, researchers reported a lower rate of confession than prior to *Miranda*. For example, Seeburger and Wettick (1967) reported that in their study of Pittsburgh, the confession rate generally dropped from 54.4 percent prior to *Miranda* to 37.5 percent after *Miranda*, though the decline varied by the type of crime reported. Yet other researchers reported only a marginal decrease in the confession rate. For example, Witt (1973) reported that in "Seaside City" the confession rate dropped only 2 percent (from 69 percent before the *Miranda* decision to 67 percent after the *Miranda* decision). And one researcher even reported an increase in the confession rate of approximately 10 percent after *Miranda* (Younger 1966*b*).

Fifth, researchers reported that clearance and conviction rates had not been adversely affected by the new *Miranda* requirements. For example, even though Seeburger and Wettick (1967) found a 17 percent decline in the confession rate in Pittsburgh, they did not find a corresponding decline in the conviction rate. Other researchers reported significant, if temporary, declines in clearance rates, but conviction rates remained relatively constant (Milner 1971). To be sure, in some instances they too dropped, but not significantly. For example, in his study of "Seaside City," Witt (1973) reported a 3 percent decline in the clearance rate and a 9 percent decline in the conviction rate (from 92 percent to 83 percent) after *Miranda* became law. If there was a significant cost to *Miranda* according to first-generation impact researchers, it appeared to be that *Miranda* may have caused the interrogation rate to drop and may also have been responsible for lessening the effectiveness of the collateral functions of interrogation such as identifying accomplices, clearing crimes, and recovering stolen property (Witt 1973).

But the consensus that emerged from the first generation of *Miranda* impact studies was that the *Miranda* rules had only a marginal effect on the ability of the police to elicit confessions and on the ability of prosecutors to win convictions, despite the fact that some detectives continued to perceive a substantial *Miranda* impact (Witt 1973). The general view of these studies is not merely that *Miranda* failed to affect the ability of police to control crime, but also that, in practice, the requirement of standard *Miranda* warnings failed to achieve the Warren Court's goal of protecting the free choice of suspects to decide for themselves whether to answer police questions.

The generalizability and contemporary relevance of the first-generation *Miranda* impact studies are undermined by two key factors. First, these studies are largely outdated. The data in each of the first-generation *Miranda* impact studies was gathered during the first three years following the 1966 *Miranda* decision. More than three decades have now passed since that time. These studies likely captured only the initial effects of *Miranda* before police officers and detectives had fully adjusted to the new procedures (Schulhofer 1996*b*). Second, many of these studies are methodologically weak, perhaps because many were conducted by lawyers or law professors without any training in the research methods of social science (Leo 1996*a*).

B. Second-Generation Studies, 1996–Present

The first generation of *Miranda* impact studies had run their course by 1973. For the next two decades, the social science and legal commu-

nity, with few exceptions (Grisso 1980; Gruhl and Spohn 1981), appeared to lose interest in the empirical study of *Miranda*'s impact on
criminal justice processes and outcomes. Gruhl and Spohn (1981) investigated the impact of *Miranda* (and post-*Miranda* rulings) on local
prosecutors, while Grisso (1980) performed a couple of empirical studies of the legal and psychological capacities of juveniles and adults to
waive their *Miranda* rights knowingly. Since the mid-1990s, however,
there has been a second flurry of empirical *Miranda* impact studies.
These studies might loosely be divided into two types: those that
seek to assess the quantitative impact of *Miranda* on confession, clearance, and conviction rates; and those that qualitatively seek to assess
Miranda's real-world impact on police—whether they comply with
or circumvent *Miranda*'s requirements, how they issue warnings and
waivers, and how they approach interrogation after securing a waiver.
Unlike their first-generation counterparts, however, the second-generation impact studies have generated considerable interpretive disagreement, debate, and commentary.

The best-known debate in the second-generation studies has been
between Cassell and Schulhofer. Selectively reanalyzing first-generation impact studies, as well as unpublished surveys conducted by prosecutors' offices in several cities immediately prior to and after *Miranda*,
Cassell speculated in 1996 that *Miranda* has caused a 16 percent reduction in the confession rate and that it is responsible for lost convictions
in 3.8 percent of all serious criminal cases. Cassell arrived at these figures by reviewing the published and unpublished surveys, ignoring
those that he claimed had major problems, and then averaging the
change in confession rate in these studies before and after *Miranda*.
Cassell did not always use the rate reported by the studies; he sometimes recalculated the rate, claiming that it was necessary to correct
methodological errors or achieve comparability with other studies.
Based on this selective reanalysis of some of these early published studies and unpublished surveys, Cassell posited that *Miranda* reduced confessions in approximately 16 percent of all cases. Cassell further posited that confessions are necessary for convictions in 24 percent of all
cases. Multiplying the two figures (0.24×0.16), Cassell argued that
Miranda is responsible for lost convictions in 3.8 percent of all serious
criminal cases. Using the FBI's Uniform Crime Reports crime index
for arrests (no figures are available for the number of individuals interrogated), Cassell concluded that approximately 28,000 violent crime
and 79,000 property crime cases are lost each year as a result of *Miranda*, and that there are an equal number each year of more lenient

plea bargains attributable to evidence weakened by *Miranda* (Cassell 1996*b*). Shortly after publishing these figures, Cassell substantially revised them and argued that each year more than one hundred thousand violent criminals (who would otherwise be convicted and incarcerated) go free as a direct result of the *Miranda* requirements (Cassell 1996*c*).

Reanalyzing the first-generation studies, Schulhofer speculated that *Miranda* may have initially caused a 4.1 percent drop in the confession rate in the immediate post-*Miranda* period. Arguing that confessions were necessary for conviction in 19 percent of all cases, Schulhofer multiplied these two figures together (0.041 × 0.19) to speculate that *Miranda* caused a 0.78 percent (seventy-eight hundredths of one percent) drop in the conviction rate, a decline, Schulhofer argued, that had probably been reversed as police learned how to comply with *Miranda* and still get confessions (Schulhofer 1996*b*). Schulhofer arrived at these figures by employing the same general approach as Cassell: Schulhofer reanalyzed the early *Miranda* impact studies, counting only those studies that he regarded as methodologically sound, and then averaging out their assessments of *Miranda*'s effect on the confession rate. Based on his analysis of these studies (as well as other adjustments such as large-city effects, trends in policing since *Miranda*, and a reanalysis of the "confessions-necessity-for-conviction figure"), Schulhofer concluded that "for all practical purposes, *Miranda*'s empirically detectable net damage to law enforcement is zero" (Schulhofer 1996*b*, p. 547).[25]

Despite Schulhofer's decisive refutation of Cassell's reanalysis of the first generation studies, Cassell continued to argue that *Miranda* has substantially depressed the confession rate and imposed significant costs on society by allowing tens of thousands of guilty suspects to escape conviction. In a study of prosecutor screening sessions involving a sample of 219 suspects, Cassell and Hayman (1996) found that 42.2

---

[25] Calling Cassell's analysis even further into question, Schulhofer pointed out that the studies on which Cassell relied suffer from significant methodological flaws and that we cannot so easily infer causation from correlation in any complex time-series analysis. Instead, Schulhofer suggested several competing alternative explanations for any decline in confession and conviction rates post-*Miranda* (long-term trends such as increasing professionalization of American police; trial courts' more rigorous reading of the Fourteenth Amendment to exclude involuntary confessions; competing causal events such as the trial rights applied to the states in *Mapp. v. Ohio*, Fourth Amendment, 367 U.S. 643 (1961), and Gideon v. Waintwright, Sixth Amendment, 372 U.S. 375 (1963); instability or random fluctuation in confession rates (i.e., regression to the mean); and shifting baselines against which to measure the effect of *Miranda*.

percent of the suspects who were questioned gave incriminating statements, a confession rate that they argued is far lower than pre-*Miranda* confession rates that they estimated to be in the range of 55–60 percent. Analyzing the same studies as Cassell, Thomas (1996*b*) found that the best estimate of the pre-*Miranda* confession rate was in the range of 45–53 percent. Arguing that Cassell and Hayman miscategorized some suspect responses that should have been counted as incriminating, Thomas speculated that the true confession rate in Cassell and Hayman's study was 54 percent, a rate similar both to Cassell and Hayman's estimate of the pre-*Miranda* confession rate as well as to the confession rate found in post-*Miranda* studies (Feeney, Dill, and Weir 1983; Leo 1996*b*).

In a subsequent law review article, Cassell and Fowles (1998) collected FBI national crime clearance rate data for violent and property crimes from 1960 (when such data first became available) to 1995. In addition, they estimated the national clearance rate data from 1950–59, thus producing a database of estimated and reported national crime clearance rates for violent and property crimes from 1950 to 1995. Cassell and Fowles visually identified a decline in national crime clearance rates in the mid-to-late 1960s and, through multiple-regression analysis, sought to test whether a variable they would call "*Miranda*" was responsible for the decline in clearance rates. Using an interrupted time series design, Cassell and Fowles developed a regression model that included thirteen other criminal justice and socioeconomic variables: number of crimes, number of law enforcement employees per capita, dollars spent on police protection per capita by state and local governments, changes to law enforcement manpower and expenditures, the interaction between these variables and the overall number of crimes (what they called "capacity of the system"), the number of persons in the crime-prone years or juveniles from ages fifteen to twenty-four, labor force participation, unemployment rate, disposable per capita real income, live births to unmarried mothers, percent of the resident population residing in urban areas, percentage of violent crimes committed in small cities, and a standard time trend variable. Cassell and Fowles then identified a dummy variable for the years 1966–68 that they called "*Miranda*," and, using an interrupted time series analysis, Cassell and Fowles found that this "*Miranda*" variable showed a statistically significant effect on estimated and collected aggregate crime clearance rates for violent and property crimes from 1950 to 1995. Disaggregating "violent" and "property" crimes and running separate regressions, Cassell and Fowles found that the only individual violent crime for which the *"Miranda"* variable showed a statistically significant effect was robbery,[26] and that the property crimes for which the *"Miranda"* variable showed a statistically significant effect were larceny, vehicle theft, and burglary.

Based on this interrupted time series, multiple-regression analysis, Cassell and Fowles argued that the *Miranda* requirements have, indeed, handcuffed law enforcement in the last thirty years. In particular, Cassell and Fowles stated that "our regression equations and accompanying causal analysis suggest that, without *Miranda*, the number of crimes cleared would be substantially higher—by as much as 6.6–29.7 percent for robbery, 6.2–28.9 percent for burglary, 0.4–11.9 percent for larceny, and 12.8–45.4 percent for vehicle theft. Moreover, applied to the vast numbers of cases passing through the criminal justice system, these percentages would produce large numbers of cleared crimes. As many as 36,000 robberies, 82,000 burglaries, 163,000 larcenies and 78,000 vehicle thefts remain uncleared each year as a result of *Miranda*" (1998, p. 1126).

Based on this analysis, Cassell and Fowles drew the more general conclusion that, "the clearance rate data collected in this study . . . strongly suggest that *Miranda* has seriously harmed society by hampering the ability of the police to solve crimes . . . *Miranda* may be the single most damaging blow inflicted on the nation's ability to fight crime in the last half century" (1998, p. 1132).

Yet as John Donahue (1998) has pointed out, there may be little relationship between *Miranda* and clearance rates since most crimes are cleared by arrest, and most interrogations occur after the arrest has been made. Moreover, Donahue cautioned that many other, unmeasured variables might be causing the effect that Cassell and Fowles attributed to *Miranda*.

My sense is that there has been some drop in actual clearance rates owing to the dramatic changes in the nature of crime, drugs, and attitudes toward authority that emerged in the late 1960s, as well as to the changes in the criminal justice system ushered in by the

---

[26] In an earlier law review article analyzing national aggregate clearance data, Cassell has asserted that "about one out of every four violent crimes that was 'cleared' before *Miranda* was not 'cleared' after *Miranda*," arguing that *Miranda* was responsible for the trend of declining clearance rates (Cassell 1997).

Warren Court's many decisions in this area, not just *Miranda*. Moreover, measured clearance rates have probably dropped also as a result of the improved quality and reliability of crime and clearance rate data. We must query how much of the measured deviation from trend found in the regressions would remain once we subtracted out the effect of these factors. (Donahue 1998, pp. 1171–72)

Floyd Feeney has systematically and exhaustively analyzed the Cassell-Fowles hypothesis about *Miranda*'s impact on clearance rates (Feeney 2000). Feeney begins by pointing out two serious errors in the Cassell-Fowles hypothesis that, he argues, render it completely defective. First, and most fundamentally, Feeney demonstrates that there was no "sharp fall" for clearance rates in 1966 or 1966–68, contrary to the assertion of Cassell and Fowles. Feeney demonstrates that Cassell and Fowles did not rely on national-level clearance data, despite their claims but, instead, relied on city-level clearance data (and only a fraction of the available city-level clearance data). When one properly analyzes all of the available city-level clearance data, argues Feeney, the "sharp fall" in clearance rates in 1966–68 (the starting point of Cassell and Fowles's analysis) quickly disappears. As Feeney demonstrates, the Cassell-Fowles contention that there was a sharp fall "in every region of the country" during this period is simply false (Feeney 2000, p. 40). Second, Feeney points out that even if the clearance rates had fallen from 1966–68, there would be no logial or empirical reason to attribute the fall to the *Miranda* decision. This is primarily because most primary clearances occur before any in-custody interrogation takes place (Feeney 2000, p. 41), and Cassell and Fowles fail to show how interrogation that takes place after a suspect has already been arrested (and thus the crime has already been cleared) leads to the initial identification and arrest itself. Clearances are driven by arrests, not the police interrogations that follow arrest. In addition, Feeney points out that other significant historical events—such as improved police management and police record keeping, a rising police workload, the 1965–68 race riots, and the heroin epidemic of the late 1960s—have been the major factors in the gradual decline in clearance rates in America, not court decisions. As a result of these logical and empirical errors in Cassell and Fowles's analysis, Feeney concludes that clearance rates are a "profoundly misleading and erroneous method" for measuring the effect of the *Miranda* decision on the ability of the police to combat crime, and that Cassell and Fowles "fail at every critical point of their argument" (Feeney 2000, p. 113).

Though he has garnered considerable attention from some of the nation's top law reviews, as well as the media, Cassell's quantitative claims have not been generally accepted in either the legal or the social science community. Instead, numerous scholars have disputed Cassell's findings or inferences and criticized his objectivity, methodology, and conclusions (Schulhofer 1996*a*, 1996*b*, 1997; Thomas 1996*b*, 1996*c*; Arenella 1997; Donahue 1998; Garcia 1998; Leo and Ofshe 1998; Weisselberg 1998; White 1998; Leo and White 1999). Schulhofer (1996*a*, 1996*b*, 1996*c*, 1997) has repeatedly criticized Cassell for selectively citing data, presenting sources and quotes out of context, and advancing indefensibly partisan analyses. Schulhofer (1996*a*, 1996*b*, 1997) has also disputed some of Cassell's factual assertions, provided alternative explanations for patterns in Cassell's data, and continued to argue that there is no empirical support for Cassell's claim that *Miranda* has measurably reduced confession rates. Other scholars have argued that Cassell oversimplifies complicated issues, presents speculation as fact, fails to discuss contrary evidence and interpretations, and, ultimately, fails to demonstrate that *Miranda* has caused a decline in confession, clearance, or conviction rates (Thomas 1996*b*, 1996*c*; Arenella 1997; Donahue 1998; Garcia 1998; Leo and Ofshe 1998; Weisselberg 1998; White 1998; Leo and White 1999).

Despite the disagreements between Cassell and his many critics, there appears to be relatively little dispute among second-generation researchers on several aspects of *Miranda*'s real-world effects. First, police appear to issue and document *Miranda* warnings in virtually all cases (Leo 1996*a*). Second, police appear to have successfully "adapted" to the *Miranda* requirements. In practice, this means that police have developed strategies that are intended to induce *Miranda* waivers (Simon 1991; Leo 1996*a*; Leo and White 1999). Third, police appear to elicit waivers from suspects in 78–96 percent of their interrogations (Leo 1998), though suspects with criminal records appear disproportionately likely to invoke their rights and terminate interrogation (Simon 1991; Cassell and Hayman 1996; Leo 1996*a*). Fourth, in some jurisdictions police are systematically trained to violate *Miranda* by questioning "outside *Miranda*"—that is, by continuing to question suspects who have invoked the right to counsel or the right to remain silent (Weisselberg 1998; Leo and White 1999). Finally, some researchers have argued that *Miranda* eradicated the last vestiges of third-degree interrogation present in the mid-1960s, increased the level of professionalism among interrogators, and raised public awareness of constitutional rights (Simon 1991; Leo 1996*a*).

The second generation of *Miranda* impact research has been far more spirited and engaging than the first round of studies. Yet despite the new energy that empirically oriented scholars have breathed into the *Miranda* debate and despite the renewed calls for more empirical research on *Miranda*'s real-world effects (Leo 1996*a*; Thomas 1996*a*; Meares and Harcourt 2001), the second generation of *Miranda* impact scholarship may be at a close. Now that the Supreme Court has resolved in *Dickerson* any question about *Miranda*'s constitutional status, it is highly unlikely that the Court will reconsider any constitutional challenges to *Miranda* for many years, if not decades, to come. As a result, there may be little incentive for either *Miranda*'s supporters or *Miranda*'s critics to continue the difficult task of gathering and interpreting data on *Miranda*'s measurable effects.

The *Dickerson* Court made its own empirical claim about *Miranda*'s impact when it stated that "*Miranda* has become embedded in routine police practice to the point where the warnings have become part of our national culture" (*Dickerson*, p. 2335). Yet it did so without considering any of the first- or second-generation research of *Miranda*'s real-world effects. This is particularly surprising in light of the fact that Paul Cassell litigated the challenge to *Miranda* before the Supreme Court in *Dickerson*. That the Court ignored even the *Miranda* impact research of one of the primary litigants might, understandably, dissuade scholars and advocates on both sides of the *Miranda* debate from pursuing another round of empirical research on *Miranda*'s real-world effects on the interrogation process, public attitudes, or confession and conviction rates. After all, *Miranda* appears to be here to stay for the foreseeable future, and the Court has made up its mind about its empirical effects.

C. Miranda *in Action: Suspects, Police, Prosecutors*

At the beginning of the twenty-first century, *Miranda*'s impact may be relatively inconsequential in practice and may have been overstated in much of the second-generation scholarship. Despite two dozen or so original studies on various aspects of *Miranda*'s impact in thirty-five years, in many ways we still lack fundamentally good data in this area (Cassell and Hayman 1996; Leo 1996*a*; Thomas 1996*a*). Nevertheless, what the first-generation researchers suggested of their era may be true of ours: *Miranda*'s impact in practice may be virtually negligible. While *Miranda* may have initially exerted a substantial effect on police practices and public attitudes, this impact may have diminished as the criminal justice system adjusted to its dictates and *Miranda* became normalized among police, prosecutors, and the public.

If so, this may explain both why police and prosecutors, for the most part, no longer complain about *Miranda*, as well as why *Miranda* is perceived by many as no longer imposing serious costs on the criminal justice system. We suggest in this essay not only that *Miranda*'s costs in the twenty-first century may be negligible, but that its practical benefits—as a procedural safeguard against compulsion, coercion, false confessions, or any of the pernicious interrogation techniques that the Warren Court excoriated in the *Miranda* decision—may also be negligible. That *Miranda* protects, in a formalistic way, the "free choice" of the suspects who understand the warnings may also be a negligible benefit. Indeed, at the risk of being overly cynical, the Supreme Court's embrace of *Miranda* in *Dickerson* may be because *Miranda* delivers few benefits to suspects and many benefits to police and prosecutors.

1. *Suspects.*   As many writers have pointed out (Baker 1983; Malone 1986; Simon 1991), the daily stream of detective shows seems to have educated everyone (in America and abroad) about the existence and content of the *Miranda* warning and waiver requirements. There has been a widespread diffusion of the *Miranda* litany in American culture not only through television programs but also through movies, detective fiction, and the popular press. It is therefore unlikely that many criminal suspects today hear the *Miranda* rights for the first time prior to police questioning; suspects are likely to have heard *Miranda* so many times on television that the *Miranda* warnings may have a familiar, numbing ring. A national poll in 1984 revealed that 93 percent of those surveyed knew they had a right to an attorney if arrested (Toobin 1987), and a national poll in 1991 revealed that 80 percent knew they had a right to remain silent if arrested (Walker 1993). With the infusion and popularity of even more detective shows in the last decade (such as *Homicide*, *N.Y.P.D. Blue*, and *Law and Order*), it is likely that these figures have only gone up. And it is because of these shows and the mass media more generally—not the police, the legal system, or Supreme Court doctrine—that *Miranda* has become so much a part of our national culture.

Despite this knowledge, however, the overwhelming majority of suspects (some 78 percent to 96 percent) waive their rights and thus appear to consent to interrogation (Leo 1998). This undisputed fact is enormously significant in evaluating *Miranda*'s contemporary real-world impact. As Malone (1986, p. 368) pointed out fifteen years ago, "*Miranda* warnings have little or no effect on a suspect's propensity to talk. Next to the warning label on cigarette packs, *Miranda* is the most widely ignored piece of official advice in our society." The same appears to be true today. This simple fact—which likely explains *Miranda*'s survival better than the doctrinal underpinnings of the Supreme Court's contorted post-*Miranda* jurisprudence—has, for years, baffled social scientists and legal scholars alike.

There are a number of theories (some suspect-centered, some police-centered) to account for why so high a percentage of suspects waive their rights and submit to police questioning. Perhaps the most obvious explanation is that some suspects—particularly juveniles, individuals of low intelligence, and the mentally handicapped or disordered—may not understand the content or the significance of the warnings. This may be due to a lack of cognitive capacity to understand, appreciate, or act on the abstract *Miranda* warning regime. For suspects with the capacity to understand the content of the warnings, the stresses of police custody and impending interrogation might cause them to fail to listen to, register, or process the meaning of the *Miranda* warnings.

Even if suspects have the cognitive capacity to understand the *Miranda* rights and register their significance, some suspects may feel that they have no choice but to comply with their interrogators. The pressures of police custody and questioning may cause suspects to perceive that they lack the power to terminate interrogation. As Ainsworth (1993, p. 261) has pointed out, "the suspect is situationally powerless inside the interrogation room because the interrogator controls the subject matter, tempo, progress of questioning and whether the suspect is permitted to interrupt questioning. The person questioned, on the other hand, has no right to question the interrogator, or even to question the propriety of the questions the interrogator has posed." Some suspects may feel as if they are under the control of their interrogator, who is trained to dominate the police-suspect encounter. Others may fear that by failing to cooperate they will anger their interrogators, who may thereby retaliate against them (Nguyen 2000). Innocent suspects may perceive that they will be prosecuted and even incarcerated if they do not cooperate with authorities; guilty suspects may believe that they can successfully divert suspicion and talk their way out of trouble. Silence in the face of an inquiry implies guilt and thus naturally evokes suspicion (Greenawalt 1980; Malone 1986; Akerström 1991; Leo 1996*a*). Whether innocent or guilty, suspects may reasonably perceive that submitting to police questioning is the only immediate way to free themselves from police custody.

Several scholars have argued, somewhat counterintuitively, that despite its enunciation of rights and cutoff rules, *Miranda* affirmatively encourages suspects to cooperate with their interrogators. Malone has suggested that "skillfully presented, the *Miranda* warnings themselves sound chords of fairness and sympathy at the outset of the interrogation. The interrogator who advises, who cautions, who offers the suspect the gift of a free lawyer, becomes all the more persuasive by dint of his apparent candor and reasonableness" (Malone 1986, p. 371). Simon (1991) has argued that *Miranda*—particularly the *Miranda* formulation of the warnings—lulls suspects into compliance by co-opting them and making them part of the interrogation process, thereby diffusing the impact of the *Miranda* warning. Leo (1994) has argued that the ritualistic *Miranda* warnings create a felt sense of obligation among suspects to show respect to the police who question them. Thomas (1996*b*) has argued that *Miranda* warnings in effect tell the suspect that he will not be released until he persuades the police that he is not involved in the crime under investigation; this message encourages suspects to attempt to provide exculpatory answers.

Some suspects may intend to invoke their rights but fail to do so in the unequivocal way the Supreme Court requires (*Davis v. United States*, 512 U.S. 452 [1994]). As Ainsworth has noted, suspects who are members of racial minorities or who are poor find it difficult to demand from powerful police officers an end to interrogation or to have the help of counsel (Ainsworth 1993). These suspects, by far the majority, use indirect and equivocal modes of expression that both police and courts fail to recognize as invocations. All of this suggests that there may be multiple and overlapping reasons why so many custodial suspects ultimately waive their rights and submit to police questioning. It is important to appreciate that these explanations are not mutually exclusive and thus that many of these factors or pressures to comply with questioning may be simultaneously present in any given interrogation.

Regardless of why suspects submit to interrogation, however, *Mi-*

randa offers little, if any, meaningful protection once a suspect has waived his rights. *Miranda* rights can be invoked at any time, even after waiver, but few suspects invoke them after they have begun to answer police questions (Cassell and Hayman 1996; Leo 1996*a*). Thus, *Miranda*, once waived, does not restrict deceptive or suggestive police tactics, manipulative interrogation strategies, hostile or overbearing questioning styles, lengthy confinement, or any of the inherently stressful conditions of modern psychological interrogation (White 2001). In addition, *Miranda* offers little, if any, protection against the elicitation of false confessions from innocent suspects or the admission into evidence of these confessions (Leo 1998). While *Miranda* may prevent some suspects from speaking to police, and while it may offer a formalistic "free choice" to those with the cognitive capacity to understand the warnings, these limited protections typically evaporate as soon as an accusatory interrogation begins—which is exactly when a suspect is most likely to feel the inherently compelling pressures of police-dominated custodial questioning. As both White (2001) and Stuntz (2001) argue, once a suspect waives his rights, *Miranda* does virtually nothing to protect suspects against abusive tactics because it provides no restrictions on postwaiver interrogation methods beyond the minimal ones already established by the cases using due process to control interrogation methods.

2. *Police.*   Law enforcement in America reacted to *Miranda* with anger (Baker 1983). Along with many others, police initially feared that *Miranda* would handcuff their investigative abilities, not only causing them to lose numerous essential confessions and convictions but also returning rapists and killers to the streets to prey again. Police chiefs predicted chaos, believing that the new *Miranda* requirements were the equivalent of a virtual ban on interrogation (Malone 1986). But police learned how to comply with *Miranda*, or at least how to create the appearance of compliance with *Miranda*, and still elicit a high percentage of incriminating statements, admissions, and confessions from criminal suspects. In this subsection, we show multiple police strategies to avoid, circumvent, nullify, or simply violate *Miranda* and its invocation rules. In sum, we will show, as one commentator has put it, that *Miranda* has become a "manageable annoyance" (Hoffman 1998).

a) Avoiding Miranda.   One police strategy to negotiate *Miranda* is to exploit the very definitions, exceptions, and ambiguities in the doctrine itself, to use *Miranda* to avoid *Miranda*. For example, because *Miranda* warnings are only required when a suspect is in custody—under formal arrest or the functional equivalent of formal arrest (*Berkemer v. McCarty*, 468 U.S. 420 [1984])—police can create circumstances in which the suspect is not in custody, and therefore *Miranda* warnings are not required. Police can recast what appears to be a custodial interrogation as a noncustodial interview by telling the suspect that he is not under arrest and that he is free to leave—even after detectives have arranged for the suspect to be questioned in the station house with the express purpose of eliciting incriminating information (*Oregon v. Mathiason*, 429 U.S. 492 [1977]). In this way, police do not have to issue *Miranda* warnings and thus lessen the risk that the suspect will terminate interrogation by exercising his right to silence or counsel (Skolnick and Leo 1992; Cassell and Hayman 1996; Greenwood and Brown 1998).

Another way police exploit legal ambiguities to minimize the risk that a suspect will terminate interrogation is to claim waiver of *Miranda* if the suspect talks without invoking his rights. To elicit this so-called implicit waiver, interrogators read to the suspect his fourfold warnings to silence and appointed counsel but do not ask whether he understands these rights or wishes to act on them (what might be called the "two-fold invocation rules"). Instead, after reading the fourfold warnings, interrogators move directly to questioning without asking the suspect for an explicit waiver of the *Miranda* rights, in effect treating the suspect's waiver as a fait accompli. If a suspect hears his rights and responds to interrogation, he can be found to have implicitly waived his rights (*North Carolina v. Butler*, 441 U.S. 369 [1979]). This strategy highlights the difference between a *Miranda* doctrine that protects a formal "free choice" and one that seeks to provide substantive protection of choice. Though the *Miranda* Court surely intended the latter, current doctrine seems to provide only the former.

b) Negotiating Miranda.   Even when police issue the fourfold *Miranda* warnings and use the two-fold invocation rules, they are enormously successful in moving past the *Miranda* moment to elicit signed waivers and control the interrogation process. Interrogators often elicit waivers by minimizing, downplaying, or deemphasizing the potential import or significance of the *Miranda* warnings (Leo 1996*a*; Leo and White 1999). One strategy is to suggest that the warnings are a mere formality to dispense with prior to questioning, a simple matter of routine, by delivering the warnings quickly in a perfunctory tone of voice or in a bureaucratic manner. Another is to engage in extensive rapport-building small talk prior to the reading of the warnings in an effort to personalize the police-suspect interaction and establish a norm of friendly reciprocation with the expectation that the suspect will comply. The purpose of these strategies is to trivialize the legal significance of *Miranda*, create the appearance of a nonadversarial relationship between the interrogators and the suspect, and communicate that the interrogator expects the suspect to passively execute the waiver and respond to subsequent questioning. As Leo and White (1999, p. 435) have written, the interrogator's "hope is that the suspect will not come to see the *Miranda* warning and waiver requirements as a crucial transition point in the questioning or as an opportunity to terminate the interrogation, but as equivalent to other standard bureaucratic forms that one signs without reading or giving much thought."

Another strategy is to suggest that the suspect will receive a tangible benefit in exchange for talking to police. For example, detectives sometimes tell a suspect that he will only be able to tell his side of the story if he waives *Miranda*, implying that the suspect will not be able to clear things up unless he first answers their questions (Leo 1996*a*; Leo and White 1999). Detectives sometimes tell a suspect that they can only inform the suspect of the charges against him, or the likely outcome of his case, if he waives *Miranda* (Leo and White 1999). Detectives sometimes accuse a suspect of committing a crime, confront him with real or alleged evidence, and then suggest that the range of possible sentences and punishments depends upon how favorably the suspect's actions are portrayed (Simon 1991; Leo and White 1999). As Arenella (1997) has pointed out, the implication is clear: if suspects waive their *Miranda* rights, the police can help them (such as by talking to the prosecutor or testifying on the defendant's behalf); if the suspect invokes his right to silence or counsel, the police communicate the message that they cannot help him. Sometimes detectives explicitly tell the suspect that the criminal justice system will treat him more leniently if he first waives his rights; otherwise, he runs the risk of being treated more punitively (Leiken 1970; Simon 1991; Leo and White 1999). As Kamisar (1999) has pointed out, all of these persuasive strategies amount to interrogation before waiver in violation of both the letter and the spirit of *Miranda*.

c) Questioning "Outside Miranda*": Interrogation after Invocation.* If the interrogator fails to elicit an implicit or explicit waiver, he may seek to change the suspect's mind by persuading him to reconsider his decision, or he may simply continue to question the suspect in direct violation of *Miranda*. This can occur even when the suspect clearly invokes one of his *Miranda* rights, as in California, where some police have been trained to question "outside *Miranda*" by suggesting that the suspect's answers will not be used against him (Weisselberg 1998). Police might, for example, falsely tell the suspect that anything he says is now off the record, that nothing he says can be used against him since he has invoked his constitutional rights, or that his answers will only be used to help the interrogator understand what happened (Weisselberg 1998, 2001; Leo and White 1999).

The purpose of questioning outside *Miranda* is to exploit the Supreme Court's ruling in *Harris v. New York* that established the impeachment exception to *Miranda*. As a result of *Harris*, police can use statements taken in violation of *Miranda* to obtain additional incriminating information against a suspect (such as the location of physical evidence, the names of witnesses, the identities of accomplices, or the suspect's modus operandi). Prosecutors can use statements taken in violation of *Miranda* to impeach the defendant at trial should he take the stand. Police question "outside *Miranda*" precisely because the Supreme Court created the incentive for them to do so. The practice of questioning "outside *Miranda*" has been extensive in the last decade, particularly in California (Weisselberg 1998, 2001; Leo and White 1999; Rosenfeld 2000).

d) The Police Advantage in Miranda.   The lost convictions and system chaos feared by law enforcement in the immediate wake of *Miranda* have not materialized (American Bar Association 1988). Instead, American police have successfully adapted to *Miranda*. They can use legal strategies to avoid the reading of rights or the invocation rules. They can use psychological strategies that result in a surprisingly high percentage of waivers. And police and prosecutors can even use statements taken in violation of *Miranda* against defendants. These developments seem inconsistent with what the Warren Court intended when it created the *Miranda* rules. If the goal of *Miranda* was to reduce the kinds of interrogation techniques and custodial pressures that create station-house compulsion and thus undermine the suspect's free choice to decide whether to answer police questions, it appears to have failed. The reading of rights and taking of waivers has become largely an empty ritual, and American police continue to use the same psychological methods of persuasion, manipulation, and deception that the Warren Court roundly criticized in *Miranda* (Malone 1986; Simon 1991; Uviller 1996).

For the most part, *Miranda* has helped, not hurt, law enforcement, and for the most part law enforcement supports *Miranda* (Leo 1996*a*; Arenella 1997). Numerous members of the law enforcement community have publicly expressed support for *Miranda* (Schulhofer 1987; Leo 1996*a*; Weisselberg 1998). As Schulhofer (1987) has pointed out, since the mid-1970s, police have consistently reported that complying with *Miranda* has not produced adverse effects for law enforcement. As others have pointed out, in the mid-1980s, none of the major police lobbying groups, such as the International Association of Police Chiefs, joined in then Attorney General Edwin Meese's call to overrule *Miranda*. In 1988, an American Bar Association survey found that an overwhelming majority of police agreed that compliance with *Miranda* did not present serious problems for law enforcement or hinder their ability to garner confessions (American Bar Association 1988). In 1993, several police organizations (the Police Foundation, Police Executive Research Forum, International Union of Police Associations, and the National Black Police Association) filed amicus curiae (friend of the court) briefs on behalf of *Miranda* in *Withrow v. Williams*, 507 U.S. 680 (1993). To be sure, a number of law enforcement organizations filed amicus curiae briefs opposing *Miranda* in *Dickerson v. United States*, but this appears to be the result of Paul Cassell's impressive lobbying and advocacy efforts, not the natural inclination of law enforcement, on its own, to abandon *Miranda*. If there is, in fact, widespread opposition to *Miranda*, police in the trenches have expressed surprisingly little desire to overrule it.

When police formally comply with *Miranda*, the existence of a waiver shields the interrogation from challenges, rendering admissible otherwise questionable or involuntary confessions (Garcia 1998; White 2001). *Miranda* not only fails to provide police with any guidelines about which police interrogation techniques are impermissible but, because it is seen as a symbol of professionalism, *Miranda* also shields police from pressures to reform their practices (Belsky 1994; Garcia 1998; Leo 1998). In sum, American police have taken the advantage in *Miranda* (Neubauer 1974).

3. *Prosecutors.* Surprisingly, the empirical study of *Miranda*'s impact has almost entirely neglected the ruling's effects on the practices, attitudes, and decision making of prosecutors. The prosecutor is probably the most powerful actor in the criminal justice system. Prosecutors decide whether to drop or file charges, the amount and type of charges to file, whether to recommend bail and at what amount, whether to engage in plea bargaining, and, if so, which charging and

sentencing outcomes to recommend to courts. Any failure to issue *Miranda* warnings properly, any violation of *Miranda*'s invocation rules, as well as any police misconduct or illegality during interrogation can be undone by the prosecutor with a stroke of a pen by, for example, dismissing charges or not filing them in the first place.

Yet, in the last thirty-five years, there has been only one academic study of prosecutorial attitudes toward *Miranda*. Gruhl and Spohn (1981) analyzed 195 questionnaires from local prosecutors in forty-three states. They found that local prosecutors overwhelmingly supported *Miranda*. Over 81 percent of the prosecutors surveyed agreed that police should be required to read suspects their rights. Gruhl and Spohn (1981) found that the primary influence on prosecuting attorneys' practices was the degree to which local judges required strict adherence to the *Miranda* guidelines, and 69 percent believed that courts should continue to reduce the strictness with which *Miranda* is applied.

Gruhl and Spohn's finding of overwhelming prosecutorial support for *Miranda* is consistent with other sources of data. The American Bar Association (1988) survey of criminal justice practitioners, for example, also found that prosecutors reported that *Miranda* was not a significant factor that impedes their ability to prosecute criminals successfully. On the contrary, as Thomas (2000) and others have pointed out, *Miranda* facilitates the prosecutor's task of getting statements admitted, gaining leverage during plea bargaining, and ultimately winning convictions (Garcia 1998; Rosenfeld 2000). Prosecutors like *Miranda* because it makes law enforcement appear more professional, causes juries to attach greater weight to confession evidence, and allows prosecutors to argue that an otherwise involuntary confession was constitutionally obtained (American Bar Association 1988; Garcia 1998). Perhaps above all, it is rare that an admission or confession will be suppressed in trial proceedings because of a *Miranda* violation (Nardulli 1983, 1987; Guy and Huckabee 1988; Cassell 1996*b*).

4. *The Bigger Picture.* Despite its influence on policing in the 1960s and 1970s, *Miranda*'s impact as we go into the twenty-first century will likely be limited (Garcia 1998). Police, prosecutors, and courts have adapted to and diluted *Miranda*, using it to advance their own objectives rather than to enforce the privilege against self-incrimination or the right to counsel (Kamisar 1996). Once feared to handcuff the police and wreak havoc on the criminal justice system, *Miranda* has become just another routine part of the status quo. Police have learned how to sidestep the necessity of *Miranda* or to use clever strategies to

elicit a high percentage of *Miranda* waivers. Prosecutors have learned to use *Miranda* to facilitate the admission of confession evidence, to add leverage to plea bargaining negotiations, and to buttress cases at trial. Trial judges have learned to use *Miranda* to simplify the decision to admit interrogation-induced statements and to sanitize confessions that might be deemed involuntary if analyzed solely under the Fourteenth Amendment due process standard of voluntariness (Garcia 1998; Thomas 2001).

Miranda imposes few, if any, serious costs on the individual actors of the criminal justice system or on the system as a whole. Contrary to the arguments of Cassell, there is no compelling evidence that *Miranda* causes a significant number of lost convictions—certainly not the tens or hundreds of thousands of convictions lost annually that Cassell imputes to *Miranda*. As Thomas (1996*b*), Weisselberg (1998), and Garcia (1998) have pointed out, the number of lost convictions attributable to *Miranda* is empirically unknowable because the very question presumes a counterfactual world that does not exist and therefore cannot be measured. It is empirically impossible to ascertain the frequency or number of "lost confessions" historically attributable to the *Miranda* warnings and cutoff rules in the manner that Cassell (1996*b*) has suggested and attempted. However, with an adequate sample size, it is possible—using chi square or multiple-regression analysis to control potentially confounding variables and statistical significance to infer probable causation—to test whether the *Miranda* warnings and cutoff rules depress, increase, or have no effect on conviction rates in a particular sample of cases. Only one study has statistically tested the effect of *Miranda* in this manner, and it found that the relationship between the suspect's response to *Miranda* warnings (waived vs. invoked) and the case outcome (convicted vs. not convicted) was not, in the sample studied, statistically significant (Leo 1996*a*). The best evidence suggests that this empirically unknowable figure is likely to be very low.

But there remains a powerful symmetry between costs and benefits. *Miranda* in 2001 imposes low costs on those whom it was intended to regulate and also offers few benefits for its intended recipients. While it might offer an impoverished, formal free choice to suspects who understand the warnings, it does not meaningfully dispel compulsion inside the interrogation room. *Miranda* has not changed the psychological interrogation process that it condemned but has only motivated police to develop more subtle and sophisticated—and perhaps more compelling—interrogation strategies. Police "work" *Miranda* in practice to undercut the original goal that a suspect be effectively apprised of his rights and have a continuous opportunity to exercise them. *Miranda* offers no protection against traditionally coercive interrogation techniques but may, instead, have weakened existing legal safeguards in this area. And *Miranda* offers suspects little, if any, protection against the elicitation, and admission into evidence, of false confessions. In short, the empirical evidence to date, though highly imperfect, suggests that as a safeguard, *Miranda* offers few tangible benefits to suspects.

The last piece of the *Miranda* puzzle has to do with the timing of the challenge to its legitimacy. Chapter 18 U.S.C. sec. 3501 had been on the books for thirty-one years before it gave rise to a challenge to *Miranda* that reached the Supreme Court. Why 1999 and not 1969 or 1979? And if no challenge issued within the first ten years of the statute's existence, why did a challenge arise at all? After having been neglected by federal prosecutors and judges for thirty years, why did section 3501 suddenly become the vehicle to challenge *Miranda* in 1999? The next section offers some thoughts about that question.

V. The Timing of the *Miranda* Challenge: Why 1999?

Miranda was decided in 1966. By 1968 it was clear that the Court was far ahead of the country in the amount, or kind, of protection of suspects' free choice that should exist in the interrogation room, perhaps too far ahead to be sustainable. Despite life tenure and the doctrine of judicial review that makes the Court the final word on constitutional issues, the Court draws its legitimacy in part from societal consensus. If the Court gets too far ahead, or falls too far behind, the developing consensus, self-correcting mechanisms come into play. One obvious self-correcting mechanism is the election of a president who promises to change the Court. Richard Nixon was that president.

It seems likely that *Miranda*'s first few years were peaceful precisely because enemies of *Miranda* were waiting for Nixon to appoint "law-and-order" judges to the Court. There would be no reason—indeed, it would be foolish—to seek review of the constitutionality of 18 U.S.C. sec. 3501 as long as the Court had a majority in support of *Miranda*. The appointment of Thurgood Marshall in 1967 to replace Tom Clark, who had dissented in *Miranda*, meant that there were six likely votes for *Miranda*. The appointment of Chief Justice Burger to replace Chief Justice Warren in 1969 brought the likely vote back to five in favor. But it was not until Harry Blackmun was appointed to replace Abe Fortas in 1970 that the likely vote shifted against *Miranda*.

By 1973, Lewis Powell had replaced another *Miranda* supporter, Hugo Black, and William Rehnquist had replaced a *Miranda* dissenter, John Marshall Harlan II. So the likely vote was now six to three against *Miranda*. Two years later, President Gerald Ford appointed John Paul Stevens to take the seat of another *Miranda* supporter, William O. Douglas. Though Stevens has become the great liberal of the Rehnquist Court, he was widely perceived in the beginning as a moderate tending toward the conservative side on criminal justice issues, and the likely vote was now seven to two against *Miranda*. Indeed, the only member of the *Miranda* majority left on the Court by 1975 was William Brennan, though Marshall also took a robust view of *Miranda*'s protections.

Despite the steady infusion of more conservative judges onto the Court, and a congressional statute that seemed to overturn part of *Miranda*'s holding, only one serious effort to overrule *Miranda* reached the Supreme Court. In 1977, the Court heard *Brewer v. Williams*, 430 U.S. 387 (1977), a case that drew twenty-two amicus curiae briefs from states "strongly urg[ing] that" *Miranda* be reexamined (*Brewer*, p. 438). The lower federal courts had reversed Williams's conviction of raping and murdering a child, in part on *Miranda* grounds. If the Supreme Court affirmed, many would recall the dire prediction of Justice White in dissent in *Miranda* that the Court's rule would return killers and rapists to the street.

The child had been abducted in Des Moines, Iowa, on Christmas Eve. An abduction warrant was issued for Williams. Upon advice of his lawyer, he surrendered to police in Davenport, Iowa, about three hours by car from Des Moines. He was arraigned in Davenport on the abduction warrant. In the car on the way to Des Moines, the police detective engaged in a strategy to get Williams to disclose the location of the child's body, a strategy that was likely "interrogation" under *Miranda*. As Williams was isolated in the police car, and no warnings were given after he left his lawyer in Davenport, it looked like a pretty easy case against waiver. But would the Court apply *Miranda* to free a child rapist and killer?

The lower courts found a *Miranda* violation but also found a violation of the Sixth Amendment right to counsel in its pretrial form (*Massiah v. United States*, 377 U.S. 201 [1964]) on the ground that the police had elicited statements from Williams after he was arraigned but without his lawyer present. The Supreme Court decided the case on that ground, five to four, in favor of Williams. Without a Sixth Amendment ground to support the lower courts' holdings, *Brewer* might have seen the overruling of *Miranda*. It seems likely that the Court chose to decide the case on Sixth Amendment grounds because it is easier to justify reversing the conviction of a child killer because he was deprived of his lawyer under the Sixth Amendment than because he was deprived of his right to remain silent. As the narrow vote shows, the Sixth Amendment waiver issue was a close one. Perhaps *Miranda* just barely escaped.

The best hope to overrule *Miranda* was always 18 U.S.C. sec. 3501. This was a considered judgment, by a coordinate branch of the federal government, that the *Miranda* remedy was too narrowly focused on the warnings. Section 3501 does not, on its face, contest *Miranda*'s central premise that police interrogation constitutes compelling pressure. It simply crafted a different procedure for determining when federal judges should find that pressure sufficient to suppress a confession. Subsection (b) provides:

> The trial judge in determining the issue of voluntariness shall take into consideration all the circumstances surrounding the giving of the confession, including (1) the time elapsing between arrest and arraignment of the defendant making the confession, if it was made after arrest and before arraignment, (2) whether such defendant knew the nature of the offense with which he was charged or of which he was suspected at the time of making the confession, (3) whether or not such defendant was advised or knew that he was not required to make any statement and that any such statement could be used against him, (4) whether or not such defendant had been advised prior to questioning of his right to the assistance of counsel; and (5) whether or not such defendant was without the assistance of counsel when questioned and when giving such confession.

Subsection (b) also provided that "the presence or absence of any of the above-mentioned factors to be taken into consideration by the judge need not be conclusive on the issue of voluntariness of the confession."

If the Court wanted to overrule *Miranda*, it now had both "cover" and a principled justification—it could acknowledge the superior ability of Congress to find facts and craft remedies, and then defer to Congress. Of course, section 3501 first had to be litigated. Only one appellate case reached the merits of the statute in the thirty years prior to *Dickerson*. That court held section 3501 constitutional, a decision that was not appealed to the Supreme Court.[27] It is difficult to know exactly why *Miranda* enjoyed this quiescent period. Perhaps it was implicit recognition that, as shown in Sections III and IV, its doctrinal and empirical effects could be sharply limited. It is not inconceivable that in the hands of a skilled interrogator, the *Miranda* warnings could actually increase the number of suspects willing to talk to police, by making them feel more at ease or even by creating subtle pressure to speak (Malone 1986; Simon 1991; Thomas 1993, 1996*b*). Without doubt, the task of prosecutors in getting confessions admitted into evidence was greatly facilitated by *Miranda*. The great protector of the rights of suspects had evolved into the prosecutor's safe harbor rule. If the police gave the warnings, admissibility was virtually assured. What prosecutor could be against that?

The criticism of *Miranda*, which had subsided in the late 1960s, began to resurface in the 1970s and 1980s, led principally by Joseph Grano's sustained scholarly attack on the doctrinal premises and ethical underpinnings of *Miranda* (Grano 1979*a*, 1979*b*, 1985, 1986, 1988, 1989).[28] A few other scholars also published scathing critiques (Graham 1970; Caplan 1985; Markman 1987, 1989). Grano's focus was on the value to the criminal process of discovering the truth. He noted the argument of some "that prosecution should be made difficult as an end in itself," that it is somehow unfair to make it easier to prove the defendant's guilt (Grano 1989, p. 404). Grano responded: "I would have thought that proving the defendant's guilt was precisely the goal [of the criminal process], at least absent a serious concern about convicting the innocent, condoning or encouraging official misconduct, countenancing violations of the defendant's dignity, or encouraging some other evil of comparable gravity" (Grano 1989, p. 404). To the extent that *Miranda* discourages guilty suspects from talking to police, it impedes the search for truth and the proving of guilt. Many weighed in to defend *Miranda* but none more forcefully than Yale Kamisar (1966, 1977*a*, 1977*b*, 1990, 1999, 2000). Kamisar argued that, though ascer-

---

[27] United States v. Crocker, 510 F.2d 1129 (10th Cir. 1975) (alternative holding). For a thorough discussion of sec. 3501 and the history of various litigation strategies by a succession of attorneys general, see Cassell (1999*b*).

[28] Grano's scholarship on *Miranda* continued into the 1990s and produced an important book on the law of confessions (Grano 1993).

tainment of truth is important, the criminal process "must be made subsidiary to the values and principles found in the Bill of Rights as a way of making *those constitutional provisions* effective in action" (Kamisar 1990, p. 542).[29]

The concern with pursuing truth, kept alive by Grano, Caplan, and Markman, led to new trouble for *Miranda* during Edwin Meese's tenure as attorney general under Ronald Reagan. Stephen Markman headed the Office of Legal Policy, which issued the Truth in Criminal Justice Series as a report to Meese in 1986 (Report to the Attorney General 1986; see also Markman 1989). The report took direct aim at several of the Warren Court criminal procedure landmarks that valued process over truth. It concluded both that *Miranda* was vulnerable and that the Department of Justice should make overruling it a top priority. The vulnerability was thought to follow from the cases that we discussed in Section III refining, and limiting, *Miranda*. The report concluded that these decisions held, "in effect, that *Miranda* is unsound in principle" (Report to the Attorney General 1986, p. 565). Noting that section 3501 was "specifically designed to overrule" *Miranda*, the report concluded, "Overturning *Miranda* would . . . be among the most important achievements of this administration—indeed, of any administration—in restoring the power of self-government to the people of the United States in the suppression of crime" (Report to the Attorney General 1986, p. 565).[30]

The report brimmed with confidence, at one point noting: "It is difficult to see how we could fail in making our case" (Report to the Attorney General 1986, p. 565). Yet little was done to implement its strategy for overturning *Miranda* (Cassell 1999b). One difficulty was finding the "right" test case. A challenge to *Miranda* needed the "right" facts to increase the chances of succeeding. An old legal cliché is that "bad facts make bad law." When reversing precedent, the Court often picks cases that have facts that seem to call for a new rule.[31] A

[29] Schulhofer argued that the largely toothless protections of *Miranda* were insufficient to protect Fifth Amendment interests of suspects: "the proper critique of *Miranda* is not that it 'handcuffs' the police but that it does not go quite far enough" (Schulhofer 1987, p. 461). Lawrence Herman (1987) argued that whatever the flaws of the *Miranda* regime, a return to the voluntariness test was even worse.

[30] For two highly critical responses to the report, see Herman (1987); Schulhofer (1987).

[31] In Mapp. v. Ohio, 367 U.S. 643 (1961), e.g., the Court reversed a holding only twelve years old and required all states to suppress evidence taken in violation of the Fourth Amendment. The facts in *Mapp* were extraordinarily friendly to that task. When Mapp refused to let the police into her home without a warrant, the police responded hours later by breaking into her home. She demanded to see a copy of the warrant. An

good case for overruling *Miranda* would have a defendant obviously guilty of a very serious crime who confessed without much prodding from the police and after an unintentional, minor violation of *Miranda*. From the early 1980s until the end of the George Bush presidency in 1992, the Department of Justice looked for a test case. Perhaps they looked too hard for a perfect one. Paul Cassell had the responsibility of finding a test case from 1986 to 1988, but his superiors always found reasons to reject all but a few of the cases he picked (Cassell 2000, personal communication). The Bush Department of Justice had finally chosen a test case and had begun the litigation when Clinton won the 1992 election. The Clinton Department of Justice terminated the litigation.[32]

Section 3501 applied only in federal court, and part of the difficulty in finding the right test case undoubtedly, if ironically, was attributable to the professionalism of the United States Attorneys and the federal law enforcement agencies. Whether section 3501 was constitutional was an unknown fact. What federal agents and prosecutors did know for certain was that *Miranda* was a safe harbor rule. If winning cases and imprisoning criminals is the most important goal, federal agents would give warnings rather than seek a test case for section 3501, and no U.S. Attorney would ask the agents to omit the warnings, particularly in serious cases. Section 3501 was raised in several Courts of Appeal beginning in 1970 (Cassell 1999*b*, pp. 199–200), but in all but one case (*United States v. Crocker*, 510 F.2d 1129 [10th Cir. 1975]), the court refused to reach the issue because it found that the agents had complied with *Miranda*.

This brings us to the Clinton years. *Miranda* is now truly "part of our national culture." Repeated thousands of times on television and in the movies, it rarely is portrayed as keeping the police from "getting their man." A whole generation of police and detectives has now been trained to use *Miranda* and still get the "bad guys." A generation of prosecutors sees the value in *Miranda*'s safe harbor rule. Once *Miranda* got through the 1980s, it could easily have expected to live out the rest of its life in peace like any other aging baby boomer.

---

officer held up a piece of paper and she snatched it from his hand. The police physically manhandled her to get the paper back. No warrant was introduced at trial. And what did they find for all this aggressive policing? Not the bombing suspect they sought but a few items of obscenity. It was an easy case to hold for the defendant.

[32] For more details on this history of the effort to challenge *Miranda*, see Cassell (1999*b*).

But it was not to be. What created a new *Miranda* controversy in the 1990s? Recalling Kant's theory that causal knowledge is structured by the mind, our observations here must be very tentative. One possibility is that the cultural climate changed sufficiently by the mid-1990s to make Joe Grano's and Paul Cassell's criticisms of *Miranda* more telling in the late 1990s than they were at any time since the early 1970s. We are not claiming that the social climate caused the issue of section 3501 to be litigated or even that it caused the Fourth Circuit to decide *Dickerson* in a particular way. We make no causal claim at all because we would not know how to prove it. That the section 3501 issue made it to the Supreme Court might be attributable to the writings of Grano and others, to the advocacy and persistence of Cassell, or to little more than random chance. What we do claim is that the climate was more fertile for *Miranda* critics.

Recall that the *Miranda* Court characterized the suspect as at least somewhat sympathetic—disadvantaged educationally and environmentally, unable to match wits (or skill) with professional police interrogators. As Gerald Caplan put it, "*Miranda* was a child of the racially troubled 1960s" (Caplan 1985, p. 1470), and of the 1960s philosophy that social forces were the root cause of crime and, more broadly, the root cause of much behavior, good and bad. This picture saw humans more or less trapped in a web of deterministic forces, unable to effect changes in the sweep of history.

Events in the 1970s reinforced this belief structure: the Nixon administration's retreat from Vietnam a step ahead of advancing North Vietnamese troops, the agonizing Watergate years, and the president's resignation. Next was the caretaker administration of Gerald Ford, followed by Jimmy Carter's plea for Americans to sacrifice more and expect less. In a much-noted address to the nation, Carter wore a sweater rather than a suit and asked Americans to turn down their thermostats so that we would not be hostage to OPEC. Then, ironically, we became literally hostage to the Iranian terrorists who held our embassy and its personnel for 444 days. In this climate, the radar screens of prosecutors might have lost sight of *Miranda*. Perhaps it had become an old piece of doctrinal furniture that had to be moved slightly every now and then for vacuuming but was a permanent part of their world.

Ronald Reagan campaigned in 1980 on the theme of "morning in America." The message of his campaign, delivered in many different ways, was that Americans are an energetic, resourceful people and that we control our destiny. We are not powerless before unknown forces.

We make our own fortune and our futures. We are able to act in the face of social pressures, including that of police interrogators.

Reagan's message that we create our own futures is, to some extent, antithetical to *Miranda*'s basic assumption that suspects are easily manipulated by police interrogators. It is perhaps no coincidence that the Reagan Department of Justice sketched the first plan for a serious sustained challenge to *Miranda*. Why it ran out of steam is a more difficult question. Perhaps the nation had not yet fully absorbed the Reagan message of optimism and free will. Perhaps there just were no good test cases. Simplest of all, perhaps Paul Cassell was not yet in position to lead the charge.

But the Reagan revolution did not stop when he left office. During the Bush presidency, despite some sour economic times, the national mood lightened, and our self-esteem was reinforced when we finally won a war (the Gulf War provided our first clear victory since 1945). Clinton defeated Bush in 1992 but quickly proved himself a centrist. During Clinton's presidency, we turned a perennial budget deficit into a large surplus, we saw a stock market boom of unprecedented proportions, we ended "welfare as we know it," and we saw the resurgence of American creativity and entrepreneurial activity in Silicon Valley and many other places. Microsoft Corporation showed the extent to which American ingenuity could dominate world markets—to the point, of course, that the Justice Department sought to put the brakes on Microsoft. Advertisements for on-line stock trading appeared on television showing twenty-somethings saying "we don't depend on the government for our retirement, we don't depend on our parents, we don't depend on anyone but ourselves." The 1990s, in sum, saw a rise in American individualism.

Whatever else *Miranda* might be, it is at heart a denial of robust individualism—at least among the population of suspects in police interrogation rooms. *Miranda* insisted that these less fortunate, relatively powerless individuals needed to be protected. This was not the message of the 1990s. So, in that sense, *Miranda* is an anachronism. The cultural context of the 1990s was less receptive to the image of the powerless suspect who surrenders his will to the powerful police interrogator. Instead, more like the 1940s and 1950s, the suspect is now likely to be seen as making a choice to engage in crime to the detriment of the innocent citizen. The "poster child" suspect once again is Lisenba torturing and murdering his helpless, hysterical wife, not a pathetic suspect cowering before relentless police interrogators. It is a paradigm shift of the first magnitude and can be seen in many concrete manifestations, including laws locking up "sexual predators" for life even though they have already served their sentence for the crime that led to the civil commitment process (*Kansas v. Hendricks*, 521 U.S. 346 [1997]); the "three-strikes" laws that incarcerate for life without parole on a third conviction (California Penal Code, sec. 667 [2000]); proposals for victims' rights laws, and even constitutional amendments to create victims' rights (New Mexico Statute, sec. 31-26-4 [2000]; Mosteller 1997; Cassell 1999*a*). The victims' rights movement is perhaps the best illustration of the shift from seeing the criminal suspect as sympathetic to seeing the crime victim as the person who needs "rights" and deserves our sympathy (Grano 1996). In this paradigm, it is not Ernest Miranda who needs rights and sympathy. It is his rape victim.

If this speculation is roughly right, it would explain why Grano's arguments against *Miranda* and in favor of crime victims, contained in the 1986 Attorney General's Report, were especially resonant in the mid- to late-1990s. Moreover, it also explains why Cassell champions victims' rights with the same fervor that he displays when attacking *Miranda* (Cassell 1999*a*). The two issues are inextricably linked by their denotation of who is the victim and who is not.

There is no doubt that Cassell was a dedicated advocate of the constitutionality of section 3501. He clerked for Justice Scalia when he was on the D.C. Circuit Court of Appeals and for Chief Justice Burger. An associate deputy attorney general under Meese, Cassell helped with the latter stages of the Office of Legal Policy Report, including the task of publicizing the report. It is clear from Cassell's law review articles that he intensely dislikes both the message and (what he thinks is) the effect of *Miranda* (Cassell 1996*a*, 1996*b*, 1996*c*, 1997, 1999*b*; Cassell and Fowles 1998). Grano's work laid the groundwork for Cassell's later successes, but Cassell's zealous advocacy might have been crucial in getting the section 3501 issue before the Supreme Court.

On appeal from the federal district court to the Fourth Circuit in *Dickerson*, the government did not raise section 3501 in its brief (once again apparently seeking to avoid a decision on the constitutionality of section 3501). Without Cassell's amicus curiae brief, the issue would not have been before the Fourth Circuit (Cassell 1999*b*, p. 222). An amicus curiae is not a party to the case, and it is unusual for a court to decide a case based on an issue not raised by either party. The Fourth Circuit's decision to address the issue raised by an amicus brief could have been influenced by the changing times. Or, once again, it could simply have been the determination of scholars and litigators (Grano, Caplan, Markman, Cassell) to keep raising the issue until some court somewhere reached the merits.

The latter explanation is perhaps most consistent with the final outcome. Cassell, after all, did not win in the Supreme Court. He did not even come close. The Court's general distaste for overruling precedent was part of the reason, as well as the perception (that the data assembled in Section IV tend to bear out) that *Miranda* does not significantly harm police while helping prosecutors get confessions admitted. We also suggested in Section III that the current Court sees itself as the author of the present somewhat narrower, though sometimes broader, *Miranda* rule and that it is particularly distasteful to overrule one's own creation.

But we suspect part of the reason *Miranda* lives is that it taps into a basic vein of fairness that transcends the opinion's assumptions about the diminished free will of suspects facing police interrogation. When the Court in *Dickerson* says that the "warnings have become part of our national culture," it does not explain why this has taken place (*Dickerson*, p. 2335). The implication is that the culture has echoed what the police say, and the police are echoing what the Court said they had to say. But the causal mechanism may be more complicated.

The right to be told one's basic rights before the government insists that they be relinquished is part of the fundamental belief structure underlying Anglo-American law. Our law assumes autonomous agents capable of acting in their own best interests. To exercise autonomy requires at least some level of information about the basic rights that we may assert against the government actor who insists we act in a certain way (Thomas 2001). Citizens, of course, have no right to full information about the consequences they face before being asked to make certain decisions, but knowing that no duty exists to answer police questions during custodial interrogation might be one piece of information that is crucial. It might not, as Sections III and IV suggest, provide suspects with much protection from police pressure, but it might be just enough to satisfy the current Court and society.

Academics and historians can debate endlessly whether there is, was, or should be a Fifth Amendment right against self-incrimination in the police interrogation room. But it might be that the culture believes, at some intuitive level, in precisely the kind of notice that *Miranda* requires. *Miranda* did not, after all, forbid police interrogation or require lawyers. It left the decision of whether to answer police questions up to presumably autonomous agents who have been given a minimum, formalistic level of information about the consequences of answering. Perhaps the American people as well as the judges find this fair enough even though we now have a different view of who is the "victim" when the police set out to solve a crime.

It is possible that the changing conception of "victim" provided a sympathetic audience among the Fourth Circuit judges for the *Miranda* criticisms but that, upon reflection, the Supreme Court viewed the *Miranda* warnings as more a matter of basic fairness than a refuge for guilty criminals. That explanation is consistent with the *Miranda–Dickerson* story. Cassell, Grano, and the other *Miranda* critics got their day in a court of appeals known to be conservative. They lost in the moderate Supreme Court because whatever the *Miranda* Court claimed as a rationale, the real basis for requiring warnings ultimately derives from the essential fairness of telling a suspect he does not have to convict himself. Perhaps even guilty suspects deserve that small bow toward the Fifth Amendment privilege against compelled self-incrimination.

REFERENCES

Ainsworth, Janet. 1993. "In a Different Register: The Pragmatics of Powerlessness in Police Interrogation." *Yale Law Journal* 103:259–322.
Akerström, Malin. 1991. *Betrayal and Betrayers: The Sociology of Treachery.* New Brunswick, N.J.: Transaction.
American Bar Association. 1988. *Criminal Justice in Crisis.* Washington, D.C.: American Bar Association.
Arenella, Peter. 1997. "*Miranda* Stories." *Harvard Journal of Law and Public Policy* 20:375–87.
Baker, Liva. 1983. Miranda: *Crime, Law and Politics.* New York: Atheneum.
Belsky, Martin. 1994. "Living with *Miranda:* A Reply to Professor Grano." *Drake Law Review* 43:127–47.
Burt, Robert A. 1969. "*Miranda* and Title II: A Morganatic Marriage." *Supreme Court Review* 1969:81–134.
Caplan, Gerald M. 1985. "Questioning *Miranda.*" *Vanderbilt Law Review* 38: 1417–76.
Cassell, Paul G. 1996a. "All Benefits, No Costs: The Grand Illusion of *Miranda*'s Defenders." *Northwestern University Law Review* 90:1084–124.
———. 1996b. "*Miranda*'s Social Costs: An Empirical Reassessment." *Northwestern University Law Review* 90:387–499.

————. 1996*c*. "True Confessions about *Miranda* Legacy." *Legal Times* (July 22, 1996), pp. 22–23.

————. 1997. *"Miranda*'s Negligible Effect on Law Enforcement: Some Skeptical Observations." *Harvard Journal of Law and Public Policy* 20:327–46.

————. 1999*a*. "Barbarians at the Gates? A Reply to the Critics of the Victims' Rights Amendment." *Utah Law Review* 1999:479–544.

————. 1999*b*. "The Statute That Time Forgot: 18 U.S.C. § 3501 and the Overruling of *Miranda.*" *Iowa Law Review* 85:175–259.

————. 2000. Personal communication with George C. Thomas III, professor of law, University of Utah College of Law, August 31.

Cassell, Paul G., and Richard Fowles. 1998. "Handcuffing the Cops? A Thirty-Year Perspective on *Miranda*'s Harmful Effects on Law Enforcement." *Stanford Law Review* 50:1055–145.

Cassell, Paul G., and Brett S. Hayman. 1996. "Police Interrogation in the 1990s: An Empirical Study of the Effects of *Miranda.*" *U.C.L.A. Law Review* 43:839–931.

Dallek, Robert. 1998. *Flawed Giant: Lyndon Johnson and His Times, 1961–1973.* New York: Oxford University Press.

Donahue, John. 1998. "Did *Miranda* Diminish Police Effectiveness?" *Stanford Law Review* 50:1147–80.

Feeney, Floyd. 2000. "Police Clearance: A Poor Way to Measure the Impact of *Miranda* on the Police." *Rutgers Law Journal* 32:1–114.

Feeney, Floyd, Forest Dill, and Adrianne Weir. 1983. *Arrests without Conviction: How Often They Occur and Why.* Washington, D.C.: U.S. Department of Justice, National Institute of Justice.

Garcia, Alfredo. 1998. "Is *Miranda* Dead, Was It Overruled, or Is It Irrelevant?" *St. Thomas Law Review* 10:461–505.

Graham, Fred P. 1970. *The Self-Inflicted Wound.* New York: Macmillan.

Grano, Joseph D. 1979*a*. *"Rhode Island v. Innis:* A Need to Reconsider the Constitutional Premises Underlying the Law of Confessions." *American Criminal Law Review* 17:1–51.

————. 1979*b*. "Voluntariness, Free Will, and the Law of Confessions." *Virginia Law Review* 65:859–945.

————. 1985. "Prophylactic Rules in Criminal Procedure: A Question of Article III Legitimacy." *Northwestern University Law Review* 80:100–164.

————. 1986. "Selling the Idea to Tell the Truth: The Professional Interrogator and Modern Confessions Law." *Michigan Law Review* 84:662–90.

————. 1988. *"Miranda*'s Constitutional Difficulties: A Reply to Professor Schulhofer." *University of Chicago Law Review* 55:174–89.

————. 1989. "The Changed and Changing World of Constitutional Criminal Procedure." *University of Michigan Journal of Law Reform* 22:395–424.

————. 1992. "Ascertaining the Truth." *Cornell Law Review* 77:1061–66.

————. 1993. *Confessions, Truth and the Law.* Ann Arbor: University of Michigan Press.

————. 1996. "Criminal Procedure: Moving from the Accused as Victim to the Accused as Responsible Party." *Harvard Journal of Law and Public Policy* 19:711–17.

Greenawalt, Kent. 1980. "Silence as a Moral and Constitutional Right." *William and Mary Law Review* 23:15–71.

Greenwood, Kate, and Jeffrey Brown. 1998. "Investigation and Police Practices: Custodial Interrogations." *Georgetown Law Journal* 86:1318–33.

Griffiths, John, and Richard Ayres. 1967. "Interrogation of Draft Protesters." *Yale Law Journal* 77:395–424.

Grisso, Thomas. 1980. "Juveniles' Capacities to Waive *Miranda* Rights: An Empirical Analysis." *California Law Review* 68:1134–66.

Gruhl, John, and Cassia Spohn. 1981. "The Supreme Court's Post-*Miranda* Rulings: Impact on Local Prosecutors." *Law and Policy Quarterly* 3:29–54.

Guy, Karen L., and Robert G. Huckabee. 1988. "Going Free on a Technicality: Another Look at the Effect of the *Miranda* Decision on the Criminal Justice Process." *Criminal Justice Research Bulletin* 4:1–3.

Herman, Lawrence. 1987. "The Supreme Court, the Attorney General, and the Good Old Days of Police Interrogation." *Ohio State Law Journal* 48: 733–55.

Hoffman, Jan. 1998. "Some Officers Are Skirting *Miranda* Restraints to Get Confessions." *New York Times* (March 29, 1998), p. A1.

Kamisar, Yale. 1965. "Equal Justice in the Gatehouses and Mansions of American Criminal Procedure." In *Criminal Justice in Our Time*, edited by A. E. Dick Howard. Published for the Magna Carta Commission of Virginia. Charlottesville: University Press of Virginia.

———. 1966. "A Dissent from the *Miranda* Dissents: Some Comments on the 'New' Fifth Amendment and the 'Old' Voluntariness Test." *Michigan Law Review* 65:59–104.

———. 1974. "Kauper's 'Judicial Examination of the Accused' Forty Years Later: Some Comments on a Remarkable Article." *Michigan Law Review* 73: 15–38.

———. 1977*a*. "*Brewer v. Williams, Massiah*, and *Miranda:* What Is 'Interrogation'? When Does It Matter?" *Georgetown University Law Journal* 67:1–101.

———. 1977*b*. "Fred E. Inbau: The Importance of Being Guilty." *Journal of Criminal Law and Criminology* 68:182–97.

———. 1990. "Remembering the 'Old World' of Criminal Procedure: A Reply to Professor Grano." *University of Michigan Journal of Law Reform* 23: 537–89.

———. 1996. "*Miranda* Does Not Look So Awesome Now." *Legal Times* (June 10, 1996):A22.

———. 1999. "Reflections: Retrospective on David Simon's *Homicide*." *Jurist* 2:1–6.

———. 2000. "Can (Did) Congress 'Overrule' *Miranda?*" *Cornell Law Review* 85:883–955.

Kant, Immanuel. 1998. *The Critique of Pure Reason*. Translated and edited by Paul Guyer and Allen W. Wood. New York: Cambridge University Press.

Leiken, L. S. 1970. "Police Interrogation in Colorado: The Implementation of *Miranda*." *Denver Law Journal* 47:1–53.

Leo, Richard A. 1994. "Police Interrogation and Social Control." *Social and Legal Studies* 3:93–120.

————. 1996*a*. "Inside the Interrogation Room." *Journal of Criminal Law and Criminology* 86:266–303.

————. 1996*b*. "The Impact of *Miranda* Revisited." *Journal of Criminal Law and Criminology* 86:621–92.

————. 1998. "*Miranda* and the Problem of False Confessions." In *The* Miranda *Debate: Law, Justice and Policing*, edited by Richard A. Leo and George C. Thomas III. Boston: Northeastern University Press.

Leo, Richard A., and Richard J. Ofshe. 1998. "Using the Innocent to Scapegoat *Miranda:* Another Reply to Paul Cassell." *Journal of Criminal Law and Criminology* 88:557–77.

Leo, Richard A., and George C. Thomas III, eds. 1998. *The* Miranda *Debate: Law, Justice, and Policing.* Boston: Northeastern University Press.

Leo, Richard A., and Welsh S. White. 1999. "Adapting to *Miranda:* Modern Interrogators' Strategies for Dealing with the Obstacles Posed by *Miranda.*" *Minnesota Law Review* 84:397–472.

Malone, Patrick. 1986. "You Have the Right to Remain Silent: *Miranda* after Twenty Years." *American Scholar* 55:367–80.

Markman, Stephen J. 1987. "The Fifth Amendment and Custodial Questioning: A Response to 'Reconsidering *Miranda.*'" *University of Chicago Law Review* 54:938–49.

————. 1989. "Foreword: The 'Truth in Criminal Justice' Series." *University of Michigan Journal of Law Reform* 22:425–36.

Meares, Tracey, and Bernard Harcourt. 2001. "Transparent Adjudication and Social Science Research in Constitutional Criminal Procedure." *Journal of Criminal Law and Criminology* 90:733–98.

Medalie, Richard J., Leonard Zeitz, and Paul Alexander. 1968. "Custodial Police Interrogation in Our Nation's Capital: The Attempt to Implement *Miranda.*" *Michigan Law Review* 66:1347–422.

Milner, Neal A. 1971. *The Court and Local Law Enforcement: The Impact of* Miranda. Beverly Hills, Calif.: Sage.

Monaghan, Henry P. 1975. "Foreword: Constitutional Common Law." *Harvard Law Review* 89:1–45.

Mosteller, Robert P. 1997. "Victim's Rights and the United States Constitution: An Effort to Recast the Battle in Criminal Litigation." *Georgia Law Journal* 85:1691–715.

Nardulli, Peter. 1983. "The Societal Cost of the Exclusionary Rule: An Empirical Assessment." *American Bar Foundation Research Journal* 3:585–609.

————. 1987. "The Societal Costs of the Exclusionary Rule Revisited." *University of Illinois Law Review* 2:223–39.

Neubauer, David W. 1974. *Criminal Justice in Middle America.* Morristown, N.J.: General Learning Press.

Nguyen, Alex. 2000. "The Assault on *Miranda.*" *American Prospect* (March 27–April 10, 2000), pp. 1–9.

Report to the Attorney General on the Law of Pretrial Interrogation. 1986. Truth in Criminal Justice, Report no. 1. Washington, D.C.: U.S. Department of Justice, Office of Legal Policy. Reprinted 1989 in *University of Michigan Journal of Law Reform* 22:437–572.

Robinson, Cyril D. 1968. "Police and Prosecutor Practices and Attitudes Relating to Interrogation as Revealed by Pre- and Post-*Miranda* Questionnaires: A Construct of Police Capacity to Comply." *Duke Law Journal* 3: 425–524.

Rosenfeld, Seth. 2000. "How an Improper Interrogation by Police Derailed a Murder Prosecution." *San Francisco Examiner* (June 18, 2000), p. A6.

Schaefer, Roger C. 1971. "Patrolman Perspectives on *Miranda*." *Law and the Social Order. Arizona State Law Journal* 1971:81–101.

Schulhofer, Stephen J. 1987. "Reconsidering *Miranda*." *University of Chicago Law Review* 54:435–61.

———. 1996*a*. "*Miranda* and Clearance Rates." *Northwestern University Law Review* 91:278–94.

———. 1996*b*. "*Miranda*'s Practical Effect: Substantial Benefits and Vanishingly Small Social Costs." *Northwestern University Law Review* 90:500–563.

———. 1996*c*. "Pointing in the Wrong Direction." *Legal Times* (August 12, 1996), pp. 21, 24.

———. 1997. "Bashing *Miranda* is Unjustified—and Harmful." *Harvard Journal of Law and Public Policy* 20:347–73.

Seeburger, Richard H., and R. Stanton Wettick. 1967. "*Miranda* in Pittsburgh: A Statistical Study." *Pittsburgh Law Review* 29:1–26.

Seidman, Louis Michael. 1990. "Rubashov's Question: Self-Incrimination and the Problem of Coerced Preferences." *Yale Journal of Law and the Humanities* 2:149–80.

———. 1992. "*Brown* and *Miranda*." *California Law Review* 80:673–753.

Simon, David. 1991. *Homicide: A Year on the Killing Streets.* Boston: Houghton Mifflin.

Skolnick, Jerome H., and Richard A. Leo. 1992. "The Ethics of Deceptive Interrogation." *Criminal Justice Ethics* 11:3–12.

Stephens, Otis, Robert Flanders, and J. Lewis Cannon. 1972. "Law Enforcement and the Supreme Court: Police Perceptions of the *Miranda* Requirements." *Tennessee Law Review* 39:407–31.

Stuntz, William. 2001. "*Miranda*'s Mistake." *Michigan Law Review* 99:975–99.

Thomas, George C., III. 1993. "A Philosophical Account of Coerced Self-Incrimination." *Yale Journal of Law and the Humanities* 5:79–111.

———. 1996*a*. "Is *Miranda* a Real World Failure? A Plea for More (and Better) Empirical Evidence." *U.C.L.A. Law Review* 43:821–37.

———. 1996*b*. "Plain Talk about the *Miranda* Empirical Debate: A 'Steady-State' Theory of Confessions." *U.C.L.A. Law Review* 43:933–59.

———. 1996*c*. "Telling Half-Truths." *Legal Times* (August 12, 1996), pp. 20–24.

———. 2000. "The End of the Road for *Miranda v. Arizona?*: On the History and Future of Rules for Police Interrogation." *American Criminal Law Review* 37:1–39.

———. 2001. "Separated at Birth but Siblings Nonetheless: *Miranda* and the Due Process Cases." *Michigan Law Review* 99:1081–1120.

Toobin, Jeffrey. 1987. "Viva *Miranda*." *New Republic* 196 (February 1987):11–12.

Uviller, H. Richard. 1996. *Virtual Justice: The Flawed Prosecution of Crime in America*. New Haven, Conn.: Yale University Press.

Wald, Michael, R. Ayres, D. W. Hess, M. Schantz, and C. H. Whitebread. 1967. "Interrogations in New Haven: The Impact of *Miranda*." *Yale Law Journal* 76:1519–1648.

Walker, Samuel. 1993. *Taming the System: The Control of Discretion in Criminal Justice, 1950–1990*. New York: Oxford University Press.

Weisselberg, Charles. 1998. "Saving *Miranda*." *Cornell Law Review* 84:109–92.

———. 2001. "In the Stationhouse after *Dickerson*." *Michigan Law Review* 99:1121–63.

White, Welsh. 1998. "What Is an Involuntary Confession Now?" *Rutgers Law Review* 50:2001–57.

———. 2001. "*Miranda*'s Failure to Restrain Pernicious Interrogation Practices." *Michigan Law Review* 99:1211–47.

Wigmore, John Henry. 1923. *A Treatise on the Anglo-American System of Evidence in Trials at Common Law*. 2d ed. Boston: Little Brown.

Witt, James W. 1973. "Non-coercive Interrogation and the Administration of Criminal Justice: The Impact of *Miranda* on Police Effectuality." *Journal of Criminal Law and Criminology* 64:320–32.

Younger, Evelle. 1966a. "*Miranda*." *Fordham Law Review* 35:255–62.

———. 1966b. "Results of a Survey Conducted in the District Attorney's Office of Los Angeles County regarding the Effect of the *Miranda* Decision upon the Prosecution of Felony Cases." *American Criminal Law Quarterly* 5:32–39.

Paul E. Mullen and Michele Pathé

Stalking

ABSTRACT

Stalking has emerged as a significant social problem. Antistalking legislation has been introduced in most Western nations. The nature, prevalence, and impact of stalking are only now being systematically studied. There are debates on how best to conceptualize stalking and how to understand what drives stalkers persistently to pursue and harass the targets of their unwanted attentions. The prevalence of being victimized by stalkers is relatively high, with those subjected to extended periods of harassment often suffering both significant psychological damage and being at risk of physical and sometimes sexual assault. A variety of strategies have been developed to curb and prevent stalking and to relieve the distress of victims.

The word "stalk" has long had the meaning of both following and walking stealthily. In the late 1980s the media appropriated "stalking" and "stalker" to describe a group of individuals who persistently followed and intruded on others. Initially those so described were pursuers and pesterers of the famous. From the outset the media linked stalking to violence. One of the earliest defining examples was the persistent pursuit and ultimate murder of the actress Rebecca Shaeffer by a disordered fan. Between 1988, when the term "stalking" began to acquire currency in the media, and 1991, stalking captured the public imagination. The use of the term ceased to be confined to those who

Paul E. Mullen is clinical director of the Victorian Institute of Forensic Mental Health, Australia, and professor of forensic psychiatry, Monash University, Victoria, Australia. Michele Pathé is a consultant psychiatrist and assistant clinical director, Victorian Institute of Forensic Mental Health, and honorary senior lecturer at Monash University.

harassed the famous and acquired a wider usage, particularly as a label for those who continued to harass and intrude on their erstwhile partners.

Star stalkers could be either men or women and were portrayed as people inappropriately obsessed with someone famous, and, by implication, stalkers were likely to be mentally disordered. These were rare and exotic creatures found only in the ecological niches inhabited by the famous. When the use of the word "stalking" broadened to incorporate the harassers of ex-partners, it was initially reframed as "a woman's issue, a widespread precursor of serious violence . . . a common problem . . . a form of domestic violence against women" (Lowney and Best 1995, pp. 42–45). This newer construction was typified by an angry and vengeful male pursuing a terrified female. In the process, a social problem that had initially been confined to the famous was transformed into an experience open to all women. Stalking as a form of female harassment became the dominant construction, though it never entirely eclipsed the media's fascination with stalkers to the stars. Eventually, stalking was generalized beyond both the confines of domestic violence and being one of the burdens of fame to encompass any extended pursuit involving attempts to communicate or intrude upon an unwilling, frightened victim (Mullen, Pathé, and Purcell 2000).

Stalking progressed rapidly from being a media neologism to becoming an established social problem and a specific form of criminal offending. The murder of Rebecca Shaeffer was the impetus for the introduction of antistalking legislation in California. Her death became virtually synonymous with the public outcry and media pressure for new laws to control such harassment. The public pressure culminated in the passage of the world's first antistalking statute in California, which came into effect on January 1, 1991 (see Gilligan 1992; Resnick 1992; Anderson 1993; Sohn 1994).

The California Penal Code Section 646.9(a) defines the offense of stalking as "any person who wilfully, maliciously, and repeatedly follows or harasses another person and who makes a credible threat with the intent to place that person in reasonable fear for his or her safety, or the safety of his or her immediate family." "Harass" was further defined by Section 646.9(e) as a "knowing and wilful course of conduct directed at a specific person which seriously alarms, annoys, torments, or terrorizes the person and which serves no legitimate purpose." The course of conduct must be such as would cause a reasonable person to suffer substantial emotional distress and must actually cause substantial emotional distress to the person. Course of conduct is defined in Section 646.9(f) as "a pattern of conduct composed of a series of acts over a period of time, however short, evidencing a continuing of purpose." Constitutionally protected activity is not included within the meaning of course of conduct. The statute's sentencing provisions initially created a maximum term of one year's imprisonment, a $1,000 fine for an initial conviction, or both. There were enhanced penalties if the perpetrator committed a further stalking offense. The courts subsequently interpreted "a series of acts" to constitute acts performed on two or more occasions (*People v. Heilman*, 25 Cal. App. 4th 391 [1994]).

Other American states followed California. States either adopted the California approach, requiring the perpetrator to engage in a course of conduct, or specified in legislation those activities that constitute stalking. Since 1992 every U.S. state has introduced antistalking legislation (McAnaney, Curliss, and Abeyla-Price 1993). Thirty states enacted antistalking legislation in 1992 and an additional nineteen in 1993. The U.S. federal government also legislated to prohibit interstate stalking and malicious communications. Canada enacted criminal harassment provisions to deal with stalking-related conduct (Manitoba Law Reform Commission 1997). Between 1993 and 1995 antistalking laws were passed in every Australian state and territory (Purcell, Pathé, and Mullen, forthcoming). In England and Wales the Protection from Harassment Act, with broadly similar purposes, came into force in June 1997, while there is a separate provision for Scotland. A number of European countries are considering or preparing such legislation.

In less than a decade a new category of offending had been established in most Western nations. Stalking has come to be seen as a new and increasingly prevalent form of criminal behavior. Stalking, having acquired meanings and connotations in the popular discourse, and having acquired a variety of legal definitions, only then attracted the interest of behavioral scientists.

In California in 1990, in conjunction with the establishment of antistalking laws, the Los Angeles Police Department (LAPD) established a Threat Management Unit whose mission was to understand the elements of stalking and implement a new approach to the management of these cases by law enforcement officials (Zona, Palarea, and Lane 1998). At an early stage in the development of this police initiative, a psychiatrist, Michael Zona, became involved, and subsequently a clinical psychologist, Russell Palarea, joined in. The data for their initial paper were based on seventy-four case files from the Threat Management Unit and provided the basis for the first behavioral science study on stalkers (Zona, Sharma, and Lane 1993). This work aimed at describing the clinical characteristics of stalkers and offered a classification of the main types. The authors drew heavily on the previous literature on what had been considered a rare psychiatric disorder, erotomania, as well as on the work of Reid Meloy who had described a more broadly based form of psychopathology that he termed "borderline erotomania" (Meloy 1989, 1992). In his turn Meloy drew on the work of Zona and colleagues to define stalking as "an abnormal or long term pattern of threat or harassment directed towards a specific individual" (Meloy and Gothard 1995, p. 259). Meloy attempted to introduce the term "obsessional following" as the clinical corollary of stalking, at least in part to avoid the sensational connotations that stalking had acquired. To date, however, the power of the word "stalking" has swept all competing terms before it. The work of Mullen and Pathé (1994a, 1994b) followed a not dissimilar course, beginning with studies on a large series of cases of erotomania. Like Meloy, they found erotomania to be defined in a manner overly restrictive and ill-suited to clinical realities. A broader notion of these disorders was attempted in the description of morbid infatuations, which in many ways overlapped with Meloy's concept of borderline erotomania (Mullen and Pathé 1994a).

The study of erotomanics and of those with morbid infatuations highlighted the extent to which these individuals became involved in the stalking of the person unfortunate enough to have attracted their disordered affections. The so-called star stalkers were drawn almost exclusively from the ranks of those with erotomania or morbid infatuations. Initially, therefore, it appeared as if these categories of disorder would encompass the majority of the perpetrators of stalking as a criminal offense. When, however, behavioral scientists began to study the wide range of individuals who were being apprehended by the new antistalking statutes, it became clear that perpetrators were not confined to those with conditions in the erotomanic spectrum but included a wide variety of individuals with states of mind varying from the virtually normal to the grossly psychotic.

The first task for behavioral scientists and mental health professionals was to derive usable definitions. The next was to generate descriptions of the ranges of behavior, motivations, and states of mind associated with the stalking, from which classifications could be derived.

Employing such definitions and descriptions, it would be possible to establish the prevalence of the behavior and the basic demographics of perpetrators and victims. Finally, from a mental health perspective, the task was to derive the type of understanding of the psychopathology and intentions of the stalker that would advance the understanding necessary to develop interventions capable of effectively stopping the stalking behaviors.

Stalking is an event that has a victim and a perpetrator. The victim is central to stalking because stalking is, in its essence, a victim-defined phenomenon. The behaviors are transformed from behavior that is inappropriate and socially inept to behavior that is damaging and criminal, by the fear and apprehension provoked in the victim. In many jurisdictions repeated communications and repeated intrusions become criminal acts, be they harassment or stalking, when such behavior could reasonably be expected to induce fear and distress and when, in fact, that behavior did produce such distress. Clearly, the dividing line between the socially inappropriate and the criminal will be influenced by the attitudes, tolerance, and reactivity of the victim. In practice most stalking that attracts the attention of the criminal justice system is of a nature that would frighten and distress all but the most stoic of individuals. Nevertheless, some complaints may well be made about behavior that others would shrug off as part of life's mundane inconveniences, but if the behavior meets the legal criteria, it is an act of stalking (here as elsewhere perpetrators have to take their victims as they find them—eggshell skulls, peculiar sensitivities, and all). The offense of stalking can also be "victim defined" in the sense that some jurisdictions do not require the perpetrator to intend to make unwanted intrusions, let alone have a wish to frighten or distress. From a mental health professional's perspective, this is a necessary consequence of attempting to criminalize stalking, given that such behaviors can arise from pathological beliefs and incorrigible assumptions about the target. The stalker may well be convinced that his or her activities will be welcomed, either now or eventually, and will discount all evidence to the contrary while continuing to pursue the fantasy of some new intimacy or hoped-for reconciliation.

Stalking is all too often a lengthy and intense harassment continuing for months or years. The effects on victims of such chronic stress have started to be studied systematically. Prior to stalking emerging as an area of legitimate interest for mental health professionals, most work on the impact of psychological trauma had been concerned with the effects of overwhelming acute stresses produced by life-threatening situations or by the horrors of such events as rape. The possible impact of ongoing fear and apprehension experienced over months or years had received little attention. For this reason the initial stalking studies by Pathé and Mullen (1997) and Hall (1998) focused on the description of the impact of such chronic fear-inducing behaviors. Pathé and Mullen (1997) found deleterious effects on the victim's psychological and social functioning in virtually all cases. Increased anxiety, sleep disturbance, significant depression, and suicidal ruminations were common, with the majority of victims having symptoms of a post-traumatic stress disorder. Major lifestyle changes—including reducing or ceasing work, curtailing social activities, and moving home—were common. The studies of the impact of stalking are only now beginning to be used to develop more effective approaches to relieving the distress of victims. In most cases where there has been extended exposure to such harassing intrusions, it is not enough simply to stop the stalking. The distress and disturbance leave lasting emotional and psychological damage that must be understood and managed in its own right.

This essay provides an overview of current knowledge about stalking in the behavioral science and mental health literatures. Section I describes stalker classifications that have been developed, mostly from clinical samples, including our own. Section II discusses the small but growing epidemiological literature on victimization by stalkers. There have been few such surveys, but their findings are broadly similar. Section III, relying on clinical and law enforcement samples, surveys what is known about stalking victims in relation to those who stalk them, and Section IV examines same-sex stalking, a phenomenon that is more prevalent than is conventionally recognized. Sections V, VI, and VII examine the effects of stalking on victims, false claims of stalking, and the prevalence of assaults by stalkers. Sections VIII and IX discuss clinical and other approaches to working with stalkers and their victims.

I. Classification

No generally accepted approach to classifying stalkers has yet emerged. A number of different typologies and groupings have been advanced that are the product of the particular experiences, theoretical commitments, and practical needs of the groups who have proposed them. As the knowledge and experience about stalkers and their behaviors, motivations, and trajectories increase, so classifications will become more firmly based in the realities of the stalking phenomena. Till then, doubtless differing constructions, typologies, and would-be classifications will contend for attention and, inevitably, that elusive preeminence.

Classifications are creatures of convenience that reflect the properties of what is being classified and the needs of those advancing the classification. Law enforcement officers, mental health professionals, and advocates for victims of domestic violence, for example, have legitimate interests in stalking, and each group has evolved classifications that advance its aims and are reconcilable with its own assumptions and language. Here we briefly examine a number of classificatory systems that have gained prominence, though no single system has yet imposed itself on the literature.

Zona, Sharma, and Lane (1993) were the first to advance a classification of stalkers. They based their proposed typology on a review of seventy-four case files processed by the LAPD's Threat Management Unit that was later augmented with a further 126 cases (Zona, Sharma, and Lane 1993; Zona, Lane, and Moore 1996; Zona, Palarea, and Lane 1998). The authors identified three groups of stalkers: the erotomanic, the love obsessional, and the simple obsessional. The erotomanic group encompassed only those subjects who, as a result of delusional disorder, believed absolutely that they were loved by those whom they were stalking. None of these subjects had a prior relationship with their victim, and as a group they focused their amorous attentions almost exclusively upon those in the entertainment industry. The second group was the love obsessionals who, like the erotomanic group, consisted to some extent of those who harbored delusions that they were loved by their victim. In contrast to the erotomanic type, however, this group's delusions arose secondarily as part of a more extensive psychotic illness (most frequently schizophrenia or bipolar disorder), rather than manifesting itself as a pure or primary delusional syndrome. Also included in the love obsessional group were those who were said to show an intense infatuation with the object of their unwanted attentions but not to claim that their love was reciprocated. Unlike the erotomanic grouping, the majority of love obsessionals were male. Both the erotomanic and the love obsessional categories were reported to share a common fascination with media figures, frequently choosing young female "bombshells" as the targets of their ardent affections. Neither the erotomanic nor the love obsessional groups had prior relationships with their victims. It was on this basis of a lack of a prior relationship that the love obsessional grouping was separated from the final group, the simple obsessionals. This simple obsessional group was reported to have pursued victims with whom they had previous contact. Their victims were typically ex–intimate partners but included neighbors, casual acquaintances, workmates, and professional contacts. Males and females were equally represented among stalkers in this simple obsessional category, and they had usually commenced their pursuit after a relationship had "soured."

Zona and colleagues (Zona, Sharma, and Lane 1993; Zona, Palarea, and Lane 1998) used a classificatory approach that drew on the *Diagnostic and Statistical Manual of Mental Disorders* (DSM-III-R) of the American Psychiatric Association. The erotomanic group overlapped with existing definitions of "delusional disorder, erotomanic type." They also extended existing notions of obsessive and compulsive behaviors to create their other two groups. It should perhaps be noted, however, that the information on which they based their typology was provided in many instances primarily, or exclusively, by the victims. The complainant to the police may well have been unaware of the pursuer's current and past mental health status. Zona and coworkers (Zona, Sharma, and Lane 1993; Zona, Palarea, and Lane 1998) approach the classification of stalking from the dual perspectives of psychiatry and law enforcement. The subjects of their studies were drawn particularly from the stalkers of the rich and famous. These authors clearly recognized that stalking was not confined to the harassment of celebrities, though they had perforce to focus to a significant degree on those who stalk people with whom they have had no, or only the slightest, relationships and who are engaged in establishing or asserting a fantasized relationship. This contrasts with the stalking subjects of those who work in the domestic violence field who deal with individuals, predominantly male, who are bent on controlling, retaining, regaining, or terrorizing their present or prior partner. The commitments of the researchers and the use to which they intend to put their classification inevitably, and quite properly, directs the nature of the classification produced (Mullen, Pathé, and Purcell 2000).

Stalking has been classified as an integral part of violence against women (Australian Bureau of Statistics 1996; Coleman 1997). Walker and Meloy (1998) suggest that stalking is often a strategy of intimidation and control used by men to force their female partners to remain in a relationship. This emphasis on stalking as an extension of domestic violence creates a view of stalking that focuses on women as victims and men as perpetrators (Burgess et al. 1997).

An alternative and more broadly based approach is illustrated by the work of Harmon, Rosner, and Owens (1995), who distinguished stalkers on the basis of the nature of the attachment to the victim and on the nature of the prior relationship. The authors reviewed cases referred to a psychiatrist attached to the criminal and supreme courts of New York following charges of criminal harassment or menacing. The majority of stalkers were described as having an "affectionate/amorous" attachment to their victims, with the rest deemed to have a "persecutory/angry" attachment. Diagnostically, these stalkers consisted predominantly of patients with erotomanic features, although subjects with narcissistic and paranoid personality traits who stalked ex–intimate partners were also represented. Those with an amorous attachment were said not infrequently to victimize third parties who were believed to be interfering with the stalker's pursuit of their supposed beloved. All subjects within the affectionate/amorous attachments commenced their stalking with romantic intentions, but their emotions could on occasion turn to anger and persecution when rejection occurred. The stalking by those who had persecutory/angry attachments was reported typically to emerge following a real or imagined mistreatment or injury and often in the context of a business or professional relationship. The victims were not only individuals but also included large institutions, placing multiple victims at risk of harassment or violence. One example provided was a fifty-nine-year-old man who indiscriminately stalked lawyers and associated staff from a law firm that had unsuccessfully represented him nearly two decades earlier. The stalkers in the persecutory/angry grouping covered a more diverse spectrum in terms of psychiatric diagnoses than the amorous group, encompassing not only those with delusional illnesses but often mood or adjustment disorders and personality disorders.

The classification proposed by Harmon, Rosner, and Owens (1995) provides a meaningful framework from which to approach the motivations of stalkers and the nature of their attachment to their victims. It unfortunately did little to distinguish the pursuit characteristics of subjects. Though the subjects in the affectionate/amorous category were more likely to be single, the groups did not differ according to age, gender, ethnicity, education, criminal charges, or psychiatric diagnoses. Furthermore, subjects in both groups showed the same propensity for seeking physical contact with their victims and making threats of violence, although there was a greater association between threats and actual assault in the amorous group.

Kienlen et al. (1997) divided stalkers into two groups on the basis of whether they were, or were not, psychotic. Psychotic stalkers were more likely to visit the home of their victim but were somewhat less inclined to send letters or keep their victims under surveillance. Non-psychotic stalkers were more often verbally threatening and also were at higher risk of perpetrating an assault. Schwartz-Watts and Morgan (1998) and Schwartz-Watts, Morgan, and Barnes (1997) compared stalkers to other violent offenders and subsequently compared violent to nonviolent stalkers. Violent stalkers were reported to be more likely to have had a prior intimate relationship with the victim. Wright and coworkers (1996), who are affiliated with the Federal Bureau of Investigation, advanced a classification of stalkers based on thirty cases that, given that six culminated in murder and seven in suicide, could be seen as an extreme and highly selected group. The classification combined five elements: the nature of the relationship between the victim and stalker (domestic or nondomestic); the content of the communications (nondelusional or delusional); the level of risk to the victim in terms of aggression (low, medium, high); the motive of the stalker (infatuation, possession, anger/retaliation, other); and the outcome of the case for the stalker (legal, suicide, psychiatric, other). The elements of the classification have face validity, but the small size and peculiar nature of the sample on which it was generated make generalization to more mundane groups of stalkers problematic.

De Becker, who also approaches stalking from a law enforcement perspective, has classified stalkers on the basis of motivation, dividing them into attachment-seekers, identity-seekers, the rejection-based, and the delusion-based (cited in Orion 1997) categories. Stalkers in the attachment-based group wish to establish a relationship with the victim while recognizing that none exists, the example offered being John Hinckley, Jr. Stalkers who are identity-seekers pursue their victim as a means to achieve attention or fame themselves; here the example suggested was John Lennon's assassin Mark Chapman. The rejection-based stalkers pursue targets they believe have injured or rejected them, with the intention of exacting revenge. This group need not necessarily be former intimate partners but can include workmates and estranged friends. The delusion-based stalkers have a major mental illness that drives their stalking. De Becker argues that the rejection-based and identity-seekers groups pose the greatest threat of violence. This classification has considerable appeal, based as it is on the motivations that drive the behavior, but to date has not been elaborated to any extent in the literature.

Mullen et al. (Mullen et al. 1999; Mullen, Pathé, and Purcell 2000) proposed a classification based on clinical evaluations of 168 cases of stalking. This approach aspires to be multiaxial. The primary axis was a typology related mainly to the stalker's predominant motivation and the context in which the stalking emerged. The nature of the prior relationship with the victim and the psychiatric diagnosis formed the other two axes.

The types proposed by Mullen et al. (1999) were the rejected, the intimacy seekers, the resentful, the predatory, and the incompetent. This typology attempts to capture the function of the behavior for the stalker in terms both of the needs and desires the stalking satisfies and the gratifications and reinforcers that perpetuate the harassment. The context in which the stalking arises is also of relevance given its relationship to the stalker's likely aims and manner of advancing those aims. The intimacy seekers are responding to loneliness by attempting to establish a close relationship and are sustained by the gratification of a fantasied closeness, which presumably is preferable to no intimacy at all. The rejected are responding to an unwelcome end to a close relationship by actions intended to lead to reconciliation or to extract reparation, or both. Their stalking is reinforced by the continuance of a semblance of the relationship, however conflicted. The resentful are responding to a perceived insult or injury by actions aimed not just at revenge but at vindication. The sense of power and control created by the stalking activities reinforces the intrusiveness. The predatory are pursuing their desires for sexual gratification and control both in and through the stalking. The voyeuristic elements, the stimulus to fantasy, and the sadistic satisfactions of inducing fear and humiliating the victim combine to extend this type of stalking. The incompetents are would-be suitors seeking a partner but, given their ignorance or indifference to the usual courting rituals, employ methods that are likely to be at best counterproductive and at worst terrifying for their target. There are few satisfactions inherent in this type of stalking, and it is rarely sustained, but, unfortunately, it is all too often repeated with a new victim.

The second axis related to the relationship to the victim and was separated into prior intimate partners, professional contacts, work related contacts, casual acquaintances and friends, the famous, and strangers who had no contact prior to the onset of the stalking. The final axis was related to psychiatric status and had two divisions: the first, a psychotic group, incorporating schizophrenia, delusional disorders, affective psychosis, and organic psychosis; and the second, a nonpsychotic grouping comprised predominantly of personality disorders and to a lesser extent depressive and anxiety disorders.

This typology, taken together with relationship and the psychiatric diagnosis, enabled predictions to be made about the duration of the stalking, the nature of the stalking behaviors, the risks of threatening and violent behavior, and to some extent the response to management strategies (Mullen et al. 1999; Mullen, Pathé, and Purcell 2000). The rejected grouping used the widest range of stalking behaviors including following, repeatedly approaching, telephoning, letter writing, and leaving notes. In contrast, the predatory stalkers concentrated almost exclusively on furtively following and maintaining surveillance, never sending letters, and rarely phoning or openly approaching the victim. Intimacy seekers were the most prolific of letter writers, and they also excelled all other groups in the sending of unsolicited gifts and other forms of material. The duration of stalking was by far the longest in the rejected and intimacy seekers and shortest, as might be expected, in the predatory stalkers and incompetent suitors. The psychotic subjects were particularly likely to send unsolicited materials and the nonpsychotic to follow and maintain surveillance. The psychotic and nonpsychotic were equally likely to threaten, but the nonpsychotic were twice as likely as the psychotic to proceed to assault. The best predictor of stalking duration was the typology. Assaultiveness was best predicted by typology that, when combined with substance abuse and a history of prior convictions (irrespective of their nature), accounted for most of the explained variance.

The typology was a guide to management, as was the psychotic/ nonpsychotic dichotomy. Intimacy seekers were largely impervious to judicial sanctions, often regarding court appearances, and even imprisonment, as the price to be paid for the pursuit of a true love. By contrast, the stalking of intimacy seekers was often based on a treatable psychiatric disorder and could effectively be ended by mental health care. In contrast, the rejected were in many cases responsive to judicial sanctions curbing their behavior when the price to them of continuing to harass was sufficiently high. Given, however, that in the rejected type there are significant levels of psychopathology, particularly connected to personality disorder, a role remains for therapeutic interventions in preventing a relapse into the stalking behaviors. The incompetent type can usually be persuaded to abandon the pursuit of their current victim with relative ease, but the challenge is to prevent them moving on to harass some new victim who catches their fancy. The predatory are drawn from the ranks of the paraphiliacs, and management of their sexual deviance is central to the prevention of stalking recidivism.

No consensus typology has emerged. Given the different objectives of law enforcement officials, clinicians, and others, this is not surprising. Given, however, the recency of attention to stalking, considerable progress has been made.

II. Epidemiology

Despite the explosion of interest in stalking in recent years, there is a dearth of published epidemiological studies. The epidemiology of stalking is, strictly, the epidemiology of the reporting of being victimized by stalkers rather than of data on those who stalk. There are several encumbrances to the development of good data on the extent of stalking. The potential prevalence and nature of stalking have shifted dramatically as the definitional constraints on the behavior changed. For instance, if the criteria for stalking include the evocation of fear, prevalence estimates will be lower than those based on stalking behaviors irrespective of their impact (see Tjaden and Thoennes 1998). Similarly, the prevalence of stalking will be substantially higher if stalking is defined as two or more episodes of the requisite harassing behavior than for definitions that set the threshold at ten or more such episodes (see Mullen et al. 1999). The manner of framing inquiries will also influence prevalence figures. Questions such as "Have you ever been stalked?" are likely to yield fewer positive responses than a series of specific questions about particular experiences. A far richer database is generated by using properly structured questions that constrain the respondent to detailing what happened, how often, and over what period.

Sample selection can also have a significant influence on estimates of prevalence. A representative random community sample is the preferred sampling method likely to produce the most generalizable prevalence estimates. To date, the bulk of information regarding the nature of stalking and the characteristics of stalkers and their victims has been derived from clinical studies conducted in forensic mental health settings. Stalking studies have typically used convenience samples, with subjects drawn from clinics (Mullen and Pathé 1994*a*), courts (Harmon, Rosner, and Owens 1995), police files (Zona, Sharma, and Lane 1993), or self-selected victims (Pathé and Mullen 1997; Hall 1998). However, the prevalence of stalking behaviors and the extent to which such behaviors are experienced by their target as fear inducing will almost certainly vary between, and even within, communities. Further, systematic errors in prevalence estimates will reflect the extent to which the willingness to participate in a survey of stalking experiences is directly influenced by whether or not the subject has been stalked. Victims may be more eager to participate or, conversely, may experience any letter containing intrusive inquiries as a revictimization to be avoided. In either case, response rates would directly reflect the experience of stalking and bias the resulting prevalence estimate.

The first epidemiological study of stalking was undertaken in Australia in 1996. The Australian Bureau of Statistics (ABS) conducted a random, nationwide survey of women's experiences of physical and sexual violence perpetrated by men (Australian Bureau of Statistics 1996). Part of this included questions related to stalking, its broad definition based on a composite of Australian State antistalking laws. The threshold to qualify as a victim was set relatively low (i.e., unwanted contacts or intrusions on as few as two occasions; the experience of fear was not a criterion). Of the 6,300 adult respondents 15 percent reported being stalked by a man at some time in their lives (implying 1 million Australian women will have experienced stalking at this level). In the twelve months preceding the survey some 2.4 percent reported having been stalked, a quarter of whom were experiencing ongoing victimization. Contrary to the findings of case reports and nonrandom studies, most of the respondents reported being stalked by a stranger rather than a former intimate or acquaintance. A third of the sample were pursued for less than a month, whereas those stalked by a prior intimate were subjected to more protracted periods of harassment. Although it could be argued that the study's broad inclusion criteria produced an overestimate of the frequency of stalking within this community, these figures may be countered to some extent by the exclusion from the study of male victims and same-gender stalkers.

The U.S. National Institute of Justice (NIJ) subsequently commissioned a survey of stalking in the United States (National Institute of Justice 1997; Tjaden and Thoennes 1998). Telephone interviews were conducted on a random sample of 8,000 men and 8,000 women, ascertaining the prevalence of stalking victimization by employing a definition based on U.S. antistalking laws that intentionally omitted the word "stalking." Under that definition, respondents could be considered as possible cases if the behaviors occurred on as few as two occasions but only if the stalking made victims significantly frightened or fearful of bodily harm. Eight percent of women responding and 2 percent of men had experienced stalking, so measured, at some time in their lives. The twelve-month prevalence was 1 percent for women and 0.4 percent for men, half the levels reported in the Australian sample. Less stringent criteria, requiring that the respondent be only a little frightened, produced an increase in lifetime prevalence to 12 percent for women and 4 percent for men, which approaches the Australian results. The NIJ survey also found that women were principally stalked by former intimates, and there was a strong association between domestic violence and stalking, though stalking also occurred in a variety of other contexts. Half the sample said they were stalked for a year or more, the harassment taking similar forms to that reported in the ABS survey (most often following, unwanted phone calls and letters, and surveillance).

These findings suggest that, at least within these two Western industrialized countries, the experience of stalking is broadly consistent in terms of patterns and methods of pursuit. Across these studies, men have emerged as the predominant offenders, but a substantial minority of victims are male. Where the community studies diverge is the nature of the prior relationship between stalkers and their victims. In Australia, victims were more likely to report being pursued by a stranger than a familiar figure (Australian Bureau of Statistics 1996), while in the U.S. intimate partner stalking predominated (Tjaden and Thoennes 1998).

Notwithstanding the caveats and the paucity of large-scale studies, it can be said that within our community stalking is a not uncommon experience. Around 8 percent of women and 2 percent of men are likely to experience at some time in their lives unwanted contacts and intrusions sufficient to cause significant fear and apprehension. Community surveys to date well capture the spectrum of stalking, from the limited yet unsettling acts that constitute legal criteria for criminal stalking to the persistent and corrosive conduct that may extend over months and years, prompting not only distress in the victims and those around them but also disruptive lifestyle changes that will be detailed later. Though undoubtedly difficult to undertake, further population-based studies are essential to the advancement of our understanding of this complex phenomenon.

III. Victims of Stalking

The stimulus for criminalizing stalking behaviors and the reason, ultimately, that they are of interest to mental health professionals is that they inflict damage on their victims. It was earlier thought that victims were drawn from a select group of celebrities and other public figures. Ordinary citizens were spared such attentions, or so it was thought. However, as researchers and legislators focus increasingly upon information from stalking victims as a source of information not reflected in official records or the few selective studies of perpetrators, a different picture is emerging. Victims of stalking present a diverse sociodemographic profile. Celebrities cannot claim exclusive membership nor can any individual be assured immunity from a stalker's attentions by virtue of social class, age, gender, occupation, cultural background, or sexual orientation.

A sizable number of studies have examined the characteristics of victims. Many of the samples are self-selected, clinical, or recruited, but the patterns they share broadly resemble those from epidemiological surveys. Stalking victims are predominantly women, but many men are also victims. A sizable minority of victims are stalked by prior intimates and another sizable minority by other prior acquaintances. Combined, most studies report that 60–80 percent of reported perpetrators are prior intimates or prior acquaintances.

In what may be the earliest empirical study of stalking victims, Jason et al. (1984) interviewed fifty Chicago women recruited primarily from advertisements or via word of mouth. All had been harassed by men after ending a relationship or refusing to enter into one. All were subject to behaviors that persisted for at least one month and would by most contemporary criteria be labeled stalking. Fourteen percent had never dated their harasser.

A later University of Toronto study (Jones 1996) analyzed data from more than 7,000 victims reporting incidents of stalking and harassment to police during 1994–95. The study analyzed data from the Uniform Crime Reporting Survey, an annual review that incorporates 130 police departments across Canada. Men were the main perpetrators though they were also at risk, accounting for 20 percent of those making reports. The majority of victims were stalked by an ex–intimate partner or a casual acquaintance, though the study documented a wide range of prior relationships between stalkers and their targets: family members, coworkers and business associates, strangers, and current spouses were identified.

Fremouw, Westrup, and Pennypacker (1997) surveyed 593 psychology undergraduates in West Virginia, finding 30 percent of female and 17 percent of male respondents met the study criteria for victimization by stalking. The stalker was known to his or her victim in 80 percent of cases, with a quarter of self-reported male victims and over 40 percent of females reporting a previous romantic involvement with their stalker. One percent of subjects (three men) admitted to having committed acts of stalking.

In the NIJ survey (Tjaden and Thoennes 1998), almost 80 percent of victims were females. Again, the stalker was known to the victim in the majority of cases, being a former intimate partner of 60 percent of the women stalked and 30 percent of men. For 23 percent of women and 36 percent of men, the perpetrator was a stranger.

Hall (1998) examined a self-selected group of 145 stalking victims recruited largely through press releases and media interviews that promoted the research in six major urban centers in the United States. Females predominated in the sample (83 percent), the majority pursued by prior intimates. The reported duration of stalking ranged from less than a month to over thirty years, with only half the sample reporting the stalking had ceased.

Pathé and Mullen (1997) reported on demographic profiles of one hundred Australian stalking victims recruited through referrals to their forensic mental health clinic and self-referrals following a series of articles on stalking that appeared in the print media in 1994 and 1995. Characteristics were similar to those found in other clinical and epidemiological studies. More than 80 percent of the sample were female, while 84 percent were previously known to the perpetrator (prior intimates in 29 percent, professional alliance such as a doctor/patient relationship in 25 percent, other work-related contexts in 9 percent, acquaintances in 21 percent, and strangers in 16 percent). The duration of stalking ranged from one month to twenty years, and for half the cohort the harassment was continuing.

The British Crime Survey (Budd and Mattinson 2000) involving nearly 10,000 sixteen-to-fifty-nine-year olds in England and Wales found that 2.9 percent of subjects had been stalked in the past year, equating to almost 900,000 victims nationally. The prevalence of victimization was higher for women (4 percent) than for men (1.7 percent). A third of cases reported a prior intimate relationship with their stalker, and in another third of cases, victim and stalker were acquaintances. A further third of cases involved strangers.

Subsequently, a random community sample (Purcell, Pathé, and Mullen, forthcoming) involving 3,700 Australian adults selected from the electoral roll found lifetime prevalence figures as high as 20 percent for women and 7 percent for men for severe stalking (ten or more incidents over a one-month period or longer, inducing fear and distress in the victim). This study also found that if the harassment extended beyond two weeks, there was a likelihood that the victim would continue to be stalked for a substantial period.

Several classifications of stalking victims have been proposed, based on the premorbid relationship between victim and stalker. Zona, Sharma, and Lane (1993) divided victims into two categories, either "prior relationship" or "no prior relationship," the former subdivided into "acquaintance," "customer," "neighbor," "professional relationship," "dating," and "sexual intimates." Meloy and Gothard (1995) advocated the categories "stranger" or "former (sexual) intimate," while Harmon, Rosner, and Owens (1995) used the classifications "personal," "professional," "employment," "media," "acquaintance," and "none" or "unknown." Subsequently, Meloy (1996) argued for a simplification of the relational typology into three broad, mutually exclusive groupings: "prior sexual intimates," "prior acquaintances," and "strangers." Fremouw, Westrup, and Pennypacker (1997) proposed the classification "friend," "casual date," "serious date," and "stranger," while Emerson, Ferris, and Gardner (1998) introduced the terms "unacquainted stalking," "pseudoacquainted stalking" (where the victim is a publicly identified figure), and "semi-acquainted stalking" (where there has been some contact between victim and stalker in the past).

We have developed a typology that is derived from our clinical experience of working with stalking victims in Australia over the past eight years. It is based on the victim's former relationship with his or her stalker and the context in which victims are targeted. The groupings are not mutually exclusive.

Prior Intimates.   This is the largest category, the most common victim profile being a woman who has previously shared an intimate relationship with her (usually) male stalker. We include only cases in which the relationship has been explicitly terminated, because in these cases the behavior is unequivocally unwanted, although approximately half the victims in this category will have been subjected to harassment while still in the relationship. This most often involves following, surveillance, and damage to personal property. Such relationships are frequently characterized by the offending partner's emotional abuse, controlling behavior, and violence. Tjaden and Thoennes (1998) found that over 80 percent of women stalked by a current or former partner were physically assaulted, and 30 percent were sexually assaulted prior to leaving the relationship. The stalking behaviors that are manifest while the relationship is still intact serve to intimidate and control the victim. Stalking isolates them from outside supports and hampers their efforts to extricate themselves from the abusive situation (Walker and Meloy 1998).

Victims in this category are exposed to the widest range of harassment methods, repeated phone calls, persistent following, and threats being more commonly experienced by this group. They are also more likely to be subject to violence, particularly if the perpetrator has prior criminal convictions (Mullen et al. 1999). Victims of ex–intimate stalkers can also expect the pursuit to be more persistent, though legal sanctions may persuade their former partners to refrain from further harassment. This is obviously more complicated if victim and stalker share children; the stalker may have legitimate visitation rights (though these are often exceeded) or may embark on a custody battle fueled by a strong sense of entitlement, vengeance, or determination to maintain contact with the rejecting party. "Date" stalkers—with whom the victim may have had only a brief romantic liaison—are less likely to be violent than are ex-partners, whose emotional investment in the victim is considerably greater. The victim of a date stalker often gives a history of feeling uneasy early in the relationship. They are, however, reluctant to hurt their (most commonly) boyfriend's feelings, and they may accept further dates beyond the point at which they perceive any future in the relationship. When they do make an assertive attempt to leave, their partner typically reacts badly, often in a pathetic, childlike manner that exploits the victim's guilt and sympathy.

The guilt frequently experienced by victims of ex-intimates can be reinforced by the propensity of others to judge their predicament. Family and friends may express their disapproval of the victim's relationship choices, and helping agencies may convey their suspicions that the victim in some way encouraged the stalking. This is particularly likely when there has been a previous intimate relationship but also in situations where the victim may have failed to respond assertively to the stalker's advances, usually as a consequence of naïveté or reluctance to upset or anger the stalker. These victims are more likely than those in other categories to seek police help and legal advice, where they may encounter similar attitudes (Pathé and Mullen 1997). The response of the judicial system does not always live up to the victim's expectations, as victims are confronted by lawyers, magistrates, and judges who are ignorant of stalking issues and who trivialize the stalker's actions. This has led to calls for comprehensive training for those who work in these areas in the special needs of the victims of prior intimate stalking (Tjaden and Thoennes 1998).

Casual Acquaintances and Friends. This may be the most common category for male stalking victims (Hall 1998). Intimacy seekers and incompetents may commence their activities after a casual social encounter, while the pursuit of the rejected may be subsequent to the breakdown of a friendship or estrangement from a family member. Neighbor stalking generally falls into this category, usually perpetrated by a resentful stalker and precipitated by a dispute with the victim over noise, a fence, or garden. The stalking neighbor frequently involves the primary victim's family or other cohabitants. In our experience the victim or victims not uncommonly resort to a change of residence to escape their highly stressful home environment, a drastic measure that is nonetheless successful in those instances where the harassment has confined itself to that neighborhood.

Professional Contacts. Health care providers, lawyers, and teachers are especially at risk of stalking (see Pathé and Mullen 1997). These professions are at increased risk of stalkers from all motivational categories, though intimacy seekers, incompetents, and the resentful predominate. The termination of a therapeutic relationship may occasionally give rise to "rejected" stalking patterns, and this group of victims can also be prone to the sexually predatory behaviors of their patients, clients, or students.

Psychiatrists and primary care physicians share an enhanced risk of being stalked by intimacy seekers and incompetent suitors by virtue of their regular contact with the lonely and mentally unstable. Any profession that comes into contact with the isolated and disordered and in whom sympathy and attention is easily misconstrued as romantic interest may be vulnerable (Mullen et al. 1999). Plastic and orthopedic surgeons and lawyers are more typically the focus of resentful individuals who feel wronged, mistreated, or misshaped.

Harassing phone calls, unsolicited gifts, and letters are more often the lot of victims in this category, with following, surveillance, and violence less commonly reported (Mullen et al. 1999). These victims typically feel shocked and ill prepared to deal with these situations, a concern that some medical educators and those in other "high-risk" professions are addressing by means of the introduction of appropriate training in their curricula.

Workplace Contacts.   The victim-stalker relationship that arises in a work-related context is characteristically that of employer/supervisor-employee, fellow employee, or service provider-customer. Almost 50 percent of all stalkers show up at their victim's workplace. Although stalking incidents incorporate prior intimate stalking where (usually) the husband harasses his estranged wife at her work or a "date" stalker pursues the object of interest at his or her workplace, these victims more properly belong to the "prior intimates" category.

Victims for whom stalking commences at work may find themselves the focus of a resentful stalker's embitterment and vengeance derived from an organizational change or disciplinary action that poses a threat to his or her ego or job security. The stalker may believe he has been unfairly passed over in favor of the victim and may contest the perceived discrimination before various tribunals and appeals boards, with escalating harassment as the complaints are dismissed. Occasionally, however, intimacy-seeking and socially incompetent individuals may focus their attentions upon a coworker, some of whom react with violence to the humiliation of persistent rejection. Simon (1996) cites the famous example of California software engineer Robert Farley who became infatuated with fellow worker Laura Black. He responded to her repeated rebuttals by stalking her and, some four years later and after he had been sacked by the company where Laura still worked, stormed his former workplace and shot seven innocent employees. Black, though seriously wounded, survived. Work environments are a purlieu for many stalkers and pose safety concerns not only for the primary victim but also for coworkers, a reality that managers and supervisors in some organizations are beginning to address through educative and safety practices.

Strangers.   In this category the victim is not aware of any prior contact with the pursuer, who is most often an intimacy-seeking or incompetent stalker. The victim may have been admired from afar for some time before being subjected to more overt forms of stalking. Victims of intimacy-seeking strangers are generally selected on the basis of their elevated social status or prominence in the stalker's environment. For these victims the stalking may be quite persistent, but it is seldom characterized by violence (Mullen et al. 1999). Occasionally, however, these stalkers will react with extreme violence to their victim's repeated rebuffs (Mullen and Pathé 1994*b*).

Those who fall victim to socially incompetent strangers find that, usually by virtue of physical attractiveness and being in the wrong place at the wrong time, they are subsequently subjected to repeated approaches and other unwanted intrusions from an unknown or little known individual of limited endowment who is unnervingly impervious to rejection. Victims report crude attempts to court them, often receiving gifts such as flowers and soft toys, especially on occasions like birthdays and St. Valentine's day. These victims recount feelings of surprise and even flattery when first approached. Their polite and often ambiguous response is perceived by the stalker as encouragement. At times victims give in to their stalker's persistence, dating them on one or more occasions, perhaps out of naive curiosity but more often in the misguided hope that their unbidden courter will then desist. This response does indeed gratify the stalker's wishes to have, and to hold onto, a relationship and reinforces the pursuit.

Predatory stalkers are also unknown to their victims in many instances. They typically pursue adult women, but, as for sexual offenders generally, men and children may also be targets. Victims of predators are generally aware only of a short duration of stalking, if they are aware of this at all, before the perpetrator declares himself. This group is subject to a range of sexually abusive behaviors, from obscene phone calls to rape and even sexual murder (Mullen, Pathé, and Purcell 2000).

Occasionally, the unknown stalker is motivated by resentment. Their victim may have done nothing specific to provoke harassment, being merely perceived as representing a particular group or class detested by the stalker. For some unfortunate victims this may be little more than epitomizing success in life.

The Famous.   These victims are most often encountered through radio, television, and film but may also include politicians, royalty, sports stars, and other prominent public figures. Their stalkers are drawn from the socially incompetent, morbidly infatuated, erotomanic, and the resentful. Just as celebrity stalkers not uncommonly target, concurrently or sequentially, a number of celebrities, high-profile victims may well have to contend with more than one stalker.

IV. Same-Gender Stalking

Stalking is usually portrayed as heterosexual activity in which men pursue women and women pursue men. Instances of same-gender stalking have been regarded as a rarity, some suggesting less than 1 percent of all cases (Meloy 1996). Recent studies, however, indicate that same-gender stalking is more prevalent than formerly estimated (Pathé, Purcell, and Mullen 2000). In our clinical experience, people stalked by individuals of the same gender meet greater skepticism and indifference from law enforcement and other helping agencies. This is not just a homophobic response, as it appears to be independent of the victim's sexual orientation. Case reports of same-gender stalkers have appeared in the popular press. These have included Mark Chapman, who stalked and killed musician John Lennon, and more recently Jonathan Norman, who stalked film director Steven Spielberg with the stated intention of raping him. Author Stephen King was reputedly the victim of two male stalkers, and actress Sharon Gless was pursued for years by a woman claiming to be in love with her. Finally, a number of personal and fictional accounts of same-gender stalking have appeared in literary circles in recent years, notably psychiatrist Dr. Doreen Orion's gripping account of being stalked by a female ex-patient in *I Know You Really Love Me* (1997) and Ian McEwan's novel *Enduring Love* (1997), which portrays the plight of a man pursued by a male stranger with an erotomanic attachment to him.

Hall's (1998) study of stalking victims found high rates of males stalking males. While females were with few exceptions stalked by men, male victims were almost as likely to be stalked by a male as a female. Pathé and Mullen (1997) reported 14 percent of their cohort of victims experienced same-gender victimization, ten of the eighty-three female victims (12 percent), and four of the seventeen male victims (24 percent). The NIJ study (Tjaden and Thoennes 1998) found that of 2 percent of male respondents reporting stalking victimization, 60 percent were stalked by a male. In the British Crime Survey (Budd and Mattinson 2000), male offenders were involved in 57 percent of stalking incidents against men.

Pathé, Purcell, and Mullen (2000) found that 18 percent of 163 stalkers referred to their Australian forensic psychiatric service were same-gender cases. A comparative analysis of same-gender ($N = 29$) and opposite-gender ($N = 134$) stalkers found more similarities than differences. However, same-gender stalkers were more likely in this study to be female, and the prior relationship between victim and stalker was less often an intimate one for same-gender cases and more likely to have originated in the workplace. Same-gender stalking was more commonly motivated by resentment, and there were no predatory same-gender stalkers. The psychopathological profiles of same-gender stalkers, other than the absence of diagnosable sexual deviations, were not significantly different from those of opposite-gender stalkers, and there was no evidence that their victims suffered any more or less than the victims of opposite-gender stalkers. Rates of threat and violence did not vary significantly between the two groups.

V. Effects

Unlike many other criminal offenses, stalking is distinguished by repetition and persistence. Most stalking involves multiple forms of harassment, engendering fear and apprehension, hypervigilance, and mistrust in its victims. Such responses can alienate victims from their customary support systems. Relationships and careers may be eroded, exacerbating social isolation and despair.

The psychological responses of stalking victims share much in common with victims of other trauma. Those who experience single, violent crimes frequently manifest an initial acute stress disorder that may give rise over time to the development of stress-related symptoms, currently conceptualized as post-traumatic stress disorder (PTSD; American Psychiatric Association 1994). Stalking, however, possesses many of the features associated with the development in its victims of chronic stress reactions and related psychological sequelae. Because of the stalker's repeated intrusions, victims experience a lack of control over their situation. The responses of the criminal justice system and helping agencies are frequently perceived as ineffectual, undermining the victims' assumptions that they live in a fair and safe society and shattering their expectations of regaining control. Stalking victims live in a state of persistent threat, with associated symptoms that may be more enduring than the harassment itself.

Pathé and Mullen (1997) provided a sobering early account of the substantial disorder and disruption that stalking can produce. All but six of the one hundred victims reported major lifestyle changes and modified their daily activities in direct response to being stalked. This included avoiding places where the stalker might be and adopting additional, often expensive, security measures such as installing video surveillance equipment and house alarms. Fear of venturing out forced a curtailment of social activities in 70 percent of respondents. Over half claimed they had changed or ceased employment as a consequence of being stalked. Such drastic measures were usually the result of the stalker's intrusions at the workplace, including threats to harm coworkers or employers, or absenteeism through the victim's attendances at court or medical appointments. Forty percent of study participants relocated their residence, some on two or more occasions. Most reported deterioration in mental or physical well-being, or both. Feelings of powerlessness and aggressive fantasies were commonly experienced, together with suicidal ideation in a quarter of the cohort. Over 80 percent reported heightened anxiety subsequent to the onset of stalking, most often manifested as "jumpiness," "shakes," panic attacks, and hypervigilance. Three-quarters suffered chronic sleep disturbance, largely due to nightmares and hyperarousal, though many were kept awake by their stalker's repeated phone calls or lay awake listening for any intrusions. Nearly half experienced appetite disturbance and weight changes, while symptoms such as nausea, excessive tiredness, weakness, headaches, and changes in bowel habits were not uncommon. Alcohol and cigarette consumption rose in a quarter of the sample, and several subjects experienced exacerbations of preexisting conditions such as asthma and peptic ulcers.

A majority of victims in the study reported one or more symptoms of PTSD. Intrusive recollections of the stalking, which were portrayed as recurrent and distressing, were acknowledged in 55 percent of victims. Avoidance or numbing responses were endorsed by 38 percent, particularly feelings of detachment from others. A third of victims met the full DSM-IV diagnostic criteria for PTSD (American Psychiatric Association 1994). A further 20 percent met all criteria but for the lack of a necessary stressor that involved actual or threatened physical harm or a threat to one's physical integrity.[1] Post-traumatic stress symptoms

[1] The constellation of symptoms that comprise a diagnosis of PTSD—avoidance, intrusive memories, numbing of responses, and excessive arousal—well captures the psychological sequelae of stalking. As a diagnostic entity, PTSD also valuably emphasizes the chronic nature of mental disorder or disturbance that can be produced by exposure to traumatic stressors. However, the current conceptualization of post-traumatic stress by the American Psychiatric Association is somewhat restrictive in that it allows for psychological decompensation following only a discrete or relatively circumscribed traumatic event that threatens or actually harms one's physical integrity. This conceptualization fails to acknowledge the psychological distress produced by prolonged trauma and repeated victimization, as occurs in stalking. While not necessarily involving explicit threats to one's physical being, a stalker's activities are clearly no less damaging to the victim's mental health. Violence was not an essential prerequisite for psychological distress and social and occupational disruption in this sample, the majority of subjects reporting chronic fear in the absence of any physical assaults, though for many fear was a response to the threat of imminent violence. More significant, the menace and persistent

were more likely to be reported by females and those subjected to following or violence. They were also more commonly observed in victims who shared a prior intimate relationship with their stalker, a reflection perhaps of the preponderance of female victims and violence in such relationships.

Systematic assessment of stalking victim populations using standardized measures of psychological distress has supported the findings of these earlier studies. Westrup et al. (1999) compared thirty-six female college-student stalking victims with forty-three who had experienced less severe to frequent harassment ("harassed" group) and forty-eight controls. Psychological impact was measured using a number of widely validated psychometric scales. Stalking victims had significantly higher scores in a number of areas, particularly depression, and they exhibited heightened interpersonal sensitivity. They scored significantly higher on post-traumatic symptoms, and these were more severe relative to the comparison groups. The Australian community survey conducted by Purcell and colleagues (forthcoming) found elevated rates of psychiatric morbidity in over a third of subjects based on standardized psychometric instruments. Significant post-traumatic stress reactions occurred in 22 percent of victims.

VI. False Claims

A small proportion of individuals who claim to be stalking victims have not been. The LAPD database suggests that false claims are rare (around 2 percent). Zona, Lane, and Moore (1996) postulated that the phenomenon arises from "a conscious or unconscious desire to be placed in the victim's role." Pathé, Mullen, and Purcell (1999) described twelve false claims. The accounts were judged to be false because they were clearly and repeatedly at odds with the available objective information. For those in whom the belief was delusional, the claims were inherently unlikely, if not impossible. The benefit of the doubt was given to marginal cases in which the victim's presentation was suspect, but the occurrence of stalking could not confidently be excluded.

False claims appear to emerge in five contexts. The first is when a stalker preempts a victim's complaints by accusing him or her of stalk-

---

intrusions that had come to dominate the victim's life, the unpredictability of the behavior, and in some instances the incomprehensible motives of the perpetrator were powerful determinants of the victim's suffering. Some stalking victims have even applied descriptors such as "psychological terrorism" and "emotional rape" to their experiences.

ing. The second is when severely mentally disordered people have delusions that they are being stalked by an imagined persecutor. The third is when individuals who have been stalked in the past become hypersensitive to a recurrence, such that they begin to see stalking in others' innocent actions. Fourth, there are factitious victims, who simulate the distress of being stalked to experience the victim role, and finally, malingerers, who fabricate accounts of being stalked for personal gain, such as monetary compensation or the avoidance of criminal responsibility.

Suspicions that claims of sexual harassment are false have been said to be heightened by "a perplexing discrepancy between the plaintiff's apparent sincerity and the objective facts that seem to discredit her allegations" (Feldman-Schorrig 1996, p. 515). This is equally pertinent to the false stalking victim. False victims' accounts lack the consistency, plausibility, and richness of detail evident in genuine cases. False victims are likely to seek help at an earlier stage than do true victims. True victims often delay because of embarrassment, fear of being disbelieved or considered mad, or a failure to appreciate the seriousness of their predicament. Other features that may alert the examiner to the false victim, irrespective of the underlying diagnosis, include disorganized or convoluted histories that cannot be verified or are falsified by the available evidence; the engagement of multiple therapists, moving from one to another at the first hint of skepticism; and the possession of dossiers of "evidence" of dubious significance. A repeated insistence that he or she is telling the truth and must be believed is found far more frequently. Care must always be exercised, for while psychotic false victims may give bizarre accounts that can be discounted at the outset, genuine victims' stories can occasionally astound, attracting skepticism from practitioners less familiar with these cases.

Mental health professionals have an important role to play in helping the courts to distinguish between valid and false allegations of stalking and the psychopathology that can underlie the latter. An improved understanding of the forces at play can assist in improving several key aspects of the criminal justice system, including developing more discerning approaches to restraining order applications and minimizing trauma to those falsely accused of stalking. The vast majority of those who report stalking, however, are genuine. Despite acknowledgment of their plight through legislation, sympathetic media coverage, and the emergence of victim information/support groups, genuine victims of stalking face many obstacles in their quest for personal safety and well-being. Those who make false claims are in most cases distressed and disturbed people. They require help, but that help becomes possible only when the fabrications are recognized.

VII. Assault

Stalking attracted attention and became a significant social issue largely because it was presented as the harbinger of violent, and potentially homicidal, assault. A downside of constructing stalking in this way is a tendency to underestimate the pain and distress occasioned by persistent stalking in which no physical violence occurs. The other unfortunate consequence is that this reinforces victims' inevitable apprehensions about being attacked. Stalking victims understandably want a realistic appraisal of the risk that they will be physically attacked. Police and courts seek guidance on the chances of stalkers attacking their targets. Therapists similarly need some guide to the probability of future violence in stalkers with whom they are working, or whose victims they are counseling. Stalking research has so far focused primarily on documenting the level of violence. Reported rates vary from 3 percent to 47 percent, most falling in the 30–40 percent range. Few studies have had sufficiently large samples to establish clear risk factors for violence.

Erotomania has from its earliest recognition been known to be associated with what we now call stalking and occasionally to lead to violence. Morrison wrote in 1848: "Erotomania sometimes prompts those labouring under it to destroy themselves, or others, for although in general tranquil and respectful the patient sometimes becomes unstable, passionate and jealous" (quoted in Enoch and Trethowan 1979, p. 204). Savage (1892) described a woman who developed an erotomanic attachment to a local doctor who she believed wished to marry her. Persuading herself that only his wife stood between her and her supposed lover, "she found the wife was fond of chocolate creams and most ingeniously managed to introduce poisoned creams into the stock from which the doctor's wife bought her sweets. This resulted in several children being poisoned though the intended victim escaped" (p. 721). Goldstein (1978, 1987) deserves credit for being the first in modern times to draw clear attention to the potential for violence as part of the stalking behavior of erotomanics.

Erotomanics can resort to overt violence against the object of their affections, motivated by rage at rejection or jealousy. Occasionally the assault may be an inadvertent by-product of the patient's clumsy attempts to approach the object of his or her attention (Mullen and Pathé 1994*b*). Those believed to impede access to the beloved may also fall victim. Taylor, Mahendra, and Gunn (1983) and Menzies et al. (1995) found the violence to be directed most frequently at someone other than the object of the patient's affections, but in studies by Mullen and Pathé (1994*b*) and Harmon, Rosner, and Owens (1995), the supposed beloved was the usual victim.

Zona, Sharma, and Lane (1993) first reported the incidence of violence in stalking. Only two of their seventy-four stalkers had physically assaulted their victims, and although many made threats, few acted upon them. The low incidence of violence precluded attempts to search for significant associations between stalkers' characteristics and assaultive behaviors. The stalkers in this study were not a representative sample because a significant proportion pursued film and television stars, and it is unclear whether the low level of violence found could be generalized to other groups of stalkers.

Harmon, Rosner, and Owens (1995, 1998) examined factors contributing to violence among stalkers referred to a New York Forensic Psychiatry Clinic for assessment. In their initial study of forty-eight individuals who had been charged with harassment offenses, 21 percent had been physically assaultive. In a subsequent study in which the sample size had been increased to 175 stalkers, 46 percent of stalkers (81) had exhibited violent conduct (Harmon, Rosner, and Owens 1998). Violence was associated with the nature of the prior relationship. Over 65 percent of stalkers with an "intimate" prior relationship (spouses, romantic partners, or family members of the victim) exhibited violent behavior compared with 37 percent of those whose victims were casual acquaintances and 23 percent whose victims were strangers. Psychiatric status was also related to violent behavior with the highest rates among those with DSM Axis II personality disorder and substance abusers, of whom 88 percent were violent. In contrast, patients who received only an Axis I mental illness diagnosis were the least likely to exhibit antisocial behavior. Contrary to the findings of Zona, Sharma, and Lane (1993), the majority of stalkers who had threatened their victims subsequently acted upon their stated intentions (Harmon, Rosner, and Owens 1998).

In an archival study of twenty-five forensic subjects (Kienlen et al. 1997) comparing psychotic and nonpsychotic stalkers, a third were reported to have committed assaults. The incidence of violence was higher among the nonpsychotic (41 percent, $N = 7$), most of whom were diagnosed with an Axis II personality disorder or substance abuse, and lower among those diagnosed as psychotic (13 percent, $N = 1$). Over three-quarters had made verbal threats. Nonpsychotic stalkers were significantly more likely to make threats (88 percent) than were psychotic stalkers (50 percent). The nonpsychotic were also more likely to follow through; over 50 percent committed acts of violence.

Schwartz-Watts and Morgan (1998) reviewed medical records of forty-two pretrial detainees charged with stalking in South Carolina between 1992 and 1996 and compared their clinical and demographic characteristics in relation to whether their harassment involved violence. There were no differences between the groups in terms of age, gender, marital status, education, history of substance abuse, or Axis I diagnoses. However, the violent stalkers were more likely to have been previously intimately involved with their victims.

Mullen et al. (1999) studied 145 stalkers to establish risk factors associated with threats and assault. Over a third of the victims had been attacked by their stalker. Another 6 percent of stalkers assaulted third parties believed, in some way, to be impeding their access to the target. The injuries inflicted were confined largely to bruises and abrasions, but serious sexual assaults also occurred. Assault was most prevalent among the rejected stalkers, 59 percent of whom attacked their former intimate. Half of the predatory stalkers were also assaultive, usually committing sexual attacks against the victim. Violence was less common among the intimacy seekers, the incompetent, and the resentful. Threats were made to the victim by 59 percent of stalkers and to third parties by 37 percent. The resentful (87 percent) and the rejected (71 percent) were the most likely to intimidate their victims with threats. Intimacy seekers made explicit threats in over 50 percent of cases. The rejected were the most likely to carry out their threats. The resentful were the least likely. Substance abuse was strongly associated with threats and violence, as was a history of prior criminal offending. Ex-partners were by far the most likely to assault (64 percent), compared with stalkers encountered in work contexts (25 percent), casual acquaintances (32 percent), and strangers (24 percent).

Farnham, James, and Cantrell (2000) examined case files of all pretrial psychiatric assessment referrals to a regional forensic service in North London, identifying fifty stalking cases over a five-year period. Serious violence (assault occasioning actual or grievous bodily harm, wounding, attempted murder, and murder) occurred in twenty-two cases. Although forensic samples are biased toward severe mental illnesses and serious offending, associations found between groups are unlikely to be affected; the authors noted that the greatest danger of serious violence from stalkers in the United Kingdom is from nonpsychotic former sexual intimates.

The studies reviewed in this section are based on samples of stalkers. Victims are, however, in our view the most reliable source of information about intimidation, threats, and violence. Hall (1998) reported 41 percent of the 145 victims had been threatened, 43 percent had their property damaged, 38 percent were hit or beaten, and 22 percent were the subjects of sexual assaults. In addition, eleven subjects were kidnapped, and two subjects were victims of arson attacks. Pathé and Mullen (1997) in their sample of one hundred victims reported that fifty-one had been threatened, with assaults being reported by 36 percent of victims, seven of whom suffered predominantly sexual attacks. Property damage was reported by 36 percent of these victims. Threats preceded assault in 70 percent of cases. Assault was significantly more likely in victims who had an intimate relationship with the stalker.

Meloy (1998, 1999), in groundbreaking reviews of the relationship between threats and assaults associated with stalking, drew the following conclusions: approximately half of all stalkers threaten the victim, the incidence being higher among those with a prior intimate relationship with the victim or those with a real or imagined injury related to a business or professional relationship. The majority of those who threaten do not subsequently commit violence. Nonetheless, threats by stalkers should be taken seriously, as those who commit assaults have usually issued prior "warnings." Violence occurs in approximately a third of cases but seldom results in serious physical injury. The most likely victim of violence is the object of attention, followed by third parties perceived as impeding access to the victim.

Attacks on victims' pets is a form of violence that should not be overlooked. Hall (1998) reported that the stalker had killed or injured family pets of 13 percent of her victims. Nearly 10 percent of victims in Tjaden and Thoennes' (1998) study claimed that their pets had been killed or threatened. A number of victims seen in our clinic have recounted horrific stories of killed and maimed pets.

Several well-publicized stalking cases have culminated in homicidal violence. There have been suggestions that the overall incidence of homicide in stalking is around 2 percent (Meloy 1998, 1999; White and Cawood 1998). Such figures seem extraordinarily high. If we accept that the overall period prevalence of being stalked exceeds 1 percent per annum, and if we assume a homicide rate of 2 percent in stalking, then stalking would, in and of itself, be expected to produce a homicide rate of one per 5,000 of the population per annum. This exceeds the known homicide rates in the United States of approximately 1:10,000, in the United Kingdom of approximately 1:100,000, and in Australia of approximately 1:50,000 (Biles 1982; Reiss and Roth 1993–94, vol. 1; Malmquist 1996). Homicide rates in stalking cannot conceivably approach rates of 2 percent or even 0.2 percent for that matter. Homicide is, fortunately, a rare event. The risk of stalking having a fatal outcome will become clear only when there are adequate epidemiological studies and large enough forensic and clinical series. For the present, the mortality associated with stalking must remain an open question.

Studies published to date indicate that being stalked by an ex-intimate carries the highest risk of being attacked (Zona, Sharma, and Lane 1993; Kienlen et al. 1997; Schwartz-Watts and Morgan 1998; Mullen et al. 1999). The levels of assault by acquaintances and strangers, however, also remain significant, and stranger stalkers include predators who are preparing for attacks of the most damaging type. A number of studies indicate that stalkers with major mental illness are less likely to become assaultive than nonpsychotic stalkers (Kienlen et al. 1997; Harmon, Rosner, and Owens 1998; Mullen et al. 1999). This finding again needs to be interpreted with caution. Among the stalkers with major mental illness are included those, for example, with delusional jealousy that is associated with remarkably high levels of assault (Mowat 1966; White and Mullen 1989; Silva et al. 1998). Substance abuse in stalkers is associated with increased rates of assault (Harmon, Rosner, and Owens 1998; Mullen et al. 1999). In the studies of stalkers, an association between a history of criminal convictions and subsequent assault has emerged (Menzies et al. 1995; Kienlen et al. 1997; Sandberg, McNiel, and Binder 1998; Mullen et al. 1999). Violent or sexual offending in the past carries the highest risk, but any significant prior criminal history, almost irrespective of the nature of the offending, increases the probability of assault in the stalking situation. Violence in stalkers has been reported to be associated with prominent narcissistic personality traits and with borderline, histrionic, paranoid, and psychopathic traits (Meloy 1996; White and Cawood 1998). Clearly this encompasses a wide range of characterological anomalies and will require refinement before it could contribute to the evaluation of the probability of future assault.

Threats should be regarded as promises. Like many promises, not all are fulfilled, but, nevertheless, they should be accepted as a commitment to future action until proved otherwise. Most stalkers who assault give warnings of their intentions by threatening (Pathé and Mullen 1997; Harmon, Rosner, and Owens 1998; Mullen et al. 1999). Threats in the stalking context should always be taken seriously. Quite apart from being a warning, threats are, in and of themselves, acts of violence issued to frighten and intimidate.

The ability to sort stalkers into high-, medium-, and low-risk categories is a first stage in establishing a useful algorithm for predicting the probability of assault. No single study to date has the numbers to allow such calculation. A metanalysis of a number of existing studies is tempting, but the populations studied, and the methods of data gathering, are still too disparate to justify combining results in this manner. The existing studies are also hampered by selection processes that almost certainly produce an overrepresentation of violent and assaultive stalkers. For prediction we need to know about who does not act violently as well as who does.

Studies of the violent behaviors associated with stalking have almost exclusively been based on highly selected populations in whom assault might be expected to be overrepresented. The victim studies of Pathé and Mullen (1997) and Hall (1998) both gathered their samples in a manner that would be likely to recruit the more severely affected and, consequently, those at greatest risk of having been attacked. In the final analysis it will be properly conducted studies on random community samples gathering data from those who have been stalked that will provide the best picture of the prevalence of threats, property damage, and assault in stalking situations. For the present we must work with the available information while retaining a healthy degree of skepticism about how far it can be generalized beyond the specific populations from which it derives.

VIII. Working with Stalkers

Ending a stalker's campaign of harassment is a critical step in alleviating the distress of victims and the disruption caused in the lives of the perpetrators. Stalking exemplifies a behavior that is criminal (in most jurisdictions) but in which mental disorder can, and not infrequently does, play a causal role. Stalking may reflect, as Emerson, Ferris, and Gardner (1998, p. 290) argue, "intricate social processes," but if the psychopathology of the stalker is a necessary, even if a far from sufficient, cause, then treating that psychopathology will end the stalking. To ignore the role of remedial mental disorders in stalking behaviors is a disservice to stalkers and to victims. Though some of these disorders are less amenable than others to currently available treatments, attending to them is a far easier task than altering society's broader social pathologies such as gender inequalities and distortions in human relatedness. In managing stalkers the choice between criminal sanctions and therapy is not either/or. Rather, the choice should be pragmatic, selecting the appropriate balance of judicial sanctions and therapy that will best end the stalking and reduce the chances of recurrences.

The assessment and management of stalkers with significant psychopathology does not differ, in most respects, from approaches to individuals with similar mental disorders who do not stalk. Those who work in forensic mental health services are no strangers to the problems of managing individuals in whom offending and mental disorder coexist and interrelate. One such dilemma is the prevention of further offending during the course of treatment. Understandably, neither victims nor the criminal justice system are inclined to allow stalking to continue while the treatment has "time to work." In some stalkers a moratorium can be negotiated on their activities. For such cases the willingness to accept this temporary cessation is facilitated by judicial sanctions or parole conditions. In others, however, stalkers recognize they have a problem that requires help and that curtailing their activities is the price of that help. In the deluded, it may also be possible to negotiate a respite from stalking by entering into a dialogue with the patient's sane part, which exists even in the maddest of minds. For others who will not, or cannot, desist, containment may be necessary in hospital, if their mental state justifies civil commitment, or in prison, if directed by the courts. In practice, the management of stalkers in the community is not infrequently punctuated by recrudescences of stalking activities, particularly in the early stages of treatment. While never colluding with nor condoning these, minor relapses cannot be an indication, in and of themselves, for abandoning therapy. Occasionally, the outpatient treatment of stalkers is interrupted or totally disrupted by their arrest and imprisonment on further charges.

The assessment of stalkers necessitates a full clinical evaluation incorporating details of past assessments and management strategies and, if possible, information from independent sources such as family, friends, or coworkers. Details of the stalking behaviors are gleaned from witness statements, victim impact reports, and police records.

The stalker's full criminal record should be obtained. Stalkers themselves are often difficult to engage and unreliable historians. Their presentation to mental health services is almost always compelled, if not coerced. They frequently lack insight, and their capacity to deny and distort is, in our experience, on a par with sex offenders. The initial phase of the assessment is usually best given over to allowing the stalker to both express resentment and provide an account of events. It is generally more productive to frame questions about the stalking in a manner that is nonjudgmental, if not frankly collusive. For example, asking "What drove you to these actions?" or employing phrases such as "attempts to communicate with" or "efforts to meet" the other person are likely to elicit more ready responses than inquiries as to why the stalker intruded or harassed. Similarly, exploring the what and why of the harassment needs to be amplified by inquiries directed at the impact of the stalking on the stalker. How much time is occupied by the stalking behaviors? How long does the stalker spend thinking about the target? What have been the costs to the stalker of his or her campaign? How long does the stalker think he or she can continue to pay the price of the quest in terms of time, money, energy, and emotional turmoil? Having explored the costs, it is then possible to explore the benefits. What has the stalker gained so far from his or her behavior?

Framing questions in this way is not simply a collusive trick to obtain more information but the beginning of an attempt to lay the groundwork for changing these behaviors. Focusing attention on the costs of the behavior for the stalker is in part beginning the process of persuading him or her to change, or in psychological parlance, cognitively restructuring his or her attributions and commitments. Having the stalker admit the personal price of the failed enterprise is a potentially important step on the path to change. The frankly deluded or totally self-deceived may well remain impervious to such approaches, however, protected as they are by an absolute conviction in the eventual success of their quest.

When completed, the assessment of the stalker should allow at least a preliminary answer to the following questions: What, if any, is the nature of the current mental disorder? Is there a history of mental disorder and how has this been managed in the past? What are the salient personality vulnerabilities? What is their substance use and misuse? What are the motivations for the stalking behaviors? What is the context from which this individual's stalking arose and the factors that tend to sustain the behavior? What is the likely future course of the harassment? What is the probability of assault (expressed curiously in terms of probable risk; there is a real danger, particularly when reporting to the courts, of covertly encouraging, or justifying, sentencing not for what the individual has been convicted but for offenses he or she might in the future commit)? What are the current social situation and the social support networks? What could be the role of therapy in ameliorating and preventing stalking behavior? What therapy is required for the individual for any mental disorder (irrespective of the likely impact of such treatment on the stalking behaviors, though fortunately it is difficult to imagine effective treatments that aggravate stalking rather than potentially ameliorate the behavior)?

Management of stalkers first requires treatment of any continuing mental disorder. Delusional disorders best respond to a combination of supportive and gently confronting psychotherapy in concert with antipsychotic medication. Depressive disorders, when successfully managed with antidepressant medication, can occasionally produce dramatic results in arresting stalking activities. Even in those stalkers where depression is thought to be reactive to the problems created subsequent to the onset of the stalking, it is still important to adequately manage the altered mood to facilitate other treatment approaches. Social deficits and personality problems are common and require focused and often long-term remedial therapy. Paraphiliacs require referral to a specialized sex offender program.

Management strategies with stalkers must also specifically target the stalking behaviors. Stalking is a time-consuming, resource-expending, emotionally draining, and ultimately futile activity. Even stalkers caught up in a delusional system generally have some realization, however remote, of the costs and self-defeating nature of their pursuit. Changing those behaviors is in part about helping them focus on the negative consequences of continuing to stalk. Strategies aimed at encouraging victim empathy, even in the deluded, should also be included. Most stalkers deceive themselves into believing their activities will further the aims of either attracting or reconciling with the object of their unwanted attentions, and even those pursuing agendas of revenge or vindication rarely admit to themselves the extent to which they are damaging their victims. Providing information about the impact of stalking in general and of their behavior in particular may be useful, together with other elements of victim empathy training borrowed from sex offender treatment programs (see Marshall 1996).

Stalking is sustained, in no small part, because the behavior is gratifying in and of itself. Despite this, few stalkers admit that they find the stalking rewarding. They explain their actions to themselves as being necessary to attain their goal (be that goal a relationship, retribution, or whatever). It can be useful to expose the intimacy seeker's use of stalking behaviors as a substitute for an intimate relationship, rather than a path to such a goal. Similarly, the rejected can sometimes be helped to understand that they have substituted the stalking for the lost relationship. As a result they can neither reestablish a connection to nor free themselves from their ex-partner. The incompetent suitor can occasionally be made to realize that the behavior is a crude caricature of establishing a relationship and is doomed to fail. The resentful stalker has poured all his or her pain and bitterness into the pursuit of someone who in practice is largely irrelevant to the real issues. They can sometimes be encouraged to an understanding that their "pursuit of justice" is being lost sight of in the short-term gratifications of punishing a minor and possibly innocent party.

By the time stalkers come into contact with mental health professionals (rarely of their own accord) they will have invested considerable personal and often financial resources in their pursuit. To abandon their course would be to lose face. It is necessary to attempt to maneuver them into a position where they can abandon the pursuit without feeling humiliated or cheated. By reframing their actions as "understandable" but ultimately counterproductive and damaging, they can sometimes forego the stalking as an act of generosity or of enlightened self-interest.

Stalkers are almost always socially impoverished and isolated people. The stalking would have been unlikely to have emerged, let alone to have been sustained, if they had adequate peer relationships. The intimacy seeker often never established adequate social networks, while the rejected, if he or she ever had such connections, often lost them with the breakdown of the relationship and as a result of the subsequent stalking. A developmental history characterized by loneliness, isolation, and lack of feedback about their behavior from those whose opinions they value, are among the prerequisites for such stalking. Improving stalkers' social networks, equipping them with the skills to acquire and maintain friendships, and helping them establish and use confiding relationships are often critical elements in ending stalking. Connecting, or reconnecting, stalkers to a social world is essential in preventing relapse.

IX. Working with Victims

Central to the amelioration of suffering in stalking victims is the provision of sound guidelines aimed at combating the stalking and ensuring the victim's personal safety. To date, it has been difficult for many victims of stalking to gain access to responsive, coordinated services, but a growing awareness of the magnitude of this problem has seen the establishment of stalking victim support organizations and specialized services within the helping professions (Pathé and Mullen 1997).

Victims are well advised to inform trusted individuals that they are being stalked, report their concerns to police, and involve helping agencies such as victim support organizations or, where applicable, domestic violence programs. They should document all suspicious incidents and retain any evidence, such as taped answering machine messages, letters, or other unsolicited material, and police reports of any illegal acts that occur during the course of the stalking. These can be invaluable in the event of legal proceedings against the stalker. Victims should inform their pursuer firmly, unambiguously, and at the earliest opportunity that they do not want any further contact. Any subsequent contact with their stalker, including attempts to reiterate or renegotiate this message, must be strictly and consistently avoided. It is important for stalking victims to understand that any contact with the perpetrator, however intermittent, will reinforce the unwanted behavior. Unfortunately, the victim's resolve may occasionally be overridden by other forces, an example being the victim who is forced to appear before his or her stalker in the courtroom to answer spurious charges concocted by the stalker. The "no contact" edict may also prove difficult in situations of neighbor or workplace stalking, or when the offender is an estranged husband awarded regular access visits to his children.

The use of restraining or nonmolestation orders is a contentious issue. When restraining orders are contemplated, it is preferable to initiate the application early in the course of the harassment. For stalkers who fail to appreciate that their behavior is a nuisance and source of distress, the issuance of a restraining order may succeed in conveying this message. Restraining orders taken out at a relatively early stage are likely to be more effective than those obtained after months or even years of stalking, when the stalker's emotional investment in the relationship has intensified and the stalker may well be left to wonder, "Why now?" De Becker (1997) cautions against the use of restraining orders in response to threats or to an escalation in stalking behaviors, as this usually signals that the perpetrator is intensely involved in the stalking dynamic and may become enraged by the added dimension of a legal rein on his or her behavior. Victims should also understand that restraining orders are a civil remedy that rarely attract prison sentences and pit the victim against the accused (the exception being antistalking legislation in the United Kingdom, which enables court-initiated restraining orders). Victims may be better advised to pursue criminal charges against their stalker, invoking antistalking laws or other charges such as theft, assault, or threats. This approach diffuses some of the fervor encountered in victim-initiated civil interventions, as the charges are brought by the state. It may also reduce demands on the victim in the court process, including face-to-face contacts between victim and defendant. Prosecution under antistalking laws offers greater flexibility in sentencing and more serious penalties than do civil approaches. Legal sanctions raise the stakes sufficiently high for a substantial number of stalkers to abandon their quest.

Those working with victims of stalking should familiarize themselves with the resources available to their clients and be prepared, when the victim is overwhelmed, to advocate on his or her behalf. Therapists should be ever mindful of security issues, especially the personal safety of the victim and significant others, and assist the victim and others at risk to take all appropriate safety measures. Victims of stalking should obtain a home security check from the local police or a reputable security company. A number of relatively simple measures, such as changing locks, installing exterior motion sensor lights and peepholes in doors, and removing potential surveillance points (e.g., trimming outside shrubbery, especially near windows) are useful. Victims should remove their contact details from all public records, including those held by professional bodies such as medical licensing boards.

Since the mid-1990s several prominent support organizations have been founded for stalking victims and their families. These organizations play an invaluable role in providing educational and safety information and emotional support for victims. Most, such as Survivors of Stalking (S.O.S.) in the United States and the National Anti-Stalking and Harassment Campaign and Support Association (NASH) in the United Kingdom were founded by stalking victims disillusioned with existing services. A range of Web sites provide information and assistance to victims of stalking and cyberstalking.

The clinical approach to traumatized stalking victims combines education about stalking in general and the provision of strategies to combat his or her particular stalker, together with psychological and occasionally pharmacological treatments. Cognitive-orientated psychological therapies often prove useful since, for many victims, stalking breaches previously held assumptions about their safety. The victim's belief in his or her strength and resilience, and confidence in the reasonable and predictable nature of the world, is often shattered, to be replaced by feelings of extreme vulnerability and an expectation of persisting danger and unpredictable harm. Cognitive restructuring methods attempt to correct the erroneous post-traumatic assumptions and evaluations about the world that threaten the victim's adaptation and functioning. These assumptions and evaluations will be well-founded in some instances of continued victimization, and in these cases cognitive therapies must focus on rebuilding a realistic and viable sense of safety for the victim. Behavioral techniques can prove particularly beneficial for victims with avoidance symptoms. Although avoidance of threatening situations or cues may be a reasonable and adaptive response, when avoidance extends to other areas of the victim's life, preventing him or her from leaving home or working, alienation from supports and social and vocational opportunities will impede the victim's recovery.

Medication is an important adjunct to nonpharmacological approaches in those victims suffering severe symptoms and in the treatment of comorbid psychiatric disorders. The selection of medication is guided by the victim's situation and the side-effect profiles of these agents, minimizing as far as possible any iatrogenic contribution to existing distress and disability. The treating clinician must also be mindful of the occasionally protracted course of stress-related syndromes and hence the potential requirement for long-term chemical treatment. Medication can prove invaluable in alleviating suffering. It may also facilitate responsiveness to psychological measures that play a longer-term role in restoring self-efficacy and control over negative emotional states.

It is useful wherever possible to involve the victim's family or partner in therapeutic interventions. They are often affected either directly or indirectly, and the provision of information about stalking and its impact on victims, together with supportive counseling, helps galvanize their support for the victim. Families can also be a valuable additional resource in the collection of information about the stalker.

Self-help groups can play an important role in victims' rehabilitation by diminishing the sense of isolation and alienation. They offer a supportive environment in which participants experience mutual understanding, validation, and trust, and a safe venue for sharing feelings of anger, frustration, and loss. Often such groups become a useful resource, especially given the paucity of dedicated, coordinated services for stalking victims, with members exchanging helpful strategies, reading material, useful contacts, and security equipment. Ideally, therapeutic support groups should be facilitated by a clinician who is well-grounded in the issues faced by victims of stalking, including its complex psychological sequelae. The role of the therapist includes enhancing and maintaining mutual support among members and retaining a focus on proactive measures that take account of members' safety and rehabilitation needs.

A further objective of therapeutic groups is reduction of psychological distress. This is achieved by instructing group members in techniques to manage anxiety symptoms, anger, and depression. The trained facilitator and group member set realistic goals, such as the gradual resumption of activities avoided or abandoned due to the stalking, which are reviewed during the course of the group. This should ideally be supplemented with objective measures to assess the progress of individuals and the efficacy of the therapeutic approach.

Some victims will require professional intervention long after the stalking has abated. Frequently, the stalker has left a trail of destruction, and the therapist can assist in sorting through the chaotic aftermath. Stalking victims must renegotiate links with family and friends and attempt to restore interpersonal, social, and occupational functioning. The imprint of their ordeal may well be indelible, affecting their capacity for trust and intimacy. While some regard their enduring caution as a safety mechanism, victims are counseled to move beyond a position of distrustful alienation to one of prudent self-protection. The path to this goal may be protracted and sometimes painful for all concerned.

Stalkers and their victims have only recently attracted the attention of the public, the legal system, and mental health professionals. Once stalking was established as a social problem the legal response was remarkably swift. Understandably less rapid has been the acquisition of a knowledge base about the nature and impact of stalking that can inform effective strategies of prevention and remediation. We have, however, the beginnings of such knowledge, and the combination of appropriate criminal justice and therapeutic interactions may be able in the future to relieve victims of stalking and rescue stalkers from their futile, and often self-damaging, pursuits.

The subject priorities for future research are, first, how best to manage stalkers to terminate their damaging activities and, second, how best to reduce the distress of those who fall victim to such behavior. To accomplish both tasks, more needs to be learned about the nature and prevalence of stalking behaviors. We are still in the process of uncovering the full extent of the problem, but, even as we do so, new systems of harassment using, for example, the Internet, are emerging. Even now, however, knowledge has reached a stage where it can better inform public policy.

Stalking merges into a multiplicity of irritating but mundane intrusions, but the distinction between rude and insensitive social interactions and stalking is usually dramatic in terms of the nature, duration, and impact of those behaviors. Those stalked for weeks, months, or years usually suffer serious psychological and social disruption and are at risk of falling victim to physical and sexual assaults. Effective legal protections for victims are essential. These laws must recognize that a significant minority of stalkers intend to pursue projects of reconciliation or affection but in the process are wreaking havoc. However repellent such an approach is to jurists, the stalker's intent must be regarded as irrelevant to the legal constructions of the crime of stalking if the law is to effectively protect victims.

Stalkers are predominantly drawn from among the mentally disturbed and socially disabled. In many cases, effective mental health interventions are essential to stop the behavior or prevent its recurrence. Those convicted of stalking-related offenses should be assessed by mental health professionals to establish what, if any, therapeutic approaches can contribute to preventing a recurrence of the offending. Courts should be prepared to order mandated treatment when relevant. Mental health professionals offering services in the forensic area should acquire the knowledge and skills to assess and manage stalkers.

Victims of stalking frequently seek advice from both legal and health professionals. Information about the effects of being stalked and what remedies and supports are available to victims should become part of professional knowledge bases in just the same way as for domestic violence and child sexual abuse. Stalking is a visible social problem and one which the criminal justice, legal, and medical professions have joint responsibility for tackling.

APPENDIX

Web sites for stalking victims:
www.stalkingassistance.com
www.suzylamplugh.org
www.antistalking.com.au
www.stalkingvictims.com
Assistance for victims of cyberstalking:
CyberAngels. Web site: http://www.cyberangels.org

REFERENCES

American Psychiatric Association. 1994. *Diagnostic and Statistical Manual of Mental Disorders*. 4th ed. Washington, D.C.: American Psychiatric Association.

Anderson, S. C. 1993. "Anti-stalking Laws: Will They Curb the Erotomanic's Obsessive Pursuit?" *Law and Psychology Review* 17:171–85.

Australian Bureau of Statistics. 1996. *Women's Safety: Australia, 1996*. Canberra: Commonwealth of Australia.

Biles, D. 1982. *The Size of the Crime Problem in Australia*. 2d ed. Canberra: Australian Institute of Criminology.

Budd, T., and J. Mattinson. 2000. *The Extent and Nature of Stalking: Findings from the 1998 British Crime Survey*. London: Home Office, Research, Development, and Statistics Directorate.

Burgess, A. W., T. Baker, D. Greening, C. Hartman, A. Burgess, J. E. Douglas, and R. Halloran. 1997. "Stalking Behaviors within Domestic Violence." *Journal of Family Violence* 12:389–403.

Coleman, F. L. 1997. "Stalking Behavior and the Cycle of Domestic Violence." *Journal of Interpersonal Violence* 12:420–32.

De Becker, G. 1997. *The Gift of Fear*. London: Bloomsbury.

Emerson, R. M., K. O. Ferris, and C. B. Gardner. 1998. "On Being Stalked." *Social Problems* 45:289–314.

Enoch, M. D., and W. H. Trethowan. 1979. *Uncommon Psychiatric Syndromes*. Bristol: John Wright.

Farnham, F., D. James, and P. Cantrell. 2000. "Association between Violence, Psychosis and Relationship to Victim in Stalkers." *Lancet* 355:9199.

Feldman-Schorrig, S. 1996. "Factitious Sexual Harassment." *Bulletin of the American Academy of Psychiatry and Law* 24:387–92.

Fremouw, W. J., D. Westrup, and J. Pennypacker. 1997. "Stalking on Campus: The Prevalence and Strategies for Coping with Stalking." *Journal of Forensic Sciences* 42:666–69.

Gilligan, M. J. 1992. "Stalking the Stalker: Developing New Laws to Thwart Those Who Terrorize Others." *Georgia Law Review* 27:285–342.

Goldstein, R. L. 1978. "De Clérambault in Court: A Forensic Romance?" *Bulletin of the American Academy of Psychiatry and Law* 6:36–40.
———. 1987. "More Forensic Romances: De Clérambault's Syndrome in Men." *Bulletin of the American Academy of Psychiatry and Law* 15:267–74.
Hall, D. M. 1998. "The Victims of Stalking." In *The Psychology of Stalking: Clinical and Forensic Perspectives*, edited by J. Reid Meloy. San Diego: Academic Press.
Harmon, R. B., R. Rosner, and H. Owens. 1995. "Obsessional Harassment and Erotomania in a Criminal Court Population." *Journal of Forensic Sciences* 40:188–96.
———. 1998. "Sex and Violence in a Forensic Population of Obsessional Harassers." *Psychology, Public Policy, and Law* 4:236–49.
Jason, L. A., A. Reichler, J. Easton, A. Neal, and M. Wilson. 1984. "Female Harassment after Ending a Relationship: A Preliminary Study." *Alternative Lifestyles* 6:259–69.
Jones, C. 1996. "Criminal Harassment (or Stalking)." Toronto: University of Toronto. http://www.chass.utoronto.ca:8080/~cjones/pub/stalking. (Last accessed 2000.)
Kienlen, K. K., D. L. Birmingham, K. B. Solberg, J. T. O'Regan, and J. R. Meloy. 1997. "A Comparative Study of Psychotic and Nonpsychotic Stalking." *Journal of the American Academy of Psychiatry and Law* 25:317–34.
Lowney, K. S., and J. Best. 1995. "Stalking Strangers and Lovers: Changing Media Typifications of a New Crime Problem." In *Images of Issues: Typifying Contemporary Social Problems*, edited by J. Best. New York: Aldine De Gruyter.
Malmquist, C. P. 1996. *Homicide: A Psychiatric Perspective*. Washington, D.C.: American Academic Press.
Manitoba Law Reform Commission. 1997. *Stalking*. Report no. 98. Manitoba: Law Reform Commission.
Marshall, W. L. 1996. "Assessment, Treatment and Theorizing about Sex Offenders." *Criminal Justice and Behavior* 23(1):162–99.
McAnaney, K. G., L. A. Curliss, and C. E. Abeyla-Price. 1993. "From Imprudence to Crime: Anti-stalking Laws." *Notre Dame Law Review* 68:819–909.
McEwan, I. 1997. *Enduring Love*. London: Jonathan Cape.
Meloy, J. R. 1989. "Unrequited Love and the Wish to Kill: Diagnosis and Treatment of Borderline Erotomania." *Bulletin of the Menninger Clinic* 53:477–92.
———. 1992. *Violent Attachments*. Northvale, N.J.: Aronson.
———. 1996. "Stalking (Obsessional Following): A Review of Some Preliminary Studies." *Aggression and Violent Behavior* 1:147–62.
———. 1998. "The Psychology of Stalking." In *The Psychology of Stalking: Clinical and Forensic Perspectives*, edited by J. Reid Meloy. San Diego: Academic Press.
———. 1999. "Stalking: An Old Behavior, a New Crime." *Psychiatric Clinics of North America* 22:85–99.
Meloy, J. R., and S. Gothard. 1995. "A Demographic and Clinical Comparison

of Obsessional Followers and Offenders with Mental Disorders." *American Journal of Psychiatry* 152:258–63.

Menzies, R. P. D., J. P. Fedoroff, C. M. Green, and K. Isaacson. 1995. "Prediction of Dangerous Behaviour in Male Erotomania." *British Journal of Psychiatry* 16:529–36.

Mowat, R. R. 1966. *Morbid Jealousy and Murder.* London: Tavistock.

Mullen, P. E., and M. Pathé. 1994*a*. "Stalking and the Pathologies of Love." *Australian and New Zealand Journal of Psychiatry* 28:469–77.

———. 1994*b*. "The Pathological Extensions of Love." *British Journal of Psychiatry* 165:614–23.

Mullen, P. E., M. Pathé, and R. Purcell. 2000. *Stalkers and Their Victims.* Cambridge: Cambridge University Press.

Mullen, P. E., M. Pathé, R. Purcell, and G. W. Stuart. 1999. "Study of Stalkers." *American Journal of Psychiatry* 156:1244–49.

National Institute of Justice. 1997. *The Crime of Stalking: How Big Is the Problem?* Washington, D.C.: U.S. Department of Justice.

Orion, D. 1997. *I Know You Really Love Me: A Psychiatrist's Journal of Erotomania, Stalking, and Obsessive Love.* New York: Macmillan.

Pathé, M., and P. E. Mullen. 1997. "The Impact of Stalkers on Their Victims." *British Journal of Psychiatry* 170:12–17.

Pathé, M., P. E. Mullen, and R. Purcell. 1999. "Stalking: False Claims of Victimization." *British Journal of Psychiatry* 174:170–72.

Pathé, M., R. Purcell, and P. E. Mullen. 2000. "Same-Gender Stalking." *Bulletin of the American Academy of Psychiatry and the Law* 28(2):191–97.

Purcell, R., M. Pathé, and P. E. Mullen. Forthcoming. "Stalking: Defining and Prosecuting a New Form of Offending." *International Journal of Law and Psychiatry.*

Reiss, A. J., Jr., and J. A. Roth, eds. 1993–94. *Understanding and Preventing Violence.* 4 vols. Washington, D.C.: National Academy Press.

Resnick, R. 1992. "California Takes Lead: States Enact 'Stalking' Laws." *National Law Journal* 4(36):3, 27.

Sandberg, D. A., D. E. McNiel, and R. L. Binder. 1998. "Characteristics of Psychiatric Inpatients Who Stalk, Threaten, or Harass Hospital Staff after Discharge." *American Journal of Psychiatry* 155:1102–5.

Savage, G. H. 1892. "Jealousy." In *Dictionary of Psychological Medicine,* edited by Daniel Hack Tuke. London: Churchill.

Schwartz-Watts, D., and D. W. Morgan. 1998. "Violent versus Non-Violent Stalkers." *Journal of the American Academy of Psychiatry and Law* 26:241–45.

Schwartz-Watts, D., D. W. Morgan, and C. J. Barnes. 1997. "Stalkers: The South Carolina Experience." *Journal of the American Academy of Psychiatry and Law* 25:541–45.

Silva, J. A., M. M. Ferrari, C. B. Leong, and G. Penny. 1998. "The Dangerousness of Persons with Delusional Jealousy." *Journal of the American Academy of Psychiatry and Law* 26:607–23.

Simon, R. I. 1996. *Bad Men Do What Good Men Dream.* Washington, D.C.: American Psychiatric Press.

Sohn, E. F. 1994. "Antistalking Statutes: Do They Actually Protect Victims?" *Criminal Law Bulletin* 30:203–41.

Taylor, P. J., B. Mahendra, and J. Gunn. 1983. "Erotomania in Males." *Psychological Medicine* 13:645–50.

Tjaden, P., and N. Thoennes. 1998. *Stalking in America: Findings from the National Violence against Women Survey*. Washington, D.C.: U.S. Department of Justice, Office of Justice Programs, National Institute of Justice.

Walker, L. E., and J. R. Meloy. 1998. "Stalking and Domestic Violence." In *The Psychology of Stalking: Clinical and Forensic Perspectives*, edited by J. Reid Meloy. San Diego: Academic Press.

Westrup, D., W. J. Fremouw, R. N. Thompson, and S. F. Lewis. 1999. "The Psychological Impact of Stalking on Female Undergraduates." *Journal of Forensic Sciences* 44(3):554–57.

White, G. L., and P. E. Mullen. 1989. *Jealousy: Theory, Research and Clinical Strategies*. New York: Guilford.

White, S. G., and J. S. Cawood. 1998. "Threat Management of Stalking Cases." In *The Psychology of Stalking: Clinical and Forensic Perspectives*, edited by J. Reid Meloy. San Diego: Academic Press.

Wright, J. A., A. G. Burgess, A. W. Burgess, A. T. Laszlo, G. O. McCrary, and J. E. Douglas. 1996. "A Typology of Interpersonal Stalking." *Journal of Interpersonal Violence* 11:487–502.

Zona, M. A., J. Lane, and M. Moore. 1996. "The Psychology and Behavior of Stalkers." Paper presented at the American Academy of Forensic Sciences annual meeting, Nashville, Tenn.

Zona, M. A., R. E. Palarea, and J. Lane. 1998. "Psychiatric Diagnosis and the Victim-Offender Typology of Stalking." In *The Psychology of Stalking: Clinical and Forensic Perspectives*, edited by J. Reid Meloy. San Diego: Academic Press.

Zona, M. A., K. K. Sharma, and J. Lane. 1993. "A Comparative Study of Erotomanic and Obsessional Subjects in a Forensic Sample." *Journal of Forensic Sciences* 38:894–903.

Anthony A. Braga, Philip J. Cook,
David M. Kennedy, and Mark H. Moore

The Illegal Supply
of Firearms

ABSTRACT

The case for focusing regulatory and enforcement efforts on the illegal
supply of firearms to criminals rests on the belief that a supply-side
approach has the potential to reduce the use of guns in violence. The case
against this focus follows from the belief that guns in America are so
readily available, and from such a variety of sources, that efforts to restrict
the supply are futile. Individuals who are proscribed from buying guns
legally (because of their criminal record or youth) tend to acquire firearms
from "point" sources, such as illegal traffickers and scofflaw dealers, and
"diffuse sources," including all sorts of informal transfers from the vast
stock of weapons in private hands. Both are important. The mix within a
jurisdiction appears to depend on the prevalence of gun ownership and
the stringency of state regulations. A variety of promising supply-side
measures are available, and some have been tried. Lessons have been
learned—for example, that gun "buybacks" are ineffective—but for the
most part any conclusions necessarily are speculative. Systematic
"experimentation" with different tactics appears warranted.

There are more than 200 million privately owned firearms in the
United States, including 70 million handguns. This vast arsenal serves
as a source of guns to youths and criminals, who may obtain them
through a variety of means. The pervasiveness of guns in American
cities suggests to some that it is simply not feasible to prevent danger-

Anthony A. Braga is senior research associate, Kennedy School of Government, Har-
vard University. Philip J. Cook is ITT/Terry Sanford Distinguished Professor of Public
Policy Studies, Duke University. David M. Kennedy is senior researcher, Kennedy
School of Government, Harvard University. Mark H. Moore is Daniel and Florence
Guggenheim Professor of Criminal Justice Policy and Management, Kennedy School of
Government, Harvard University.

ous people from obtaining them if they are so inclined—that "gun control," in the sense of restrictions on commerce and possession of firearms, is futile. A more sanguine view holds that some good could be accomplished by supply-side measures directed at reducing access by those who are legally proscribed; that even in an environment where guns are plentiful it is feasible to increase the transaction costs in the types of gun markets relevant to youths and criminals, thereby reducing the prevalence of gun possession and use by these groups.

Both of these perspectives claim the support of research findings. Those who favor the "futility" view stress the power of markets to circumvent legal obstacles and note surveys of youths and criminals that provide data suggesting that their guns are often stolen or in some other way diverted from private (and more-or-less legitimate) ownership—the tens of millions of guns in private hands form a vast pool that is readily tapped. Those who view supply-side measures more positively offer as evidence the recent data from federal gun tracing and trafficking investigations that indicate that some percentage of the guns used in crime come directly from licensed dealers; in effect criminals are being supplied by dedicated "pipelines" as well as the pool. That being the case, it is plausible that closer regulation of those dealers could be effective in reducing access by youths and criminals.

Thus, the two sources of primary data, surveys of criminals and gun traces, are used to support contrasting conclusions concerning the potential efficacy of supply-side interventions. Yet a close look at these data demonstrates that they are compatible with each other with respect to estimating the importance of alternative sources of guns to criminals. Both sources suggest that a substantial minority of crime guns come from close-to-retail diversions from licensed dealers, while a majority of crime guns come from thefts and informal transfers from the existing pool of guns. The disagreement is in the interpretation and emphasis that analysts have given the results. And since there is little in the way of direct evidence on the potential for reducing the effective availability of guns to proscribed people, that disagreement cannot easily be adjudicated.

While the available evidence does not provide a strong basis for resolving the fundamental dispute about supply-side policy, it does provide some guidance about how to direct supply-side efforts. In particular, the trace data help identify licensed dealers who are involved in diverting guns to criminals, either knowingly or through negligence, and hence provide a basis for initiating regulatory actions and criminal investigations. In turn, data generated from these investigations provide further insight into the structure and functioning of illicit gun markets, as documented by a recent analysis of over 1,500 federal criminal investigations.

In what follows, we synthesize existing research on the structure and operations of firearms markets that supply youths and criminals and review alternative supply-side strategies on the way to extracting some policy lessons. We begin with an account of the legal framework that governs firearms commerce, together with an empirical characterization of transaction flows and ownership patterns. The second section then summarizes the empirical research on the sources of guns to delinquents and criminals. Section III assesses policy alternatives for reducing the availability of guns for criminal use. A final section looks to the future with respect to research and policy.

I. The Structure of Legal Firearms Markets

Federal, state, and local governments regulate commerce in firearms and the possession and use of firearms. Most jurisdictions occupy the middle ground between laissez faire and prohibition in order to preserve legitimate uses of guns while preempting their use as an instrument of criminal violence (Zimring 1975, 1991; Cook and Blose 1981).

A. Regulations

A primary purpose of federal law is to prevent lax firearms controls in one state from undermining more restrictive regulations in another state. The Gun Control Act of 1968 (GCA) established a system of federal licensing for gun dealers, requiring that all individuals engaged in the business of selling guns must have a Federal Firearms License. The act limits shipments of firearms to licensed dealers, who are required to obey state and local regulations (Zimring 1975). Direct sales of handguns to out-of-state residents are prohibited. The McClure-Volkmer Firearms Owners Protection Act of 1986 (FOPA) repealed the ban on out-of-state purchases of rifles and shotguns, which are now permitted as long as the transfer complies with the regulations of both the buyer's and seller's states of residence. Although the 1968 Gun Control Act limited Federal Firearms Licensees (FFLs) to conducting business only from their licensed premises, the FOPA allowed licensees to conduct business at occasional gun shows held in the same state as their business premises.

The U.S. Bureau of Alcohol, Tobacco, and Firearms (ATF) is charged with regulating firearms commerce and enforcing federal firearms law. The ATF is a small agency whose jurisdiction includes regulatory inspections of gun dealers and, often in partnership with state and local law enforcement agencies, criminal investigations of violations of federal firearm laws.

The Gun Control Act of 1968 established a set of requirements designed to allow the chain of commerce for any given firearm to be traced from its manufacture or import through its first sale by a retail dealer (Cook and Braga 2001). Each new firearm, whether manufactured in the United States or imported, must be stamped with a unique serial number. Manufacturers, importers, distributors, and retailers are required to maintain records of all firearms transactions. Licensed dealers are also required to report multiple sales and stolen firearms to the ATF and provide transaction records to the ATF on request. When FFLs go out of business, they are required to transfer their transaction records to the ATF, which then stores them for tracing. Thus, a paper trail for gun transactions is created that at least in principle can be followed by ATF agents. In reality, the tracing procedure used by the ATF is rather cumbersome, as most of the relevant transaction records are not centralized but are kept piecemeal by dealers, distributors, and retailers (Cook and Braga 2001). This arrangement reflects the intention of the U.S. Congress to ensure that there be no national registry of firearms (explicitly prohibited by the FOPA), yet there be some mechanism in place that would allow investigators to trace a firearm used in crime.

Federal law establishes a minimum set of restrictions on the acquisition and possession of guns. Several categories of people are denied the right to receive or possess a gun, including convicted felons and those under indictment, illegal aliens, illicit drug users, fugitives from justice, people ever convicted of domestic violence, and those who have been involuntarily committed to a mental institution. Licensed dealers are not allowed to sell handguns to persons younger than twenty-one or long guns to persons younger than eighteen. Licensed dealers are required to ask for identification from all prospective buyers and have them sign a form indicating that they do not have any of the characteristics that would prohibit them from acquiring a firearm. (In 1986, the FOPA amended the GCA to allow the possession of firearms by convicted felons whose civil rights have been restored or "convictions" have been pardoned, set aside, or expunged.) Finally, the Brady Handgun Violence Prevention Act of 1994 requires licensed dealers to initiate criminal-history background checks of all would-be purchasers.

Beyond these federal requirements, some states impose more stringent requirements for handgun transfers (Peters 2000). State laws may require buyers to obtain a special permit or license, and licensed dealers to observe a waiting period before transfer, conduct more extensive record checks, and limit the number of guns that can be sold to any one buyer in a specified period (such as one handgun per month). The District of Columbia and some other cities ban handgun commerce and possession, with limited exceptions. All states except Vermont either ban carrying a concealed firearm or require a special permit or license.

Federal and state laws regulate certain types of firearms more stringently than others. The National Firearms Act of 1934 mandated registration and a $200 tax on all transfers of gangster-style firearms, including sawed-off shotguns and fully automatic firearms (such as the Tommy gun). More recently, Congress has prohibited the manufacture of these firearms. The Gun Control Act of 1968 banned the importation of small, cheap handguns commonly known as "Saturday night specials," while permitting domestic production. Congress banned the importation and manufacture of certain military-style "assault" weapons in 1994 (Roth and Koper 1997). Since handguns account for the vast majority of firearms used in crime, states typically regulate them more closely than long guns.

About 30–40 percent of all gun transactions do not involve a licensed dealer (Cook and Ludwig 1996), but rather occur on the "secondary market" (a term coined by Cook, Molliconi, and Cole [1995]). Under current federal law, unlicensed private citizens are permitted to sell firearms without initiating a criminal-history background check or even establishing the identity of the prospective buyer and are not required to keep any record of the transaction. One result is that tracing the transactions history of a firearm recovered in crime is very difficult after the initial sale by an FFL. Prosecuting unlicensed sellers for transferring a firearm to a felon, teenager, or other prohibited person is difficult, since federal law bans such transactions only if the seller had reason to know that the buyer was not entitled to buy the gun.

Although unlicensed sellers may sell firearms without keeping records or conducting background checks, they are not permitted to "engage in the business" of manufacturing, importing, or dealing in firearms. The Gun Control Act of 1968 did not provide a definition of "engaged in the business." Until 1986, the ATF's operating rule was that individuals selling five guns or more per year were to be considered firearms dealers and required to obtain a federal firearms license. But the FOPA barred any such quantitative standard and explicitly exempted individuals who sell firearms from their "private collections," a loophole that has been hard for prosecutors to overcome. It remains true, however, that the federal licensing system is fairly effective in preventing unlicensed individuals from acquiring guns directly from wholesale distributors or shipping guns directly to customers.

B. Stocks and Flows

Firearms commerce is composed of transactions made in the primary firearms market and in the largely unregulated secondary firearms market. Transactions of new and secondhand firearms conducted through federal licensees form the primary market for firearms (Cook, Molliconi, and Cole 1995). Retail gun stores sell both new and secondhand firearms and, in this regard, resemble automobile sales lots. Transfers of secondhand firearms by unlicensed individuals form the secondary market. Economic analysis suggests that primary and secondary markets are closely linked, with buyers moving from one to the other depending on relative prices and other terms of the transaction (Cook and Leitzel 1996).

Firearms manufacturers, importers, distributors, and dealers are required to obtain a license from the ATF, which screens applicants and regulates the licensees to ensure that they comply with firearms laws. Between 1975 and 1992, the licensee population grew from 161,927 to 284,117 (ATF 2000b). During this time period, the ATF was understaffed and lacked political support for their firearms mission. Almost all applications for firearms-dealer licenses were approved without review (Sugarmann and Rand 1992). A large number of these licensees were not actively engaged in a firearms business (ATF 2000b). In 1993, the ATF estimated that 46 percent of licensees were not retail dealers but rather used their licenses only to buy firearms for their own use by mail order. Of greater concern was that some of these FFLs were scofflaws who used their licenses to supply criminals with guns (ATF 2000b). Noting that it was easier to get a gun dealer license than a driver's license (ATF 2000b), the Clinton administration initiated a review and tightening of licensing procedures. In 1993 and 1994, federal law was amended to provide more restrictive application requirements and a hefty increase in the licensing fee, from $30 to $200 for three years (ATF 1997). These new safeguards reduced the number of federal licensees to 103,942 in 1999, of which 80,570 were retail dealers or pawnbrokers (ATF 2000*b*). Despite this remarkable decline in the number of licensees, those that remain include a large number who are not operating a business. Fully 31 percent of retail licensees in 1998 had not sold a single firearm in the previous year (ATF 2000*b*).

There has been a long decline in the percentage of households with guns. Based on the General Social Survey conducted by the National Opinion Research Center, the percentage of American households reporting ownership of at least one gun has decreased from 48 percent in 1980 to 36 percent in 1999 (Smith 2000). However, the percentage of individuals with guns has remained near constant at about 28 percent since 1980, with 44 percent of men and 12 percent of women reporting gun ownership in 1999. The drop in household ownership reflects the trend in household composition rather than a trend in individual gun ownership. During this period households shrank and became less likely to include an adult male.

Whites are more likely to own guns than blacks, and rural residents are far more likely than urban residents to own firearms, including handguns. On a regional basis, gun ownership is highest in the South, followed by the Rocky Mountain states, the Midwest, and the Pacific states. New England has the lowest levels of gun ownership. This geographic pattern is remarkably stable over time (Azrael, Cook, and Miller 2001).

There are currently about 200 million privately owned firearms in the United States (Cook and Ludwig 1996; Kleck 1997), with several million new guns sold each year. The influx of new guns has partly gone to increase the size of the average owner's collection (Wright 1981). The most detailed national survey on the subject (the National Survey of the Private Ownership of Firearms, or NSPOF [Cook and Ludwig 1996]) revealed that gun-owning households averaged 4.4 firearms in 1994, up substantially from the 1970s (Cook and Ludwig 1996). Owners of four or more guns (about 10 percent of the nation's adults) are in possession of 77 percent of the total stock of firearms. Handguns, which are most often acquired for self-protection, have been the new additions to many gun-owning households. The increase in handgun prevalence corresponds to a large increase in the importance of handguns in retail sales. The ATF has estimated that half of the new guns sold in the United States in the early 1990s were handguns, up from one-third in the early 1970s. In the late 1990s, however, the handgun share of all new gun sales fell back to about 40 percent (ATF 2000*b*).

Some 4.5 million new firearms, including about 2 million handguns (ATF 2000*b*), and about 2 million secondhand guns are sold each year in the United States (Cook and Ludwig 1996). According to the national survey (NSPOF), most guns acquired in the previous two years were either purchased by the respondent (73 percent) or received as a gift (19 percent) (Cook and Ludwig 1996). The predominant source of guns was a store (60 percent), followed by family members (17 percent), and acquaintances (12 percent).

Firearms thefts from households are common and represent a major source of illegal diversions from the existing legal stock of firearms.[1] The NSPOF data suggest that there were 269,000 incidents in which guns were stolen from a residence in 1994, and that the total number of guns taken was over 500,000 (Cook and Ludwig 1996).

Guns are durable goods that may remain in circulation for many years. However, there are several avenues by which guns are removed from circulation, including breakage and confiscation by law enforcement agencies. According to ATF tracing records, police departments submit information on more than 150,000 guns recovered in crime per year (Cook and Braga 2001), which places a lower bound on the yearly number of guns recovered since not all recovered guns are traced. Owners discard some 36,000 guns per year (Cook and Ludwig 1996). There may also be a substantial drain on the existing stock due to unrecorded exports of firearms associated with the international drug trade. Anecdotal evidence suggests that the United States may be a primary source of illegal firearms for organized crime networks, drug traffickers, and terrorists in other countries (Lumpe 1997; United Nations Commission on Crime Prevention and Criminal Justice 1997).

Figure 1 presents a conceptual scheme of the flow of firearms to criminals and juveniles. Other than theft, there are three broad mechanisms through which criminal consumers acquire firearms from licensees: straw purchase, "lying and buying," and buying from a dealer who is willing to ignore regulations. A straw purchase occurs when the actual buyer, typically someone who is too young or otherwise pro-

---

[1] Guns are also stolen from businesses. The Violent Crime Control and Law Enforcement Act of 1994 requires licensed dealers to report firearms lost and stolen from their inventory. In 1998 and 1999, licensees filed reports on over 5,000 incidents involving 27,287 lost or stolen firearms (ATF 2000*b*). These included the following incidents: inventory errors, record-keeping errors, and employee theft (39 percent of incidents and over 11,000 guns); burglary (21 percent of incidents and nearly 11,000 guns); larceny (38 percent of incidents and over 3,500 guns); and robbery (2 percent of incidents and about 1,000 firearms).

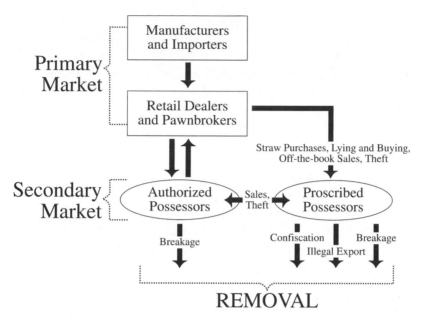

Fig. 1.—Firearms flows

scribed, uses another person to execute the paperwork. Prohibited persons can purchase firearms directly by showing false identification and lying about their status. In some cases the seller is knowingly involved and may disguise the illegal transaction by falsifying the paper record of sale or reporting the guns as stolen.

After firearms are diverted from legal commerce, it is quite likely that they will be put to use in criminal activity. It appears that most guns used by criminals, especially by youth offenders, have been acquired relatively recently, reflecting the fact that street criminals tend to have brief careers (Blumstein et al. 1986).

Guns have value in exchange as well as in use. On the basis of interviews with youth offenders, Cook, Molliconi, and Cole (1995) report that guns were valuable commodities for youth to trade for services, money, drugs, or other items. Youth offenders may be active both as sellers and buyers of guns through informal networks of family, friends, and street sources (Wright, Sheley, and Smith 1992). Incarcerated felons who reported selling or trading stolen guns identified a varied list of customers including friends, fences, drug dealers, strangers on the street, pawnshops, retail gun stores, and family members (Wright and Rossi 1994).

II. Research on Illegal Firearms Markets

There are three main sources of evidence on the operations of illegal firearms markets: surveys of criminals and youth, ATF firearms-trace data, and ATF firearms-trafficking investigation data.[2] These sources have been used to support seemingly contradictory conclusions concerning the value of supply-side interventions. In fact, the alternate sources of information illuminate different aspects of the same basic phenomenon.

A. Survey Research on Gun Acquisition

The importance of theft and the secondary market in supplying youths and criminals has been documented by three surveys: Wright and Rossi's (1994) survey of prisoners, the survey of state prisoners reported by the Bureau of Justice Statistics (BJS) (1993), and Sheley and Wright's (1995) survey of youths in juvenile correctional institutions. Some of the results of these survey data are summarized in table 1.

Some respondents in these surveys admitted that they stole their most recent gun, although that occurs less frequently than might be supposed. Sheley and Wright (1995) found that just 12 percent of their juvenile inmates had obtained their most recent handgun by theft, while BJS (1993) found that only 9 percent of the handgun-using state prison inmates had stolen their handgun. Wright and Rossi (1994), however, found that 32 percent of the most recent handguns acquired by their prison respondents were stolen by the respondent himself, and that a total of 46 percent of these handguns had, in the opinion of the respondent, been stolen at some time (Kleck 1999, p. 39). And while the juvenile respondents of Sheley and Wright (1995) were much less likely to have stolen their most recent handgun, they had in many cases stolen guns at some point in their "careers": "About 30 percent of the inmates said they had stolen rifles, shotguns, and military-style weapons; 50 percent had stolen revolvers; and 44 percent had stolen automatic or semiautomatic handguns at some point in their criminal careers" (Sheley and Wright 1995, p. 47). More recently, Decker,

---

[2] It is important to clarify the term "firearms trafficking" here. Since all crime guns initially start off as legally owned firearms, firearms trafficking refers to the illegal diversion of legally owned firearms from lawful commerce into unlawful commerce, often for profit (ATF 2000d, p. 3). The term "trafficking" has a different meaning in the firearms context than in the context of drug trafficking, where it usually refers to the illegal manufacture, transportation, and smuggling of large quantities of illicit drugs. In contrast to their drug running counterparts, firearms traffickers include those who move just a few guns from time to time for the purpose of making an illegal transaction.

TABLE 1

Sources of Guns to Criminals: Results from Three
Inmate Surveys (in Percent)

	Most Recent Handgun		
	Male Prisoners in 1982*	Prisoners in 1991[†]	Juvenile Male Inmates 1991[‡]
Purchase from retail outlet	21	27	7
Black market, "street"	26	28	43
Theft	(32)	9	12
Family or friends	44	31	36
Other	10	5	2

SOURCE.—Cook and Braga 2001.

* Survey of inmates in ten states; 1,032 respondents admitted to ever owning a handgun (Wright and Rossi 1994, p. 183). Note that "theft" in their tabulation is not a source but rather a means of obtaining the gun. Only 970 male prisoners reported the means of acquiring the gun; of these, 32 percent stole their most recent handgun.

[†] Survey of state prisons; BJS 1993.

[‡] Survey of juvenile inmates of six facilities located in four states; 640 juvenile male inmates reported the source of their most recent handgun (as opposed to the more than 800 who admitted to ever owning a handgun) (Sheley and Wright 1993, p. 6).

Pennell, and Caldwell (1997) analyzed the results of interviews with arrestees in eleven cities that were conducted as part of the Drug Use Forecasting system and found that 13 percent of arrestees admitted to having stolen a gun. Among juvenile males, one-quarter admitted to theft of a gun (Decker, Pennell, and Caldwell 1997). Indirect evidence of the importance of theft in supplying the black market comes from the low prices inmates typically report paying for their guns in the informal market (Sheley and Wright 1995; Kleck 1999).

The survey data also suggest a fairly substantial role, either direct or indirect, for the FFLs. About one-quarter of the respondents in the survey of state prisoners said that they had acquired their most recent gun from a retail outlet (BJS 1993).[3] While the percentage of juvenile-inmate respondents who acquired their most recent gun from a retail outlet is much lower (just 12 percent), Sheley and Wright (1995, p. 48)

[3] Note that survey-response data may understate the importance of FFLs. A firearm counted in surveys as having been obtained from a "family member or friend" may have been acquired though a straw purchase from an FFL. "Street" firearms purchasers "cannot be expected to know how, and from whom, street gun vendors acquire their wares," argues Julius Wachtel (1998, p. 223). "Incomplete depictions of gun pedigrees can lead to the misattribution of sales that should be assigned, at least in part, to [retail] sources."

note that 32 percent of these inmates had asked someone to purchase a gun for them at a retail outlet at least once in their career. In most cases, these straw-purchase arrangements involved a family member or friend as the purchaser. All three survey studies found that black market sources are important; these may well include traffickers who acquire their guns from licensed retail outlets (Kennedy, Piehl, and Braga 1996*b*; Wachtel 1998).

Survey findings may be challenged on the grounds that the samples are not representative of the relevant populations of criminals and that the respondents' self-reports on their criminal activities are not reliable.[4] The survey samples are what are known as "convenience samples." They are selected from just a few institutions and the respondents who are selected from those institutions are those who were willing and available to participate. More generally, prisoners are not representative of the population of active criminals.

B. Firearms Trace Data

Best practice in the police investigation of a gun homicide or assault often includes submitting the gun (if available) for tracing, in the hope of identifying a suspect or developing a case against a suspect. Analyzed properly, firearms trace data can also be used as a statistical basis for gaining some insight into the supply side of the gun violence problem. However, trace data analyses are subject to a number of widely recognized problems (see Congressional Research Service 1992; Blackman 1999; Kleck 1999). All are based on firearms recovered by police and other law enforcement agencies, which may not be representative of firearms possessed and used by criminals. Furthermore, a substantial percentage of recovered firearms cannot be traced for various reasons. The trace-based information that results is biased to an unknown degree by these factors.

Firearms trace data have been used to gain insights on the illegal supply of firearms since the early 1970s. In 1973, the ATF began a study, known as Project Identification, of handguns confiscated by po-

---

[4] For example, the incarcerated felons surveyed in Wright and Rossi's (1994) research had a strong preference for large, well-made handguns. These findings on the gun preferences of felons contrast with the observation that many guns recovered in crime tend to be small, cheap handguns (see, e.g., Kleck 1997). Kennedy, Piehl, and Braga (1996*b*) suggest taking survey findings on gun preferences with caution. In Boston, youth reported strong preferences for larger caliber, high-quality handguns, such as Glock 9mm pistols, but actually tended to possess small, low-quality handguns (Kennedy, Piehl, and Braga 1996*b*, p. 171).

lice departments in sixteen cities (ATF 1976). The ATF received more than 10,000 handguns and successfully traced 74 percent to the first retail purchaser. Most of these were small, cheap handguns known as "Saturday night specials." The ATF's analyses of the trace data suggested that many handguns recovered in cities with restrictive state and local firearms laws (e.g., Boston and New York) were first purchased in states with less restrictive firearms laws. Conversely, in those jurisdictions with lenient gun laws (e.g., Atlanta and Dallas), most recovered firearms were first purchased in-state.

In his careful examination of ATF handgun trace data, Franklin Zimring (1976) concluded that a disproportionate number of handguns seized by police in major metropolitan areas had been first sold at retail in the relatively recent past. Zimring (1976) tentatively concluded from these data that interventions targeting the retail supply of firearms would be more useful than might be expected in reducing firearms availability on the street. These findings were replicated and extended in a major study by the Police Foundation, which emphasized the importance of interstate firearm trafficking in undermining the more stringent state and local firearms laws (Brill 1977).

In any event, the quality of firearms trace data has improved in recent years. In 1996, the ATF initiated the Youth Crime Gun Interdiction Initiative (YCGII) with commitments from seventeen cities to trace all recovered crime guns (ATF 1997). This program expanded to thirty-eight cities in 2000, with additional cities added in 2001 (ATF 2000c). Other jurisdictions have also expanded their use of gun tracing; six states, for example, have recently adopted comprehensive tracing as a matter of state policy, by law (California, Connecticut, North Carolina, and Illinois), executive order (Maryland), or law enforcement initiative (New Jersey) (ATF 2000c). Comprehensive tracing of all firearm recoveries reduces some of the bias in trace data introduced by police decision making. Jurisdictions that submit all confiscated guns for tracing can be confident that the resulting database of trace requests is representative of a well-defined "population" of guns recovered by police during a particular period of time and a reasonable "sample" of guns used in crime (Cook and Braga 2001).[5]

---

[5] Using recovered crime guns as a basis for estimating the characteristics of all guns used in crime is analogous to using arrestees as a basis for estimating the characteristics of all criminals. Although both are unrepresentative of the relevant populations in various ways and both are influenced heavily by police priorities and procedures, both types of data may yield valid insights in certain applications.

TABLE 2

Gun-Trafficking Indicators from Three Recent Analyses of ATF Firearms Trace Data

	Boston Youth Guns*	YCGII Handguns 1999[†]	Los Angeles Area Guns[‡]
Guns recovered	1,550	54,363	5,002
Successfully traced (in percent)	52	54	55
New guns (percent of successful traces)	26[§]	32[‖]	pistols: 52 revolvers: 24[§]
Purchased out of state (percent of successful traces)	66	Total YCGII—38 Washington, D.C.—100 New York—89 Boston—69	19
New guns recovered in possession of first retail buyer (in percent)	0	18	14[#]
Obliterated serial numbers (in percent)	20	pistols: 9 revolvers: 5[**]	N/A

* Comprehensive tracing of firearms recovered from Boston youth ages twenty-one and under between January 1991 and May 1995 (Kennedy et al. 1996a).

[†] Comprehensive tracing of handguns recovered in thirty-eight cities participating in ATF's Youth Crime Gun Interdiction Initiative (YCGII) program (Cook and Braga 2001).

[‡] Firearms recovered and submitted for tracing between 1988 and 1995 (Wachtel 1998). These analyses were not based on comprehensive tracing. Eighty-two percent of these firearms were recovered by the Los Angeles Police Department and the rest were recovered by law enforcement agencies in nearby communities.

[§] Less than twenty-four months from purchase.

[‖] Less than thirty-six months from purchase.

[#] This study did not unravel the extent to which new guns were recovered from the first retail purchaser. The 14 percent represents all traced guns recovered from the first retail purchaser.

[**] These figures come from eleven YCGII cities that reliably submitted information on guns recovered with obliterated serial numbers.

Table 2 summarizes some of the main findings of three recent analyses of firearms trace data in Boston (Kennedy, Piehl, and Braga 1996b), cities participating in YCGII in 1999 (Cook and Braga 2001), and the Los Angeles area (Wachtel 1998). The three studies found that a noteworthy proportion of traced crime guns had a "time to crime" (the period from first retail sale to recovery by the police) of a few months or years. In particular, recovered crime guns tend to be quite new in comparison with guns in public circulation (as assessed on the basis of annual firearm production figures). For example, Pierce et al. (2001) found that guns manufactured between 1996 and 1998 represented about 14 percent of the firearms in private hands, but they accounted for fully 34 percent of traced crime guns recovered in 1999.

"Fast" time-to-crime firearms that are recovered from possessors who are not the first retail purchasers present particularly strong evidence that these firearms may have been illegally diverted from legal firearms commerce. The three studies found that relatively few crime guns were recovered in the possession of the first retail purchaser. None of the firearms recovered from youth in the Boston trace study were recovered from persons who had legal permits to buy the guns (Kennedy, Piehl, and Braga 1996b). Fast time-to-crime guns were also concentrated among a few manufacturers of relatively cheap guns such as Lorcin Engineering, Bryco Arms, Raven Arms, and Davis Industries.[6]

The percentage of crime guns imported from out-of-state is closely linked to the stringency of local firearm controls. Overall, 62 percent of traced YCGII handguns were first purchased from licensed dealers in the state in which the guns were recovered (Cook and Braga 2001), but this fraction was far lower in tight-control northeastern cities such as Boston, New York City, and Washington, D.C., where less than half of the traceable firearms were sold at retail within state. Many firearms originated from southern states with less restrictive legislation such as Virginia, North Carolina, Georgia, and Florida (ATF 2000c).

The recovery of firearms with obliterated serial numbers is viewed by the ATF as a key indicator of firearms trafficking. Guns with thoroughly obliterated serial numbers are untraceable, and hence they offer protection for a criminal who is concerned about being tied to an illegal use of the gun; gun traffickers use this tactic to conceal the source of the firearm (Kennedy, Piehl, and Braga 1996b), even though possession of

[6] The preferences of criminal consumers for certain types of guns may partially explain why semiautomatic pistols have quicker time-to-crime distributions. In Boston, interviews with youthful probationers revealed that they preferred modern and stylish semiautomatic pistols that were "new in the box" (Kennedy, Piehl, and Braga 1996b, p. 169). The preference for newer semiautomatic pistols arose from "street wisdom" that an older, less expensive firearm may have a "body" on it, and they wished to avoid being caught and charged with crimes they did not personally commit (Kennedy, Piehl, and Braga 1996b, p. 170). In the YCGII trace reports, the median time-to-crime of firearms recovered from youth ages eighteen to twenty-four (4.8 years) is shorter than for adults (5.6 years) and juveniles (6.3 years) (ATF 2000c).

a gun with an obliterated serial number is a federal felony. The Boston trace study revealed that one-fifth of the firearms recovered from Boston youth had obliterated serial numbers. Obliterated firearms recovered from Boston youth were found closely to resemble newer crime guns as they were mostly semiautomatic pistols, concentrated among particular brands and calibers (Kennedy, Piehl, and Braga 1996b).

In 1999, eleven YCGII cities reliably submitted information on guns with obliterated serial numbers: of these guns, 9 percent were semiautomatic pistols and 5 percent were revolvers (Cook and Braga 2001). As Kleck (1999) observes, the prevalence of obliterated serial numbers among crime guns is not great. However, as suggested by the Boston trace study, the prevalence of obliterated serial numbers was higher among guns recovered from youth than from guns recovered from adults in the eleven YCGII cities (ATF 2000c). The percentages for cities where interstate trafficking is most important appear to be higher—13 percent of recovered handguns had obliterated serial numbers in New York and 16 percent in Boston (Cook and Braga 2001).

At the national level, a 1995 study of all trace data contained in the ATF's Firearm Tracing System at the National Tracing Center found a very high concentration of traces associated with a small number of licensed dealers: nearly half of all traces came back to only 0.4 percent of all licensed dealers (Pierce, Briggs, and Carlson 1995). Of course, it is possible that the concentration of trace data may simply reflect the concentration of firearms sales among FFLs, which are also highly concentrated: in California, the 13 percent of FFLs with more than 100 sales during 1996–98 accounted for 88 percent of all sales (Wintemute 2000b). Handgun trace volume from 1998 was strongly correlated with handgun sales volume and is highly concentrated among high-volume dealers, but that is not the whole story: "trace volume varied substantially among dealers with similar sales volumes" (Wintemute 2000b, p. 567). However, Wintemute did not determine whether this variation was greater than could be explained by chance alone.

Multiple sales of firearms by FFLs may also be a potential indicator of firearms trafficking. Trace data analyses conducted by the ATF suggests that handguns that were first sold as part of a reportable multiple sale are much more likely than others to move quickly into criminal use (ATF 2000c).

C. Firearms Trafficking Investigation Data

Although trace studies provide useful information on the age and origin of crime guns, they do not describe the pathways through which firearms were illegally diverted to prohibited persons. Analyses of ATF firearms-trafficking-investigation data provide insights on the workings of illegal firearms markets. An early study by Mark Moore (1981) examined 131 closed cases of "dealing without a license" between 1974 and 1976 in seven ATF regional offices. The trafficking organizations involved in the ATF cases were supplied both by thefts from residences and through purchases from licensed dealers. The study concluded that the trafficking organizations involved were quite small and did relatively little business; only 10 percent had more than twenty firearms in "inventory" when the arrest was made, and the majority appeared to sell fewer than five firearms a month. Some were in the general business of fencing stolen goods.

A more recent analysis examined all trafficking investigations conducted by the ATF in the Los Angeles area between 1992 and 1995 that led to a conviction or were still proceeding through the courts (Wachtel 1998). These twenty-eight cases charged the diversion of more than 19,000 firearms, primarily .380 and 9mm handguns. Three-quarters of the diverted firearms were purchased at wholesale—more than 90 percent by licensed dealers who then sold them illegally, and 1,200 through the use of a forged license. Fourteen percent were initially acquired at retail from a licensed dealer; straw purchasers acquired nearly half of these guns, and the rest were acquired from licensed dealers acting illegally. The balance were stolen from commercial outlets; no instances of residential theft were reported. The picture of trafficking that emerged was one of both large-scale and concentrated activity. Eight of the cases examined involved more than 1,000 firearms. The obliteration of serial numbers was extensive, with one case involving the obliteration of the serial numbers on 1,200 firearms.

The Moore (1981) and Wachtel (1998) studies present strikingly different pictures of the nature of gun trafficking. Neither study is representative of the current illegal firearms trafficking patterns. The Moore (1981) findings are dated. The Wachtel (1998) findings are specific to one geographic area and may not reflect general firearms trafficking patterns in the United States.

In an attempt to provide a more representative look at firearms trafficking, ATF and academic researchers conducted a comprehensive examination of all firearms trafficking investigations—a total of 1,530 cases involving the illegal diversion of more than 84,000 guns—conducted between July 1996 and December 1998 by ATF special agents in all ATF field divisions in the United States (ATF 2000d; see also Braga and Kennedy 2001).

This study found that 43 percent of the trafficking investigations involved the diversion of ten firearms or less (ATF 2000*d*) but confirmed the existence of large trafficking operations including two cases involving over 10,000 firearms. The distribution of trafficker size may look like the distribution of FFL size. The great majority of FFLs, even those that are active, sell only a handful of guns each year. However, most of the yearly sales originate from a handful of large FFLs (ATF 2000*b*). Similarly, the illicit market may consist of a large number of small, transitory opportunists and a few large operators, with the latter accounting for the bulk of the sales.

Among the largest traffickers are corrupt FFLs, who accounted for just 9 percent of the ATF investigations but almost half of the guns that were accounted for in these investigations (see table 3). Violations by licensed dealers in these investigations included "off paper" sales, false entries in record books, transfers to prohibited persons, illegal out-of-state transfers, and obliterated serial numbers.

Nearly half of the ATF investigations involved firearms being traf-

TABLE 3

Volume of Firearms Diverted through Trafficking Channels

Source	N (percent)	Total Guns	Mean	Median
Firearms trafficked by straw purchaser or straw purchasing ring	695 (47)	25,741	37.0	14
Trafficking in firearms by unregulated private sellers*	301 (20)	22,508	74.8	10
Trafficking in firearms at gun shows and flea markets	198 (13)	25,862	130.6	40
Trafficking in firearms stolen from FFL	209 (14)	6,084	29.1	18
Trafficking in firearms stolen from residence	154 (10)	3,306	21.5	7
Firearms trafficked by FFL, including pawnbroker	114 (8)	40,365	354.1	42
Trafficking in firearms stolen from common carrier	31 (2)	2,062	66.5	16

SOURCE.—Adapted from ATF 2000*d*.

NOTE.—*N* = 1,470 investigations. Since firearms may be trafficked along multiple channels, an investigation may be included in more than one category. This table excludes 60 investigations where the total number of trafficked firearms was unknown from the total pool of 1,530.

* As distinct from straw purchasers and other traffickers.

ficked by straw purchasers either directly or indirectly. Straw purchasers may be instruments of criminals or traffickers who obtain the straw purchaser's services, or they may be unlicensed dealers who set out to use their nonprohibited status to sell guns illegally to other persons for profit. In those instances where straw purchasers were working for traffickers, they were often friends or relatives of the firearms traffickers. Trafficking investigations involving straw purchasers averaged a relatively small number of firearms per investigation, but collectively accounted for 26,000 firearms.

Firearms stolen from manufacturers, FFLs, residences, and common carriers (such as the United Parcel Service) were involved in more than a quarter of the investigations (ATF 2000d). Organized rings of thieves that specialize in stealing firearms often characterized these cases.[7] Depending on the type of theft involved, stolen firearms ranged from new to quite old. For example, a burglary of a licensed dealer may yield a cache of new and secondhand firearms, while a residential burglary or a series of home invasions may yield only older firearms. The diversion of firearms from gun shows and flea markets by FFLs and unlicensed sellers characterized 14 percent of the ATF trafficking investigations and were associated with the illegal diversion of some 26,000 firearms (ATF 2000d). An earlier review of ATF gun show investigations revealed that prohibited persons, such as felons and juveniles, do personally buy firearms at gun shows and that gun shows are sources of firearms that are trafficked to prohibited persons (Braga and Kennedy 2000; see also U.S. Department of the Treasury and U.S. Department of Justice 1999). The gun show research found that firearms were diverted at and through gun shows by straw purchasers, unlicensed private sellers (some of whom were previously licensed dealers whose licenses were revoked), and licensed dealers (Braga and Kennedy 2000).

D. The Structure of Illegal Firearms Markets

In the parlance of environmental regulation, illegal gun markets consist of "point sources"—ongoing diversions through scofflaw dealers, trafficking rings, and gun thieves—and "diffuse sources"—acquisitions through direct theft and informal voluntary sales. The investiga-

[7] In one noteworthy 1994 case, which predated the investigation data collection and analysis, some 14,000 .25, .380, and 9mm semiautomatic pistols were stolen from Lorcin Engineering's manufacturing plant by four plant employees (Vanzi 1998). Since these handguns were freshly produced, none were stamped with serial numbers and authorities believe that most disappeared into the illegal firearms market (Vanzi 1998).

tion data and trace data provide evidence that point sources are quite important in supplying criminals, thus strengthening the case for supply-side interventions.

These patterns stand side by side with data indicating that more than a half million guns are stolen each year and survey findings that most criminals and juveniles obtain their guns from casual, informal sources. A reasonable conclusion is that, as in the case of pollution, both point sources and diffuse sources are important. Our own speculation is that the mix of point and diffuse sources differs across jurisdictions depending on the density of gun ownership and the strictness of gun controls. Systematic gun trafficking may well be more important in strict-control jurisdictions such as Boston and New York than in looser-control jurisdictions such as Atlanta and Dallas. As a result, the potential effectiveness of supply-side enforcement may be greater in jurisdictions where guns are relatively scarce.

To some observers, the broad lesson of the available research is that guns are available to criminals and juveniles from a variety of sources, so that even if one or two of them (straw purchases, trafficking) were to be curtailed it would make little difference to the use of guns in crime (Kleck 1999). That interpretation should be viewed as speculation, rather than as fact. The available evidence is simply not conclusive. And economic reasoning indicates that under some circumstances curtailing some sources of guns will influence the terms on which guns are available from other sources (Cook and Leitzel 1996).

The three sources of data on the illegal supply of firearms are not incompatible and do not contradict the belief that stolen guns and informal voluntary transfers predominate in supplying criminals and juveniles with guns. But FFLs also play an important role, as indicated by the survey data as well as the trace and investigation data.

These observations on the importance of direct retail purchases as a source of crime guns fits well with other evidence that prohibited persons often attempt to acquire firearms by deceiving licensed dealers. Background checks resulted in about 320,000 rejections of applications to purchase handguns made by prohibited persons between March 1994 and December 1998 (BJS 1999).

In his critique of the role of organized gun running, Kleck (1999) scrutinizes the potential sources of sample bias in the Boston trace study (Kennedy, Piehl, and Braga 1996b) and contrasts the Boston results with survey research findings to raise doubts about the importance of close-to-retail diversions of firearms in supplying criminals and youth with guns. We believe that his synthesis is inappropriate on two counts. First, analyses of trace data collected from multiple jurisdictions provide evidence of large differences among jurisdictions in the importance of various sources of guns for criminals and youth (ATF 2000c; Cook and Braga 2001). These differences are concealed in the survey research studies where the authors pool all the data. The survey data provide a picture of the "average" ways criminals and youth acquire firearms. However, this average is not representative geographically, and the trace data provide a clearer assessment of local variations associated with gun ownership among criminals and youth. Second, when the methodological limitations of the various types of illegal gun market research are considered, we believe that it is very difficult to compare the disparate types of research and make convincing arguments that privilege certain sources of guns over other sources.

Although the three sources of data on the workings of illegal gun markets are not directly comparable, they are broadly compatible. We have produced a list of grounded conclusions about the illegal supply of guns that are supported by at least one source and are not contradicted by another. Most guns used in crime have changed hands since the first retail sale. Guns used in crime are disproportionately new when compared with the stock of guns in private hands. Still, the majority of guns used in crime are more than three years old. The temporal connection between transactions and criminal use is no doubt much tighter yet, but that supposition is difficult to document in the absence of data on any transactions except the first retail sale. Theft from residences and dealers is an important source of crime guns, both directly (violent criminals and youths sometimes arm themselves through theft) and indirectly (the guns sold by street dealers have often been stolen). One earmark of trafficking is obliterated serial numbers. The guns preferred by youthful offenders in tight-control areas are quite likely to have obliterated numbers. The illicit market is served to some extent by dealers—people making money off buying and selling guns on an ongoing basis—including those both licensed and unlicensed. Guns are diverted from retail sources through a variety of means including scofflaw FFLs, straw purchases, and "lying and buying." Illicit dealers and traffickers cover a wide spectrum with respect to scale of activity— just as do FFLs. Scofflaw FFLs tend to be associated with the diversion of higher numbers of firearms than other traffickers. In tight-control jurisdictions, crime guns are relatively likely to be imported from other states and to be recovered in the hands of someone other than the first retail purchaser.

III. Supply-Side Interventions to Reduce the Availability of Guns

The supply-side approach seems futile if one accepts the common view that "guns are everywhere," that almost anyone can quickly and cheaply obtain a gun regardless of age or place of residence. However, much evidence suggests otherwise. For example, according to victim reports, 75 percent of robbers do not use a gun, despite the tactical advantage of doing so (Cook and Leitzel 1996). A longitudinal study of teenage gang members in Rochester, New York, found that only one-third owned a gun (Bjerregaard and Lizotte 1995). Similarly, about one-third of juvenile male arrestees in eleven cities reported owning a gun (Decker, Pennell, and Caldwell 1997). These statistics suggest that many active criminals and a majority of crime-involved youth do not own a gun.

Effective supply-side efforts would help increase the price of guns sold to prohibited persons and increase the "effective price" of acquiring guns—the time and hassle required to make a "connection" to buy guns (see Moore 1973, 1976). The benefit of this approach would be an increased incentive for criminals and youths to economize on gun possession and use. As guns become scarcer and more valuable, they will be slower to buy and quicker to sell, thus reducing the percentage of their criminal careers in which they are in possession of a gun (Kennedy 1994).

Thus, the potential for attacking illegal firearms markets has promise. Definitive evidence-based conclusions are scarce, but there is no lack of ideas.

A. Putting Trace Data to Work

Until recently, most law-enforcement agencies did not trace firearms unless they needed the information to solve a particular crime. In 1993, about 55,000 trace requests were submitted to the ATF (ATF 2000b). As described earlier, the ATF, with the support of the Clinton administration, embraced a supply-side approach to reducing gun violence. A key component to this approach was improving the ATF's capacity to trace firearms and increasing the volume of trace requests submitted to the ATF. With three dozen cities now comprehensively tracing all firearms recovered by law enforcement, more than 150,000 trace requests were submitted to the ATF in 1999.

Strategic analyses of trace data provide more focused information on the identity of FFLs and others who are most active in diverting guns into criminal use. These data have become an increasingly important tool in enforcement efforts. The use of trace data as an investigative tool has been enhanced by the development of Project LEAD beginning in 1993 (ATF 1995). Project LEAD is a computerized software application that contains information on all traced firearms in ATF's National Tracing Center's Firearms Tracing System. The system provides ATF agents with data useful in identifying gun traffickers, straw purchasers, and scofflaw FFLs. The ATF also analyzes multiple sales data for suspicious purchasing patterns suggestive of gun trafficking. Nearly 30 percent of 1,500 ATF firearms trafficking investigations reviewed between July 1996 and December 1998 were initiated through strategic analyses of information—analyses of trace data, multiple sales data, or both (ATF 2000d). After initiation of investigations, tracing was used as an investigative tool to gain information on recovered crime guns in 60 percent of the 1,500 ATF firearms trafficking investigations.

Another interesting application of strategic analyses of trace data has been as a guide to licensing and regulatory enforcement. As described earlier, federal dealers' licenses are now being issued far more selectively, and the number of active licensees has dropped from more than 260,000 to about 100,000. With the elimination of some 160,000 marginal dealers, ATF regulatory and enforcement resources are spread less thinly. Moreover, relatively few dealers are associated with the bulk of crime gun traces. The ATF has focused its investigations on this small group. In 2000, the ATF conducted focused compliance inspections of dealers who had been uncooperative in response to trace requests and of FFLs who had ten or more crime guns (regardless of time to crime) traced to them in 1999 (ATF 2000a). The inspections disclosed violations in about 75 percent of the 1,012 dealers inspected. Nearly half (47 percent) of the dealers had at least one inventory discrepancy. While the majority of the discrepancies were resolved during the inspection process, some 13,271 missing guns could not be accounted for by 202 licensees. Sixteen FFLs each had more than 200 missing guns. More than 57 percent had at least one violation relating to a failure to execute transaction paperwork properly, and 54 percent failed to maintain a complete and accurate record book.

The focused compliance inspections identified sales to more than 400 potential firearms traffickers and nearly 300 potentially prohibited persons, resulting in 691 referrals sent to ATF agents for further investigation (ATF 2000*a*). The overall ratio of trafficking referrals to licensees was more than three times higher in the group of licensees with ten or more firearms traces with short time-to-crime than in the group of licensees who did not have at least ten traces with short time-to-crime. Some 45 percent of the inspected dealers were recommended for follow-up administrative action, including 2 percent for license revocation. The licensees subjected to the focused compliance inspections had significantly higher rates (75 percent) of Gun Control Act violations than a random sample of licensees inspected in 1998 (37 percent) (ATF 2000*a*).

B. Regulating Licensed Dealers

States have generally paid little attention to regulating gun dealers, leaving that effort to the ATF. But there are some exceptions that suggest a fruitful role for state and local government. In 1993, North Carolina found that only 23 percent of ATF-licensed dealers also possessed its required state license (Cook, Molliconi, and Cole 1995). Noncomplying dealers were required to obtain a state license or forfeit their federal license. Alabama also identified FFLs who did not possess the required state license: 900 claimed not to know about the state requirements and obtained the license; another 900 reported that they were not currently engaged in the business of selling firearms and 200 more could not be located (Cook, Molliconi, and Cole 1995)—Alabama officials scheduled the licenses for these 1,100 dealers for cancellation.

The Oakland (California) Police Department worked with the ATF to enforce a requirement that all licensed dealers hold a local permit that requires dealers to undergo screening and a criminal background check (Veen, Dunbar, and Ruland 1997). This effort caused the number of license holders in Oakland to drop from fifty-seven to seven in 1997. Officials in New York City found that only 29 of 950 FFLs were operating in compliance with local ordinances. In cooperation with the ATF, all local license applications were forwarded to the New York City Police Department, which assumed responsibility for screening and inspections. The increased scrutiny reduced the number of license holders in New York City from 950 to 259 (Veen, Dunbar, and Ruland 1997). Unfortunately, these interventions have not been evaluated to determine if they affected rates of gun misuse.

C. Limiting Gun Sales

Analyses of multiple purchase data revealed that handguns acquired in multiple purchase transactions are relatively likely to be associated with gun trafficking (ATF 2000c). In July 1993, Virginia implemented a law limiting handgun purchases by any individual to no more than one during a thirty-day period. Prior to the passage of this law, Virginia had been noted as one of the leading source states for guns recovered in Northeast cities such as New York, Boston, and Washington, D.C. (Weil and Knox 1996). Using firearms trace data, Weil and Knox (1996) showed that during the first eighteen months the law was in effect, Virginia's role in supplying guns to New York and Massachusetts was greatly reduced. For traces initiated in the Northeast corridor, 35 percent of the firearms acquired before one-gun-a-month took effect and 16 percent purchased after implementation were traced to Virginia dealers (Weil and Knox 1996). Although the number of guns originating from Virginia decreased, the number of guns originating from other states increased, which suggests that this approach would be most effective if a national one-gun-a-month law was adopted. Maryland adopted a one-gun-a-month law in 1996, and California followed suit in 1999 (Wintemute 2000a).

D. Screening Gun Buyers

Implemented in February 1994, the Brady Handgun Violence Prevention Act required licensed dealers to conduct a background check on all handgun buyers and mandated a one-week waiting period before transferring the gun to the purchaser. In November 1998, waiting periods for background checks were eliminated for a National Instant Check System (NICS).[8] Over a five-year period (1994–99), 13 million Brady criminal background checks were conducted of prospective handgun purchasers (BJS 1999). Nearly 320,000 requests were denied, of which 220,000 were due to prior felony convictions or pending indictments (BJS 1999). Nevertheless, it seems easy enough for criminals to circumvent the provisions of the Brady Act by acquiring guns through the unregulated secondary market (Jacobs and Potter 1995).

---

[8] The NICS system suffers from two key problems: the national registry of convicted felons is not complete, and there is no national registry of other prohibited persons such as drug addicts (Tien and Rich 1990).

The Brady Act did not affect licensed dealers operating in eighteen states because state law already required a background check; licensed dealers operating in the thirty-two remaining states were required to institute the change. The Brady Act thus created a natural experiment, with the "no change" states serving as a control group. Ludwig and Cook (2000) evaluated the Brady Act and found that there were no discernible difference in homicide trends between the thirty-two "Brady" states as compared to the eighteen "non-Brady" states. Criminals acquiring firearms from the unregulated secondary market may have undermined the effectiveness of the Brady Act in preventing homicide.

Cook and Braga (2001) demonstrate that criminals in Chicago were being supplied to a large extent by organized gun trafficking from south-central states, in particular Mississippi, and that a modest increase in regulation—imposed by the Brady Act—shut down that pipeline. However, this large change in trafficking channels did not have any apparent effect on gun availability to violent people in Chicago, as the percentage of homicides with guns did not drop after 1994 (Cook and Braga 2001).

Some observers suggest, however, that screening prospective buyers can be an effective way to keep guns out of the wrong hands. In Florida, McDowall, Loftin, and Wiersema (1995) reported a significant decrease in homicide rates after the state adopted mandatory waiting periods and background checks for prospective handgun buyers. A recent California study compared 170 felons whose handgun purchases were denied to 2,470 handgun buyers who had felony arrests but no felony convictions (Wright, Wintemute, and Rivara 1999). After a three-year period, the felony arrestees whose purchases were approved were 21 percent more likely to be charged with a new gun offense and 24 percent more likely to be charged with a new violent offense than were the convicted felons.

Since 1994, persons subjected to domestic violence restraining orders have been restricted from purchasing or possessing handguns. The 1997 Omnibus Consolidated Appropriations Act banned the purchase or possession of firearms by persons convicted of a misdemeanor domestic violence offense. Some eighteen states and Washington, D.C., prohibit persons convicted of selected misdemeanors, usually violent crimes and alcohol and drug offenses, from purchasing firearms (Wintemute 2000a). Research has revealed that certain misdemeanants, although legally entitled to buy firearms, are at substantial risk for committing crimes (Wintemute et al. 1998). A California study of violent misdemeanants who sought to purchase handguns found that denying these purchases reduced their risk of committing new gun crimes or violence by 20–30 percent (Wintemute et al. 1999).

E. Gun Buybacks

Gun buyback and exchange programs have been popular in a number of jurisdictions, but they appear to have only symbolic value (Kennedy, Piehl, and Braga 1996a). Evaluations indicate that they have had no observable effect on either gun crime or firearm-related injury rates (see, e.g., Callahan, Rivara, and Koepsell 1994).

F. The Boston Story

Local problem-oriented policing projects hold great promise for creating a strong response to illicit firearms markets. Problem-oriented policing works to identify why things are going wrong and to frame responses using a wide variety of often untraditional approaches (Goldstein 1990). This approach provides an appropriate framework to uncover the complex mechanisms at play in illicit firearms markets and to develop tailor-made interventions to disrupt the gun trade. The famous illustration of this approach was the Boston Gun Project, launched during the early 1990s. It included an interagency problem-solving group that sought to disrupt the illegal supply of firearms to youth through the following efforts: systematically expanding the focus of local, state, and federal authorities to include intrastate trafficking in Massachusetts-sourced guns, in addition to interstate trafficking; focusing enforcement attention on traffickers of those makes and calibers of guns most used by gang members, on traffickers of guns showing short time-to-crime, and on traffickers of guns used by the city's most violent gangs; attempting restoration of obliterated serial numbers, and subsequent trafficking investigations based on those restorations; and supporting these enforcement priorities through analysis of crime gun traces generated by the Boston Police Department's comprehensive tracing of crime guns and by developing leads through systematic debriefing of, especially, arrestees involved with gangs and/or involved in violent crime (Braga et al. 2001, p. 199). The Boston supply-side approach was implemented in conjunction with a powerful deterrence-based demand-side strategy to reduce youth violence. Unfortunately, the gun-trafficking investigations and prosecutions followed the implementation of a very successful deterrence strategy and their effects on gun violence could not be independently established (Braga et al. 2001).

The U.S. National Institute of Justice (NIJ), in partnership with the ATF, recently funded a demonstration program in Los Angeles to examine the effects of disrupting the illegal supply of guns on the nature of the illegal market and on gun violence (Riley et al. 2001). In addition to addressing LA's gun violence problem, this interagency law enforcement project was developed to provide other jurisdictions with guidance on how to analyze and develop appropriate problem-solving interventions to control illegal gun markets. The NIJ also recently revised the gun-addendum to its Arrestee Drug Abuse Monitoring (ADAM) program to address the shortcomings of other gun acquisition survey instruments in providing information on the illegal pathways through which criminals acquire guns. The ADAM program currently operates in thirty-five cities, and results of the gun addendum survey will be used to guide local law enforcement agencies in unraveling and responding to illegal gun markets.

G. Reducing Theft through Personalization

Reducing the flow of guns from theft, a major diffuse source of guns, might be accomplished by obligating or encouraging gun dealers and owners to safeguard their guns. More promising over the long run would be to require that new guns be "personalized" (Cook and Leitzel 2002). Millions of dollars of public and private funds have been invested in developing such a gun, one that could only be fired by the owner. A variety of designs are under development, including fairly traditional combination and keyed locks, or, more intriguing, a lock that is released by application of a preprogrammed thumbprint. If it were difficult to overcome the locking mechanism, then a personalized gun would be of little value to a thief. If a personalized safety lock became standard equipment, the long run effect would be to reduce theft and other unauthorized transfers of guns, thus cutting into an important source of crime guns.

For all of the above possibilities, the lack of definitive experience should encourage an experimental orientation, open to fresh possibilities and to evaluating the results.

IV. Learning by Doing

Criminal misuse of guns kills or injures tens of thousands of Americans every year. The threat of such violence imposes a heavy burden on our standard of living, not only on groups that have the highest victimization rates but also on the entire community. By one estimate this burden amounts to $80 billion per year (Cook and Ludwig 2000). Reducing gun violence would provide correspondingly great benefits, as indeed we have experienced during the 1990s. The unparalleled reductions in lethal violence, much of it with guns, has raised property values and given many communities the chance to reclaim a more civilized lifestyle, while reducing violence-related costs to the taxpayers. To achieve still further reductions, or fend off the next epidemic of violence, may require a concerted effort directed in part at separating guns and violence. In our judgment, that effort should include a variety of efforts to reduce the availability of guns to youths and dangerous adults.

However, the will to pursue this approach may not be available at the federal level. While some modest innovations were put in place during the Clinton administration, there appears to be little appetite for doing more now. And the existing legal framework actually impedes effective action.

In particular, prosecuting gun traffickers is remarkably difficult (Braga 2001). Since the telltale paperwork is not available for unregulated transactions in the secondary market, unlicensed dealers illegally engaged in the business of selling firearms can avoid prosecution by claiming that they were selling only a handful of firearms from their private collection. Corrupt FFLs who illegally divert firearms face very small penalties. (The FOPA reduced most of these record-keeping violations from felonies to misdemeanors in 1986.) Straw purchasers are also difficult to prosecute, given various legal loopholes. As a result, U.S. attorneys typically prosecute gun traffickers on charges unrelated to trafficking such as "felon in possession" or drug trafficking (ATF 2000d).

The enforcement of laws against gun trafficking is also hindered by the rather cumbersome procedure that the ATF is forced to use to trace firearms (Braga 2001). The limits of current record-keeping procedures thwart routine firearms tracing of secondhand firearms sold by licensed dealers and prevent the ATF from identifying straw purchasers and scofflaw dealers who divert secondhand firearms. Trace data also provide ATF investigators with little support in examining the robust trade in secondhand firearms on the secondary market. Modest statutory changes in the system for tracking firearm purchases and sales could make a big difference in developing an effective supply-side strategy (Travis and Smarrito 1992). For example, a requirement for licensed dealers to report serial numbers for all sales to the ATF would greatly facilitate the tracing process without creating a central registry of gun owners. A requirement that all secondary market transactions pass through federally licensed dealers—with the same screening and paperwork provisions as if the gun were being sold by the dealer— would be useful in a variety of ways, including in detecting gun traffickers. However, both proposals would likely be vigorously challenged as infringing on the rights of lawful gun owners and as violating the FOPA, which prohibits the ATF from establishing any national system of gun registration (Braga 2001).

More promising, politically speaking, is the possibility of action at state and local levels. There is much that can be done at those levels. States could assume some of the responsibility for tracing crime guns and investigating dealers. Local police departments can quite possibly be effective at disrupting local gun markets, but only if they concern themselves with gathering the necessary intelligence and acting on it. Most police departments have been focused on getting guns off the street instead of focusing on where the guns are coming from (Moore 1980, 1983). In recent years, however, police practices have changed in many major cities due in part to efforts by ATF and the U.S. Department of Justice to form partnerships to reduce the availability of guns to youth and criminals (see, e.g., ATF 2000c, 2000d).

A major contribution of the research community in this setting should be evaluation of interesting policy changes at the state and local level. Only through systematic assessment of actual experience in the field are we going to be able to move past the cacophony of speculation to firm conclusions about what supply-side strategies are likely to be effective, and under what circumstances.

REFERENCES

Azrael, Deborah, Philip J. Cook, and Matthew Miller. 2001. "State and Local Prevalence of Firearms Ownership: Measurement, Structure and Trends." Unpublished manuscript. Durham, N.C.: Duke University, Sanford Institute of Public Policy.
Bjerregaard, Beth, and Alan Lizotte. 1995. "Gun Ownership and Gang Membership." *Journal of Criminal Law and Criminology* 86:37–58.
Blackman, Paul H. 1999. "The Limitations of BATF Firearms Tracing Data

for Policymaking and Homicide Research." *Proceedings of the Homicide Research Working Group Meetings, 1997 and 1998*. Washington, D.C.: U.S. Department of Justice, National Institute of Justice.

Blumstein, Alfred, Jacqueline Cohen, Jeffrey A. Roth, and Christy Visher. 1986. *Criminal Careers and "Career Criminals."* Washington, D.C.: National Academy Press.

Braga, Anthony A. 2001. "More Gun Laws or More Gun Law Enforcement?" *Journal of Policy Analysis and Management* 20:545–49.

Braga, Anthony A., and David M. Kennedy. 2000. "Gun Shows and the Illegal Diversion of Firearms." *Georgetown Public Policy Review* 6(1):7–24.

———. 2001. "The Illicit Acquisition of Firearms by Youth and Juveniles." *Journal of Criminal Justice* 29:379–88.

Braga, Anthony A., David M. Kennedy, Elin J. Waring, and Anne M. Piehl. 2001. "Problem-Oriented Policing, Deterrence, and Youth Violence: An Evaluation of Boston's Operation Ceasefire." *Journal of Research in Crime and Delinquency* 38(3):195–225.

Brill, Stephen. 1977. *Firearms Abuse: A Research and Policy Report*. Washington, D.C.: Police Foundation.

Bureau of Justice Statistics (BJS). 1993. *Survey of State Prison Inmates, 1991*. Washington, D.C.: U.S. Department of Justice, Bureau of Justice Statistics.

———. 1999. *Presale Handgun Checks, the Brady Interim Period, 1994–1999*. Washington, D.C.: U.S. Department of Justice, Bureau of Justice Statistics.

Callahan, Charles M., Frederick P. Rivara, and Thomas D. Koepsell. 1994. "Money for Guns: Evaluation of the Seattle Gun Buy-Back Program." *Public Health Reports* 109:472–77.

Congressional Research Service. 1992. *"Assault Weapons": Military-Style Semi-Automatic Firearms Facts and Issues*. Report 92-434. Washington, D.C.: Library of Congress.

Cook, Philip J., and James Blose. 1981. "State Programs for Screening Handgun Buyers." *Annals of the American Academy of Political and Social Sciences* 455:80–91.

Cook, Philip J., and Anthony A. Braga. 2001. "Comprehensive Firearms Tracing: Strategic and Investigative Uses of New Data on Firearms Markets." *Arizona Law Review* 43:277–309.

Cook, Philip J., and James A. Leitzel. 1996. "Perversity, Futility, Jeopardy: An Economic Analysis of the Attack on Gun Control." *Law and Contemporary Problems* 59:91–118.

———. 2002. "'Smart' Guns: A Technological Fix for Regulating the Secondary Gun Market." *Contemporary Economic Problems* 20:38–49.

Cook, Philip J., and Jens Ludwig. 1996. *Guns in America: Results of a Comprehensive National Survey on Firearms Ownership and Use*. Washington, D.C.: Police Foundation.

———. 2000. *Gun Violence: The Real Costs*. New York: Oxford University Press.

Cook, Philip J., Stephanie Molliconi, and Thomas Cole. 1995. "Regulating Gun Markets." *Journal of Criminal Law and Criminology* 86:59–92.

Decker, Scott H., Susan Pennell, and A. Caldwell. 1997. *Illegal Firearms: Access and Use by Arrestees.* Washington, D.C.: U.S. Department of Justice, Bureau of Justice Statistics.

Goldstein, Herman. 1990. *Problem-Oriented Policing.* Philadelphia: Temple University Press.

Jacobs, James B., and Kimberly Potter. 1995. "Keeping Guns out of the 'Wrong' Hands: The Brady Law and the Limits of Regulation." *Journal of Criminal Law and Criminology* 86:93–120.

Kennedy, David M. 1994. "Can We Keep Guns Away from Kids?" *American Prospect* 18:74–80.

Kennedy, David M., Anne M. Piehl, and Anthony A. Braga. 1996*a*. "Gun Buy-Backs: Where Do We Stand and Where Do We Go?" In *Under Fire: Gun Buy-Backs, Exchanges, and Amnesty Programs,* edited by Martha R. Plotkin. Washington, D.C.: Police Executive Research Forum.

———. 1996*b*. "Youth Violence in Boston: Gun Markets, Serious Youth Offenders, and a Use-Reduction Strategy." *Law and Contemporary Problems* 59: 147–96.

Kleck, Gary. 1997. *Targeting Guns: Firearms and Their Control.* New York: Aldine de Guyter.

———. 1999. "BATF Gun Trace Data and the Role of Organized Gun Trafficking in Supplying Guns to Criminals." *Saint Louis University Public Law Review* 18:23–45.

Ludwig, Jens, and Philip J. Cook. 2000. "Homicide and Suicide Rates Associated with the Implementation of the Brady Handgun Violence Prevention Act." *Journal of the American Medical Association* 284:585–91.

Lumpe, Lora. 1997. "Global Black-Market Arms Trade Should Be Next Target of Non-Governmental Organizations." *Journal of the Federation of American Scientists* 50:1–15.

McDowall, David, Colin Loftin, and Brian Wiersema. 1995. "Easing Concealed Firearms Laws: Effects on Homicides in Three States." *Journal of Criminal Law and Criminology* 86:193–206.

Moore, Mark H. 1973. "Achieving Discrimination on the Effective Price of Heroin." *American Economic Review* 63:270–77.

———. 1976. *Buy and Bust: The Effective Regulation of an Illicit Market in Heroin.* Lexington, Mass.: Heath.

———. 1980. "The Police and Weapons Offenses." *Annals of the American Academy of Political and Social Sciences* 452:22–32.

———. 1981. "Keeping Handguns from Criminal Offenders." *Annals of the American Academy of Political and Social Sciences* 455:92–109.

———. 1983. "The Bird in Hand: A Feasible Strategy for Gun Control." *Journal of Policy Analysis and Management* 2:185–88.

Peters, Rebecca. 2000. *Gun Control in the United States: A Comparative Survey of State Firearms Laws.* New York: Open Society Institute, Soros Foundation.

Pierce, Glenn L., Anthony A. Braga, Christopher Koper, Jack McDevitt, David Carlson, Jeffrey Roth, and Alan Saiz. 2001. "The Characteristics and Dynamics of Gun Markets: Implications for a Supply-Side Enforcement Strategy." Final report submitted to the National Institute of Justice. Boston: Northeastern University, Center for Criminal Justice Policy Research.

Pierce, Glenn L., LeBaron Briggs, and David Carlson. 1995. *The Identification of Patterns in Firearms Trafficking: Implications for a Focused Enforcement Strategy.* Washington, D.C.: U.S. Bureau of Alcohol, Tobacco, and Firearms.

Riley, Kevin Jack, Glenn L. Pierce, Anthony A. Braga, and Garen J. Wintemute. 2001. *Strategic Disruption of Illegal Firearms Markets: A Los Angeles Demonstration Program.* Funded proposal to the National Institute of Justice. Santa Monica, Calif.: RAND Corporation.

Roth, Jeffrey A., and Christopher S. Koper. 1997. *Impacts of the 1994 Assault Weapons Ban, 1994–1996.* Research in Brief. Washington, D.C.: U.S. Department of Justice, National Institute of Justice.

Sheley, Joseph F., and James D. Wright. 1993. *Gun Acquisition and Possession in Selected Juvenile Samples.* Research in Brief. Washingtion, D.C.: U.S. Department of Justice, National Institute of Justice.

———. 1995. *In the Line of Fire: Youth, Guns, and Violence in Urban America.* New York: Aldine de Guyter.

Smith, Tom W. 2000. "1999 National Gun Policy Survey of the National Opinion Research Center: Research Findings." Unpublished manuscript. Chicago: University of Chicago, National Opinion Research Center.

Sugarmann, Josh, and Kristen Rand. 1992. *More Gun Dealers than Gas Stations: A Study of Federally Licensed Firearms Dealers in America.* Washington, D.C.: Violence Policy Center.

Tien, J., and Thomas Rich. 1990. *Identifying Persons, Other than Felons, Ineligible to Purchase Firearms: A Feasibility Study.* Washington, D.C.: U.S. Bureau of Justice Statistics.

Travis, Jeremy, and William Smarrito. 1992. "A Modest Proposal to End Gun Running in America." *Fordham Urban Law Journal* 19:795–811.

United Nations Commission on Crime Prevention and Criminal Justice. 1997. *Criminal Justice Reform and Strengthening of Legal Measures to Regulate Firearms: Report to the Secretary-General.* Vienna: Economic and Social Council, United Nations.

U.S. Bureau of Alcohol, Tobacco, and Firearms (ATF). 1976. *Project Identification: A Study of Handguns Used in Crime.* Washington, D.C.: U.S. Bureau of Alcohol, Tobacco, and Firearms.

———. 1995. *Project LEAD: How to Generate Investigative Leads.* Washington, D.C.: U.S. Bureau of Alcohol, Tobacco, and Firearms.

———. 1997. *Gun Dealer Licensing and Illegal Gun Trafficking.* Washington, D.C.: U.S. Bureau of Alcohol, Tobacco, and Firearms.

———. 2000a. *ATF Regulatory Actions: Report to the Secretary on Firearms Initiative.* Washington, D.C.: U.S. Bureau of Alcohol, Tobacco, and Firearms.

———. 2000b. *Commerce in Firearms in the United States.* Washington, D.C.: U.S. Bureau of Alcohol, Tobacco, and Firearms.

———. 2000c. *Crime Gun Trace Reports (1999): National Report.* Washington, D.C.: U.S. Bureau of Alcohol, Tobacco, and Firearms.

———. 2000d. *Following the Gun: Enforcing Federal Laws against Firearms Traffickers.* Washington, D.C.: U.S. Bureau of Alcohol, Tobacco, and Firearms.

U.S. Department of the Treasury and U.S. Department of Justice. 1999. *Gun*

Shows: Brady Checks and Crime Gun Traces. Washington, D.C.: U.S. Department of the Treasury and U.S. Department of Justice.

Vanzi, Max. 1998. "Legislature OKs Bill to Boost Security at Some Gun Plants." *Los Angeles Times* (August 7), p. B3.

Veen, John, Stacie Dunbar, and Melissa Stedman Ruland. 1997. *The BJA Firearms Trafficking Program: Demonstrating Effective Strategies to Control Violent Crime.* Washington, D.C.: U.S. Bureau of Justice Assistance.

Wachtel, Julius. 1998. "Sources of Crime Guns in Los Angeles, California." *Policing: An International Journal of Police Strategies and Management* 21:220–39.

Weil, Douglas S., and Rebecca Knox. 1996. "Effects of Limiting Handgun Purchases on Interstate Transfer of Firearms." *Journal of the American Medical Association* 275:1759–61.

Wintemute, Garen J. 2000a. "Guns and Gun Violence." In *The Crime Drop in America,* edited by Alfred Blumstein and Joel Wallman. Cambridge: Cambridge University Press.

———. 2000b. "Relationship between Illegal Use of Handguns and Handgun Sales Volume." *Journal of the American Medical Association* 284:566–67.

Wintemute, Garen J., Christiana M. Drake, James J. Beaumont, Mona A. Wright, and Carrie Parham. 1998. "Prior Misdemeanor Convictions as a Risk Factor for Later Violent and Firearm-Related Criminal Activity among Authorized Purchasers of Handguns." *Journal of the American Medical Association* 280:2083–87.

Wintemute, Garen J., Mona A. Wright, Christiana M. Drake, James J. Beaumont, and Carrie A. Parham. 1999. "Effectiveness of Expanded Criteria for Denial of Firearm Purchase." Paper presented at the annual meeting of the American Society of Criminology, November 17–20, Toronto.

Wright, James D. 1981. "Public Opinion and Gun Control: A Comparison of Results from Two Recent National Surveys." *Annals of the American Academy of Political and Social Science* 455:24–39.

Wright, James D., and Peter H. Rossi. 1994. *Armed and Considered Dangerous: A Survey of Felons and Their Firearms,* 2d ed. New York: Aldine de Guyter.

Wright, James D., Joseph Sheley, and M. Dwayne Smith. 1992. "Kids, Guns, and Killing Fields." *Society* (November/December), pp. 84–89.

Wright, Mona A., Garen J. Wintemute, and Frederick Rivara. 1999. "Effectiveness of Denial of Handgun Purchase to Persons Believed to Be at High Risk for Firearm Violence." *American Journal of Public Health* 89:88–90.

Zimring, Franklin E. 1975. "Firearms and Federal Law: The Gun Control Act of 1968." *Journal of Legal Studies* 4:133–98.

———. 1976. "Street Crime and New Guns: Some Implications for Firearms Control." *Journal of Criminal Justice* 4:95–107.

———. 1991. "Firearms, Violence, and Public Policy." *Scientific American* 265(5):48–54.